Personhood

PERSONHOOD

THE NEW CIVIL WAR OVER REPRODUCTION

● ● ●

MARY ZIEGLER

Yale

UNIVERSITY PRESS

New Haven and London

Published with assistance from the foundation established in memory of Henry Weldon Barnes of the Class of 1882, Yale College.

Yale University Press books may be purchased in quantity for educational, business, or promotional use. For information, please e-mail sales.press@ yale.edu (U.S. office) or sales@yaleup.co.uk (U.K. office).

Set in Gotham and Adobe Garamond types by IDS Infotech Ltd. Printed in the United States of America.

Library of Congress Control Number: 2024946274
ISBN 978-0-300-27304-5 (hardcover : alk. paper)

A catalogue record for this book is available from the British Library.

This paper meets the requirements of ANSI/NISO Z39.48-1992 (Permanence of Paper).

10 9 8 7 6 5 4 3 2 1

Contents

Preface

In the summer of 2022, a conservative supermajority of the United States Supreme Court overturned *Roe v. Wade*, the famed 1973 decision recognizing a right to choose abortion. Many Americans struggled to understand how something they considered a fundamental right could simply be wiped away. Still others were terrified that the Court's decision in *Dobbs v. Jackson Women's Health Organization* would make pregnancy in the United States more dangerous than it already was. For abortion foes, of course, *Dobbs* brought a very different kind of news. Reporters described the decision as a stunning win for the American right, a sign of American abortion opponents' strength and the conservative legal movement's savvy.[1]

Where will antiabortion advocates turn next? Will they move to dismantle rights to birth control or do more to target in vitro fertilization? What will happen to interstate travel for abortion? Will conservatives be able to shut down abortions that rely on mifepristone, a pill used in more than half of procedures in the United States, when the pill can easily be ordered online?

These are important questions, but we cannot answer any of them without understanding that the reversal of *Roe* was never the U.S. antiabortion movement's ultimate goal. From its inception in the 1960s, it has always been a fetal-personhood movement.[2]

I should pause here to clarify what I mean by *fetal personhood*. There are divergent conversations in which personhood has high stakes. Lawyers use the idea of personhood to sort through individual obligations and entitlements, applying the term to corporations, partnerships, and other entities. Bioethicists debate the extent to which legal personhood is coextensive with moral personhood and discuss what care persons are owed—such as being treated as autonomous actors or protected from harm. In philosophical debates, some assign personhood only to those who currently possess certain attributes, such as rationality or consciousness, while others suggest that any being with the theoretical capacity for these attributes qualifies as a person. Certain faith communities, including those heavily invested in struggles over abortion, associate personhood with the possession of a soul.[3]

This book is not primarily a study of moral or religious understandings of personhood. Instead, fetal personhood, in the sense I intend, is a claim about the meaning of the nation's Constitution. The term has taken on various meanings that have shifted over the past half century, reflecting broader cultural, religious, political, and economic developments. Nevertheless, over the course of five decades, fetal-personhood claims have involved two core arguments: first, that a fetus is a separate, unique human individual from the moment of fertilization, and second, that because of that biological and moral uniqueness, the Constitution gives (or at least should give) that individual rights.

Neither of these claims has anything like universal support. Polling, for example, suggests that Americans hold complex views about when human life begins, how and when that life gains value, and how these questions connect to support for the criminalization of abortion or IVF. Majorities appear to support the idea of a right to choose abortion. As important, there have always been disagreements about what it *means* to recognize personhood. Which rights does personhood confer? How should they be enforced? And how can the rights of fetal persons be balanced against those of other persons, including pregnant women? Even within the antiabortion movement, there have been disagreements about whether the Constitution can properly be interpreted as already protecting fetal rights or whether the only way to secure those rights is through a constitutional amendment. Throughout the past half century, abortion opponents have disagreed about how to guarantee fetal equality. But there has been no difference of opinion among abortion foes on the *importance* of securing personhood, whether through a constitutional amendment or a judicial decision. The fight for it has become one of the major American political mobilizations of the past fifty years.[4]

The fight for constitutional fetal personhood began in the 1960s, when states started reforming their criminal abortion laws. Attitudes about sex outside of marriage were shifting, and discrimination against gays and lesbians had begun to come under fire. Some reformers saw abortion regulations as the reflection of a similarly outdated sexual morality. Others stressed that criminal bans led women to pursue dangerous illegal procedures that could cost them their lives or health. By the later 1960s, the reform movement had gained momentum in state legislatures and among medical professionals.[5]

The struggle for personhood began as a countermovement. At first, a primarily Catholic group of activists and lawyers insisted that because of advances in medical care, there was no longer such thing as a medically necessary abortion. Some of these advocates asserted that abortion itself actually undermined women's physical and mental health. Ultimately, however, these arguments were not enough to persuade legislators in critical states to reject abortion reform. Moreover, a growing group of voters seemed open to the idea that decriminalizing abortion would address real health-based harms, particularly for low-income women and patients of color. Opponents of abortion did not simply deny the truth of these claims. The early antiabortion movement also replied that reform itself was unconstitutional because the fetus qualified as a person under the Fourteenth Amendment, and liberalizing abortion laws denied that person equality and due process of law.[6]

Over the course of five decades, abortion opponents took varying positions on what *equal* personhood required. Did recognizing fetuses as persons mean that they must have rights identical to other persons', including women? If a fetus was a person, was it right to punish those who performed abortions less severely than those who committed murder, or even permissible not to punish anyone involved in abortion at all? While members of the antiabortion movement supplied different answers to these questions, and while the meaning of personhood evolved throughout the decades, advocates' commitment to the idea of personhood did not waver. By advocating for it, abortion opponents sought to establish how the nation and the Constitution should change.[7]

Anyone skeptical about the need to study personhood may have in mind questions about the sincerity of those demanding fetal rights. There is no question that those who invented and later relied on personhood arguments were sometimes hoping to gain a tactical edge. But antiabortion activists made these claims even when there was no obvious strategic benefit, in internal conversations with one another, or when fetal rights stood no chance of gaining recognition from legislatures or courts. For a period of fifty years, organizations and individuals had multiple motives in pursuing personhood. Studying their ideas can help us map the emerging constitutional agenda of abortion opponents in the years to come.

Anyone closely following the abortion debate in the United States will likely equate fetal personhood with the criminalization of abortion. The history of struggles over fetal personhood suggests that this preoccupation with criminalization was never inevitable. Indeed, ideas of personhood have changed over time, as have broader struggles over equality in America.

What abortion opponents meant by fetal personhood shifted in the face of questions about racial justice, sex discrimination, the treatment of civilians in wartime, and even corporate power. Some members of the antiabortion movement explored other ways of enforcing personhood—including those that would require more support for pregnant women—and continue to do so at the time of this writing. Even today, some Americans express in polls that they oppose additional restrictions on abortion despite their belief that a fetus is a person, or that life begins at conception. And yet we have come to take for granted that fetal personhood requires criminalization. This book challenges that assumption and explains how we got to the present moment.[8]

If we understand personhood to be more than a shorthand for banning abortion, we can recognize that personhood is fundamentally a claim about *equality* in the United States, one with stakes beyond abortion. If a fetus is a person under the Constitution, lawmakers may feel compelled to introduce new restrictions on in vitro fertilization or contraceptives. Recognizing fetal personhood could also—and more fundamentally—reshape how courts approach ideas of liberty and equality in other areas of the law.

Those calling for personhood have stressed that in states where abortion is legal, the fetus has suffered the most egregious discrimination of any person in America. At the same time, proponents of personhood argue that the law has long venerated and protected life, even or especially in the womb. Personhood proponents have thus aimed to redefine equality not to focus on addressing prejudice against those at society's margins or correcting past injustice—as courts would sometimes suggest in the context of race or sex discrimination—but on restoring long-standing protections for the weak and vulnerable, chief among them the fetus.

Looking to the past to understand the meaning of the Constitution became increasingly common for abortion opponents as their movement aligned with legal conservatism. Personhood proponents eventually championed constitutional approaches to the recognition of rights under the Fourteenth Amendment yoked to ideas of history and tradition—and suggested that the Constitution should be interpreted to preserve long-standing rights and customs, not primarily to eliminate the vestiges of past discrimination. And over time, personhood advocates increasingly came to see criminalization as a necessary remedy for discrimination against the unborn. To truly treat fetuses as equals, they argued, was to criminalize acts of violence committed against them.

For the past fifty years, the priority for the antiabortion movement has been the recognition of fetal rights. If the movement never strayed from this objective, however, the agenda the antiabortion movement pursued had far-reaching effects—and could yet produce far more consequential changes in American constitutional law and politics. At stake is how courts identify which fundamental rights Americans have and what it means to enjoy equal protection under the law.

The antiabortion movement of the nineteenth century championed the idea that human life begins at conception. But the physicians who led the campaign to criminalize abortion throughout pregnancy made arguments about biology and morality, not the Constitution.

It was not until the 1960s that abortion opponents argued that the word *person* in the Fourteenth Amendment applied to the fetus. At the time, a growing group of reformers argued that existing criminal bans had deeply unequal effects. While wealthier women could access safe therapeutic procedures, low-income patients, many of them patients of color, still induced their own abortions and suffered comparably high rates of maternal morbidity and mortality. Reformers pointed to these deaths and injuries in demanding new exceptions to criminal laws. Antiabortion lawyers, theologians, and activists first replied that the exceptions were unnecessary or immoral. When these claims were unavailing, abortion opponents argued that reform itself was unconstitutional.

Fetal-personhood politics took shape at a time when the constitutional law of equal protection was in flux. Following a series of decisions, including the landmark desegregation ruling in *Brown v. Board of Education* (1954), race became the classic "suspect classification," and the Supreme Court scrutinized laws that distinguished among people on that basis. As the battle over abortion reform continued, competing ideas about equality multiplied—in the context of abortion and well beyond it. While the lawyers of the National Association for the Advancement of Colored People worked to enforce *Brown*'s desegregation mandate in the courts, local Black leaders sought to increase the number of Black teachers, improve the quality of schools in Black neighborhoods, and achieve socioeconomic equality. Writing in 1962, the Black feminist Pauli Murray drew an influential analogy between discrimination on the basis of race and of sex, suggesting that a history of subordination had ensured "women's inferior status" and rendered laws classifying Americans on the basis of sex constitutionally suspect.[9] The National Organization for Women, founded in 1966 to demand "a fully equal partnership of the sexes," called for the legalization of abortion in 1967, and two years later, the organization's president, Betty Friedan, argued that without a right to control reproduction, "there is no freedom, no equality, no full human dignity and personhood possible for women."[10] These ideas of equality were complex and varied but shared a focus on the legacy left behind by past injustice.[11]

As the 1960s continued, an antiabortion movement took shape, with single-issue groups forming across the country. In seeking to defeat abortion reform, these advocates proposed their own vision of equality, one that read *Brown* and its approach to "suspect classifications" very differently. In the 1960s, antiabortion lawyers and grassroots activists were overwhelmingly Catholic, white, and middle class, but they saw faith-based arguments as a liability. Arguments about sexual promiscuity or maternal responsibility also increasingly fell flat as sexual mores and gender roles began to change.

Rather than defining their cause by reference to religion or gender politics, antiabortion activists more often argued that the legalization of abortion threatened to make the unborn more marginalized than any group in America. The courts, in interpreting the Equal Protection Clause, had begun pointing to the fallout a group faced from years of discrimination. Antiabortion activists, by contrast, believed that American law and culture had long defended the unborn child. But a lack of historic prejudice struck the antiabortion leaders of the 1960s as of at most secondary importance: physical dependence and weakness, not past injustice or present political powerlessness, should be the central concern of the Equal Protection Clause.

As the decade continued, the reform movement largely gave way to a fight to repeal all criminal abortion laws. Feminist activists and other proponents of repeal contended that both old abortion bans and new attempts to write fetal rights into the law involved sex discrimination because they reflected damaging stereotypes and denied women even medically needed care—and constituted discrimination based on religion because such laws imposed a minority theology on everyone else. Abortion-rights supporters also insisted that criminal abortion laws disproportionately harmed the poor, who were least able to circumvent restrictions placed on the procedure.

Antiabortion groups, for their part, echoed ideas articulated by those challenging affirmative action programs or judicial integration orders. These advocates contended that certain remedies for racial bias were themselves discriminatory because they categorized people by group without honoring their individuality.

As they formed single-issue groups in the late 1960s and early 1970s, abortion opponents claimed that the fight for fetal personhood combatted the kind of insidious classification denounced by white litigants, scholars, and commentators decrying what they called reverse discrimination. True equality was not about membership in a marginalized group. What mattered was the failure to treat anyone, including an unborn child, as a unique individual, and that, antiabortion activists argued, was precisely what the repeal of abortion laws accomplished by categorizing the fetus based on residence in the womb.

Nevertheless, members of the antiabortion movement remained divided about the relationship of personhood to other equality struggles of the day, from the fight for new civil-rights legislation to the struggle to end sex discrimination through ratification of a federal Equal Rights Amendment. The idea of personhood was fluid enough to allow activists who disagreed about the meaning of equality to fight for the same cause.

Beginning in the 1980s, the antiabortion movement championed a vision of equality defined by claims about tradition and history. This new rhetorical agenda partly reflected the rising influence of white conservative Protestants in the movement, as well as an increasingly important partnership with the conservative legal movement and the Federalist Society. Leading Federalist Society figures advocated for originalism, a method of constitutional interpretation that revolved around what its proponents described as the original intent of the Constitution's framers or, later, the original public meaning of its text. Christian conservatives and single-issue antiabortion activists borrowed from originalism but did not always warmly embrace it. Some were unsure that originalist interpretations would deliver the victories they sought. Others wanted to incorporate traditions, including Christian ones, that predated the founding—or look to evidence from decades long after the Constitution's ratification.

These antiabortion activists and their allies therefore looked to other judicial approaches, suggesting that courts should protect rights under the Fourteenth Amendment only if they were deeply rooted in unchanging national traditions. Disagreements about the meaning of fetal personhood remained. Advocates, for example, clashed about whether the prosecution of pregnant drug users advanced the recognition of fetal personhood, but there was broad consensus on the importance of a constitutional approach centered on a particular idea of unchanging national tradition.

In the 1990s, antiabortion leaders defined themselves as champions of equality for both women and the unborn, portraying both as victims of an industry as well funded and unscrupulous as "Big Tobacco." The antiabortion movement advocated for "right-to-know" laws that transformed arguments for fetal rights into information wrongly denied women considering abortion. Defining both women and fetuses as victims helped the antiabortion movement to soften its image at a time when the murder of doctors made headlines—and when those doctors' attackers claimed that they had justifiably used force to protect the lives of fetal persons.

Divides about the nature of women's victimhood also emerged in struggles over welfare reform. Across the antiabortion movement, advocates condemned what they saw as a surge in sexual promiscuity and teen pregnancy. But while some groups, like the Christian Coalition, a voter-mobilization organization launched by the televangelist Pat Robertson in 1987, favored eliminating benefits for adolescent unmarried mothers, other abortion opponents argued that doing so would incentivize abortion and unfairly penalize young women who did not understand their own choices. Parallel arguments about a right to know united the movement but did not resolve what should happen to women who *did* embrace the choice to end a pregnancy. The answer to this question would divide the movement in the years to come. In the 2000s and 2010s, ideas of equality for the fetus also shaped and reflected conversations about whether conservative Christians suffered from or perpetuated discrimination, what defined religious liberty, and what it meant to recognize rights for major corporations.

The struggle for fetal personhood began in the 1960s in reaction to demands for more liberal criminal abortion laws, but it became something more lasting. Fetal personhood, this book shows, became and remained a symbol of what a range of socially conservative Americans saw as fundamental injustices in American society. Remarkably, calls for fetal personhood captivated many on the American right for more than half a century, from the passage of the Civil Rights Act to the decision of *Roe* to the demise of abortion rights and the ascendancy of new bans. As I write this, the idea of fetal rights is no less compelling to those opposed to abortion rights than it was decades ago.

Personhood has this hold on the American imagination because abortion opponents and social conservatives, too, saw themselves as champions of equality, committed to eradicating discrimination in the United States, and because they have offered quite different ideas about what equality is and how it can be achieved. In the pursuit of equal justice for the fetus, antiabortion groups drew on debates about race, reverse discrimination, and affirmative action, about criminal justice, victims' rights, and the welfare state, about consumer protection and sex discrimination, and about religious liberty and corporate power. At times, abortion opponents, in developing these ideas of equality, disagreed not only with other Americans and other movements but also with one another.

Because antiabortion groups ascribed so many different meanings to fetal personhood, the fight for it can tell us something important about the changing ideas of equality and injustice that have defined both antiabortion activism and American conservatism over the course of half a century. And while focusing on the unborn, the champions of personhood proposed changes to American law and politics that would have far-reaching consequences in struggles over race, sex, and disability. The personhood battle has been a battle about whose wrongs deserve redress, about the role of history and tradition in the interpretation of the Constitution, and about the nature of discrimination itself.

For decades, antiabortion Americans insisted that the struggle for fetal personhood was the civil-rights battle of a generation. This claim has so far failed to convince most Americans to endorse the kind of criminal abortion ban the movement favors. But regardless of anyone's beliefs about reproductive rights, the struggle for fetal personhood *has* transformed what civil rights mean, both to those who believe in fetal personhood and to those who do not. It has fundamentally changed how Americans debate the path to equal protection under the law.

Those championing fetal personhood have already succeeded in eliminating what many viewed as a fundamental right. In the next fifty years, the movement's quest for personhood could have even further-reaching effects. From the beginning, abortion opponents sought with their vision of equality to establish that the fetus, an entity that they often described as invisible and voiceless, had at least the same worth as a pregnant woman. And to establish the equal worth of the unborn, abortion opponents increasingly insist that the violence of performing or aiding an abortion must be answered with the full weight of the criminal law.

Acknowledgments

I could not have completed this book without the support of many people. The John Simon Guggenheim Foundation provided me with tremendous support, as did the University of California, Davis. Thanks to the staff at the libraries of the American Philosophical Society Library, Catholic University, the Cincinnati History Library and Archives, Columbia University, the Concordia Seminary of the Lutheran Church Missouri Synod, the Connecticut State Library, Duke University, the George H. W. Bush Presidential Library and Museum, Harvard University, the Phyllis Schlafly Center Library Archives, Princeton University, the Southern Baptist Historical Library and Archives, the University of California, Berkeley, the University of California, Los Angeles, the University of Kansas, the University of Michigan, the University of Missouri, St. Louis, the University of Notre Dame, the University of Wyoming, and the William J. Clinton Presidential Library and Museum. I am especially indebted to those who allowed me to canvass private collections, including James Bopp, Mark Lee Dickson, Kristan Hawkins and Students for Life, and Bob and Marie Meyers.

Many wonderful people have shared comments on the ideas advanced in the book. Glenn Cohen, Anna Lvovsky, Ken Mack, Serena Mayeri, and Laura Weinrib offered invaluable help with the framing of the project. Others closely read parts of the manuscript, often more than once, including David Cohen, Patricia Cohen, Greer Donley, Richard Fallon, Dov Fox, Gillian Frank, Michele Goodwin, Jennifer

Holland, Amanda Hollis-Brusky, Courtney Joslin, Laura Kalman, Kenneth Kersch, Felicia Kornbluh, Lauren MacIvor-Thompson, Martha Minow, Rachel Rebouché, Carol Sanger, Reva Siegel, Brian Soucek, Ann Southworth, Marc Spindelman, Aaron Tang, and Daniel K. Williams. I am also grateful for feedback from workshops hosted by the faculties of the Georgetown University Law School, Harvard Law School, Ohio State University School of Law, Stanford University School of Law, University of Colorado School of Law, and the University of Southern California Gould School of Law.

I thank my editor at Yale University Press, Bill Frucht, for seeing the potential in this book and doing everything in his power to improve it. The people at Yale University Press, including Amanda Gerstenfeld, have been unfailingly helpful. Kristin Brandt and the library staff at the UC Davis Mabie Law Library were tireless in helping me hunt down documents. I also thank my tremendous research assistants, Michelle Calcany Blair, Elena Cullen, Caleb Gonzales, Kirin Gupta, Lauren Haumesser, Emma Hynes, Katrina Kim, Emily Marcus, Soojin Park, Marlen Renderos, Taylor Russ, Sam Spurrell, Alex Waugh, and Yifan Xia.

This book would not be the same without those who agreed to share their stories. I am often asked why people trust me with their experiences. I attribute this to my good fortune and the generosity of those who are shaping an unprecedented moment in the long struggle over abortion and reproduction in the United States. To all of those who shared experiences and memories, thank you.

Finally, I thank my husband, Dan, my daughter, Layla, and my mom and dad. My father, who made me want to be a professor and a writer, still reads my drafts and makes them immeasurably better. My mother, who is the best writer in the family, lent her time and sharp eye to improving this manuscript. If the two of them are proud of me, that will have made this book worthwhile.

As for Dan, he helped me realize that this was a book I needed to write. When the everyday politics of a deeply divisive topic were too much, he made me take a break. He is the cure for my imposter syndrome, the love of my life, and my biggest reminder that history can help us to see how we got here and where we might go.

Layla, who is writing her own books at age seven, is the strongest person I know. She made me feel proud of myself when I was despondent and reminded me of what is more important than work. For teaching me the meaning of resilience and showing me why I am writing in the first place, this book is for her.

Personhood

1

Before Personhood

In modern constitutional law, for the past several decades, originalism has been the preferred interpretive method of the conservative legal movement in the United States. Originalists disagree about how best to apply their method and what it requires, but many today claim that the text of the Constitution should be interpreted as it would be understood by a well-informed reader at the time of enactment. It was only in recent years that antiabortion lawyers prioritized originalist arguments. Today, however, prominent antiabortion advocates more often reason that the authors of the Fourteenth Amendment understood the word *person* in the Equal Protection and Due Process Clauses to apply—and to confer constitutional protection—from the moment an egg is fertilized. That means, these abortion foes assert, that the state and federal government may not deny fetal persons equal protection or due process—for example, by protecting abortion as a right.[1]

In making this argument, these abortion opponents look first to the text of the Constitution. While some parts of the Fourteenth Amendment, like the Privileges and Immunities Clause, apply to "citizens," the Equal Protection and Due Process Clauses apply to "persons"—a term, the movement claims, that was intended to apply to the unborn. Abortion foes further point to older treatises and cases that heavily influenced the thinking of the Fourteenth Amendment's architects. These texts spoke of protecting life before birth. While the

authors of these venerable cases and treatises proposed legal protections only at quickening, the point at which fetal movement could be
detected, personhood proponents see this as a simple matter of ignorance about when human life begins. Besides, the Fourteenth Amendment became part of the Constitution at a time when states were
passing laws criminalizing abortion throughout pregnancy—a sign,
say abortion opponents, that the unborn counted as persons under
the amendment.[2]

Skeptics of this argument respond with arguments of their own
about the Constitution's text and structure. The Fourteenth Amendment does not mention abortion, and contemporary champions of
personhood have not surfaced any evidence that its framers were
thinking about fetal protection when crafting the constitutional text.
Fetal-personhood skeptics next stress that use of the word *person* in the
Constitution does not support the inferences that fetal-personhood
advocates draw from it. In some passages, such as in the three-fifths
clause of Article I, Section 2, which explains how enslaved "persons"
will be counted for the purpose of legal representation and taxation,
the word quite clearly applies only to those already born.[3]

What of the fact that states were criminalizing abortion at the time
of the Fourteenth Amendment? In that era, some critics argue, understandings of pregnancy and pregnancy loss were radically different
from our own, and personhood arguments impose twenty-first-
century ideas that would have been unfamiliar, if not incoherent, to
the authors of the Fourteenth Amendment. Moreover, Americans were
still quite attached to the idea that life began at quickening, fetal-
personhood critics insist, and not just because they failed to understand when life began—Americans also seemed to want smaller
families, a phenomenon reflected by falling birth rates in the era. Even
Horatio Storer, the leader of the nineteenth-century antiabortion
movement in the United States, wrote with dismay in the 1860s that

Americans believed that there was nothing wrong with abortion until quickening—a state of affairs he worked to change, but one that hardly suggests that his contemporaries universally regarded the fetus as a rights-holding person. And if state lawmakers criminalized abortion because they felt the Constitution compelled them to do so, it is hard to explain why states moved at such a leisurely pace. Many did not pass bans for years or even decades after the amendment was ratified.[4]

That the originalist case for personhood is contested should not surprise us, but there is one point of agreement: the framers of the Fourteenth Amendment did not discuss abortion as a constitutional issue. Perhaps more strikingly, leaders of the nation's first antiabortion movement did not invoke the Constitution as a source of rights for the unborn child—even at a time when those seeking freedom and equality for people of color *did* focus on the rights owed to constitutional persons. When antiabortion lawyers and grassroots activists created a constitutional fetal-personhood movement in the 1960s, they developed something new.

The Early Law

In *Dobbs v. Jackson Women's Health Organization*, the decision in which the Supreme Court reversed the landmark 1973 abortion-rights ruling in *Roe v. Wade*, Justice Samuel Alito's majority opinion asserted that abortion had traditionally been viewed with disfavor throughout pregnancy. The *Dobbs* Court vowed to recognize rights under the Due Process Clause of the Fourteenth Amendment only if they were deeply rooted in the nation's history and tradition. But how, Alito asked, could an abortion right be deeply rooted in history and tradition if states had long viewed abortion as a crime? This historical account led the *Dobbs* majority to conclude that the *Roe* decision had been "egregiously wrong."[5]

Most historians question Alito's account of the nation's past. At the time of the nation's founding, many argue, courts often reasoned that intentionally causing miscarriage was a crime only after quickening. Whatever the law said, women in the era had no obvious way of confirming an early pregnancy—a state of affairs that persisted well into the twentieth century. In the colonial period, women and healers discussed blocked or obstructed menstruation as a serious health concern and advised the use of remedies, including some with abortifacient properties, to make menstruation more regular. In the nineteenth century, widely available remedies marketed for female troubles or obstructions might have functioned as contraceptives, abortifacients, or emmenagogues, medicines to regulate menstruation. Some concoctions could be fatal if taken in the wrong doses, and between the 1820s and 1840s, in a first wave of regulation, states began expanding their anti-poison laws to cover abortifacients.[6]

In the 1840s, the press began to call more attention to abortion. The story of Caroline Clark, an eighteen-year-old Michigan woman, was representative. Clark frequently socialized with her stepfather's daughter and her husband, Alonzo Plumstead, who impregnated Clark and then took her to get an abortion. She grew ill and died at the home of one of Plumstead's acquaintances. The press demonized the brother-in-law as a "heartless seducer and murderer" and praised Clark as "beautiful and accomplished." It was a travesty, one reporter complained, that there was "serious doubt" that Plumstead could "be convicted of any offense."[7]

At the time of Clark's death, abortion had become a big business. Ann Trow Lohman, a British immigrant who went by the name Madame Restell, offered abortions, contraceptives, emmenagogues, and other services for over thirty years. Restell became a sort of celebrity, known for her jaw-dropping wealth and frequent letters defending her work in the pages of New York's daily newspapers. While some targeted self-described female doctors like Restell in the 1840s and 1850s, legislators also expressed concern about the deaths of women like Caroline Clark, and some states, including New York and Massachusetts, introduced a second wave of abortion laws, authorizing harsher penalties when a woman died as the result of terminating a pregnancy.[8]

At a time when abortion drugs and devices were widely available, a new antiabortion movement mobilized, led by physicians in the recently formed American Medical Association (AMA). The early AMA, led by young, ambitious doctors, was a small organization that had trouble winning over established practitioners. For decades after the group's founding, medical schools applied wildly different standards, and few states had any criteria at all for licensing physicians.[9]

The young doctors who gravitated to the AMA thought it crucial to distinguish themselves from the druggists, salesmen, midwives, and homeopaths who also claimed to cure illnesses. Horatio Storer, a young Boston doctor, saw the abortion issue as a way to set regular physicians apart. A professor at Harvard Medical School, Storer was a contrarian, one of the first to establish gynecology as a standalone discipline. In an 1855 lecture to his medical school class, his father, David Humphreys Storer, also a professor of obstetrics at Harvard Medical School, had argued that abortion rates were unacceptably high and urged his fellow physicians to discourage the practice. But when Storer Sr. tried to publish these comments, he ran into trouble; his colleagues disagreed with his stance and worried that the lecture would cause controversy.[10]

Two years later, Storer Jr. created a committee to study abortion rates in Boston's Suffolk County. As he began his quest to regulate abortion, Storer had more than his fair share of enemies in the Boston medical establishment, but it did not hurt that many of the AMA's early recruits were much like Storer himself: white, Protestant men from well-to-do families, drawn from across the United States, who loudly proclaimed their personal piety. For example, Nathan Smith Davis, one of the organization's founders, described himself as a member of "the Protestant Methodist Church, contributing by precept and example to the advancement of its interests, and the dissemination of true piety."[11] The men drawn to the AMA also asserted, as a South Carolina member of the group put it in 1842, that absent exacting standards, "every old woman, savage Indian, or Guinea Negro could choose to start up and call themselves doctors." They argued that the profession of medicine should be restricted to people—men like themselves—who were better able to care for patients.[12]

In May 1859, Storer and other members of a special committee on criminal abortion delivered their report at a national AMA gathering held in Louisville. It proclaimed that "physicians have long been united in condemning the act of producing abortion," which was nothing less than "an unwarrantable destruction of human life."[13] Storer planned to send a memorial on criminal abortion to President James Buchanan as well as to the governors and legislators of every state. He and his allies made other arguments too. In an 1867 book, *Why Not?*, Storer observed that abortions were "infinitely more frequent among Protestant women than among Catholic." Legal abortion, he predicted, would shape the demographic future of the country, especially with the opening of "the great territories of the far West." Would these lands, Storer asked in referencing abortion laws, "be filled by our own children or those of aliens?" He also argued that women who chose abortion abdicated their responsibilities in marriage. "Marriage where the conception or birth of children is intentionally prevented," he wrote, "is in reality, but legalized prostitution"—and acceptance of legal abortion was little more than the "public confession of cowardly, selfish, and sinful lust." The doctors crusading against abortion were certainly interested in the nature of fetal life—and insisted that the fetus was a biological person "endowed with all that appertains to man." But the AMA, like Storer, did not suggest laws permitting abortion before quickening were unconstitutional.[14]

To begin with, if a fetus was a rights-holding person, it was not clear how much of a practical difference that would make. Before the Civil War, courts, politicians, and even activists did not approach rights claims in the way their twentieth- or twenty-first-century counterparts would. Consider, for example, *Corfield v. Coryell*, an 1823 decision involving a Pennsylvania man whose ship was seized after he harvested oysters in New Jersey waters. Corfield, the oysterman, argued that the seizure violated the Privileges and Immunities Clause of Article IV, Section 2 of the Constitution, which Corfield claimed protected the right to pursue his profession and harvest oysters. In his opinion, Justice Bushrod Washington made clear that citizens held rights beyond those spelled out in the text of the Constitution. These rights, however, were ill defined and seemingly limited—only those so "fundamental" that they belonged to "the citizens of all free governments." And the purpose of these rights, as Washington framed it, was not so much to protect individual liberty but to "secure and perpetuate mutual friendship and intercourse among the people of the different states of the Union." Moreover, these privileges and immunities belonged only to citizens—at a time when states could decide how and when to confer citizenship and excluded most of their Black and Native American residents.[15]

When it did recognize a right, the antebellum Supreme Court often concluded that states were free to regulate it. Historians like Kate Masur and Martha Jones have studied the efforts by Black Americans to claim rights in the antebellum United States, suggesting, as Jones writes, that "free African Americans became rights holders when they managed to exercise those privileges that rights holders exercised." But even for these Americans, claiming citizenship often served as a way to demand the rights that white people already enjoyed, and those rights were both limited and easy for the government to restrict.[16]

At the time Storer's campaign got underway, however, there was a debate about whether constitutional rights applied only to citizens or if some were also available to "persons," a category that included enslaved Americans and free Americans of color. Later generations of antiabortion activists would see a clear parallel between laws that denied the rights of people of color and those they claimed denied the personhood of the fetus. But in the nineteenth century, antiabortion doctors did not make these arguments, even after the Supreme Court's 1857 decision in *Dred Scott v. Sandford*. That case involved an enslaved man who claimed that when his owners brought him to Illinois, where slavery was illegal, he was automatically emancipated. In a 7-2 decision, the Court ruled that people of African descent "were not included, and were never intended to be included, under the word 'citizens' in the Constitution." Scott's case had come to the Supreme Court because under the doctrine of "diversity of citizenship," if the plaintiff and defendant in a suit came from different states, the federal courts had jurisdiction. But because Scott was not a citizen, Chief Justice Roger Taney wrote in his majority opinion, there was no "diversity of citizenship," so the Supreme Court had no jurisdiction over the case. Taney then moved beyond the immediate issue to rule that the Missouri Compromise, which limited the spread of slavery north of 36 degrees latitude in the western states, was an unconstitutional limit on slaveowners' property rights.[17]

Abolitionists, Republican politicians, and others opposed to slavery insisted that Taney was mistaken: the Constitution provided at least some rights for all *men* (or *persons*), a category that included those of African descent. Abraham Lincoln, a trenchant critic of *Dred*

Scott, contended in 1857 that the Court should recognize that all persons enjoyed the rights spelled out in the Declaration of Independence, which applied to "all men," who were "equal in 'certain inalienable rights, among which are life, liberty, and the pursuit of happiness.' "[18] Lincoln and other Republicans did not think that the Constitution guaranteed Black Americans equality in all spheres of life, but nevertheless argued that personhood itself provided them with some protection. Frederick Douglass, the most well-known abolitionist of the era, maintained in 1860 that the key determinant of constitutional rights was whether enslaved Americans were "persons, or . . . beasts of burden." If they were persons, Douglass wrote, "then all the thunders of the constitution may be launched at the head of him who dares to treat them contrary to the rights sacred to persons."[19]

Given this raging debate over the legal status of free Blacks and the legitimacy of slavery, members of the AMA could have drawn a comparison between the unborn child and the enslaved person, as abortion opponents so often would after *Roe:* just as *Dred Scott* denied the rights of Black Americans, legalized abortion denied the rights of the unborn by deeming them non-persons. But even this analogy presupposed that enslaved people and free people of color *did* hold rights, and that point might have fractured the AMA's regionally divided membership. The organization's desire to avoid questions about slavery and race only grew after the Civil War began. The AMA prioritized its self-preservation, stressing, as Dr. Wilson Jewell stated in 1863, that it was an "organization that eschewed all politics."[20]

Storer, in his antiabortion rhetoric, never talked about the Constitution, only about biology and morality. He treated the fetus as a biologically separate human being and insisted that abortion violated a "higher than human law" that treated "the willful killing of a human being, at any stage of its existence, as murder." Not only were

Catholic immigrants having many more babies than native-born Protestant women, he claimed; abortion also damaged women's health, mental well-being, and future fertility, and subverted women's biological destiny of producing potentially unlimited numbers of children. "Were women intended as a mere plaything," Storer wrote, "there would have been need for her of neither uterus nor ovaries."[21]

Abortion in Obscenity Regulation

In addition to the criminal laws championed by the AMA, state and federal obscenity laws also began to address abortion. In the eighteenth and early nineteenth century, courts generally punished speech defined as obscene only when it was also blasphemous or seditious. By the mid-nineteenth century, however, in both the United Kingdom and the United States, courts had begun recognizing "obscene libel" as an independent crime. But courts offered little guidance about what made speech or images obscene—and applied the term *obscene* to profanity-laced public tirades, erotic images, public nudity, and even images of monsters. The anti-vice crusader Anthony Comstock and his allies advocated for a different definition. If Storer grew up around Harvard men, Comstock had been less privileged. His mother had died in childbirth when he was ten. Comstock quit high school to work as a clerk at a Connecticut store before signing on to fight for the Union. By the time he moved to New York after the Civil War, his father had started a new family, and Comstock himself had only a few dollars to his name, but he soon found wealthy patrons in the city's Young Men's Christian Association. Obscenity, he and his colleagues asserted, encompassed not just speech but *items*, like condoms or sex toys. And anti-vice activists defined obscenity to include not only erotic images, objects, and writings but also drugs, devices, and information related to abortion and contraception. All of these things, Comstock's allies argued, encouraged illicit sex and, in the case of abortion and contraception, allowed "women to conceal their lapse from chastity."[22]

In 1873, Comstock got Congress to pass a sweeping obscenity bill that made it a federal crime to receive or mail any "obscene, lewd, or lascivious book, pamphlet, picture, paper, print, or publication, or any article or thing designed or intended for the prevention of conception or the procuring of abortion." Societies for the suppression of vice spread across the country, targeting those who performed abortions alongside supporters of women's suffrage, pool hall operators, lottery organizers, art dealers, crime newspapers, free lovers, suffrage advocates, anarchists, civil libertarians, political dissidents, novelists, atheists, and pornographers. But neither Comstock nor his allies generally spoke of protecting unborn children, let alone of vindicating fetal constitutional rights. Instead, they primarily argued that "the sole purpose of abortionists"—a term Comstock also applied to those who dealt only in contraception— was the "promotion or concealment of licentiousness."[23]

In the later nineteenth century, states passed obscenity bills like the Comstock Act as well as the kind of abortion ban advocated by Storer. The state abortion statutes championed by Storer and introduced after 1850 criminalized abortion throughout pregnancy but allowed an exception if the life of a woman was endangered. Other states retained some version of a quickening rule, but there was no question that Storer and Comstock's campaigns left a mark. Increasingly, the law treated at least some abortions as a crime.[24]

An Uneasy Compromise

Horatio Storer retired from the practice of medicine in 1872 after recovering from a life-threatening infection. For years, he had complained about how much higher the birth rates of Catholic immigrants were compared to "native-born" women. Then, in 1876, he himself married a Catholic woman, a former nun who had tended to him during his infection. He moved to Newport, Rhode Island, a town of seaside mansions, and later converted to Catholicism. He would live until 1922, long enough to see every state enact a ban like the ones he had championed. Anthony Comstock, who died in 1915, saw his name become an epithet: Comstockery, a phrase that signaled a Victorian prudishness that the country had outgrown. But like state abortion bans, the Comstock Act remained on the books. Both kinds of law seemed at least somewhat ineffective: while precise figures are hard to come by, it is clear that illegal abortions continued in the late nineteenth century and first few decades of the twentieth—likely even more than before the practice was criminalized. Prosecutions of abortion doctors under state law remained rare unless a woman died during the procedure, and enforcement of the Comstock Act in cases of abortion or contraception seems to have dropped off considerably.[25]

This uneasy compromise—that abortion remained common, but no one was pushing to legalize it—persisted into the 1910s and 1920s, when an organized birth control movement took shape. In 1912, Margaret Sanger, practicing as a nurse on New York's Lower East Side, encountered a woman, Sadie Sachs, suffering from complications after a self-induced abortion. Sachs recovered with Sanger's help but confided that although she could not survive another pregnancy, her physician refused to prescribe a contraceptive. Sachs's death a mere three months later from the complications of a botched abortion convinced Sanger that laws limiting access to birth control had deadly consequences. Sanger tied her cause to women's equality: if woman "must break the law to establish her right to voluntary motherhood," she wrote in 1917, "then the law shall be broken." Soon after Sanger opened the first birth control clinic in the United States, she and her sister were arrested for fitting a birth control device. After she was released, Sanger increasingly experimented with other tactics, including pursuing support from an ascendant eugenics movement, popular across the ideological spectrum, that sponsored laws requiring the compulsory sterilization of "defectives," vaguely defined to include not only people with certain physical or psychological conditions but also women who had sex outside of marriage.[26]

Eugenicists, for the most part, rejected strategies based on contraception because they wanted the government and the self-proclaimed experts it consulted, not individual patients, to decide who reproduced and when. Moreover, opponents of birth control also reasoned in the language of eugenics: in 1905, for example, President Teddy Roosevelt called motherhood "the duty of women" and chided wealthy and middle-class women for having small families, labeling this "race suicide" the "chief cause as well as chief symptom of what is evil in nations." Other birth control advocates, like the peace and suffrage activist Mary Ware Dennett, did not stress claims tied to eugenics but framed contraception as an issue of equality for women, intimately connected to freedom of speech.[27]

Sanger had better luck when she aligned with the medical profession. Her position gradually gained support from mainline Protestants and Jews as well as from some members of the Black elite, like W.E.B. Du Bois and the suffrage proponent Mary Church Terrell. Not all proponents of contraceptive access endorsed Sanger's approach: Dennett, for example, rejected the doctor-centered model and demanded the repeal of laws, like the Comstock Act, that treated contraception as obscene. Ultimately, both Dennett and Sanger failed in Congress, but their ideas influenced the courts. Even in the nineteenth century, when courts permitted the prosecution under the Comstock Act of a wide variety of Americans for mailing love letters, contraceptive information, and medical textbooks, judges reasoned that the act did not permit the prosecution of doctors who communicated directly with their patients. By the 1930s, federal judges began describing a broader "health" exemption from the statute that pro-tected over-the-counter access to condoms and other contraceptive and abortifacient drugs.[28]

Catholic leaders remained among the most vocal critics of legal birth control and abortion during the Depression, though they did not invoke constitutional fetal rights. In his 1930 encyclical on the subject, Pope Pius XI argued that "the taking of the life of the off-spring hidden in the women's womb" was part of a broader attack on the dignity of life and the family. Some Catholics also drew on eu-genicists' arguments about "race suicide" in opposing legal contracep-tion. Father Charles Coughlin, the Nazi-sympathizing "radio priest" whose sermons at times reached almost one in four Americans, testi-fied before Congress in 1934 that legal contraception would devastate the white race because "negroes [were] out-begetting the Anglo-Saxon and Celtic races in this country."[29]

Countering Abortion Reform

While few openly supported the decriminalization of abortion in the 1930s, medical research and surveys done during the Great De-pression established that abortion had become more common across economic classes and age groups. The visibility of abortion changed prosecutorial practices. For decades, doctors had usually faced crimi-nal charges for performing abortions only when they negligently killed their patients. But in the 1940s, prosecutors began casting a much wider net. Their newfound zeal reflected a growing pronatalist undercurrent in the 1940s. World War II and the start of the Cold War reinforced the belief that a high birth rate would make the nation more secure, both economically and militarily.[30]

Beginning in the mid-1950s, a growing number of non-Catholic hospitals instituted therapeutic abortion committees intended to insulate doctors from civil suits and criminal charges. Growing numbers of these committees began approving procedures when a pregnant woman claimed to be suicidal. In theory, these abortions fell under the life-of-the-patient exception, but there was no easy way to verify that someone was truly suicidal, and some patients with other reasons for seeking an abortion managed to convince committees.[31]

These committees sparked concern among Catholic physicians, but they argued that life-of-the-woman exceptions were no longer justified, not that they violated constitutional fetal rights. In 1951, Dr. James Beaton, the chair of obstetrics at St. Mary's Hospital in Grand Rapids, Michigan, argued that "with modern medical knowledge, therapeutic abortion is practically extinct in all good hospitals."[32]

Beaton might have been surprised to learn that women were still dying from pregnancy-related conditions a decade later—not infrequently due to illegal abortion. By the early 1960s, abortion accounted for nearly half of maternal deaths in New York City, even as evidence mounted that the procedure was safe with a skilled practitioner. Abortion opponents saw figures like these as further reason to suppress the procedure, but they struck other doctors and advocates quite differently: if the procedure could be performed safely, every death due to illegal abortions was a scandal and a tragedy.[33]

In 1959, discontent in the medical community helped prompt the American Law Institute (ALI), an elite body of lawyers, judges, and scholars, to propose a model law that would allow abortions in cases of rape, incest, fetal abnormalities, and threats to maternal health. Reformers like Mary Steichen Calderone argued that ALI-style reform could address grave public health concerns. From a young age, Calderone's aristocratic bearing and forthrightness had made her an imposing presence. She had pursued a career on the stage before going to medical school, practicing for several years before becoming the medical director of Planned Parenthood in 1953. Later in the decade, she took an interest in illegal abortion, organizing a confidential conference and then penning a book on the subject. At the time, Planned Parenthood still officially kept its distance from the subject of abortion reform. "Voluntary parenthood through child spacing," explained William Vogt, Planned Parenthood's national director, in 1955, "is directly opposite to the whole traumatic experience of abortion." Calderone, like Vogt, did not initially call for sweeping changes to abortion laws, but she had become convinced that they were deeply discriminatory. In an influential 1960 article, she wrote of the "inequity of the application" of the criminal laws: a woman with means could more easily get an abortion, while "her poorer, less influential sister . . . in exactly the same physical and mental state . . . is turned down." The previous year, Alan Guttmacher, a prominent physician and family planning proponent, published a book advocating for abortion reform that received attention everywhere from *Reader's Digest* to the *New York Times.* Guttmacher, like Calderone, insisted that abortion reform would advance "the general health."[34]

Calderone and Guttmacher picked an opportune time to challenge criminal abortion laws. In the United States, wildly popular studies of human sexuality published by Alfred Kinsey in 1948 and 1953 presented sex practices and reproductive decisions once viewed as obscene as common. The Rockefeller Foundation, which had subsidized Kinsey's research, also supported the work of the ALI. And the ALI itself recommended not only loosening criminal abortion bans but also decriminalizing a great deal of private consensual sex, including adultery, fornication, and same-sex intimacy. As attitudes about sexual morality began to shift, the framers of the ALI, like some other Americans, started to see criminal abortion laws, sodomy laws, and fornication laws as of a piece: reflecting outdated views about sex. "Restrictive attitudes toward premarital sex," argued the sociologist Alice Rossi in 1966, "bear a decided relationship to opposition to legal abortion."[35]

Changes to the religious landscape made it easier for civil libertarians to call for abortion reform. By this time, the Protestant-led antiabortion movement of the nineteenth century had faded away. Mainline and evangelical Protestants at times endorsed at least some narrow abortion reforms, while others said little about the issue. Views among Catholics were hardly monolithic either.[36]

But the movement to defeat the reform bills was populated overwhelmingly by white Catholic religious leaders and scholars. Initially, these advocates did not discuss the Constitution. Some explicitly referred to questions of faith. When the Stanford legal scholar Ralph Gampell, for instance, argued in 1960 that doctors should not be "forced to practice medicine by courtesy of the district attorney," the *Catholic Standard and Times* responded that physicians "should be required to practice medicine according to the law of God." But the most prominent antiabortion advocate of the time, Eugene Quay, went to great lengths to stress that his hostility to the ALI had nothing to do with Catholicism because he recognized that arguments rooted in Catholic teachings would be a strategic liability. Americans held strong concerns about the separation of church and state. Besides, anti-Catholic sentiment still ran high in the early 1960s, and the Catholic Church often tied abortion to contraception, which was increasingly common and accepted. But Quay, too, did not focus on the Constitution. He and his wife, Effie, stressed arguments about the role of women and the nature of America's long-standing traditions.[37]

In 1961, in the twilight of his long career, Quay was an idealist, an iconic figure in the Chicagoland legal community who had cofounded the *Georgetown Law Journal* almost half a century before. But by the 1960s, his health was declining, and his campaign against the ALI was a joint venture with his wife. Quay had been deeply devout throughout his adult life, but Effie had not been a believer for much of their marriage, even though she agreed to raise their two children in the Catholic Church and to pause her career as a reporter until they were older.[38]

But in 1948, after Effie went back to work, the Quays' nineteen-year-old daughter died in a car accident—a tragedy that reshaped Effie's religious convictions and inspired her later involvement with the antiabortion movement. By the 1960s, Eugene Quay's sight was failing badly, so Effie did much of the research and writing of his argument against the ALI.[39]

The key, as they saw it, was to establish that opposition to abortion was a matter of American tradition, not Catholic doctrine. "Protecting the life of the unborn child," the Quays contended, "has been a major concern of the earliest laws known to us."[40]

While the Quays wanted to focus on tradition, they had a great deal to say about women's roles in the family and in public life. They insisted that exceptions for rape were unnecessary and invited fraud. "The present pressure," they contended, "is for freedom to have abortions for the convenience of the mother." While they acknowledged that some women felt suicidal upon learning they were pregnant, the Quays dismissed these impulses as due to hormonal shifts during pregnancy. Even actual suicides were not a reason to change the law. "If there could be any authority to destroy an innocent life for social considerations," they wrote, "it would still be in the interests of society to sacrifice such a mother rather than the child who might otherwise prove to be normal and decent."[41]

As the ALI model gained influence, similar arguments about gender and morality became more visible. In 1961, when New Hampshire state representative Genevieve Neale proposed a bill that would add an exception for the life of the mother—the norm in virtually all state bans—an emerging Catholic antiabortion movement condemned it. The thirteenth-century Catholic theologian Thomas Aquinas had developed the doctrine of double effect, which suggested that there was a moral distinction between intending and foreseeing the consequences of a course of action. Catholic antiabortion advocates applied this doctrine to distinguish "direct abortion"—the intentional and unjustifiable taking of a fetal life—from what they saw as legitimate medical procedures intended to save the life of the mother that nevertheless foreseeably resulted in the death of the unborn child. That did not mean, however, that early activists supported life exceptions, which theoretically permitted some direct abortions. Archbishop Ernest J. Primeau of New Hampshire, for example, opposed the reform of his state's law. He insisted that there was no scenario in which a life exception was needed because "leading medical authorities" believed that abortion was never necessary to save a patient's life. But even if medical experts rejected Primeau's claim, his view remained steadfast. The movement to legalize abortion, he explained, reflected "secularism, worldliness, and outright paganism." "Medicine," he explained in rejecting a life exception, "should go hand in hand with morality."[42]

The governor of New Hampshire vetoed Neale's bill, but the momentum for the ALI grew, especially after Sherri Finkbine's story gained a national following. Finkbine, a young white woman known as "Miss Sherri" on the local version of the children's TV show *Romper Room*, had taken a pill her husband brought back from London to help with insomnia while she was pregnant. But then she read a story suggesting that the medication she took, thalidomide, caused serious birth defects. She began a deliberately public journey to end her pregnancy, litigating all the way to the Arizona Supreme Court before deciding to travel abroad for the procedure.[43]

Finkbine's abortion changed the conversation. A Gallup poll conducted in 1962 found that 52 percent of Americans believed she had "done the right thing" by terminating her pregnancy. While few women in the United States had taken thalidomide, there was widespread concern about fetal abnormalities due to a recent outbreak of rubella, which caused thousands of disabilities and miscarriages in the United States.[44]

The Quays might have assumed that their readers shared certain beliefs about sex and gender that made legal abortion seem deeply immoral, even in cases like Finkbine's. By the mid-1960s, however, it was no longer clear that most Americans saw sex or abortion in the same light. Now, antiabortion advocates would seek to strip away arguments about gender to focus on the fetus and draw attention away from pregnant women altogether—and to reframe the unborn child not just as a biological person but also as a holder of rights. The new answer given to stories like Finkbine's by antiabortion lawyers and theologians was that even if women wanted to get abortions, legalizing the procedure was unconstitutional. Father Francis Filas, the chair of the theology department at Chicago's Loyola University, had already been outspoken in opposing every direct abortion, even when the mother's life was at risk. He now argued that liberal abortion laws violated the Constitution. "Every unborn child," he contended in 1962, "must be regarded as a human person with all the rights of a human person from the moment of conception."[45]

Due Process

If advocates like Filas needed new inspiration for their arguments, they were in luck: in the early 1960s, the federal courts were recognizing new rights, developing stronger protections for criminal defendants, and demanding more scrutiny of laws that classified people on the basis of race. The new constitutional protections created by the courts opened up the possibility of future litigation—and in the short term, pointed to alternative ways of justifying criminal abortion laws. Rather than discussing religion or even immorality, antiabortion lawyers could present themselves as champions of new liberties. These arguments, however, were not just a strategic convenience. Evolving claims about the vulnerability and rights of the fetus struck a nerve with a growing group of Catholic theologians and lawyers who had their own deeply held beliefs about the Constitution.[46]

William Kenealy, one of the architects of these new arguments, had experience arguing about civil rights. A Jesuit priest who had served as dean of the Boston College Law School from 1939 to 1956, Kenealy had a dry sense of humor that endeared him to the press. Talking to the media was not new for him: he was arguably best known for speaking out against racial segregation. In 1954, in *Brown v. Board of Education*, the Supreme Court struck down laws requiring the racial segregation of public schools, ruling that they violated constitutional guarantees of equality under the law. Kenealy criticized President Dwight Eisenhower for not taking a stronger stand on the racist violence that greeted *Brown*. In the early 1960s, he became one of the nation's most vocal opponents of legal abortion. He contended that the unborn child was a person like any other. Surely, he reasoned, if the Supreme Court was expanding procedural protections for those accused of serious crimes, then innocent unborn children deserved the same respect. "Our plea for the unborn," he testified in 1962, "is for the very same legal fairness accorded all our citizens."[47]

That abortion opponents like Kenealy would make constitutional claims was no surprise. The rhetoric of human rights had become more visible in the aftermath of World War II. After the revelation of the atrocities in Hitler's Germany, the United Nations began the project of detailing universal human rights that every nation should honor, releasing the Universal Declaration of Human Rights in 1948.[48]

The civil-rights movement made rights claims far more politically salient. Following the *Brown* decision, southern legislatures passed dozens of laws intended to nullify *Brown*, authorizing school closures, funding all-white private schools, and suspending mandatory attendance requirements. White resisters threatened violence and economic reprisals against families trying to integrate local schools. This backlash intensified civil-rights organizing and increased northern whites' sympathy for the cause. Kenealy's colleagues in the early antiabortion movement held a wide range of views on civil-rights legislation. Nevertheless, reasoning in the language of rights seemed likely to resonate in politics in ways that arguments about gender roles or sexual morality did not—and, perhaps later, to persuade the Supreme Court. But using the language of constitutional rights was more than a practical move. The civil-rights movement forced white Americans to confront the possibility that laws and practices long taken for granted were in fact viciously biased. In unsettling the meaning of equality, debates about racial justice prompted a wider variety of Americans to rethink what qualified as discrimination and why. Activists like Kenealy, too, believed that the definition of equality had to change, while concluding that segregation was neither the only nor the worst form of discrimination that the country had to uproot.[49]

Kenealy and his colleagues first argued that a fetus was a person entitled to protection under the Due Process Clause of the Fourteenth Amendment, which prohibits the states from depriving "any person of life, liberty, or property, without due process of law." The Bill of Rights further set out specific safeguards for defendants in criminal trials. In the early 1960s, the Supreme Court began holding that more of these criminal protections bound states as well as the federal government, declaring the same about the Fourth Amendment's protections against unreasonable search and seizure in 1961 and the Eighth Amendment's protections against cruel and unusual punishment in 1962. But Kenealy and his colleagues were not initially focused on persuading judges. When speaking to legislators, they stressed that courts were doing more to protect criminal defendants—and told state lawmakers that they should do at least as much for the innocent unborn child.[50]

The failure of several ALI bills in 1962 convinced abortion opponents of the value of such arguments. In March 1963, when Kansas considered its own version of the ALI bill, Emmet Blaes, an antiabortion attorney whose Wichita firm represented four local Catholic dioceses, opposed the proposal by stressing that it would deprive an unborn child of life without due process of law. "No judge presides," he argued, "no advocate speaks, no jury stands to be convinced 'beyond a reasonable doubt' before the sentence of death is pronounced."[51]

Throughout the 1960s, the Supreme Court continued to expand protections for criminal defendants. In *Gideon v. Wainwright* (1963), the Court unanimously held that the Fourteenth Amendment created a right for criminal defendants who could not afford a lawyer to have the state appoint counsel on their behalf. Later in the decade, the Court also held that protections against self-incrimination applied to the states. Antiabortion lawyers like Kenealy hoped that the courts would hand down a sort of *Gideon* for the unborn child—a declaration that fetuses were entitled to their day in court.[52]

By the mid-1960s, as states like California continued debating the ALI model, pro-reform witnesses maintained that antiabortion due process arguments were bunk because fetuses were unique. A fetus had not been born, they stressed, and might never be; and because they depended on their mothers for survival, fetuses were not really biologically separate persons. Lester Kinsolving, an Episcopal minister and prominent reform advocate from Monterey, California, was one of the most visible early proponents of this argument. He claimed that personhood was only a religious teaching of "the Roman Catholic hierarchy," a relic from a time "when women didn't have the right to vote."[53] Anthony Beilenson, the state representative leading the fight to reform California's law, agreed with this assessment, stressing that the only obstacle to reform was "the hierarchy of the Roman

Catholic Church." To his colleagues, Kinsolving wrote that "the strongest opposition to our cause (a religious denomination) is best countered with contrary theological expression."[54]

In the mid-1960s, mainline Protestants like Kinsolving were increasingly likely to speak up in favor of bills patterned on the ALI, as were rabbis from Reform congregations. Despite misgivings about the sexual revolution or the women's movement, conservative Protestants did not join Catholics either. These religious alignments energized a pro-reform movement adamant that opposition to abortion was purely sectarian and had no place in American politics.[55]

Kenealy responded that fetal rights were rooted in biology. Constitutional rights, he reasoned, belonged to anyone who was genetically human, and that included the fetus. "Reason premised on scientific evidence," he wrote, "concludes that the child is essentially the same human being before as after its birth." Kenealy hinted that understandings of equality under the law had to change too. He compared his work on segregation to his new campaign against abortion, describing unborn children, not people of color, as members of the "most voteless, voiceless, helpless, unrepresented and unorganized minority in the land."[56]

Connecting constitutional rights to genetics captivated a growing group of abortion opponents. But from antiabortion lawyers' standpoint, procedural due process arguments were hardly perfect. To rectify a violation, the law usually required more process. Antiabortion attorneys could stress that therapeutic hospital committees were too secretive, or that fetuses lacked representation, or that a full trial was necessary before an abortion could take place. But most of those rallying against the ALI did not want to allow *any* direct abortions, with or without procedural protections, except perhaps in cases of threats to life. Kenealy certainly counted himself in that camp. "The direct and deliberate killing of an innocent human being, even as a means to preserve the life of another human being, is immoral," he wrote in 1963, urging lawmakers to ensure that the law "prohibit abortion for *any* reason." Relying on process left open the possibility that judges would let abortions continue.[57]

A Right to Life

Perhaps, some thought, the alternative was to claim a right to life for the unborn person. The Constitution spells out certain liberties, especially those written into the Bill of Rights. But since the 1900s, the Supreme Court had periodically looked to the Due Process Clause as a source of other substantive rights not made explicit in the constitutional text. Some of these, such as the right to freedom of contract recognized in *Lochner v. New York* (1905), had already been dismantled by the Court. *Lochner*, which had invalidated a maximum working hours law for bakers, had come for many to symbolize an unprincipled approach to judging whereby courts constitutionalized their own policy preferences. But other substantive due process rights still enjoyed respect, such as the right of parents to shape the upbringing of their children, recognized in the 1920s in *Pierce v. Society of Sisters* and *Meyer v. Nebraska*.[58]

The idea of a right to life had tremendous emotional resonance for early antiabortion activists. Some antiabortion lawyers looked to the Declaration of Independence as the source of such a right. By the early 1960s, veneration of the Declaration was already taking off in some conservative circles, promoted by the era's most visible "declarationist," Harry Jaffa, a professor at Claremont McKenna who had trained with the famous political philosopher Leo Strauss. In 1959, Jaffa published a book, *Crisis of the House Divided*, contending that the Constitution protected the rights laid out in the Declaration. The reference to "life, liberty, and happiness" as "unalienable rights" sounded, to abortion opponents, like protection of a fetus's right to life. It was easy to harmonize Jaffa's declarationism with the writings of prominent Catholics like John Courtney Murray, a Jesuit theologian writing in the 1960s who saw the Declaration as evidence that the Constitution was "conceived in the tradition of natural law."[59] Kenealy, for example, insisted that "all human beings have an essentially and fundamentally equal right to life." Antiabortion activists also leaned on a widely publicized 1964 book by Norman St. John-Stevas, a British member of Parliament and columnist for the *Economist*, who argued that the right to life was the foundation "not only of liberty, but perhaps even more of equality."[60]

But to some antiabortion lawyers, right-to-life arguments had drawbacks. To begin with, Stevas was hardly an ideal ally. His position on abortion was too moderate—he suggested, for example, that it would be morally acceptable to allow abortion "on the grounds that it would benefit the life or health of the mother." As important, his views of the law—and even his personal style—felt foreign to those seeking to establish protection for an unborn child as an American principle. He adored the British monarchy and filled his home with papal memorabilia, and could not have seemed less American (or more Catholic) if he tried.[61]

Nor was it clear in 1964 that the Supreme Court would recognize any new due process right, much less a right to life. The most visible effort to secure a new due process right had begun when birth control advocates challenged a Connecticut law modeled on the Comstock Act that barred married couples from using contraception. By the 1960s, this statute was an outlier, and the Food and Drug Administration's approval of the birth control pill in 1960 had made contraception far more widespread. Connecticut's law was also singularly divisive. Most remaining laws prohibited only the sale or manufacture of birth control. Connecticut targeted *use*, and by married couples at that. A challenge to the Connecticut law, *Poe v. Ullman*, had gone to the Supreme Court in 1961, but the justices had decided the case was not ripe for challenge since Connecticut rarely enforced the law.[62]

The Planned Parenthood League of Connecticut did not give up, and the question was soon back before the Court in the case of *Griswold v. Connecticut*. Estelle Griswold, the affiliate's executive director, had worked with doctors, lawyers, and professors supportive of birth control to create a test case, opening a birth control clinic that patently violated the state law. It did not take long for the police to turn up (an enthusiastic Griswold offered information she hoped would be used in a court challenge). When the Court heard arguments in the case in March 1965, some Catholics sided with those challenging the law, arguing that Connecticut had improperly interfered with the private decisions of married couples.[63]

The following June, the Court issued its decision, holding that Connecticut's law violated a constitutional right to privacy. In his majority opinion, Justice William O. Douglas acknowledged that the Constitution's text did not mention such a right, but constitutional amendments protecting the freedom of association and freedom from illegal search and seizure implied that the Constitution safeguarded the right to privacy too. Douglas had no trouble concluding that this right to privacy protected married couples' decision to use contraception. Marriage was "older than the Bill of Rights," and sex was the most intimate part of it.[64]

Griswold established that the Supreme Court was sometimes willing to recognize new constitutional rights, like a right to life, found nowhere in the document's text. But for the antiabortion movement, developments in the mid-1960s increased the importance of arguments based on equality. At the time, the abortion reform movement was growing, and new single-issue organizations were starting to make a more compelling case for legalization.[65]

One national abortion-rights organization, the Association for the Study of Abortion, began operating in 1965 for the purpose of "educating the public in all aspects of abortion as it relates to community life in our country." Its messaging emphasized the impact of criminal abortion laws on low-income Americans. Therapeutic abortion was quite safe when performed in private hospitals that primarily served white patients (between 1943 and 1962, for example, more than 90 percent of women who had therapeutic abortions in New York City were white). The municipal or public hospitals that served most patients of color performed significantly fewer abortions, and many low-income women relied on dangerous at-home methods. Even as pregnancy-related mortality declined, poor women, many of them women of color, used everything from lye injections to off-label vaginal suppositories to end their pregnancies.[66]

The effects of criminal abortion laws on low-income patients became a centerpiece of the argument for reform. Alan Guttmacher, who had become a leader of the Association for the Study of Abortion, described the differences in abortion mortality rates as "class privilege for survival." The sociologist Alice Rossi made a similar point. After marrying in 1951 and bearing three children, she did not give up on pursuing an academic career. At a 1963 gathering of the American Academy of Arts and Sciences, she presented an explosive paper, "Equality between the Sexes," that argued that consigning women to only full-time motherhood was socially destructive—and that a different division of caretaking responsibilities between men and women was necessary. By the mid-1960s, Rossi also stressed that criminal abortion laws had created a public health crisis. The result of such laws, she wrote, was more women forced to undergo "the unsafe and traumatic experience of illegal abortion."[67]

Across the country, feminist reformers also began linking concerns about health equity to sex discrimination. In 1962, Pat Maginnis launched the Citizens Committee for Humane Abortion Laws to fight for reform in California. She had grown up poor in Oklahoma, the daughter of a veterinarian who struggled throughout his life with the fact that he had been born out of wedlock. Maginnis was relieved to be shipped off to convent school, after which she got a job at the Bureau of Mines, joined the army, and was sent to Panama, where she was horrified by the experience of women hospitalized after an illegal abortion. When she returned to the United States, she joined the re-form movement in California. By 1965, her organization had ex-panded, formally incorporated as the Society for Humane Abortion, and Maginnis was framing abortion as part of a broader fight against sex discrimination. "If the woman seeks an abortion, she faces public condemnation," Maginnis testified about a typical pregnant woman before the California state legislature in 1963. "If she happens to be unwed and decides to keep the pregnancy, she will be subject to social stigma, and finally if she carries the child to term and gives it out for adoption, she again suffers the stigma that society uses as a peculiar vengeance."[68] Her organization also began to emphasize that criminal abortion policy hurt the poor and "discriminated against those who can least afford its outrageous costs."[69]

Arguments about a right to life or procedural due process did not fully address these concerns about abortion and equality. Antiabor-tion lawyers had argued that liberal abortion laws were fundamentally unfair because they denied the fetus a lawyer or a hearing, but abor-tion-rights supporters replied that criminal abortion laws were even more profoundly unequal.

A Suspect Classification

What was needed, thought Robert Byrn, was an equality argu-ment *for* fetal rights. The son of a salesman, Byrn had grown up in the Bronx, where he and his brother, Francis, both became lawyers. Francis worked for one of the nation's largest maritime firms, Robert at Hughes, Hubbard, and Reed, the ultimate Manhattan white-shoe law firm. In 1963, Robert returned to teach at his alma mater, Fordham Law School, which had become a hub of antiabortion activity. Byrn was a compulsive volunteer, looking for new assignments at homeless shelters and hospitals. Convinced that the unborn child faced the most daunting discrimination of any group in the country, he began writing about fetal personhood.[70]

Byrn wanted to frame abortion as a matter of discrimination against unborn children. He began by asking not just whether the fetus was human but whether it was "an *inferior* being." As he saw it, there were three leading arguments about why fetuses should be treated differently from people who had been born: (1) fetuses were not recognizable as human, (2) fetuses depended on others for survival, and (3) fetuses were at most a potential life, because a pregnancy might not continue to term.[71]

Byrn rejected each argument by drawing an analogy between fetuses and Black Americans. This strategy was no accident. Racial discrimination was becoming the classic example of unconstitutional bias. In 1954, in *Brown*, the Supreme Court had held that the legal segregation of public schools by race violated the Equal Protection Clause. A decade later, in *McLaughlin v. Florida*, the Court concluded that all laws that classified people on the basis of race were suspect "in light of the historical fact that the central purpose of the Fourteenth Amendment was to eliminate racial discrimination emanating from official sources in the States." Protections for people of color expanded in Congress as well, with the Civil Rights Act passing in 1964 and the Voting Rights Act the following year. The Supreme Court had yet to recognize any other legal classifications that were as suspect as race, but for Byrn, it made no difference. He hoped to argue that classifying someone on the basis of residence in the womb was analogous to racial discrimination.[72]

Fetuses did not look like other persons, Byrn acknowledged, but what did that matter? "Like a person whose skin pigment is other than white," he wrote, "the unborn child is recognizable as a human being simply because he is a human being."[73]

What about the fetus's dependence? People of color did not depend for their survival on physical connection to another person, as fetuses and embryos did. And some pregnancies would end in miscarriage or stillbirth. These real differences could justify differing treatment under the Equal Protection Clause: if two groups of people were not similarly situated, then the genuine differences, rather than discrimination, could account for differing treatment under the law.[74]

Byrn turned this argument on its head, arguing that dependence or vulnerability was the core justification for protecting people of color—or even defining any legal classification as "suspect." "The more dependent and helpless a person is," he wrote, "the more solicitous the law is of his welfare." Black Americans were vulnerable because of past injustice and present-day discrimination. Fetuses were even more so because of their location in the womb. Antiabortion activists, including Byrn, continued to argue that the law had long shown special solicitude for the interests of unborn children. But past prejudice was not central to his argument. For him, the main issue in equality law was physical vulnerability.[75]

In the years to come, the Supreme Court's developing race-discrimination jurisprudence would be both forward and backward looking, asking whether a marginalized group had suffered a history of oppression and if it still struggled with its aftermath. Byrn's model would have required a revolution in thinking about the effects of discrimination on the basis of race and potentially much more. In the years to come, antiabortion advocates would disagree intensely about what personhood required. Nevertheless, the core ingredients of Byrn's vision of personhood—framed as scientific, and fusing ideas of equality, due process, and dependence—would soon attract a wide variety of conservative Americans—and transform the antiabortion movement itself.

2

Individualizing the Fetus

In the mid-1960s, a new model of antiabortion organizing emerged, one led by single-issue groups focused on the fight for constitutional fetal personhood. It all started in San Diego, a city bouncing back from a postwar industrial slump. Dave Tomshany, a Michigan native, opened a public relations firm in town and quickly rose up the ranks of the state Republican Party. By the mid-1960s, he was the go-to campaign manager for the California GOP. In 1966, he was often spotted driving gubernatorial candidate Ronald Reagan from one campaign stop to another in the candidate's powder-blue convertible. When Reagan defeated the two-term incumbent Democrat Edmund Brown that November, it was a major coup for Tomshany.[1]

Maybe Tomshany was intent on making the Right to Life League of Southern California, a group founded in 1967, a success too, and he ran it just like a political campaign. Although the group's early leaders were primarily male, Tomshany's first recruits were often women, many of them self-described homemakers who considered abortion cruel and unnecessary. The Right to Life League bused these women to legislative hearings, handed out brochures, tutored prospective speakers, and oversaw campaigns for the state legislature. Tomshany and his colleagues never missed a chance to stress that they were fighting for the idea of fetal personhood articulated by lawyers like Robert Byrn, and for equality under the law.[2]

What they meant by *equality* was complicated. Tomshany's colleagues agreed with Byrn that the unborn child was a unique, separate human being, and as such was entitled to the same basic legal protections as other Americans. They thus argued that liberal abortion laws—which allowed the killing of fetuses but not other Americans—violated the unborn child's right to equal protection of the laws. But how equality for the fetus fit in with other struggles over civil rights was disputed. Some compared abortion to present-day racism. Others championed equality for the unborn while asserting that hard-working citizens were being taken advantage of by welfare recipients and those Reagan called "malcontents, beatniks, and filthy speech advocates" in the state's universities. For California's abortion foes, the ambiguity of personhood was a virtue. The idea attracted a range of Americans who thought equality was a distant dream but disagreed fundamentally about what had to change.[3]

Struggles over racial justice were shifting in the late 1960s and early 1970s, and core ideas about fetal personhood changed too. As conflict about segregation raged on, some white academics argued that *Brown* would be less controversial if it were understood to bar racial classifications rather than addressing the oppression of Americans of color. Opponents of affirmative action argued that race-based hiring preferences or admissions programs were themselves discriminatory because they defined applicants as members of a racial group rather than judging them as unique individuals. Antiabortion advocates like Tomshany and Byrn came to frame abortion as creating a similar form of discrimination. If white and Black Americans could not constitutionally be categorized on the basis of race, abortion opponents asked, how could the fetus be classified on the basis of residence in the womb?[4]

The Invention of the Right to Life League

The Right to Life League of Southern California was not the first nominally secular antiabortion group. Robert Byrn had founded the Metropolitan Right to Life Committee in New York City in 1963, but he ran it out of a local diocese and did not try especially hard to distance the group from the Catholic Church. Tomshany and his colleagues, though mostly Catholic, wanted to do things differently.[5]

Other abortion opponents thought Tomshany was on to something. Just weeks after the Right to Life League of Southern California was founded, Edward Golden, a Catholic air force veteran who worked in his family's construction business, announced the formation of New York State Right to Life. A few months later, a right-to-life league opened its doors in Northern California, and in October 1967, a Virginia group described by its leaders as 90 percent Catholic—but "trying to keep the church out of it"—began fighting to preserve the state's criminal abortion law.[6]

Tomshany and his colleagues responded to new arguments developed by feminists and other supporters of legal abortion, who increasingly demanded a *right* to end a pregnancy. This new campaign partly reflected a growing conviction among reformers that the exceptions written into state laws were not working. Justifying an abortion under one of the new laws was expensive and complicated, and generally, only relatively wealthy women managed to do it. The number of illegal abortions continued to run high, and deaths from botched procedures were disproportionately concentrated in communities of color.[7]

Feminists led a new fight for the complete repeal of criminal abortion laws. One of the leading women's liberation organizations, the National Organization for Women (NOW), began in 1966 in a Washington, DC, hotel room. The women present at NOW's inaugural meeting believed that the bureaucrats charged with enforcing civil-rights law did not see sex discrimination as a serious problem. Pauli Murray, a pathbreaking Black attorney who had long worked on issues of civil rights and sex discrimination, co-founded NOW to pressure the government to act. Alice Rossi, the sociologist who published a widely circulated article on abortion the same year, was one of the group's early leaders. The group tapped Betty Friedan as its first president. Friedan had emerged as a kind of celebrity since the publication of her best-selling feminist book, *The Feminine Mystique*, in 1963. She helped lead NOW to endorse a resolution calling for the repeal of all abortion laws the year after the organization's founding.[8]

In a position paper for NOW, feminist Ti-Grace Atkinson asserted that fetal-personhood arguments reflected nothing more than "the Catholic position on abortion." "The denotative definitive characteristic of what it is to be a person," Atkinson argued, "is existence as a *separate* man, woman, or child." Atkinson wrote that personhood, properly understood, required bodily integrity—something that a fetus in the womb lacked. A California feminist organization called Abolish All Abortion Laws similarly stressed that personhood began only when a child "survives separation" from the mother. Fetuses may be genetically distinct, feminists acknowledged, but they insisted they could not be persons as long as they lacked bodily autonomy.[9]

The Right to Life League of Southern California responded with arguments that paralleled those emerging in new challenges to integration. In striking down school-segregation laws in the 1954 *Brown* decision, the Supreme Court had discussed the dignitary harms inflicted by segregation. In *Loving v. Virginia* (1967), in invalidating a ban on interracial marriage, the Court likewise spotlighted cultural and legal practices "designed to maintain White Supremacy." But in the climate of intense racial conflict prevailing in the 1960s, some scholars and judges embraced what they saw as a less divisive idea of equality (and, they believed, a less polarizing interpretation of *Brown*): one that prohibited racial *categorization.* In 1964, legal scholar John Kaplan asserted that the harm at issue in *Brown* was "separation by classification." Judge John Minor Wisdom, writing for the Fifth Circuit Court of Appeals in 1966, likewise explained that "state-imposed separation by race" was "an invidious classification and for that reason alone, unconstitutional." Classification, the argument went, harmed Black and white Americans alike by failing to treat them as individuals. The Right to Life League of Southern California articulated a similar view of equality. If fetuses were genetically human, they must be treated like any other unique individual, not classified and thus devalued because of their age or location in the womb.[10]

Related equality claims became a staple of antiabortion advocacy in California. "If anything is fundamental about the American system of life under the law," explained a Right to Life League of Southern California pamphlet, "it is the fact that we all have equal protection of the law. Since the unborn child is really a living human being, we must offer him equal protection too."[11]

Concerns about gender roles and sex still circulated in the Right to Life League. A strategy document mocked feminist claims about past injustice, asserting that 80 to 90 percent of those seeking abortions were married women who had "forgotten or goofed their artificial birth control devices or rhythm." This assumption was not borne out by data. Between 1971 and 1972, for example, the abortion rate for *unmarried* women was between 14 and 18 times higher than that of married women. But Americans might be more sympathetic to the plight of pregnant unmarried women, who were still more often shunned by their peers or denied child support. Married women, of course, could also struggle economically or face domestic violence. But focusing on them allowed Tomshany and his colleagues to paint abortion-seeking women as frivolous and lazy. Other California activists also stressed that legal abortion served the interests of "the married woman who wants the privileges of marriage, but not its responsibilities."[12]

To refute accusations that fetal personhood was "the Catholic position on abortion," however, Tomshany urged his colleagues to focus not on gender politics but on "modern scientific evidence." As far as the science was concerned, Tomshany argued, it did not matter whether a fetus had bodily integrity or not. The unborn child was a *genetically* distinct person, he argued, and any genetically distinct person had constitutional rights. Other antiabortion commentators echoed these points. "From the moment the baby is conceived," wrote Rev. John S. McLaughlin in a 1968 editorial, "it bears the indelible stamp of a separate, distinct personality, an individual different from all other individuals."[13]

A National Movement

In 1966, Monsignor James McHugh, who headed the Family Life Bureau of the National Conference of Catholic Bishops, gathered a handful of Catholic leaders to discuss a national strategy to defend existing abortion laws. One attendee complained about the lack of prior action from the church itself: "Everyone seems to be waiting for everyone else to start a program." But when a program got underway, McHugh stressed, it could not highlight arguments based on religion, gender, or morality. His colleagues thought it far better to make sure that "the key issue revolves around 'when human life begins.' "[14]

McHugh had reached this conclusion after surveying Catholic theologians and church leaders about abortion strategy, who concluded that claims based on science could "elicit support from non-Catholics." To win over more Americans, an emerging movement against legal abortion would present its cause as a fight for the equality of the individual and "protection for the rights of the unborn." In

1967, headlining a conference for Catholic lawyers alongside Robert Byrn, McHugh hinted that the church was preparing for "a long-term campaign" against legal abortion. Byrn added that equality arguments would have to be central—and that any genetically unique human being was entitled to equal protection of the laws. "The basic function of lawyers in this dispute," he stated, "is to demonstrate the relevance of the child's humanity."[15]

To many, it might have seemed that the Right to Life League's model was failing. In June 1967, the California legislature voted for a modest reform of the state's abortion law, and Tomshany's friend and ally Ronald Reagan signed it into law. But McHugh, who had been considering the idea of a national antiabortion organization for some months, thought the time had come for a national version of the California experiment. In April 1968, he announced the formation of the National Right to Life Committee, a secular national organization meant mostly to coordinate the many local groups that were emerging. Its first president, Juan J. Ryan, a conservative former navy man, worked as an attorney in tiny New Providence, New Jersey, where he represented everyone from construction companies to a pair of brothers accused of being surly toward the police. While lawyers for the National Right to Life Committee gave speeches, and the group hosted national conferences, the leaders of the fight for fetal personhood were unquestionably the leaders of state groups.[16]

In Minnesota, a new power couple emerged. St. Paul native Marjory Mecklenburg had grown up on the state pageant circuit, winning the title of Health Queen and Style Queen as a teen in back-to-back years. She met her husband, Fred, in high school when the two teamed up to win statewide debate contests. By the late 1960s, Fred seemed like the ideal leader of an antiabortion organization. An obstetrician-gynecologist, he was a Protestant veteran with a direct line to local papers, where he dispensed tips on maintaining a healthy pregnancy. Over time, however, Marjory emerged as the guiding force in Minnesota's movement, rising to prominent positions in national organizations and advocating for benefits for pregnant women, including those who were not married.[17]

New recruits to the antiabortion movement shared Robert Byrn's view that abortion was the worst form of discrimination. He had been traveling the country participating in abortion debates in cities from Honolulu to Hartford. It was his understanding of equality under the law for the fetal person that convinced Byrn that abortion should not be allowed in cases of rape or incest. The fetus was "far more helpless at the hands of the abortionist," he told an audience in Fort Lauderdale in 1967, "than his mother was at the hands of the rapist."[18]

Racial Justice

Antiabortion leaders saw themselves as fighting for equality at a time when the meaning of that term was deeply divisive. That was certainly true of Robert Byrn. He had maintained a steady speaking schedule, working closely with antiabortion groups just opening their doors. At Fordham, he had gained a certain notoriety because of his high-profile views. Nothing, even racism, matched the discrimination faced by the fetal person, he told a Connecticut crowd in 1968. "What we are countenancing is the death of a human being," he said, drawing a comparison between his movement and the struggle for civil rights. "Nobody cries out for fetal power."[19]

Byrn referenced changing ideas about racial equality. In 1966, at the March Against Fear in Jackson, Mississippi, the charismatic civil-rights leader Stokely Carmichael called for "black power for black people."[20] The idea quickly spread, and while it signaled many things, from demands for economic autonomy to expressions of cultural pride, many whites were repulsed. In 1966, the *Washington Post* called

Black power activists "black supremacists." For some people of color, however, Carmichael's demand spoke to ongoing injustices. The passage of the Civil Rights Act, the Voting Rights Act, and later the Fair Housing Act represented important milestones, but deep structural inequalities remained. More than four in ten Black Americans lived below the poverty line in 1966. Anger about persistent segregation, poverty, and police violence prompted civil-rights leaders to define equality in new ways.[21]

Martin Luther King Jr., the best-known leader of the civil-rights movement, also discussed the unfinished work of racial equality, tying the question to the war in Vietnam. The United States had first intervened in Vietnam, Laos, and Cambodia in the mid-1950s, after a Soviet-supported independence movement drove out the French army and took control of North Vietnam. Over time, the U.S. military had significantly escalated its involvement, with troop levels rising from under 20,000 in 1964 to more than 550,000 in 1969. In 1967, breaking with his ally Lyndon Johnson, who as president had supported those major civil-rights bills, King argued that the war had sent "black and white boys to kill and die together for a nation that was unable to seat them together in the same schools."[22] Later that year, King unveiled a Bill of Rights for the Disadvantaged, denouncing "the tenacious poverty that so paradoxically exists in the land of plenty." King portrayed war and poverty, like racism, as dehumanizing people of color.[23]

These shifting ideas played out against a background of tremendous civil unrest. In July 1964 in Harlem, Thomas Gilligan, a police lieutenant, killed James Powell, a fifteen-year-old Black child, in front of his friends and a group of witnesses. The shooting set off a wave of protest that led to the arrest of 465 New Yorkers and the injury of many others. The Harlem disturbance was the first of several dozen uprisings that deepened many whites' resistance to the civil-rights movement. Then in 1968, James Earl Ray, an escaped convict, murdered Martin Luther King Jr. when he was standing on the balcony of his Memphis hotel. The riots that followed King's assassination marked the most intense period of civil unrest since the Civil War.[24]

Polls taken in the late 1960s and early 1970s showed that Black Americans were more likely to oppose legal abortion than their white counterparts. Intense debate within the Black community helps to make sense of this divide. In the late 1960s, Black nationalists denounced both birth control and abortion not primarily because they violated fetal rights but because they worried that they could lead to "Black genocide." Some of these leaders argued that legal abortion or birth control would thin the numbers of a community that needed to grow to attain political power; others worried that the government offered Black families access to abortion or contraception instead of addressing racism or poverty. Prominent Black feminists responded that access to abortion and birth control would improve the lives of women of color seeking racial uplift. The feminist attorney and civil-rights activist Florynce Kennedy, one of these advocates, observed that many women of color had spoken out against "the oppressiveness of enforced pregnancies."[25]

Kennedy wrote at a time when some Black Americans identified the push to legalize abortion with what some saw as a racist population control movement. That movement got its start with the discrediting of eugenics after the Second World War, when observers noted parallels between U.S. compulsory sterilization laws and Nazi policies. But the supporters of eugenics hardly went away. Frederick Osborn, a former general who co-founded the Population Council in 1952, was a former head of the American Eugenics Society, and in an early draft of the Population Council's charter, the group vowed to stop "a downward trend in the genetic quality of the population." The Association for Voluntary Sterilization, founded in the 1930s under a different name to fight for compulsory sterilization, advocated looser limits on hysterectomy and vasectomy procedures. As late as 1962, its president, the eccentric Dixie Cup founder Hugh Moore, said that the organization still "favored the sterilization of imbeciles and the like." After 1945, a wave of involuntary sterilizations targeted Black women, a phenomenon some linked to the rise of calls for population control. The ascendancy of a population control movement did not make fetal personhood attractive so much as it convinced Black Americans that abortion reform might harm them.[26]

In truth, many of those who gravitated to population control did not have eugenic aims. Cold warriors worried that the Soviet Union would exploit overpopulation to draw developing countries into its orbit. Other population controllers focused on environmental preservation or women's liberation. Nor did all population controllers endorse legal abortion. And the movement to repeal criminal abortion laws reached well beyond the population controllers: it included not just liberal feminists in groups like NOW but also radical feminists, like the members of the Redstockings who stormed the 1969 legislative hearings in New York on whether to repeal the state's abortion ban and then created a speak-out of their own to tell the stories of the "real experts, women."[27]

Nevertheless, given the popularity of calls for population control, some supporters of abortion rights argued that decriminalizing abortion would curb demographic growth—an argument that held little appeal for Americans of color. For example, Planned Parenthood, which had renamed itself Planned Parenthood–World Population in 1961, distributed brochures arguing that legal abortion would lower welfare costs and illegitimacy rates at a time when welfare recipients were disproportionately people of color.[28]

Despite community debate about abortion, very few Black Americans joined the fetal-personhood movement. That was no surprise: those who championed personhood were divided about civil-rights policy. Some agreed with Robert Byrn's colleague Charles Rice, a law professor who helped form New York's Conservative Party, which had harshly criticized federal civil-rights legislation. James Buckley, the brother of commentator William F. Buckley Jr. and a Conservative Party candidate for a New York Senate seat in 1968, ran full-page ads in New York newspapers denouncing federal civil-rights statutes as "bills [that] abridge the rights of every American to give 'rights' to a few." Buckley, who would win election in 1970 and go on to sponsor one of the first constitutional personhood amendments, was born into oil money and lived most of his life on a gracious estate in Sharon, Connecticut, but he projected the image of a fed-up military veteran ready to fight on behalf of white, middle-class New Yorkers. On the campaign trail, he praised George Wallace, the former segregationist governor of Alabama, for his "strong stand on civil disorders" and called for the government to "stop patronizing and condescending to the Negro" by passing civil-rights legislation.[29]

Other proponents of fetal personhood supported further steps toward integration and voting rights for people of color. Ferdinand Buckley (no relation to James or William) was a well-heeled Atlanta lawyer who had served as a fighter pilot in World War II, flying under the cover of the famed Tuskegee Airmen, a group of primarily Black pilots. Buckley was the living embodiment of the Atlanta establishment: a booster for local businesses who belonged to the Cherokee Town and Country Club, a member-owned golf facility for Atlanta's white elite. But he also hosted campaign events for John F. Kennedy and led a local effort to write in a moderate Democrat when the two finalists in Georgia's 1966 gubernatorial race ended up being self-congratulatory segregationists. (The winner, Lester Maddox, rose to fame in the state after refusing to serve Black seminary students at his fried chicken restaurant.) Buckley especially opposed the stereotyping of Americans of color and the exclusion of qualified Black Americans from clubs and from positions of power.[30]

The claim that real equal treatment required that each American be treated as a unique individual, rather than as part of a group, united abortion opponents who otherwise disagreed on civil-rights policy. "The essential premise of Anglo-Saxon jurisprudence, the affirmative doctrine of democracy, the conception of the Constitution of the United States," explained a prominent antiabortion pamphlet, all rested "on the fundamental proposition of the integrity of the individual." Robert Byrn emphasized the same point. "All life, even unborn," he told an audience in New York, "deserves equal protection of the law."[31]

Born outside of Marriage

The meaning of equality was also up for grabs as the courts and voters grappled with the treatment of children born outside of marriage. Some abortion opponents believed that discrimination against unmarried mothers and their children led to abortion and campaigned to eliminate these kinds of biases from the law. Other anti-abortion advocates argued that the ultimate cause of abortion was a "contraceptive mentality"—a view that sex was for pleasure rather than procreation—and that lifting penalties faced by unmarried women and their children would lead to more nonmarital sex and, inevitably, to more abortion. The debate about the treatment of children born outside of marriage came to the fore because of new legal challenges. For centuries in American law, children could not inherit or even use the last names of their biological fathers unless their parents were married. By the 1960s, some states had softened this stance, but reforms were uneven, and anger about "unwed mothers," much of it suffused with racism, came to a boil.[32]

The Aid to Families with Dependent Children (AFDC) program provided grants to low-income families with children, but in the late 1960s, "welfare mothers" had become a coded term for racial animus, especially because the birth rates of unmarried women were higher in communities of color. A 1965 Gallup poll asked respondents what should be done when "unwed mothers on relief continue to have illegitimate children." About half of those polled favored cutting off financial support; roughly 20 percent favored compulsory sterilization. By the late 1960s, however, organizations from the NAACP Legal Defense Fund to the American Civil Liberties Union (ACLU) argued that discrimination against children born outside of marriage was indefensible.[33]

It was no accident that the first case on the subject to reach the Supreme Court came from Louisiana, which had recently passed a law denying AFDC aid to entire families when a woman had a child outside of marriage. The case, *Levy v. Louisiana* (1968), involved a wrongful death statute that authorized surviving family members to sue if a loved one were negligently or intentionally killed, but that did not allow such suits by children born outside of marriage. Louise Levy, a white New Orleans mother of five, died after a doctor failed to diagnose her hypertensive kidney failure. Her attorney argued that her children deserved the same benefits as any other child.[34]

In *Levy* and a companion case, *Glona v. American Guarantee & Liability Insurance Company*, the Court held Louisiana's wrongful death law to be unconstitutional. In a 6-3 majority opinion by Justice William O. Douglas, the Court began by explaining that children born outside of marriage are persons under the Constitution. "They are humans, live, and have their being," he reasoned. "They are clearly 'persons' within the meaning of the Equal Protection Clause." There was no justification for treating children born outside of marriage differently from anyone else. It was "invidious to discriminate against them," Douglas wrote, "when no action, conduct, or demeanor of theirs is possibly relevant."[35]

Robert Byrn, who had taken on a prominent role in the early National Right to Life Committee, saw the *Levy* decision as a boon to the fetal personhood movement. Instead of focusing on the effects of poverty or racism experienced by unmarried mothers, the Court had based its ruling on the rights of children. And it had recognized the significance of biology, saying that any living "human" might qualify as a person under the Fourteenth Amendment. Byrn thought an identical argument could be made on behalf of the fetus. "Unborn children too are 'humans, live, and have their being,'" he wrote in 1968, quoting *Levy*. "Thus, they are 'persons within the meaning of the Equal Protection Clause of the Fourteenth Amendment,' and no public opinion poll, no popular vote . . . can overcome this constitutional hurdle."[36]

Byrn's personhood language appealed to the growing antiabortion movement while sidestepping the growing conflict over legitimacy, race, and nonmarital sex. Activists like Marjory Mecklenburg believed that support for abortion stemmed partly from the mistreatment of unmarried mothers. Few, if any, abortion foes were comfortable with the sexual revolution, but Mecklenburg and others like her believed that discrimination at work, at school, and in the broader community was one factor driving unmarried women to terminate their pregnancies. She favored removing information about legitimacy from birth certificates and believed the government should protect fetal persons by doing more to support their mothers, including giving them better health care and contraceptive access.[37]

Other abortion opponents saw out-of-wedlock sex as a threat to fetal personhood. Charles Rice bemoaned "birth control fever," a mindset, he believed, that led people to devalue fetal life and have sex with no concern for anyone but themselves. Unmarried mothers had bought into a "new philosophy of man and sex" that counseled "the abandonment of self-control over sexual urges." Rice reasoned that one of the best ways to stop abortion was to stop fornication, and one of the best ways to stop fornication was the fear of pregnancy. Those leading the movement to legalize abortion and those fighting to destigmatize illegitimacy, he suggested, both wanted the same thing: "promiscuity with impunity."[38]

The idea of personhood appealed to those with a wide range of views on the treatment of unmarried mothers. It also helped to unify antiabortion activists across political parties at a time when neither the Republican nor Democratic leadership consistently opposed abortion. In 1968, President Richard Nixon had won the popular vote and carried thirty-two states. While he believed he could have done better with Catholics, he still was not ready to say much about abortion. Other Republicans, like Governor Nelson Rockefeller of New York, fully supported abortion reform.[39]

The Democratic Party's position was not any clearer. When New York legislators began to consider restoring previously repealed abortion restrictions, most of the support for the idea came from Democrats. In Congress, however, prominent supporters of abortion rights identified with the political left. With neither party taking a consistent position, members of the antiabortion movement were left to pick candidates based on other issues, and that was hardly a recipe for unity.[40]

These partisan divides made fetal-personhood arguments that much more important in the fight against abortion. How restrictions would be enforced—and how fetal personhood related to questions about race or legitimacy—remained unclear, but sometimes that lack of clarity could be a virtue. A broad idea of personhood allowed activists to paper over their disagreements and work together.

Personhood in Court

By the late 1960s, some courts had begun to embrace the idea that abortion was a fundamental right. In 1969, the California Supreme Court said as much in rejecting the criminal conviction of Dr. Leon Belous for performing an abortion. The law he had broken, the court wrote, abridged "women's right to life and right to choose when to bear children."[41]

The *Belous* decision energized proponents of repeal. A California advocate called it "a single episode in a long endeavor to obtain appropriate freedom for women and licensed physicians." Then, in 1970, Hawaii became the first state to make abortion legal before viability, the point at which there was a reasonable chance of survival outside the womb, as long as it was performed in a hospital by a licensed physician. In New York, Governor Nelson Rockefeller convened a commission to study the state's abortion law. Constitutional challenges were underway in courtrooms across the country.[42]

How would antiabortion activists translate personhood arguments into a legal strategy? Robert Byrn and other attorneys quickly arrived at a consensus: they would ask courts to appoint guardians to represent either individual unborn children or entire classes of fetuses. Illinois attorney Dennis Horan raised the idea of seeking the appointment of what he called a guardian for the unborn in 1970 in a Washington, DC, case that was headed to the U.S. Supreme Court. Horan was a textbook workaholic, a former linebacker, a lecturer at the University of Chicago, a legal advisor to the National Conference of Catholic Bishops, and a sometimes-scowling perfectionist with a fearsome reputation for representing plaintiffs in personal injury cases. His wife, sister, and brother-in-law were all active in the antiabortion movement.[43]

In the Washington, DC, case, prosecutors had indicted Dr. Milan Vuitch for violating a district ordinance that outlawed abortion except when "necessary for the mother's life or health." Vuitch, who made no secret of his willingness to perform abortions, sought to have the indictment dismissed, arguing that the DC ordinance was unconstitutionally vague. Horan, representing his brother-in-law, a physician who was trying to intervene in the case, asserted that there was nothing "vague in Congress exercising its inherent legislative authority to protect the civil rights of the unborn." The same year, when a Georgia woman challenged that state's ALI-style bill, Ferdinand Buckley sought to be named guardian of the fetus, arguing that an unborn child was a "legal person" entitled to "equal protection of the law." In 1971, Horan also sought the appointment of a guardian for the unborn in Illinois when the ACLU challenged the constitutionality of that state's abortion law.[44]

As other lawyers had done in the 1960s, Horan emphasized that courts had recognized fetal rights in some cases involving inheritance, prenatal injuries, wrongful death, and the refusal of unwanted medical treatment. Mostly, however, Horan insisted that abortion was the equality issue of the era. In *Dred Scott*, he wrote, "a black man was deprived of his right to bring suit in a federal court because he could not qualify as a citizen." Absent the appointment of a guardian for the unborn, "every child who is unwanted by his or her mother may be deprived of his civil right to life because he or she cannot qualify as a 'person.'"[45]

By the 1970s, ultrasound technology was becoming widespread, and Horan, like other antiabortion lawyers, believed that fetal imaging helped to make the case for personhood. A guardian for the unborn could put an ultrasound image before a court—and, ideally, before the media and the public. Calling for the appointment of a guardian also made sense to Horan and Byrn because courts nominated guardians to protect children and others who were unable to represent their own interests. By demanding the appointment of a guardian, antiabortion lawyers stressed that the fetus was similar: weak and vulnerable, but a person entitled to equal rights.[46]

Discrimination Based on Residence in the Womb

Whatever the courts thought about appointing guardians for fetuses, some antiabortion organizations felt that they were gaining an edge in state legislatures. In April 1970, when New York governor Rockefeller signed into law a statute allowing access to abortion for any reason until the twenty-fourth week of pregnancy, the setback helped to transform New York State Right to Life into a lobbying force.[47]

The main players in New York State Right to Life tended to be white, conservative, and fond of confrontation. Few had patience for women who sought abortions. Representative Neil Kelleher, one of the movement's staunchest supporters, liked to entertain New York State Right to Life rallies with the story of his mother. Told that she might die if she continued the pregnancy, Mrs. Kelleher chose to proceed and passed away thirty days after the birth of Kelleher's younger brother. Kelleher and members of New York State Right to Life held her up as an ideal that all women should aspire to. "That," Kelleher declared at one rally, "is what I call a real mother."[48]

The members of Mecklenburgs' Minnesota Citizens Concerned for Life, by contrast, presented themselves as advocates for poor women as well as the unborn. One of the group's members, Carole Nichols, told the Minnesota press that pro-liberalization lawmakers were "really saying, 'We don't want to do anything positive for the poor, so we'll get rid of poor people's children.' "[49]

In demanding guardians for the unborn, Robert Byrn hoped to appeal to both of these constituencies. He had long referred to the fetus as his "client" and maintained that human biology gave rise to personhood and thus to constitutional rights. He mocked the idea that courts might recognize rights for corporations, which were wealthy, powerful, and not even human in the first place, while ignoring the personhood of powerless unborn babies. Byrn and some of his colleagues were suspicious of corporate power, believing that abortion itself was becoming a big business—and that most corporations supported what they saw as a pro-abortion political establishment. Writing in 1971, for example, the conservative philosopher Russell Kirk mocked the "baby-food and baby-product companies" that would never "force the media to give equal time to pro-life" while advertising to expecting parents. "It would be the ultimate in irony," Byrn wrote, "if the corporation which manufactures the instruments used to abort the unborn human child was entitled, as an artificial person, to equal protection of the law, while the unborn child, who is in all respects qualitatively human, is deprived of that protection."[50]

But Byrn's ideas of equality for the fetus also tracked shifting arguments about race. In the late 1960s, some white parents organized to resist the enforcement of school integration orders, dismissing these practices as "busing." States began proposing anti-busing bills, and in 1972, Nixon emphasized his opposition to the "busing of our Nation's schoolchildren to achieve racial balance." That year, Irene McCabe, a white anti-integration activist from Michigan, became a media sensation when she mounted an anti-busing "march on Washington" to protest what she called "the long arm of the federal government reaching into my home and controlling the children I gave birth to."[51]

In the late 1960s and early 1970s, as the federal government began to more clearly authorize race-based affirmative action, some labor union activists, white liberals, and conservatives denounced what they called "reverse discrimination," arguing that affirmative action unfairly ignored individual merit. As academic jobs and seats in graduate schools became more scarce, reverse discrimination lawsuits multiplied. Richard Nixon picked up on the call to stop reverse discrimination at the 1972 Republican National Convention, proclaiming: "The way to end discrimination against some is not to begin discrimination against others." Critics of affirmative action argued that it failed to treat each individual as an individual. "Because one is a member of high achieving groups," asked the sociologist Nathan Glazer regarding affirmative action in 1972, "should he or she as an individual be penalized?"[52]

Byrn echoed these arguments about equality, individual rights, and meritocracy. He contended that liberal abortion laws effectively classified the unborn based on their age or location in the womb, rather than valuing them as unique individuals. While the "original intent" of the Fourteenth Amendment was "to safeguard Negroes against discrimination by whites," he wrote, the Equal Protection Clause had "evolved into a broad guarantee of equality both to artificial persons and to all natural persons irrespective of citizenship, sex, or race." Equality under the law no longer focused on past injustice or group identity but guaranteed individual treatment for each human being. "Natural human beings," Byrn wrote, "cannot be denied equality by the simple expedient of categorizing them as non-persons."[53]

Americans United for Life

As the 1970s began, antiabortion leaders were unsure precisely what the courts were making of their arguments. The Supreme Court's January 1971 decision in *Vuitch* was hardly clarifying. The Court had rejected a constitutional challenge to the DC ordinance, but not by embracing Horan's personhood arguments. Instead, it interpreted the ordinance as requiring prosecutors to prove that an abortion did not protect a patient's life or health. To antiabortion lawyers' dismay, it interpreted "health" to include mental as well as physical well-being. Understood in this way, the Court explained, the law was more than clear enough.[54]

Nor did it appear that any judge would appoint a guardian for the fetus. In Georgia, a district court had revoked Ferdinand Buckley's guardianship before deciding that the state's law violated the Constitution. Horan lost the first round in the Illinois case *Doe v. Scott*, after which he complained that lawyers for the unborn had received "thirty minutes to argue, and our demand for a jury was ignored."[55]

Some courts were even ruling that existing criminal abortion laws violated the Constitution. Texas, like most states at the time, still prohibited abortion except in cases of threats to life when Norma McCorvey, who had already given up two children for adoption, decided she wanted to end her third pregnancy. A lawyer who had helped arrange her previous adoptions recommended that she contact Sarah Weddington and Linda Coffee, two attorneys who were planning a constitutional challenge to Texas's law. Like their colleagues, they raised a wide variety of constitutional arguments against the law, but primarily, they stressed that the right to privacy extended to the abortion decision. The district court agreed, ruling that the Texas law "infringes upon plaintiffs' fundamental right to choose whether to have children." In the spring of 1971, the Supreme Court agreed to hear an appeal in McCorvey's case, *Roe v. Wade*, as well as *Doe v. Bolton*, a challenge to Georgia's law.[56]

Some antiabortion activists did not think the National Right to Life Committee was doing enough to advance fetal personhood or prepare the movement for a win or loss at the Supreme Court. At an emergency summit in March 1971, a group of antiabortion leaders proposed the formation of a new national group named Americans United for Life. L. Brent Bozell II, a champion of the new organization, was the sort of conservative who thought most other conservatives were too soft. A passionate anti-Communist who idolized Joseph McCarthy and Francisco Franco, the Fascist leader of Spain, he had first fashioned himself a radical as an undergraduate at Yale in the late 1940s. He went on to ghostwrite Barry Goldwater's book *The Conscience of a Conservative* and defend Jim Crow segregation as an expression of states' rights. He married the sister of William F. Buckley Jr. and became Buckley's close friend and colleague on *National Review* before quitting because he thought the magazine was too moderate on abortion. Charles Rice and Marjory Mecklenburg joined Bozell in helping to organize Americans United for Life (AUL). The group chose as its chairman George Huntston Williams, a self-identified progressive Unitarian professor at Harvard Divinity School who opposed the Vietnam War. It seemed hard to believe that one organization could represent the views of people as disparate as Bozell, Mecklenburg, and Williams, but the equality-based idea of personhood appealed to all of them. "We believe, in the words of the Declaration of Independence, that 'all men are created equal,'" Americans United for Life proclaimed in its declaration of purpose. "To be true to its heritage, this nation must guarantee to the least and most disadvantaged among us an equal share in the right to life."[57]

While the group's leaders were finding their bearings, the contraception issue arrived at the Supreme Court. In November 1971, the Court heard arguments in *Eisenstadt v. Baird*. Bill Baird, the defendant, was working as the clinical director of a contraceptive manufacturer in 1963 when he saw a hospitalized mother of nine die from complications from an illegal at-home abortion. Radicalized by the experience, he set out to expose what he saw as the absurdity of birth control bans.[58]

Following a 1967 speech, Baird gave a condom and contraceptive foam to a student and was promptly arrested. He appealed his conviction all the way to the Supreme Court, where the justices were also set to hear a pair of cases on abortion, the Texas case of *Roe v. Wade* and *Doe v. Bolton*, the Georgia case in which Ferdinand Buckley had been involved. Horan hoped that *Roe* and *Doe* would offer the Court the chance to weigh in on whether the fetus was a rights-holding person.[59]

Guardians for the Unborn

Robert Byrn had similar hopes. In December 1971, he sought to be named the guardian for all fetuses scheduled for abortion in New York and asked the court to declare the state's recently passed liberal law unconstitutional. The New York City Health and Hospitals Corporation responded that the suit was nothing more than "a device for the presentation in another forum of the plaintiff's social, religious, and moral views on abortion." Were fetuses persons? The hospital corporation responded that they were "humanoid organisms," but being genetically human did not make the fetus a rights-holder.[60]

The hospital was right that Byrn wanted to capture media attention and was using the suit to do it. "The baby is never part of the mother," stated one of his star witnesses, Dr. Dennis Procaccini. "In the biological sense, he is always a complete individual."[61] Byrn made the same point in his complaint, describing the "Infant Roe" and the class of unborn children he represented as "irreversibly individual, living human beings." If the Equal Protection Clause prohibited the categorization of individuals by race, he argued, it seemed natural that any "irreversibly individual human being" deserved the full spectrum of rights. He maintained that Infant Roe and all fetuses in the state of New York enjoyed "a fundamental and inalienable right to life, liberty, and personal security and a right to due process and equal protection of the law." On December 3, a Queens judge agreed, appointing Byrn guardian of Infant Roe and a class made up of other fetuses.[62]

Guardianship turned Byrn into a media sensation. Students at Fordham published interviews of Byrn and his attorney, who described fetuses as the ultimate victims of bias, "voiceless, voteless, and friendless." Others on campus denounced Byrn, arguing that his "sexist affront to the dignity of women" was nothing more than an attempt to return the law "to the dark ages." Reporters took a prurient interest in the fact that he had never married and still lived with his mother. He no doubt minded the prying but mostly seemed to enjoy the attention. Byrn's newfound celebrity brought greater awareness to the idea of fetal personhood while making it seem that abortion foes agreed on what it was. He vowed to "give the unborn child his day in court."[63]

Byrn seemed to be making headway. In January 1972, the same Queens judge granted his request for a preliminary injunction, temporarily halting abortions while the case continued. Abortion foes saw hopeful signs elsewhere too. While abortion-rights lawyers had their share of wins, district courts in Louisiana, Utah, North Carolina, and Ohio had rejected constitutional challenges to abortion bans. The Ohio court, in *Steinberg v. Brown*, reasoned that "once human life has commenced, the constitutional protections found in the Fifth and Fourteenth Amendments impose upon the state the duty of safeguarding it." But in Byrn's New York case, the Health and Hospitals Corporation appealed, and in February, the New York Appellate Division reversed the lower court's decision. Byrn appealed to New York's highest court.[64]

While that appeal was pending, a fight within Americans United for Life exposed just how much disagreement lay behind the embrace of fetal personhood. At an early meeting, George Huntston Williams argued that as a matter of political necessity, the group should accept exceptions for the life of the mother and for cases of rape and incest. Together with Marjory Mecklenburg, he also stressed that promoting fetal personhood was consistent with endorsing all forms of contraception. That did not sit well with Bozell, Rice, and their allies, who believed that some kinds of birth control, including intrauterine devices, blocked the implantation of a fertilized egg and therefore killed rights-holding persons. Many obstetricians argued that these drugs and devices delayed or prevented ovulation. Williams agreed, and he asserted that his movement would never win over many Protestants or Jews unless it supported birth control.[65]

If Williams had expected an easy conversation, he was mistaken. Bozell, always drawn to the nuclear option, wrote Williams that if Americans United for Life tolerated any exceptions to abortion bans, he would accuse its leadership of fraud, because in its early fundraising, it had characterized itself as a no-exceptions organization. (Later he changed tactics and promised Williams a tony fundraiser with William F. Buckley Jr. if the group took Bozell's position.)[66] Charles Rice also wrote to Williams, saying he was horrified by the idea of supporting rape and incest exceptions and believed that use of IUDs was tantamount to murder.[67]

The immediate upshot of the dispute was chaos. Invoking the distinction between direct abortion and foreseen but unintended life-taking, Rice proposed a resolution stating that Americans United for Life opposed "all direct abortion without exception." At a March 1972 meeting, the group's leaders voted 7-6 to table the motion. Rice responded with an alternative, opposing all abortion except in cases where a mother's life was at risk. This proposal was also defeated. The fallout was swift. Bozell, Rice, and the rest of their faction resigned.[68]

Williams quickly turned to personhood claims to unify those who remained. He took a particular interest in the forthcoming report of a commission on population control chartered by President Nixon. The commission's final report, issued in March 1972, concluded that "the availability of abortion on request causes a reduction in the number of illegal abortions, maternal and infant deaths, and out-of-wedlock births, thereby greatly improving the health of women and children."[69]

Williams rallied AUL around a letter to Nixon denouncing the commission's findings. In it, he compared abortion to racism. "The Founding Fathers of our republic . . . reckoned the black man to be 3/5 of a person for the purposes of establishing white representation in Congress," Williams warned the president. "Your commission runs the risk of making a comparably huge blunder today."[70]

Equality on the Basis of Sex

Fortunately for Williams, Nixon was finally ready to take sides on the abortion issue. In April 1971, Senator Edmund Muskie of Maine, running for the Democratic nomination, said in an interview with the journalist David Frost that abortion should be illegal after the sixth week of pregnancy. Muskie's interview lit a fire under Nixon. He rolled back an earlier policy allowing abortion on military bases. In March 1972, when the population commission released its report recommending the liberalization of abortion laws, Nixon wasted no time condemning it.[71]

Antiabortion leaders could not have been more excited by Nixon's newfound zeal, but the Supreme Court's March 1972 decision in *Eisenstadt v. Baird* brought disagreements over contraception back to the surface. In a 6-1 majority decision by William Brennan, the Court agreed with Bill Baird that Massachusetts's contraceptive ban violated the Constitution. The opinion relied on the Equal Protection Clause, ruling that Massachusetts had no basis for treating unmarried people differently from anyone else. But the meaning of a due process privacy right was at the center of the case. "If the right of privacy means anything," Brennan wrote, "it is the right of the individual, married or single, to be free from unwarranted governmental intrusion into matters so fundamentally affecting a person as the decision whether to bear or beget a child."[72]

Also, that March, Congress voted to send the Equal Rights Amendment to the states for ratification. The ERA, as it was called, established that "equality under the law shall not be abridged or denied by the United States or any state on account of sex." Feminists Alice Paul and Crystal Eastman of the National Women's Party had drafted such an amendment in 1921, and Congress first considered passing it two years later. Between the 1930s and the 1950s, Congress occasionally considered an ERA bill, but for some time, feminists themselves had been divided about the idea. By the late 1960s, however, pro-ERA feminists had gained the upper hand. In August 1970, more than fifty thousand Americans participated in the Women's Strike for Equality, a protest that built support for the ERA. In October 1971, the House overwhelmingly voted to pass the ERA, and in March 1972, the Senate did the same.[73]

Some antiabortion advocates endorsed the ERA and insisted that advancing equality for women would further the fight for fetal personhood. These activists stressed that women and the unborn suffered from similar forms of oppression: being denigrated for traits over which they had no control. The ERA, they claimed, would create a more defensible definition of equality under the law. At the same time, pro-ERA abortion opponents believed that addressing sex discrimination would help fetal persons by lifting some of the pressures that led women to terminate their pregnancies. One such activist was Mary Alice Duffy, a pioneering lawyer in Philadelphia in the 1950s who was famous for terrifying those she encountered in court (decades later, her colleagues would remember her as the living embodiment of her initials, M.A.D.). Duffy loved to represent underdogs, accused murderers with reams of evidence against them, or pacifists refusing to be drafted to fight in Vietnam. She identified as a feminist and called on lawmakers to do more to prevent sex discrimination. "We believe in equal rights for women," she argued in outlining her opposition to legal abortion, "but we cannot demand equal rights for ourselves unless we are willing to recognize and protect the rights of others." Patricia Goltz, a college student in Ohio, also supported the ERA and founded Feminists for Life in 1972 with a local professor, Cathy Callaghan.[74]

Other antiabortion activists argued that the ERA undermined fetal personhood by creating a new constitutional foundation for abortion rights and denigrating motherhood. An emerging anti-feminist movement was beginning to depict the ERA as the most visible sign of what was wrong with the women's movement. Phyllis Schlafly, who would become the ERA's most visible opponent, had failed in several runs for public office, but she had a knack for energizing conservative Americans. If anyone rivaled Brent Bozell in hating Communism and loving Barry Goldwater, it was Schlafly. In the 1970s, she made it her mission to destroy the ERA and take down feminists, whom she described as "radicals waging a total war on the family, on marriage, and on children." Her mission resonated with some abortion opponents. For example, Barbara Jones, a Kansas activist, linked Schlafly's opposition to abortion with her opposition to feminism, writing that both jeopardized the rights of the unborn because of the whims of "women unhappy with life, home, love, parents, and fellowmen." For activists like Jones, abortion and the ERA were of a piece: both undermined the privileges wives and mothers had long enjoyed in the name of an equality no one really wanted. Some abortion foes further argued that ratification of the ERA would lead some courts to strike down criminal abortion laws, holding that such bans discriminated on the basis of sex.[75]

The ERA debate roiled the movement. At least abortion opponents had a clear champion in the 1972 presidential campaign. Richard

Nixon had become more vocal about his opposition to abortion, partly to outflank a potential Democratic rival, Hubert Humphrey, who tried to boost his campaign against frontrunner George McGovern by attacking McGovern as too liberal on abortion. Nixon, who wanted to capture the Catholic vote, sent a letter to New York's archdiocese praising the fight to repeal New York's liberal abortion law. The letter was then leaked to the press by a Nixon staffer. Abortion opponents felt optimistic as a result of Nixon's support and a string of political victories. In New York, the legislature voted to undo its liberal abortion law, and only Nelson Rockefeller's veto prevented its repeal. In November, Michigan voters rejected Proposal B, which would have legalized abortion up to twenty weeks.[76]

Generally, though, the question of abortion appeared to have reached a stalemate, with both sides making uneven progress both in politics and the courts. Robert Byrn's guardianship gambit failed in July when the New York Court of Appeals, the state's highest court, ruled against him. Some mocked Byrn. True, he was willing to stand in as guardian for every fetus in New York, but would he assume responsibility for all of those children if they were born? Byrn and his attorney, for their part, framed the very fact that his case had made its way to the state's highest court as a victory of sorts. Byrn vowed to appeal his case on fetal personhood immediately. It seemed that the U.S. Supreme Court would have the final word on the matter.[77]

3

Victims' Rights

In his second inaugural address, on a frosty day in January 1973, Richard Nixon proclaimed a new era of self-sufficiency. He promised to end the Vietnam War, reset the welfare system, make the criminal system tougher, and ensure equality for Americans who had been short-changed by an excessive focus on the marginalized. "Let us remember," he intoned, "that America was built not by government, but by people—not by welfare, but by work."[1]

Robert Byrn had bigger things on his mind than Nixon's reelection. He had appealed his loss in New York to the U.S. Supreme Court, insisting, as the press explained, "that liberal abortion laws deny fetuses the equal protection of the law." Byrn asked the courts to imagine the fetus as an "astronaut in a uterine spaceship"—a person like the rest of us, albeit one traveling through a very foreign environment. But before the Court said a word about Byrn's appeal, the justices handed down a decision in *Roe v. Wade* recognizing a right to choose abortion. Byrn's allies would remain divided about whether Nixon's ideas about equality made sense. But in the next decade and a half, the movement's leadership would change as the antiabortion cause became more closely associated with the conservative legal movement, the Republican Party, and conservative Protestantism. As the antiabortion movement evolved, so did dominant visions of fetal personhood, with more insisting that the Fourteenth Amendment only protected rights that were deeply rooted in history and tradition.

Proponents of fetal personhood also more often contended that equality under the law required justice for crime victims who had long been forgotten by American society—chief among them, the unborn child.[2]

Roe

It seemed that the Supreme Court would weigh in on the issue of fetal personhood when the Court heard oral argument in *Roe v. Wade* in October 1972. Sarah Weddington, who led the oral argument for Jane Roe, fielded several questions about whether the "law give[s] rights to unborn children." Robert Byrn's appeal was pending too.[3]

Less than week before the *Roe* decision came down, the Court decided what feminists saw as a related case, *Frontiero v. Richardson*, which involved a federal law making it harder for male military spouses to qualify as dependents than it was for females. The Court ruled the law to be unconstitutional by a vote of 8-1 but fractured about the rule that should apply to sex classifications. (Writing for a plurality, Justice William Brennan concluded that the Court should apply the most exacting standard, strict scrutiny, to sex as well as race classifications, while several justices, including Justice Harry Blackmun, endorsed a less demanding approach.) Robert Byrn and his colleagues had long hoped that the Court would recognize the fetus as the next protected class. In *Frontiero*, it was *sex* that a divided Court saw as being like race. As Brennan explained, sex classifications too often reflected "gross, stereotyped distinctions."[4]

Roe said relatively little about the issue of sex discrimination raised in *Frontiero*. Instead, a 7-2 majority ruled that the right to privacy recognized in earlier cases about contraception, procreation, parenting, and marriage protected a woman's decision to terminate her pregnancy. The Court began with a history of medical and legal attitudes toward abortion. Justice Harry Blackmun, the author of the *Roe* majority, wrote that for centuries, "abortion performed before 'quickening' . . . was not an indictable offense." While acknowledging that over the course of the nineteenth century, states overwhelmingly chose to criminalize abortion throughout pregnancy, Blackmun presented the bans as a recent phenomenon.[5]

At some points in his majority opinion, Blackmun stressed the "detriment that the State would impose upon the pregnant woman." Often, he focused on physicians, suggesting that prior to viability, "the attending physician, in consultation with his patient, is free to determine, without regulation by the State, that . . . the patient's pregnancy should be terminated." The Court laid out what would become known as the trimester framework, which allowed little regulation in the first trimester of pregnancy and permitted the state to advance an interest in fetal life only after viability.[6]

The Court also considered the possibility that the word *person* in the Fourteenth Amendment applied before as well as after birth. Were this to be established, Blackmun wrote, the case for a right to abortion would collapse, "for the fetus' right to life would then be guaranteed specifically by the Amendment." But Blackmun observed that in most of the Constitution, *person* applied "only postnatally." Moreover, the Court argued, abortion had been more common and less stigmatized in the 1860s, when the Fourteenth Amendment was ratified, than it would become later in the nineteenth century. That made it less likely that the framers of the amendment would have intended the word *person* to apply before birth. In a dissenting opinion, Justice William Rehnquist criticized the Court for recognizing a right that "was apparently completely unknown to the drafters of the [Fourteenth] Amendment."[7]

The Supreme Court's January 1973 decision did not immediately transform Norma McCorvey's life. By then, McCorvey, who was scraping by cleaning houses, had given birth to a daughter, given her up for adoption, and fallen in love with her long-term partner, Connie. The *Roe* decision, as Joshua Prager writes, did not strike her as important enough to record in her datebook. The same was not true for many Americans. Supporters of abortion rights set to work to make abortion accessible—no small feat in a nation where most abortions took place in hospitals and only 17 percent of public and 28 percent of private, non-Catholic hospitals offered the procedure. Despite these hurdles, the decision changed the lives of American women. At least nine hundred thousand legal procedures took place in 1974, and the number increased again by 11 percent the following year. Abortion-related maternal mortality also declined, particularly as more women seeking a termination did so early in pregnancy.[8]

Robert Byrn saw *Roe* as a cruel joke. If everyone agreed that the fetus was human—as he would later quip, the unborn child was obviously not a bat or a cat—how could the *Roe* Court have rejected personhood? Byrn and his attorney filed an emergency motion, asking for a hearing before "an entire class of human beings is deprived of the protection of the law." Byrn insisted that the *Roe* decision was simply not fair because fetuses had never had their day in court. "The framers of the Constitution," he contended, "intended every human being, every member of the human race, even the most unwanted, to fall within the aegis of the due process and equal protection clauses." None of it was any use: the Supreme Court dismissed Byrn's appeal almost exactly a month after *Roe* came down. But the Supreme Court's ruling did not discourage Byrn or other proponents of fetal personhood. They wrote their legislators. They picketed when they heard that a doctor might be performing an abortion. And almost as soon as the ink was dry on the *Roe* decision, members of Congress began proposing constitutional amendments to undo it.[9]

The Human Life Amendment

In February 1973, Byrn and other leading antiabortion activists gathered in Washington, DC, to plot their next steps. Some of them shared ideas proposed by sympathetic state lawmakers like Henry Hyde, then toiling away in obscurity in the Illinois legislature. A hulking figure who relished the rough and tumble of local politics, Hyde had already proposed a bill requiring a woman to get a court order before receiving an abortion in the second trimester. He also wanted wives to obtain their husbands' consent. There were other measures: waiting periods, laws requiring minors to gain their parents' permission, and limits on how and by whom an abortion could be performed. But no matter how well-liked Henry Hyde was among those present that day, the kind of incremental restrictions he proposed did not excite anyone. Many activists had joined the antiabortion movement to demand constitutional rights for the unborn, and the meeting attendees unanimously voted for a resolution calling on Congress to pass a personhood amendment.[10]

Those championing such an amendment sometimes drew on broader conversations about the Vietnam War. That long-running conflict was increasingly unpopular, especially after the media reported in 1968 that American soldiers had murdered more than five hundred people in the village of My Lai, many of them women and young girls who had been sexually assaulted and mutilated. The My Lai massacre fed a broader conversation about the dehumanization of civilians during wartime, especially those who were not white. So did the widespread use of napalm, a kind of "liquid fire" mixed with a gel that would stick to victims and prove almost impossible to extinguish. Scientists protested against its use, and against the weaponization of herbicides like Agent Orange, which destroyed entire ecosystems during the war.[11]

In the mid-1970s, some in the antiabortion movement infused these concerns about war into their claims about personhood. "In some instances," explained Indiana activist Roland Chamblee of the need to protect the unborn, "we declared the North Vietnamese 'nonpersons.'" Thomas Hilgers, a young physician affiliated with the movement, made a similar point. "We as a nation," he said in 1974, "have been appalled by the ongoing destruction in Southeast Asia. At the same time, however, we have promoted the destruction of unborn humans at a rate which makes Vietnam look like the Boston Tea Party." The National Youth Pro-Life Coalition, a left-leaning antiabortion youth group, called on President Nixon to "prove that peace with honor applies to the war on the unborn." Not all abortion opponents agreed about the war—the movement had its share of hawks—but the comparisons to Vietnam underscored the dehumanization of the vulnerable. The point of these analogies was the same: the unborn child was a person like any other, one uniquely vulnerable and therefore entitled to particular constitutional protection.[12]

It was not easy for antiabortion leaders to frame a perfect constitutional amendment. As Representative G. William Whitehurst found out, some ideas were dead on arrival. Whitehurst, whose friends fondly called him Dr. Bill, had been a history professor at Virginia's Old Dominion University before running for the House of Representatives. Thinking a personhood amendment would never get through the Senate, he proposed an alternative: a states' rights amendment that would allow, but not require, states to criminalize abortion.[13]

Almost everyone in the antiabortion movement hated the idea. Robert Byrn objected that a states' rights amendment would put "the right to live at the mercy of shifting legislative majorities." The National Right to Life Committee, still the largest national antiabortion group, passed a resolution suggesting that a states' rights proposal would not "effectuate . . . rejection of [*Roe*] but would rather reaffirm the Court's decision."[14]

But what would a perfect amendment involve? Antiabortion attorneys agreed on the big picture. They demanded an amendment that would define the term *person* in the Fourteenth Amendment to apply from the moment of fertilization. Fleshing out the details, especially on enforcement, would prove trickier.[15]

Charles Rice, the ultra-conservative law professor who had recently moved to Notre Dame, thought that any amendment to redefine *person* under the Fourteenth Amendment would largely set the clock back to the 1950s, reviving all the nineteenth-century criminal laws against abortion and invalidating any subsequent liberalization. But some of Rice's colleagues disagreed with that interpretation. Others thought the amendment should aspire to something more than reviving the old laws that twentieth-century antiabortion activists had inherited.[16]

Having long compared the fetus to people of color, many antiabortion lawyers now proposed to pattern their personhood amendment on the Thirteenth Amendment, whose wording, "Neither slavery nor involuntary servitude . . . shall exist within the United States . . .," applied to private citizens as well as to the government. Such an amendment seemed indispensable to antiabortion lawyers given that private citizens, not government actors, performed most of the nation's abortions.[17]

Joseph P. Witherspoon of the University of Texas was one of the most vocal proponents of looking at the Thirteenth Amendment for inspiration. Witherspoon was a law professor's professor, fond of abstruse constitutional theories. In Austin, he fought for a city ordinance requiring the desegregation of its public schools, served as a local advisor to the NAACP, and advocated measures to ameliorate housing segregation. He still connected his views on race and abortion after

Roe, noting that he saw a "very close resemblance between killing human beings through abortion and submitting them to slavery and involuntary servitude." Witherspoon favored adding a life exception that required physicians to make every reasonable effort to save both the unborn child and the woman. Absent such an exception, he argued, no amendment would pass.[18]

Witherspoon believed that the framers of the Thirteenth and Fourteenth Amendments had considered the fetus a "person" deserving equal protection and due process of law. In a friend of the court brief in the *Roe* case, he had stressed that "a person simply is and has his being by virtue of an act of creation by God himself." His preferred amendment, he wrote, would restore "full protection for the life of unborn children under the Constitution."[19]

Robert Byrn worried that if his colleagues followed Witherspoon's advice, some would accuse the antiabortion movement of pursuing *special* rights for the unborn, not equal treatment. If a constitutional amendment prohibited private citizens from denying due process or equal protection to the fetus, the unborn child would enjoy more expansive rights than other persons, who could raise equal protection or due process claims only against the government and its agents because of the state action rule, which the Supreme Court applied in interpreting the Fourteenth Amendment. Byrn also wanted more attention paid to the enforcement of such an amendment. He thought the movement should simply use the playbook he had already developed: seeking "the appointment of a guardian for unborn children" who could go to court to seek an injunction before any abortion took place.[20]

Still others thought that equal treatment for the unborn required the elimination of any exception to abortion bans. Nellie Gray, the most vocal champion of this approach, grew up poor in Big Spring, Texas, joined the Women's Army Corps during World War II, went to night school, and became a lawyer for the Department of Labor. After the *Roe* decision, she quit her job to start a new organization, March for Life, in her basement. Gray saw compromise as a weakness, her zeal earning her the nickname "the Joan of Arc of the pro-life movement." Her proposed amendment would not include an exception for the life of the patient, which Gray argued was medically unnecessary and morally unprincipled. The principle of self-defense, she argued, did not apply because "the unborn child could not be called an 'unjust aggressor.'"[21]

Other antiabortion activists began to question whether the movement had fixated too much on banning abortion and too little on other ways of respecting fetal personhood. By 1974, when she pursued this idea, Marjory Mecklenburg had quit the National Right to Life Committee and founded American Citizens Concerned for Life to advocate for a vision of personhood that involved more support for pregnant women. In congressional testimony on a personhood amendment, Warren Schaller, one of the new group's leaders, suggested that in addition to abortion bans, real enforcement of personhood would require more support for pregnant women.[22]

Schaller, an Episcopal minister, preached at Gethsemane Episcopal Church, a graceful Gothic Revival building in downtown Minneapolis. He took a deep interest in civil rights, traveling from Minneapolis to Selma, Alabama, in 1965 to join Black Americans protesting for voting rights. He was also an ardent supporter of the Equal Rights Amendment, finding it hard to believe that anyone would oppose equality for women. He believed in fetal personhood and served for a time as the executive director of the National Right to Life Committee. In 1974, after joining Mecklenburg's group, Schaller argued that recognizing fetal rights would require "mandatory maternity insurance benefits, . . . AFDC payments for [the] unborn child as soon as pregnancy is diagnosed, low-cost housing, [and] day care facilities."[23]

Abortion-rights feminists and their allies organized to defeat the human life amendment. The National Abortion Rights Action League (NARAL) launched a project to discourage state legislatures from ratifying it. Advocates of abortion rights argued that writing fetal personhood into the Constitution would be unworkable, requiring what Harriet Pilpel of Planned Parenthood called "a drastic overhaul of our entire legal system." Pilpel was in her sixties when *Roe* came down. A long-standing member of the ACLU, she did not see herself as a feminist but fought to get the ACLU to take a position in favor of abortion rights as early as 1964. By the late 1970s, she was a regular on conservative William F. Buckley's debate program, *Firing Line*, an elegantly dressed and fearsome advocate. After *Roe*, she was ready to fight against a personhood amendment. How would a fetus be counted for the purposes of the census, she asked in 1974, or the apportionment of congressional seats? Would a woman have to face criminal charges if she abused alcohol or drugs during pregnancy? Recognizing fetal personhood was not just about imposing a minority religious view on the nation, she suggested. It was opening Pandora's box.[24]

Informed Consent

The 1976 presidential candidates wanted to steer clear of the abortion issue. Following the Watergate scandal and Nixon's resignation, Gerald Ford, the new president, had studiously avoided the subject. White House talking points created in 1974 clarified that Ford disagreed with *Roe* but believed "in abortion for limited situations such as rape or illness."[25]

If Ford took a middle ground that pleased no one, Jimmy Carter's position was simply muddy. A *New York Times/CBS News* poll taken in February 1976 showed that 36 percent of voters thought the Democratic frontrunner opposed an abortion ban, while 21 percent thought he would be sympathetic. Most respondents understandably had no idea what Carter really believed.[26]

The only major candidate willing to embrace the idea of personhood was Ronald Reagan, the former California governor who proclaimed in 1975 that "the unborn human being is entitled to the same protection as the rest of us." Reagan linked personhood to a particular vision of equality in America. On the stump, he regaled audiences with the tale of a "welfare queen" from Chicago who had used more than eighty aliases, claimed veterans' benefits from four nonexistent husbands, and collected welfare under each of her assumed names, defrauding the government of some $150,000. (Not much is known about the real person to whom Reagan referred, Linda Taylor, who may have gotten as little as $8,000 from the government.) Another favorite yarn centered on "working people" waiting in line at the grocery store to buy hamburger meat while "some strapping young buck" "purchased T-bone steaks with food stamps." Reagan denounced aggressive remedies to desegregate schools. When he invoked equality for the unborn child, he linked the idea to a defense of the white American majority and anger at a government that, he claimed, doled out welfare to the undeserving.[27]

In July 1976, a month before the Republican National Convention, the Supreme Court issued its first opinion on abortion since *Roe*, *Planned Parenthood of Central Missouri v. Danforth*. Missouri had passed a wide-ranging set of restrictions, requiring minors to get their parents' consent, married women to get their husbands', and doctors to get written consent from abortion seekers themselves. The state also regulated the procedures that doctors could use. The Supreme Court held unconstitutional everything but the provision mandating their patients' written consent. *Danforth* demonstrated that the Court was open to upholding certain abortion restrictions, some of which seemed quite promising. In 1976, Henry Hyde, who had made his way to Congress, helped push through a ban on Medicaid reimbursement for abortion. Measures like the Hyde Amendment would significantly limit access to abortion.[28]

For now, however, the movement still had no friend in the White House. At the Republican National Convention, Reagan made a last-ditch effort to win over moderate Republicans by selecting Pennsylvania senator Richard Schweiker as his running mate, but the move backfired, and Ford secured the nomination. Later that year, Carter squeaked past Ford, winning just over half the popular vote.[29]

Carter tried to stake out a middle-ground position on abortion rights. In the summer of 1977, in *Maher v. Roe*, *Poelker v. Doe*, and *Beal v. Doe*, the Supreme Court upheld a series of state and local laws banning the use of public money or facilities for abortion. Carter praised the decisions, but he was no supporter of fetal personhood, and a constitutional amendment to protect fetuses was not going anywhere.[30]

A group of antiabortion lawyers began trying different ways to convince Americans that unborn children were rights-holding persons. James Bopp Jr., a young Indiana lawyer, was one of them. He had been drawn to conservative politics well before he thought much about abortion. After campaigning for Barry Goldwater in high school and running for student body president at Indiana University, Bopp found kindred souls when he returned to Indianapolis after law school. If anything excited him more than conservative politics, it was winning. He loved to dwell on the details of tactics and strategy. In 1978, he took a job as the general counsel of the National Right to Life Committee and helped the group launch the Pro-Life Legal Action Project, telling an antiabortion newsletter that while abortion opponents had neglected litigation, "anti-life groups had gone wild." He proposed a plan for advancing fetal personhood that would build on *Danforth* by prioritizing informed consent.[31]

Bopp and other antiabortion attorneys experimented with this idea in drafting a model ordinance for Akron, Ohio, a town of tire factories long known as the "rubber capital of the world." The architects of the ordinance acknowledged that "when the Supreme Court legalized abortion, it declared that the unborn were not persons, thereby removing protection under the law." That did not mean, however, that the law could not build toward *later* recognition of personhood. If the Akron ordinance could mandate that patients hear certain information and thereby convince the public that a fetus was a biologically distinct person, that could be a foundation for persuading Americans to think that the fetus should have constitutional rights. "Human life begins at conception," the talking points explained. "This is basic human biology, and knowledge of it should not be denied to any woman."[32]

The debate over the Akron law became a national story. Reporters from major metropolitan areas trudged through the snow and packed the hearings for the ordinance. When it passed, in March 1978, abortion-rights supporters immediately challenged its constitutionality.[33]

Most personhood proponents pinned their hopes on the 1980 election. Ronald Reagan was back, and antiabortion activists could not have been happier about it. When he defeated Carter in a landslide, Republicans benefited down the ballot, gaining thirty-five seats in the House and taking control of the Senate.[34]

The Human Life Bill

By the time Reagan took office, feminists had gained more power in leading abortion-rights organizations. Population control reasoning had become associated with racism and fallen out of fashion. In 1981, NARAL chose a second feminist, Nanette Falkenberg, a veteran labor organizer, to replace its outgoing executive director, Karen

Mulhauser; Planned Parenthood's leader, Faye Wattleton, a Black feminist former nurse, had run the organization since 1978.[35]

Increasingly, the women leading the abortion-rights movement argued that fetal-personhood laws violated the Establishment Clause of the First Amendment, which prohibited the government from making any law "respecting an establishment of religion." Across the country in the late 1970s, attorneys filed challenges to the constitutionality of the Hyde Amendment, insisting that it advanced the religious beliefs of faith groups committed to fetal personhood. In *Harris v. McRae*, the first case to reach the Supreme Court, the plaintiffs argued that the Hyde Amendment sought to impose on Medicaid recipients "the central teaching of the anti-abortion faiths that the fetus is a person." Feminists and other abortion-rights supporters made this argument in the political arena too. "The only purpose of the Hyde Amendment," argued an ACLU pamphlet in the late 1970s, "is to promote a particular religious view of when life begins."[36]

In June 1980, the Supreme Court upheld the Hyde Amendment. In a 5-4 majority opinion in *McRae*, Justice Potter Stewart concluded that the plaintiffs did not have the standing to raise questions about the free exercise of religion because none of them showed that they were seeking an abortion for reasons of faith. The Court also rejected the idea that the Hyde Amendment involved an establishment of religion, reasoning that beliefs about personhood reflected not religious teachings but " 'traditionalist' values towards abortion." Stewart also reiterated that the privacy right recognized in *Roe* did not entitle anyone to an actual abortion. If a woman was too poor to afford the procedure, the Court reasoned, that was not the government's fault, and the Constitution had nothing to say about it.[37]

McRae came down at a time of backlash to the civil-rights movement. A 1980 National Opinion Research Center poll revealed that two-thirds of white respondents attributed the struggles of Black

Americans to their own lack of "motivation or will power." The Supreme Court had also begun sending a different message about racial equality. In 1974, in *Milliken v. Bradley*, the Court rejected a constitutional challenge to the segregation of Detroit schools. White families had fled the city, creating majority white school districts in the suburbs and majority Black urban districts. Together with several parents and students, the Detroit NAACP sued, seeking to desegregate local schools by bringing students across district lines. In *Milliken*, the Court ruled against the NAACP by a vote of 5-4, holding that the lower court could not order this kind of remedy because there was no evidence that the segregation at issue stemmed from intentional bias. In *Washington v. Davis* (1976) and *Personnel Administrator of Massachusetts v. Feeney* (1979), the justices concluded that laws could be challenged under the Equal Protection Clause only if a litigant could prove animus, no matter how grievous the disproportionate harm a law did to a marginalized group.[38]

At the same time, the increasingly visible disability-rights movement was promoting new ideas about discrimination. In 1977, protestors with disabilities had staged a sit-in at the offices of the Department of Health, Education, and Welfare to push for regulations implementing the Rehabilitation Act of 1973, a law that prohibited entities receiving federal funds from discriminating on the basis of disability. The following year, to protest a lack of access to public transport, a group of protestors in Denver got out of their wheelchairs and blocked traffic. The issue of ageism also drew attention. Congress had passed the Age Discrimination in Employment Act in 1967, but in the early 1980s, prominent companies embarked on rounds of layoffs that disproportionately affected older workers.[39]

These ideas of equality took center stage when Republicans mounted a new effort to write fetal personhood into the law. In January 1981, Jesse Helms proposed a Human Life Bill that would strip the federal courts of jurisdiction in certain abortion cases and establish that human life began at conception. A segregationist and self-proclaimed anti-politician who had haunted the halls of the Senate since 1972, Helms worked with Ron Mazzoli, a Democrat from Louisville, to craft the legislation. The two saw that abortion opponents lacked the votes to get a constitutional fetal-personhood amendment through Congress and put the bill forward as a workaround. Since the *Roe* Court had not offered an answer as to when life began, they reasoned, that meant that Congress could supply one, making an unborn child a rights-holding person whose life could not be taken.[40]

John Willke, the president of the National Right to Life Committee, put a new spin on his movement's ideas about equality in testifying before Congress in support of the Human Life Bill. Before becoming an antiabortion leader, Willke had been a celebrity in Catholic sex education circles, a photogenic doctor who traveled the country with his wife, Barbara. After *Roe*, Willke quickly rose up the movement's ranks, but in his testimony to Congress in 1981, he less often compared fetuses to people of color or to women. Drawing an analogy to race or sex discrimination was not as strategically advantageous when courts were retreating from decisions strongly policing either one—and when conservative white Americans had increasingly soured on the idea of additional civil-rights laws. At the same time, disability and age discrimination resonated more strongly with an antiabortion movement convinced that physical weakness, not a history of past prejudice, was the central concern when it came to equal protection. As with age and disability discrimination, Willke suggested, fetuses were rights-holding persons harmed by "discrimination on the basis of physical or mental [im]perfection."[41]

At least in principle, leading lawyers in the antiabortion movement were inching toward consensus on a "unity amendment" that would declare the fetus a person. The National Right to Life

Committee board of directors tapped a committee of leading anti-abortion lawyers, including James Bopp, to draft an amendment. Unity, in practice, was not so easy to find. The idea of incremental restrictions on abortion, which had originally had a broad appeal across the movement, now struck some absolutists as counterproductive: an excuse that lawmakers would use to indefinitely postpone the push for a constitutional fetal-personhood amendment. Judie Brown spoke for many of these absolutists. Growing up in Los Angeles in the 1950s, she developed a fiercely independent streak when her birth father abandoned her, her mother, and sister when Judie was a year and a half. She worked as a bookkeeper to put herself through college, took a job at the Kmart Corporation, and married a man, Paul Brown, she met on the job. The two became active in the pro-life movement, but as the 1970s wore on, Judie became convinced that her movement compromised too much on everything from contraception to abortion exceptions. She started the American Life League in 1979.[42]

Activists like Brown made the work of creating a unity amendment anything but easy. When Willke announced that the lawyers had managed to agree on the details of an amendment, the members of the National Right to Life Committee's board of directors erupted in applause. The unity amendment contained an exception for the life of the mother—seen by many lawyers as a political necessity—but required "that every reasonable effort be made to preserve the life" of both women and fetuses. The amendment also declared that rights and personhood began at fertilization and that the right to life was paramount and would take precedence over any other constitutional protection. Willke, always fond of a turn of phrase, attributed the lawyers' consensus to "good, old-fashioned prayer."[43]

However much antiabortion leaders wanted the unity amendment, it was not going anywhere in Congress. The federal personhood statute was also in trouble. Helms and Mazzoli argued that

Congress had the authority to pass it under section 5 of the Fourteenth Amendment, which gave Congress the power to enforce the Due Process and Equal Protection Clauses. But Robert Bork, a prominent conservative Yale law professor and outspoken critic of the *Roe* decision, testified that while Congress had the authority to address "violations of . . . constitutional guarantees, as they are defined by the courts," it had no "power to define the substantive content of the guarantees, themselves." If the federal courts agreed with Bork, they would strike down the Human Life Bill as unconstitutional. Bork was not alone: many members of the antiabortion movement agreed with Helms that a fetus was a rights-holding person but did not think the Court would uphold a federal statute declaring that to be true.[44]

Victims' Rights

While Congress debated the Human Life Bill, Ronald Reagan contributed to a new rhetoric of equality. The liberal federal government, he argued, had long failed to protect the law-abiding majority. Reagan claimed to be an innovator, but draconian anti-crime policies began well before he took office. Richard Nixon increased surveillance programs, encouraged states to build more prisons, and helped to militarize local police departments. Jimmy Carter had continued disinvesting in welfare programs, privatizing services, and expanding police departments. Reagan's punitive policies continued this bipartisan tradition, but he tapped into a new argument centered on the victims of crime.[45]

Reagan's push for victims' rights began with violence. On March 30, 1981, he was leaving a lunch talk at the Washington Hilton when John Hinckley Jr. tried to assassinate him. Hinckley, mentally ill and obsessed with the actress Jodie Foster, hoped to get her attention by killing the president. The president proclaimed National Victims'

Rights Week from his hospital bed, and charged a task force with considering how to help crime victims.[46]

State legislators introduced laws and even constitutional amendments codifying the rights of crime victims. Mothers Against Drunk Driving, a group founded in 1980 to advocate for tougher penalties for driving under the influence, was expanding. The decade before, the fight for better protections for victims of sexual assault had gained momentum. These movements all suggested that the law—and society as a whole—had denied the humanity of crime victims. "We are tired of being nonpersons in the courtrooms," complained one advocate at a New York rally.[47]

In August 1981, a Justice Department task force charged with considering victims' rights came back with sixty-four proposals. Rather than offer support for victims, most of the proposals involved harsher punishment of offenders: abolishing the parole system, creating new mandatory minimum sentences, and building new prisons. Reagan embraced these measures as a way to beat "back a jungle that threatens to reclaim the clearing that we call civilization."[48]

The more enmeshed the antiabortion movement became with the Republican Party, the more important it became to talk about personhood in a way that resonated with conservatives. In the Reagan era, antiabortion groups began emphasizing that the fetus was the one crime victim the law had yet to protect. "We have laws to protect other victims," wrote an antiabortion correspondent to the *Chicago Tribune* in 1981, "but we no longer have laws to protect the unborn child." The National Right to Life Committee's debate guidelines framed the personhood of the fetus in a similar way. When asked whether a law treating the unborn child as a person or banning abortion was "imposing one's own moral values on another," the manual advised responding: "No more than insisting that there should be laws prohibiting assault, battery, and theft." For the National Right to

Life Committee, the bottom line was simple: "The unborn is a living human being, and his personal safety should not be made to depend on the personal goodwill of others."[49]

The Fall of Personhood Amendments

In the fall of 1981, Orrin Hatch, Utah's conservative junior senator, proposed a constitutional amendment that would allow states to ban abortion. A few years earlier, the Hatch Amendment would have been a nonstarter because it did not prohibit abortion outright. Now, Willke and his colleagues were desperate for any sign of progress. Asked how the National Conference of Catholic Bishops could endorse the Hatch Amendment, Archbishop John Roach explained that there was "a strong urgency to get something." Members of the National Right to Life Committee shared this impulse: the organization's board of directors voted 31-24 in favor of supporting the amendment. Willke's bromides about prayer did not go over as well after the vote. Judie Brown and her allies resolutely opposed the Hatch Amendment. Some of Willke's colleagues, seeing him as a turncoat, mounted a campaign to force him out.[50]

For a time, it looked as if the Human Life Bill had more support, but it never came to the floor for a vote. Some antiabortion advocates thought that the bill did not go far enough. Others argued that the Supreme Court would strike it down if it passed. The Hatch Amendment did not fare any better. Following a filibuster, the Senate voted 47-46 to kill it, and Hatch temporarily withdrew it.[51]

The antiabortion movement also struggled to find partners in the legal community, which remained predominantly liberal in the early 1980s. Conservative lawyers had been bitterly disappointed by Richard Nixon's Supreme Court nominees, who had joined or authored decisions legalizing abortion, permitting some forms of race-conscious affirmative action, and strengthening the freedom of the press in defamation lawsuits. In 1982, three conservative law students, fed up with what they saw as liberal legal orthodoxy, launched a new group they called the Federalist Society. The students, Steven Calabresi, Lee Liberman, and David McIntosh, had the idea for a conference that would bring together right-leaning lawyers, professors, judges, and students from across the country and raised $24,000 to make it happen. At the April 1982 event, Robert Bork, whom Reagan had recently nominated to the DC Circuit Court of Appeals, gave a speech insisting that the questions of abortion and contraception were best left to the states—and that Supreme Court justices had been "legislating morality based on their own 'middle-class values.'"[52]

Bork's remarks were certainly welcome to antiabortion leaders, but their movement still had no obvious way of recruiting students to their cause. The Christian Legal Society, founded at the 1961 American Bar Association convention as a support group for Christian attorneys, had chapters on some law school campuses and took a stand against abortion, but the organization was small and mostly focused on other things, like the launch of a Christian counseling alternative to mediation.[53]

With the Human Life Bill stalled, antiabortion groups looked for another way to advance the idea of fetal personhood. They found an opportunity in Bopp's home state of Indiana, when a baby was born in 1982 with Down syndrome and a tracheoesophageal fistula, an abnormal connection between the esophagus and the windpipe, that required surgery. The obstetrician told the parents that their child would never have a reasonable quality of life and advised against the surgery. The parents agreed, and Baby Doe died six days later. The case caught the attention of the Reagan administration, which promulgated regulations in March 1983 outlining penalties for physicians who refused to care for newborns with disabilities. The American

Academy of Pediatrics sued, arguing that the administration had failed to allow adequate time for public comment before the rules became final, and that the rules stripped physicians of needed discretion. In April, a district judge invalidated the rules because the administration had not allowed for the requisite sixty-day comment period. The administration tried again, waiting for the comment period to end and then enacting strikingly similar rules.[54]

It did not take long for a second Baby Doe case to make headlines. In October, parents in Long Island decided against corrective surgery for a daughter born with spina bifida, a condition in which the spine does not form properly in utero. Antiabortion attorney Lawrence Washburn filed a lawsuit in New York to challenge the parents' decision, and the case went all the way to New York's highest court, which reasoned that Washburn, a stranger, had no right to override the decision of the child's parents.[55]

The Baby Doe cases struck a nerve with activists who believed in fetal personhood, seeding an idea that the movement would later explore: even if the antiabortion movement could not convince courts to recognize fetal personhood in the context of abortion, the movement could change other areas of the law. And if other areas of the law treated the *fetus* as a rights-holder, the antiabortion movement could more easily argue that *Roe* was an outlier—and that the Constitution should recognize fetal rights too.[56]

If Reagan had eagerly tackled the Baby Doe cases, administration insiders advised the president to say nothing about either Hatch's or Helms's proposals. Hatch was not entirely ready to admit his idea was dead. In 1983, he joined forces with Senator Thomas Eagleton, a Democrat from Missouri, to propose a slightly different version of the amendment. But he was deluding himself. Two members of the Senate Judiciary Committee who had often sided with the antiabortion movement, including Democrat Joe Biden of Delaware, switched sides and opposed the Hatch-Eagleton Amendment. When it came up for a vote in June 1983, the Senate rejected it, 49-48, with one abstaining.[57]

Reversing *Roe*

To outsiders, it might have seemed that the fight for fetal personhood was losing out to a quest to undo *Roe v. Wade*. At first, the leaders of the antiabortion movement had little regard for Ronald Reagan's first Supreme Court nominee, Sandra Day O'Connor. But when the Supreme Court released a decision in June 1983 striking down Akron's abortion ordinance, O'Connor dissented. The Akron ordinance had been the model for a new generation of multi-restriction abortion laws. It required that all abortions take place in a hospital after the first trimester, imposed a twenty-four-hour waiting period, dictated that minors involve their parents, regulated the disposal of fetal remains, and mandated that physicians read a script detailing claims about the psychological and physical risks of abortion. In a 6-3 majority opinion, Justice Lewis Powell concluded that the statute's provisions were unconstitutional. The Court easily struck down the informed-consent mandate that so many abortion opponents found promising, reasoning that its "parade of horribles" was "designed not to inform the woman's consent but rather to persuade her to withhold it altogether." Powell also took the opportunity to reaffirm *Roe*.[58]

In her dissenting opinion, O'Connor seemed far more skeptical. "Even assuming," she wrote, "that there is a fundamental right to terminate pregnancy in some situations, there is no justification in law or logic for the trimester framework adopted in *Roe* and employed by the Court today."[59]

Americans United for Life seized on the O'Connor dissent, announcing a 1984 conference, "Reversing *Roe v. Wade* through the

Courts," aimed at developing a "clear understanding of strategy and tactics for reversal." Prominent speakers at the event included Joseph Dellapenna, an expert on water law at Villanova's law school, who believed *Roe* got the history of abortion wrong and was planning to write a book about it.[60]

The conference also made it clear that the antiabortion movement had begun to prioritize control of the Supreme Court and the reversal of *Roe*. Victor Rosenblum of Americans United for Life wanted to focus on the Court's conclusions about fetal viability. "Without *Roe*'s arbitrary requirement that viability be present before the state's compelling interest could override the privacy right," he argued, "the legal framework that protects the practice of abortion topples."[61]

The conference marked a turning point in the antiabortion movement's composition. By the mid-1980s, it was increasingly hard to believe that the kind of conservative Protestants who were joining the antiabortion movement in large numbers had once been seen as a marginal force in politics. *Newsweek* magazine proclaimed 1976, the year Jimmy Carter, a born-again Protestant, won the race for the White House, to be the "year of the evangelical." In the late 1970s, celebrities, football stars, and rock musicians all claimed to be "born again." But until the early 1980s, precisely what conservative Protestants thought about abortion remained unclear. The Southern Baptist Convention, the largest conservative Christian denomination in the United States, held a middle-ground position, rejecting "abortion on demand" without embracing a right to life.[62]

By the early 1980s this ambiguity had vanished. Francis Schaeffer, a goateed theologian-philosopher, helped convince many to change their minds. Schaeffer worked with his son, Franky, and C. Everett Koop, a prominent physician and the future surgeon general, on *Whatever Happened to the Human Race?*, a 1979 film that excoriated supporters of legal abortion, which they portrayed as a clear sign of the "impending moral chaos that faces society divested of its Judeo-Christian foundations." Conservative Protestants had advanced a Christian vision of the nation's founding for years, and these ideas had new salience after the 1950s, when figures like Billy Graham filled football stadiums, and theologians like R. J. Rushdoony called for the restoration of the death penalty for gay sex. But Schaeffer and his son revived the story of a Christian founding, and a generation of conservative Protestants grew up on his ideas about abortion. Others tuned in to the sermons and radio broadcasts of Jerry Falwell, the head of the recently founded Moral Majority, who barnstormed cities and small towns as part of his "I Love America" tour, denouncing abortion and denigrating gays, lesbians, feminists, and liberals. In 1980, the Southern Baptist Convention passed a new resolution endorsing "a constitutional amendment prohibiting abortion except to save the life of the mother." Conservative Protestants started crisis pregnancy centers and participated in the annual March for Life.[63]

As growing numbers of conservative Protestants joined antiabortion groups, leading organizations did not abandon the idea of fetal personhood; they began searching for indirect paths to persuade Americans to view the unborn as a holder of constitutional rights, especially after 1986, when the Supreme Court held unconstitutional a Pennsylvania multi-restriction ordinance in *Thornburgh v. American College of Obstetricians and Gynecologists.* The law at issue included provisions mandating informed consent, limiting the use of certain medical procedures after viability, and requiring a second physician to be present at post-viability abortions. The Court agreed with those challenging the law, but the margin of victory for the abortion-rights side was close: only five justices held the Pennsylvania law unconstitutional. With the addition of one or two more conservative justices, the Court might be ready to reconsider *Roe.*[64]

The Federalist Society and the Conservative Christian Legal Movement

Antiabortion leaders looking to build on the *Thornburgh* decision hoped to capture the support of powerful new allies. By 1986, the Federalist Society had become something of a power broker, with seventy law school chapters, an office in Washington, DC, and members in high places (all three of the group's founders held powerful positions in the Reagan Department of Justice). The organization got another boost that year when Reagan nominated Antonin Scalia, a federal judge who had long served as an advisor to the organization, to fill an empty seat on the Supreme Court. The Federalist Society's vision seemed almost deliberately vague in the 1980s: to advance "individual liberty, traditional values and the rule of law." Edwin Meese III, Reagan's attorney general, began to fill in more details at a 1985 speech before the American Bar Association. Echoing ideas expressed in Bork's writing, Meese asserted that judges interpreting the Constitution should focus on "the text of the document and the original intention of those who framed it." Meese's idea of originalism intrigued those who joined the early Federalist Society. These conservative lawyers might have had different views about the law, but they all agreed that the Supreme Court in recent years had been a failure, handing down decisions that a wide variety of conservatives despised. For the antiabortion movement, partnering with the Federalist Society could bring their movement closer to power. And as the Federalist Society expanded across law school campuses, aligning with the organization could provide the antiabortion movement with fresh recruits and legitimize the movement's arguments about *Roe*.[65]

What the personhood movement needed was a way to speak to the concerns of the emerging conservative legal movement. Conflicts around LGBTQ rights and death and dying raised the possibility of an effective approach: one based on history and tradition. Following a series of favorable rulings in the late 1970s and early 1980s, litigators for the American Civil Liberties Union and Lambda Legal Defense and Education Fund, a group committed to the rights of gays and lesbians, thought the time was right to take on sodomy laws, which still criminalized oral or anal sex in half the states and Washington, DC. The case that ultimately reached the Supreme Court, *Bowers v. Hardwick*, began when Michael Hardwick received a citation for throwing away a beer can outside the Atlanta gay club where he tended bar. After he failed to appear in court to answer the charges against him, a law enforcement officer entered his house early one morning, observed Hardwick and another man having sex, and arrested Hardwick. When the Supreme Court agreed to hear *Bowers*, Georgia defended its sodomy law primarily by stressing that the Court had rejected a challenge to a sodomy ban in 1976.[66]

The Rutherford Institute, a conservative Christian law firm in Virginia, had a different plan. In 1982, when John W. Whitehead launched the Rutherford Institute, he was already well known in Christian publishing, and he had a gift for selling his own story. He had led a quiet life practicing law before he read a Christian book on the Apocalypse and Second Coming, Hal Lindsey's *The Late Great Planet Earth*. The book turned Whitehead's life upside down: he quit his law job to pursue a calling in ministry. He soon was publishing books of his own, arguing that America was a Christian nation with "Christian influence . . . written into the Constitution."[67]

Publicly, the Rutherford Institute presented itself as a champion of the little guy, "doing all it can to preserve our religious liberties and the strength of our Constitution." But Whitehead wanted Rutherford to advocate for more than religious liberty. The Constitution, he believed, should be interpreted in keeping with his vision of the nation's Christian founding. "It is up to this generation," he explained in 1986, "to insist that a man has value because he was created in God's image and has been redeemed by Jesus Christ."[68]

When Whitehead got involved in the struggle over sodomy bans, the central issue for the courts was the scope of the constitutional right to privacy. Attorneys for groups like the ACLU and Lambda Legal argued that the right logically extended to decisions about sexual intimacy. In their amicus brief in *Bowers*, Rutherford attorneys replied that the Fourteenth Amendment protected only rights that had been "historically and traditionally basic to our society." This formulation echoed Justice Lewis Powell, believed to be the swing vote in the case, who had written in 1977 that the Due Process Clause protected rights that were "deeply rooted in this Nation's history and tradition."[69]

Powell himself invoked an idea articulated by Justice John Marshall Harlan II's 1961 dissent in *Poe v. Ullman*, a decision that left in place Connecticut's ban on the use of contraception for married people. Harlan spoke of tradition as "a living thing." Powell, following this lead, described a fluid, contestable tradition to which many could lay claim. But in citing Powell's opinion, Rutherford argued that a tradition was "deeply rooted" only if it was already fixed at the time of the nation's founding.[70]

Similar arguments had begun to circulate among antiabortion activists intent on preventing recognition of a right to die. Gains in life expectancy over the twentieth century meant that more Americans were spending their final weeks and months in hospitals, sometimes receiving invasive and painful treatments that did little to extend their lives. Courts were seeing more and more plaintiffs requesting the withdrawal of artificial hydration and nutrition. Antiabortion groups argued that there could be no right to die because the Constitution recognized a narrow subset of rights beyond those spelled out in the text: those rooted in "Western Tradition," as lawyers working with the National Right to Life Committee wrote in 1985, "in which the

American constitutional order is firmly embedded." Proponents of fetal personhood saw a parallel to the right to die: as one pamphlet explained, the "unborn" was a "non-person" in the abortion context, while in the context of a right to die, the "non-person" was anyone with a "terminal condition."[71]

Rutherford brought related ideas about an unchanging Judeo-Christian constitutional tradition to the Supreme Court. In a 5-4 decision joined by Justice Powell, the Court in *Bowers* upheld the Georgia sodomy ban. Justice Byron White, in his majority opinion, acknowledged contemporary attitudes about sodomy as well as old common-law rules. But while he did not cite Rutherford's brief, White echoed the claim that "proscriptions against [sodomy] have ancient roots." In his concurring opinion, Chief Justice Warren Burger noted that hostility to gay sex was "firmly rooted in Judeo-Christian moral and ethical standards." After *Bowers*, it seemed that arguments about history and tradition might sway the Supreme Court where claims about fetal equality had failed.[72]

Fetal Homicide and the Right to Die

In the short term, antiabortion lawyers tried to paint *Roe* as an outlier by writing fetal personhood into laws on subjects other than abortion. In the 1980s, one particular context captured the movement's attention: homicide laws. Clarke Forsythe, a young AUL lawyer, helped to lead the push for new feticide laws. As a student, Forsythe had been something of a libertarian, volunteering for the campaign of John Anderson, a pro-choice Republican running for president as an independent, over spring break in 1980. But in law school, at Valparaiso, he became concerned about "how far American political policy and philosophy has come from the founding fathers." The most disturbing departure, he believed, involved *Roe v. Wade*. As a law student, he applied twice for an AUL internship, and when the organization twice rejected his application, he offered to work for free after graduation. Eventually, he rose to the position of general counsel.[73]

Roe ruled out prosecutions of women who chose abortion or of their doctors, but Forsythe and his colleagues hoped that others who took fetal life might be a different story. Most state courts at the time followed the so-called born-alive rule, which allowed prosecutors to pursue homicide or assault charges on behalf of fetuses only if they were subsequently born alive. Forsythe believed this rule was a legal anachronism based on primitive medical understandings of when life began. Americans United for Life had experimented with fetal-homicide strategies as early as 1975, but in the mid-1980s the subject gained political momentum because of Jannet Johnson, a Minnesota woman who was eight and a half months' pregnant when a car accident with a drunk driver caused the stillbirth of her child. Prosecutors pursued homicide charges against the driver, but Minnesota, like most states at the time, applied the born-alive rule, and the state supreme court held that a homicide prosecution could not proceed. But Johnson and her husband, Chris, opposed abortion, and their case rallied antiabortion groups around the idea of writing personhood into fetal-homicide laws. "Unborn children," Chris Johnson testified before the state legislature in 1986, "must be protected by the laws of the state."[74]

The Johnson case increased interest in making fetal-homicide laws a vehicle for beliefs about personhood. Clarke Forsythe wrote a law review article in 1987 attacking the born-alive rule. Americans United for Life began tracking fetal-homicide prosecutions, submitting amicus briefs, and writing model legislation.[75]

At times, these claims did not clearly pit women and fetuses against one another—after all, in many fetal-homicide cases, women with *wanted* pregnancies like Jannet Johnson suffered miscarriages or stillbirths. Americans who supported abortion rights sometimes endorsed feticide laws, and liberal states passed them. But for Forsythe and his colleagues, feticide laws set an important precedent for recognizing rights for the unborn in other contexts.[76]

Advocates like Forsythe began anchoring these arguments in claims about history and tradition—a move that seemed likely to appeal to the growing conservative legal movement. Although the abortion issue divided the early Federalist Society, antiabortion groups made headway with the organization by emphasizing a point of consensus: judicial activism posed a danger to American democracy, and *Roe v. Wade* was a quintessential example of it. Robert Bork bridged the two sides. When Ronald Reagan nominated him for the Supreme Court in 1987, his hearings and subsequent defeat made him a martyr to many conservatives. Bork considered *Roe* a deeply unprincipled decision, and his stand made it easier for conservative movement lawyers to forge an alliance with those opposed to abortion.[77]

Within a few years of Bork's defeat, the Federalist Society also began promoting a distinctive approach to constitutional interpretation that built on Edwin Meese's 1985 speech about originalism. A growing group of conservative lawyers agreed with Robert Bork that the "only way in which the Constitution can constrain judges is if judges interpret the document's words according to the intentions of those who drafted, proposed, and ratified its provisions." In 1988, Antonin Scalia, quickly emerging as one of the Court's most conservative justices, published an influential article suggesting that originalism was the best method of constitutional interpretation available to judges, because it "establish[ed] a historical criterion that is conceptually quite separate from the preferences of the judge himself." Originalism was intellectually appealing to a wide variety of conservative lawyers, even as some began to argue that judges should focus on the original public meaning of the Constitution's text rather than the intent of its framers. Promoting originalism had strategic benefits too. The Federalist Society could easily have seemed to be a reactionary group, challenging a legal status quo then taken for granted by many in the legal community. But by embracing originalism, the Federalist Society maintained that its opponents were the ones politicizing the judiciary.[78]

Making a historical argument for fetal rights seemed more likely to appeal to Scalia and the leaders of the Federalist Society. But an approach based on history and tradition differed from the kind of originalism that Scalia had in mind. The so-called new originalism that began to emerge in the 1980s focused on the public meaning of the Constitution at the time of ratification. In practical terms, it seemed hard to establish this kind of originalist case for fetal personhood, given that the authors of the Fourteenth Amendment said little or nothing about the subject in or before 1868. If the courts considered a looser concept of history and tradition, by contrast, antiabortion lawyers could look at evidence from other historical periods to make their constitutional case, such as nineteenth-century statutes criminalizing abortion *after* the amendment's ratification—or at Christian teachings that predated the amendment's ratification by centuries.[79]

At a minimum, antiabortion lawyers could argue that a right to abortion was not deeply rooted in the nation's history and traditions. And because of the Court's decision in *Webster v. Reproductive Health Services*, it seemed reasonable to believe that the Court would soon reverse *Roe. Webster* involved a Missouri law with a preamble that declared life began at conception—and that unborn children had "protectable interests in life, health, and wellbeing." The law prohibited the use of public dollars or hospitals for abortion and required any doctor who believed that a patient was twenty or more weeks pregnant to do certain tests to ascertain fetal viability. In a fractured 5-4 majority opinion, the Court upheld each challenged provision. Writing for the Court, Chief Justice William Rehnquist reasoned that it was too soon to weigh in on the application of the preamble because the justices had no idea how Missouri courts would interpret it. The question of whether the funding and facilities restrictions were constitutional struck the majority as easy: these regulations closely resembled others the Court had already upheld. While acknowledging that there was some tension between the viability regulation and *Roe* because the state chose to "superimpose state regulation on the medical determination whether a particular fetus is viable," Rehnquist wrote that these tensions exposed flaws in the reasoning of *Roe* itself. The Court nevertheless declined to reverse the 1973 decision, reasoning that the case did not require the justices to make such a monumental decision, and Sandra Day O'Connor seemed unconvinced that the viability provisions even conflicted with the Court's past precedents. But Rehnquist's opinion made it seem that a majority of justices believed *Roe*'s trimester framework to be fatally flawed.[80]

The Scope of Punishment

Webster energized proponents of fetal personhood. The influence of Operation Rescue, a group committed to blockading abortion clinics, was more complex. By the late 1980s, protests outside abortion clinics were nothing new, but Randall Terry wanted to perfect the process. He had chased a career in rock music before finding God in a roadside religious conversion. He became a minister and plunged into the antiabortion movement.[81]

Terry called on his supporters to peacefully prevent anyone from entering a clinic—but to break the law if necessary. He believed that the act of blockading a clinic made good on the idea that the fetus was a person with equal rights. A clinic blockader, he argued, was doing "what any Christian would do if a child was being dismembered in front of him."[82] He thought such lawbreaking would "create the national political pressure to hasten the political establishment of a national Constitutional Human Life Amendment."[83]

Operation Rescue was the latest reflection of a divide within the antiabortion movement about what the enforcement of personhood required. By the late 1980s, key advocates like Marjory Mecklenburg, who had argued that recognizing personhood required more support for pregnant women, had often been sidelined or changed their views. Mecklenburg herself had become the director of Adolescent Pregnancy Programs for the Department of Health and Human Services in 1981. A long-standing supporter of better contraceptive access and a stronger safety net for pregnant women, Mecklenburg became the face of the Reagan administration's focus on abstinence-only sex education and regulations that required minors to notify their parents before accessing birth control. She later resigned in 1985 after admitting that she had used government money to take unauthorized trips, including to see her son play for the Denver Broncos of the National Football League. Others, like Mecklenburg's former colleague Warren Schaller, left the movement altogether because it no longer represented their beliefs about what personhood required.[84]

What would be a more politically consequential divide in the late 1980s involved those who did not think larger groups were going far enough in promoting the rights of fetal persons. These advocates had rallied to groups like Judie Brown's American Life League, which denounced contraception, sex education, and exceptions to criminal abortion laws. Terry's Operation Rescue provided a new outlet for movement absolutists. Some Catholics strongly supported Operation Rescue, but the blockade movement primarily appealed to white conservative Protestants—an increasingly influential cohort in the movement. Blockaders refused to give their names when arrested, identifying themselves as Baby John Doe or Tar Baby One, and often turned down plea bargains. In court, they presented the legal defense of necessity, arguing that they broke laws to prevent a greater wrong—the murder of rights-holding persons. Their hearings often took place in a circus atmosphere. In Atlanta, Georgia, for example, prosecutors held preliminary hearings in a warehouse at the local fairgrounds, with the cost of arraignments alone topping $500,000.[85]

Operation Rescue compared its members to the civil-rights protestors of the 1960s, brutalized by the police and victimized by the justice system. Significantly, however, the mostly white and middle-class Operation Rescue blockaders were often arrested because they wanted to be, and then acquitted or given a slap on the wrist. The same was not true for other Americans. For much of the 1980s, the rate of fatal police encounters stood at .81 per one hundred thousand for Black Americans, compared to only .15 per one hundred thousand for white Americans. Black Americans were also especially likely to face arrest during Reagan's war on drugs. While making up only 13 percent of the nation's population, Black Americans comprised between 40 and 42 percent of all drug arrestees in 1992, up from 21 percent in 1980. These numbers notwithstanding, Operation Rescue claimed that the criminal system reserved the most persecution for the unborn and pro-life Americans.[86]

While they offered to defend blockaders against some charges, the emerging antiabortion establishment argued that Operation Rescue was not pursuing the best long-term strategy. In 1990, Clarke Forsythe and his colleagues were focused on another case, *Cruzan by Cruzan v. Director, Missouri Department of Public Health*, that at first did not seem to have much to do with abortion. Nancy Cruzan had fallen into a persistent vegetative state following a serious car accident. Her parents wanted the hospital to withdraw artificial hydration and nutrition, but Missouri law allowed for this step only if there was clear and convincing evidence of a patient's wishes—something her parents could not provide. Cruzan's parents filed a lawsuit, arguing that Missouri had ignored Nancy's humanity and violated her right to refuse unwanted medical treatment.[87]

Cruzan represented an important opportunity for antiabortion groups to promote a new constitutional approach based on history and tradition. In an amicus brief written for the evangelical group Focus on the Family, for example, Americans United for Life stressed the long pedigree of laws prohibiting suicide and punishing caretakers who harmed their dependents. The National Right to Life Committee argued that "where a guardian has abused his ward, his action has traditionally been punishable under the criminal law."[88]

The Court in *Cruzan* held that the Constitution protected Americans' right to refuse unwanted medical treatment. But in a 5-4 majority opinion for the Court, Justice William Rehnquist concluded that while a conscious person had a right to refuse food and water, Missouri's law—which permitted the termination of artificial hydration and nutrition only when there was clear and convincing evidence of a patient's wishes—was constitutional. The state had important interests in preventing the abuse of sick or elderly people, the Court reasoned, as well as in protecting "human life," and it could apply an exacting standard to advance those interests. The decision began a new round of litigation over the rights of those who received aid in dying.[89]

Clarke Forsythe, who worried about the fallout from *Cruzan*, believed that feticide laws would not be the only way to write fetal personhood into criminal laws unrelated to abortion. He also took an interest in the prosecution of pregnant drug users. Reagan had already called attention to what he called the war on drugs. On a speaking tour in 1982, Nancy Reagan was asked by an elementary school student in Oakland, California, what he should do if invited to use drugs, and she answered that young Americans should "just say no." The administration quickly turned this offhand remark into a press extravaganza. The Just Say No campaign came amid a surge in cocaine usage. Crack, a mixture of cocaine and baking soda, sold for

$5 to $20 per vial, making it affordable for low-income Americans. The Anti–Drug Abuse Act of 1986 made the penalties for possession of crack cocaine equal to the sentence for possession of one hundred times the same amount of powder cocaine.[90]

Feticide laws had not punished women, but now prosecutors began charging pregnant drug users under existing laws on drug-dealing, child abuse, neglect, or manslaughter. By 1989, eighteen such cases were pending in the nation's courts; a year later, the number was thirty-five. Some abortion opponents did not endorse such prosecutions. The United States Catholic Conference, which stressed that both substance abuse and abortion threatened unborn children, argued instead in 1992 for "the provision of prenatal and other health care, and treatment and rehabilitation of abusers of alcohol and other drugs." Leading legal players in the antiabortion movement, by contrast, sometimes lobbied for such prosecutions. "A clear, high standard should be placed on the prosecutor to determine willful, malicious child abuse before any woman is charged," Clarke Forsythe told the press in 1988. "The principle that the unborn child in the criminal law is a person should be upheld."[91]

These prosecutions primarily affected women of color, who were more likely to be screened for illegal drugs during pregnancy and to face criminal charges when tests came back positive. Kimberly Hardy was one of these women. Her case was not unique, but her story captured the attention of the national media. Hardy grew up in Mississippi and got pregnant her senior year of high school. After graduation, she moved to Michigan with her infant son and took a job on the assembly line in the factory town of Muskegon, but she quit when she became pregnant again because the smell of burning oil made her uncontrollably sick. Soon after she gave birth, a friend introduced her to crack, and Hardy became addicted. She was struggling to get clean when she gave birth to a third child. Her doctor, who knew of Hardy's substance abuse, immediately screened her for illegal drugs, and when Hardy tested positive for cocaine, the state charged her with second-degree child abuse and felony delivery of a drug, a charge often used against drug dealers. Combined, the charges could lead to twenty-five years in prison. The state also placed Hardy's children in foster care.[92]

Hardy's experience was not unusual. Many pregnant drug users temporarily or permanently lost custody of their children, and some faced time in prison, fines, or probation. Hardy, who had become a public figure, had an unusually happy ending. She became sober and vowed to fight the charges. The trial court judge had already concluded that the state could not prove the child abuse charges against Hardy because there was not enough evidence that her drug use had harmed her child, but the judge allowed the drug delivery charge to proceed. In 1991, her attorneys successfully appealed that decision to the Michigan Court of Appeals, which quashed the remaining charges against her. She then regained custody of her three children. As the case drew to a close, Hardy told reporters that she was attending community college with the hope of becoming a drug counselor who could help pregnant women struggling with addiction.[93]

For many personhood proponents, Hardy's case offered a different reason for optimism: prosecutions of pregnant drug users treated a fetus in utero as a child, and equated substance abuse with drug dealing or violence against children. After the *Webster* decision, the death of abortion rights seemed inevitable. But eliminating abortion rights would not, by itself, establish constitutional protection for the fetus. Fetal abuse prosecutions had already upended the lives of women like Kimberly Hardy, who had almost lost both her children and her liberty. But as far as fetal personhood was concerned, these prosecutions seemed like they could be the start of something bigger.

4

Abortion's Second Victim

With a decision pending in the Court's next major abortion case, *Planned Parenthood of Southeastern Pennsylvania v. Casey*, it seemed that the constitutional right to choose abortion would soon be wiped away. At its most basic, the case involved the constitutionality of a Pennsylvania abortion regulation. The law required the involvement of parents, spousal notification, a waiting period, and the written consent of women—provisions quite similar to others that had been invalidated by the Court in 1983 and 1986. But everyone expected the Court to uphold Pennsylvania's regulations and overturn *Roe v. Wade*.[1]

Paige Comstock Cunningham, like many in the antiabortion movement, had been confident that the Court would undo a right to choose abortion. The daughter of missionaries to Latin America, Cunningham had attended Taylor University, an evangelical liberal arts school in tiny Upland, Indiana, that required students to sign a pledge not to smoke, drink, or dance. She went on to law school at Northwestern and took a job at Americans United for Life. Cunningham, who considered herself a feminist, was deeply ambivalent about Ruth Bader Ginsburg, the trailblazing former ACLU attorney then serving on the DC Circuit Court of Appeals. As Cunningham put it later, she had reaped from the "seeds sown by Judge Ginsburg in her efforts to abolish sex discrimination" but was dismayed that Ginsburg supported legal abortion. Cunningham hoped the *Casey* decision would entrench a very different idea of equality from Ginsburg's, one that would reject "an elective surgery that makes second-class citizens of the voiceless."[2]

As the 1990s continued, attacks on abortion providers increased the prominence of a personhood claim very different from the one Cunningham wanted to spotlight: if fetuses were persons, lethal force could justifiably be used to defend them. The murder of several abortion providers put these ideas in the spotlight and damaged the reputation of an antiabortion movement already struggling to explain its relationship to organizations like Operation Rescue. Leading antiabortion groups like Americans United for Life worked to rehabilitate their image and reframe personhood by describing both women and their unborn children as victims of abortion.[3]

Cunningham and her colleagues drew on debates about the abuses of big tobacco companies and the reform of federal welfare policy. Smokers were winning lawsuits against tobacco companies in the 1990s by establishing that the tobacco industry had consciously misled them. In the face of Republican vows to reduce childbearing outside of marriage by blocking welfare payments, some antiabortion groups defended programs for the poor by stressing that welfare recipients did not know that nonmarital sex was intrinsically wrong. Leading antiabortion groups like Americans United for Life forged a similar idea of victimhood in the context of abortion: women who terminated their pregnancies deserved mercy because they had been denied information about the humanity and personhood of the fetus. While leading antiabortion groups would maintain in the decades to come that women should not be punished, this idea of victimhood was inherently unstable. If women were innocent because they did not understand what they chose, what should happen to women who knew or even celebrated what they had done?[4]

Whatever the answer to this question, Cunningham and her colleagues still equated equality for the unborn with the enforcement of criminal abortion laws. By framing women as victims of a misinformation campaign that denied the reality of personhood, advocates like Cunningham reiterated that criminal abortion laws were needed to deter violence, restore the nation's traditions, and deliver justice for those who had been wronged.

Casey

Most in the antiabortion movement felt betrayed when the justices announced their decision in *Casey.* Three Republican nominees, Anthony Kennedy, Sandra Day O'Connor, and David Souter, wrote a joint opinion for the Court confirming "the essential holding" of *Roe*—that there was a constitutional right to choose abortion before viability.[5]

The *Casey* decision did not leave *Roe* unscathed. The Court did away with the trimester framework—which appeared to prohibit almost any abortion restriction early in pregnancy—and replaced it with the "undue burden" test, which allowed states to regulate abortion unless a law created a substantial obstacle for those seeking to end a pregnancy. In real terms, this test seemingly made it easier for states to restrict abortion—and in fact, the Court upheld every part of Pennsylvania's law but one, a requirement that most married women notify their husbands.[6]

Roe had extended a privacy right recognized in earlier decisions on contraception, marriage, and parenting, but some commentators found the Court's reasoning in *Roe* unconvincing. In its discussion of when to overrule a precedent, the *Casey* opinion implied that the Equal Protection Clause of the Fourteenth Amendment might also justify abortion rights. Since the 1970s, the Supreme Court had relied on the Equal Protection Clause in ruling that sex-based classifications must serve an important government purpose and use means substantially related to the government's ends—a relatively demanding test that the government could not always meet.[7]

Ruth Bader Ginsburg, whom Bill Clinton would nominate to the Supreme Court in 1993, had long argued that an equal protection argument for abortion rights would be more convincing than one based on privacy. Scholars made a number of equality arguments for abortion rights in the first quarter century after *Roe*, noting that abortion laws compelled women to assume caretaking roles that had long justified discrimination. Other feminist commentators contended that abortion restrictions reflected pernicious stereotypes about women, or pointed to historical evidence that the framers of the Thirteenth and Fourteenth Amendments had been worried about forced child-bearing among enslaved people.[8]

Casey did not fully embrace an equal protection analysis, but the Court's discussion of *stare decisis*, the factors that bear on whether the Court overturns a precedent, showed a connection to sex-discrimination jurisprudence. As part of this analysis, the Court often evaluates whether people have relied on the legal status quo in ordering their lives. In *Casey*, the Court concluded that "the ability of women to participate equally in the economic and social life of the Nation, has been facilitated by their ability to control their reproductive lives."[9]

Everyone seemed to be talking about women's rights in 1992. Reporters called it the Year of the Woman because of the success of female political candidates. By the end of the election season, the number of women in the Senate had almost tripled (reaching the still-unimpressive total of five, including the only Black senator, Carol Moseley Braun). For the first time, women were serving as the nation's attorney general, secretary of state, and even the CEO of a Fortune 500 corporation. In December, NARAL unveiled what it called a "comprehensive pro-choice agenda" designed to "make abortion less necessary" by simplifying adoption procedures and expanding access to contraception and sex education. Women would soon lead major antiabortion organizations too. Wanda Franz, a psychology professor at West Virginia University, became president of the National Right to Life Committee, and Paige Cunningham took the helm at Americans United for Life. At the time, Cunningham was a mother of three in Chicago, a self-identified feminist who believed that mainstream feminist organizations had made disastrous mistakes. Defending access to abortion, she reasoned, gave employers an excuse not "to accommodate . . . women who have children."[10]

Most Americans certainly seemed to support the right to choose. A 1995 study in the *Journal of Politics* found that for voters in 1992 who were aware of a candidate's position on abortion, it was the most crucial factor in candidate selection—even more than the state of the economy. Only 34 percent of voters polled by Gallup in 1992 believed that *Roe v. Wade* should be overturned. Bill Clinton, who had stressed his support for abortion rights, carried thirty-two states plus the District of Columbia and won the popular vote. Whatever fetal personhood meant, it seemed that most voters had not embraced the idea.[11]

Identifying the Persecuted

At the start of the 1990s, Randall Terry, Operation Rescue's leader, still defined himself as God's warrior for fetal personhood, but he found his organization $70,000 in debt, most of it owed to abortion-rights organizations that had sued to stop blockades. Terry himself had been sentenced to two years in prison based on charges stemming from protests at the 1988 Democratic National Convention. (A judge had offered to reduce Terry's sentence to probation if he paid a $1,000 fine, but Terry refused.) At first, Terry was ecstatic about his prison sentence. "Going to jail," he wrote, "is probably the best statement we can make at this time." The injustice of his imprisonment, he believed, would convince others who had stayed on the sidelines of the injustice of the treatment of the fetal person. But most Americans were unmoved by Terry's absence. In the meantime, after Terry officially closed Operation Rescue, feminists saw the move as a ploy to shield the group's assets, especially after a virtually indistinguishable group, Operation Rescue National, began operating. The new organization's leader, a pastor named Keith Tucci, soon made national news by copying the blockades that had made Terry a household name. Like its predecessor, Operation Rescue National maintained that "the Christian Church" could no longer "co-exist with child-killing."[12]

At first, Operation Rescue members looking for legal representation had to rely on smaller outfits like the Thomas More Society, a Chicago-based group founded by the corporate attorney Tom Brejcha. Others turned to the American Center for Law and Justice (ACLJ), a conservative Christian public interest law firm launched by Pat Robertson in 1990. Robertson, who had the quiet manner of a country preacher, presided over a business empire that included a conservative Christian university, a law school, and a cable channel. He envisioned a symbiotic relationship between the American Center for Law and Justice and his Regent University School of Law, and he tapped Jay Sekulow to lead it. Sekulow grew up in a Jewish family in Brooklyn before moving to Atlanta and converting to Messianic Judaism, a movement that incorporates some Jewish traditions and teachings into Christian evangelicalism. After law school, he worked briefly for the Internal Revenue Service before launching a business that restored historic properties for resale. But after the tax rules changed, the business collapsed, and Sekulow reinvented himself as the counsel for the best-known Messianic Jewish organization, Jews for Jesus. In 1988, he launched a new group, Christian Advocates Serving Evangelism, which litigated cases involving the free speech and religious liberty of conservative Christians. Sekulow believed that liberal politicians, media outlets, and even medical groups were trying to undo the country's long-standing Christian traditions, including those involving fetal personhood. "America's founders," the American Center for Law and Justice explained in a brochure, "did not create a nation where God was separated from law."[13]

In the 1990s, when Sekulow was fighting for Operation Rescue in court, some pro-choice feminists were developing strategies to stop the organization. Fay Clayton was one of those women. She had grown up on a New Jersey farm, married her high school math teacher, moved to Chicago, and became a mother to three young children. When she found herself longing for more, she went to law school, got a job at a big law firm, and then started her own practice. Before long, Clayton had become heavily involved in fighting Operation Rescue. The National Organization for Women, the group she represented, had in another case relied on the federal Ku Klux Klan Act, a law passed to suppress racist violence in the aftermath of the Civil War. NOW argued that Operation Rescue represented just the kind of conspiracy that the Ku Klux Klan Act existed to stamp out and sought injunctions to prevent blockades from taking place. A different strategy compared antiabortion protest groups to organized crime. Invoking the federal Racketeer Influenced and Corrupt Organizations Act, Clayton and the National Organization for Women accused Joe Scheidler, Randall Terry, and other blockaders of engaging in a criminal conspiracy.[14]

In the political arena, those battling Operation Rescue asserted that abortion was a critical form of health care, delivered at clinics that provided other necessary services. At a 1989 strategy session, for example, leading abortion-rights groups described Operation Rescue's call for personhood as an extremist demand. "Since the majority of the Operation Rescue leadership are men," the session leaders advised, "project the image of men trying to prevent women from exercising their rights." Feminists organized networks of clinic escorts to steer patients through crowds of protestors, argued that blockades were ineffective, and insisted that Operation Rescue members championing fetal personhood really sought to prevent women from "obtaining abortions and other health care." As the feminist clinic owner and advocate Merle Hoffman explained in 1992, "The right to abortion is not about states' rights [or] fetal rights" but "foremost and forever about women and women's lives."[15]

Paige Cunningham had become increasingly alarmed about the legal attacks on Operation Rescue, which she feared might undermine the broader fight for fetal personhood. The federal government, of course, was not always hostile. At least the Supreme Court wasn't. It handed the antiabortion movement a major win in *Bray v. Alexandria Women's Health Clinic* (1993), which involved the federal Ku Klux Klan Act. Under that law, plaintiffs could seek an injunction and money damages when anyone conspired to violate protected rights based on discriminatory animus against a marginalized group. Feminists had claimed that blockades denied women their right to access abortion and other forms of health care. In a 6-3 majority opinion for the Court, Justice Antonin Scalia held that it was impossible to prove that blockades were an animus-driven conspiracy to strip women of their rights because "there are common and respectable reasons for opposing [abortion], other than hatred of, or condescension toward (or indeed any view at all concerning) women as a class." Americans United for Life celebrated the decision. Cunningham seemed especially happy, observing that the antiabortion movement would succeed only if it "waged a nationwide grassroots campaign to eliminate abortion through education."[16]

That task seemed considerably harder after Dr. David Gunn, an abortion provider, was murdered in March 1993. Gunn commuted hundreds of miles from Eufaula, Alabama, to Pensacola, Florida, and a host of other communities where no one else was willing to perform abortions. His murderer, Michael Griffin, had worked at a local chemical plant before getting involved in Rescue America, another group that organized clinic blockades. John Burt, a Pensacola minister and former Ku Klux Klan member, operated a branch of Rescue America in the Pensacola area, where he preached that violence against abortion providers was justified. (Burt would later die in prison while serving a sentence for molesting a fifteen-year-old girl staying at the maternity home that he operated.)[17]

After Gunn's death, Paul Hill, an unemployed ex-minister, captured media attention by circulating a document he called the *First Defensive Action Statement*. Hill argued that Griffin should not be prosecuted. The law, Hill stressed, generally allowed the use of lethal force to defend oneself or other persons from imminent death or serious bodily injury. If fetuses were persons, he explained, then anyone could use lethal force to defend them. "Whatever force is legitimate to defend the life of a born child," Hill wrote, "is legitimate to defend the life of an unborn child." Most antiabortion groups were horrified by Hill's claims and the publicity they received, but some activists aligned with the blockade movement quickly signed on to Hill's manifesto. Hill, with his soft voice and constant smile, soon seemed to be on every talk show in America. The leaders of Operation Rescue did not openly embrace him, but they suggested that if the government continued to crack down on blockades, it was only a matter of time before more doctors died. "Wherever the moderates have been crushed and swept from the streets," said Joseph Foreman of Operation Rescue, "the way is paved for the true extremists like Michael Griffin to step up to the plate."[18]

Loving the Wrongdoer

Paul Hill argued that killing abortion doctors was no different than using lethal force to defend the lives of other persons. The activists who joined blockades in Cleveland or San Jose or Dallas were told that abortion was murder—and they believed it. But if Randall Terry was right—if abortion was murder, and if the unborn child had the same rights as any other person—why were women who had abortions not guilty of a crime?[19]

In the nineteenth century, Horatio Storer and his colleagues had advocated for laws punishing women as well as doctors, but prosecutors had generally focused on charging doctors. After *Roe*, in the late 1970s and early 1980s, activists like James Bopp had championed informed-consent laws by claiming that women misunderstood abortion. Antiabortion leaders organized support groups, like Women Exploited by Abortion or Rachel's Vineyard, for women who regretted the decision to terminate a pregnancy. For the most part, however, movement strategies had not primarily focused on women, so in the 1990s, some antiabortion leaders began searching for a new way to discuss their role in abortion more prominently without abandoning demands for fetal personhood. Guy Condon of Americans United for Life agreed in 1991 that the time had come not only to "personalize the unborn child" but to "personalize the woman as victim." This strategy appealed to women in the movement who themselves had chosen abortion. At the same time, presenting women as victims might allow the antiabortion movement to reach a broader audience.[20]

After *Casey*, the leaders of Americans United for Life elaborated on this strategy of "loving the wrongdoer without embracing the wrong," as Paige Cunningham put it in 1993. She and her colleagues took the position that unlike doctors, women did not know what they were doing. Yes, the unborn child was human, and thus entitled to constitutional rights, but women who sought abortions generally failed to understand either the nature of life in the womb or the procedure itself.[21]

Working with Americans United for Life, Cunningham launched an initiative to promote so-called "right-to-know" laws requiring doctors to provide certain information before performing an abortion. These laws, as Cunningham explained it, would "guarantee that women receive the facts about their unborn children." But abortion opponents had spent more than two decades circulating images of aborted fetuses and making arguments about life in the womb. How could women still not know what abortion was?[22]

The right-to-know campaign echoed ideas developed in emerging lawsuits against tobacco companies. In the 1980s, consumers suffering from cancer and other devastating health consequences began going to court to hold tobacco manufacturers accountable, but jurors had often sided with the defendants because they had no sympathy for smokers themselves. Tobacco companies did not force anyone to smoke, they reasoned, and those who did had only themselves to blame.[23]

Beginning in the early 1990s, state attorneys general began to find ways around this obstacle by looking to the argument that "Big Tobacco" had deceived smokers about the dangers of smoking. These arguments began to pay off: juries in Mississippi and New York sided with tobacco plaintiffs. Soon, other states announced their own investigations and lawsuits.[24]

Cunningham saw that the war against Big Tobacco could provide a model for the struggle against "Big Abortion." Women who had abortions were victims in the same way tobacco users were victims: a massive industry had actively misled them. These new laws presented a woman-protective image of the antiabortion movement, all while advancing the belief that a fetus was a rights-holding person by "educating the American public on the humanity of the unborn child." The goal remained unchanged: "constitutional protection for the unborn child as a person." Rather than demanding recognition of personhood from courts or legislatures, however, antiabortion lawyers would write related concepts into right-to-know laws.[25]

At the time, no prominent antiabortion group, even the most absolutist, formally called for the punishment of women for abortion itself. Indeed, Keith Tucci of Operation Rescue, like Cunningham, argued that abortion doctors manipulated and exploited women—and that criminalizing abortion would "restore justice to children and mothers." But the blockade movement attracted a large number of Americans who publicly argued that abortion was murder. If women were innocent because they did not understand abortion, would those who embraced their decision deserve some kind of punishment? The right-to-know strategy did not offer a clear response to this question. "When I emphasize compassion for the women exploited by abortion," Cunningham explained in 1993, "it doesn't mean I condone abortion."[26]

Right-to-know laws also entered the conversation about whether abortion should be covered in a universal health-care bill. On the campaign trail, former Arkansas governor Bill Clinton had promised to fight for health-care reform. Abortion-rights groups pushed to ensure that abortion services were included in any legislation.[27]

Identifying abortion as an important medical service seemed even more crucial when fewer and fewer doctors were willing to perform it. In 1990, Barbara Radford of the National Abortion Federation, a group that represented abortion providers, told the *New York Times* that even in some left-leaning urban areas, it was hard to find a willing provider. By 1995, fewer than 15 percent of OB-GYN training programs even required instruction in the procedure.[28]

Abortion-rights supporters responded that the procedure was a critical form of health care. "Abortion is not a luxury item," stated "Choices," a NARAL debate manual. A later debate manual, "Talking about the Freedom to Choose," sought to refute Cunningham's arguments that abortion victimized women. NARAL insisted that providers were "subject to the same professional, ethical standards as other physicians." "Making abortion illegal," the manual explained, "is the true menace to women's health."[29]

Antiabortion groups lobbied for a version of universal health care that did not include abortion. Paige Cunningham argued that Clinton's bill required "abortion, discrimination, and euthanasia" and should be rejected. The quest to defeat the proposal—or at least remove abortion from it—made right-to-know laws seem even more important. By promoting them, antiabortion groups could reinforce the claim that women inevitably suffered after abortion because they had taken the life of a rights-holding person. "If advocates of legal abortion were pro-choice rather than pro-abortion," argued Massachusetts Citizens for Life (MCFL), "they would not oppose giving women with unintended pregnancies all the facts."[30]

This strategy did not go far enough for some antiabortion absolutists. Judie Brown mocked right-to-know laws, arguing that these laws did not even require women to be told that "nobody should be paid to murder another person." Brown and others like her also thought that any kind of consent law—even when it included information supportive of fetal rights—was inconsistent with the *idea* of personhood. "The consent of one person to another's killing," she wrote, "does not legitimize or legalize the taking of that human life." For many in the movement, however, right-to-know laws were the best way to advance personhood in the short term. These laws promised to force women to confront the arguments supporting personhood. Cunningham believed that if women came to see some abortions as wrong, they could be persuaded to embrace fetal rights. "If unborn children are worthy of legal protection in some circumstances," she wrote in 1994, "they are deserving of legal protection in all circumstances."[31]

In the mid-1990s, feminists of color increasingly began challenging this idea of victimhood. What would become known as reproductive-justice activism had roots that reached back decades. A more centrally organized fight began after the 1994 United Nations International Conference on Population and Development in Cairo, Egypt. An umbrella organization called the Women of Color Coalition for Reproductive Rights sent a delegation to Cairo committed to discussing not just reproductive choice but a lack of access to health care produced by "racism, political oppression, classism and gender bias." Peggy Saika, a leader of one of the groups that co-founded the coalition, had been born to Japanese-American parents in an Arizona internment camp during the Second World War. Saika worked as a hairdresser to put herself through college, opened the first shelter for Asian-American domestic violence survivors in Northern California, and then founded Asians and Pacific Islanders for Choice in 1989. Like her coalition colleagues, she wished to emphasize the ways that "racism, class segregation, patriarchy, and immigration status impact and limit the multitude of reproductive choices that a woman must make in her lifetime."[32]

While Cunningham argued that abortion doctors victimized women by ending their pregnancies and denying them information about the fetal person, advocates like Saika insisted that women of color knew what they were doing and sought out abortions when they needed them. At the same time, coalition members stressed that abortion access alone was not a solution for those who lacked a living wage, good health care, or the means to raise the children they already had. To members of the reproductive-justice movement, painting women as victims of abortion was just another way to silence them.[33]

Suing Big Abortion

To Mark Crutcher, the emerging reproductive-justice critique was another reason to find a better way to promote fetal personhood. Crutcher grew up in Denton, Texas, a college town outside Dallas best known as the hometown of Miss America 1971. When the

Supreme Court decided *Roe v. Wade*, Crutcher was selling Datsuns and Chevrolets at a local dealership, but he soon immersed himself in the antiabortion movement. By 1990, he had become the president of North Texas Right to Life. He believed that Americans could be convinced to support fetal personhood if the idea were marketed the right way. He began his own campaign by sending a comic book entitled "Bottom Feeder" to over thirty thousand medical students. A representative joke asked what someone should do if they were in a room with Hitler, Mussolini, and "an abortionist." The correct answer was "shoot the abortionist twice."[34]

Crutcher saw his campaign as an alternative to the declining clinic-blockade movement. First, in August 1993, came the attempted murder of George Tiller, a Wichita doctor who offered abortions later in pregnancy. Then, in Pensacola, Paul Hill, the smiling evangelist for violence, murdered Dr. John Britton and his bodyguard outside a clinic. Britton, who had begun flying across the state to Dr. David Gunn's former facility, wore a bulletproof vest, worked with a bodyguard, and carried a firearm. It did not matter. Hill, who had been a fixture at protests outside the clinic, approached Britton one sweltering July day in 1994, killed his bodyguard, injured the bodyguard's wife, and shot Britton in the head.[35]

Paige Cunningham and her colleagues condemned Paul Hill's action and worried about the political fallout from it. "Assassinating abortionists," Cunningham wrote her colleagues, "diverts attention from the brutality of abortion itself." Clarke Forsythe, Cunningham's colleague and the primary architect of the movement's fetal-homicide laws, agreed that antiabortion violence resulted "in media portrayals of abortionists as heroes"—and forced the movement to use resources that "should be reserved for responding to the violence of abortion itself."[36]

Within the broader movement, however, Britton's murder exposed a rift about the legitimacy of violence. There had always obviously been some in the blockade movement who believed that Hill's arguments had to be correct if a fetus was a rights-holding person. Before the murders of the 1990s, other extremists in the early 1980s had carried out clinic bombings and argued they were justified. Paul Hill's legal brief—which was republished by the law review of Pat Robertson's Regent University—reiterated that Hill had acted justly because fetuses were persons. "Had the decedents attempted to do to Paul Hill what they were planning to do to unborn children that day, Hill could have responded with deadly force," Hill wrote. "These unborn children, children who medically, scientifically, and logically were in imminent peril, needed a defender." In July 1994, in response to Britton's murder, members of the blockade movement gathered at a Chicago Radisson to debate topics like "violence and nonviolence: how to work within disagreement." Father Frank Pavone, the head of Priests for Life, suggested that the discussion was merely philosophical, but with three killed in Pensacola, the damage to the movement's public image had been done.[37]

The spike in attacks on doctors accelerated passage of the 1994 Freedom of Access to Clinic Entrances Act (FACE Act), which prohibited the use of force, threats of force, or physical obstruction to prevent anyone from providing or receiving reproductive health services; typical penalties for a first-time nonviolent offender ran to up to a year in prison and a $10,000 fine, with more stringent punishment authorized for repeat or violent violators. The FACE Act struck a blow against the blockade movement, which depended on the involvement of large numbers of protestors. For years, Operation Rescue had been an easy sell for people who wanted to feel that they could stop abortion immediately, but many activists were not committed enough to face prison sentences or big fines.[38]

Mark Crutcher believed that right-to-know laws were at most a partial solution to the unraveling of the blockade groups. If the antiabortion movement wanted to establish the personhood of the fetus, his allies needed lawsuits. He sent a glossy seventy-two-page how-to-sue guide to sympathetic lawyers. The primary vehicle for such suits was a claim of medical malpractice, but if a woman sued a doctor, she had to show that she suffered a concrete injury. Because *Roe v. Wade* was the law, courts would not likely recognize injuries to the fetus as the basis of a claim, and very few women suffered physical complications.[39]

Crutcher claimed that women could bring suit for "post-abortion syndrome," a depression-like condition that abortion opponents had publicized since the early 1980s. Vincent Rue, a family therapist and antiabortion researcher, first publicly discussed the syndrome at a congressional hearing in 1981. He had graduated from the University of North Carolina's School of Home Economics and began work as a family therapist. In 1990, he and his wife launched the Institute for Abortion Recovery and Research in Portsmouth, New Hampshire, and Rue himself became a kind of professional expert witness, testifying and recruiting colleagues. He claimed that abortion damaged "the very fabric of femininity" because women were destined to be mothers. "By her very anatomy," he argued, "the role of childbearing is clearly the domain of the woman."[40]

In the late 1980s, an electrical engineer and inventor named David Reardon set out to popularize research on the syndrome. He concluded that trauma was evidence that abortion violated the rights of the unborn child, both in Scripture and under the Constitution. "The dangers of abortion to women are evidence of God's natural law," he wrote in 1989. "Sin injures the sinner as well as the victim."[41]

Crutcher thought the syndrome was a concrete enough injury to justify a malpractice suit. Most such suits ultimately did not go anywhere, but for Crutcher, that was no problem. The threat of litigation could drive doctors away from providing abortions or increase the cost of insurance for those who remained in the practice. Nor did the fact that peer-reviewed studies generally failed to find evidence of such a syndrome dissuade Reardon, who believed that most scientists were biased against his movement. He began publishing studies of his own and promoting the work of others who agreed with him. Reardon argued that women instinctually understood that an unborn child was a separate, rights-holding person and suffered trauma as a result. "It is precisely because women and men struggle with the realization that they killed their own children," he wrote, "that they experience increased levels of substance abuse, suicidal behaviors, [and] a host of other self-destructive behaviors."[42]

The 1990s were an opportune time to demonize doctors. Employers searching for a way to curb costs were increasingly turning to health maintenance organizations (HMOs): networks of doctors, hospitals, and other care providers who agreed to accept payment at a certain level so that employers could control their expenses. While covering only approximately 18 percent of U.S. employer-based health insurance enrollments in 1988, HMOs accounted for more than half of all such enrollments just a decade later.[43]

Patients navigating this new landscape found that the for-profit businesses running the HMOs sometimes cut off access to essential services; others complained about the rationing of care and obstacles to seeing specialists on request. Fewer than half of Americans polled in the decade approved of the service delivered by HMOs, compared to more than 70 percent of those who were happy with the service they received from car manufacturers or even telephone companies.[44]

Paige Cunningham spoke to Americans' unhappiness with HMOs in attacking Clinton's health-care reform, insisting that it would force physicians to "abandon treatment for some . . . patients." HMOs reinforced the idea that medicine was an industry, focused more on profits than on patient need. It was an easy step for some conservatives to imagine that an abusive abortion industry was the seamiest segment of an increasingly heartless medical profession.[45]

Welfare Reform

Physicians' greed, Cunningham insisted, was particularly evident in growing demands for assisted suicide. The *Cruzan* decision in 1990 had inspired some right-to-die groups to advocate for the legalization of aid in dying for terminally ill patients. After Oregon voters approved a law authorizing aid in dying in 1994, James Bopp of the National Right to Life Committee sued, arguing that the law violated both federal disabilities law and the Constitution. Americans United for Life was involved in cases in New York and Washington, where right-to-die advocates contended that laws criminalizing aid in dying were themselves unconstitutional. Cunningham expected at least one of these cases to end up at the Supreme Court in the next few years.[46]

In 1995, Clarke Forsythe stepped in to take Cunningham's place as the president of Americans United for Life. He stressed that the organization's mission had not changed: to limit abortion access, increase "protection for the unborn child in areas of law outside of abortion," and pass right-to-know laws to translate "compassion for women and unborn children" into support for a "Human Life Amendment."[47]

Forsythe still presented women as victims denied the truth about abortion and fetal personhood—an idea of victimhood that reflected arguments made in the era about welfare recipients. In 1991, on the campaign trail, Bill Clinton had pledged to "end welfare as we know it." As many then "knew it," welfare had long been tangled in debates about race and racism—and about gender and sexuality. In 1993, one in four Black and one in five Latina women of childbearing age received support from Aid to Families with Dependent Children (AFDC), against only 7 percent of their white counterparts. The arguments that low-income people of color had a dysfunctional "culture" had been prominent for decades.[48]

After the 1994 midterm elections, when Republicans made sweeping gains in Congress, Newt Gingrich, the Speaker of the House, and his ally Dick Armey proposed to hand over management of federal AFDC, food stamp, and nutrition programs to the states and to bar unmarried mothers under eighteen from receiving benefits. With the money saved, Gingrich suggested, the government could build orphanages for the children whose parents, as a result of the bill, could no longer take care of them. The goal was not only to lower the costs of the welfare system but also "to reduce out-of-wedlock pregnancies." Robert Rector, a senior research fellow at the Heritage Foundation, a prominent conservative think tank that had shaped the GOP proposal, similarly focused on discouraging sex outside of marriage. Rector argued that illegitimacy was "the primary factor driving most other social problems." Bill Clinton, who favored work requirements as a reform strategy, also condemned sex and childbearing outside of marriage. "You shouldn't have a baby before you're ready," he told a large gathering of Baptists in 1994, "and you shouldn't have a baby before you're married."[49]

In truth, rates of adolescent pregnancy in the United States had been declining since 1990, but some conservative Protestant groups like Pat Robertson's Christian Coalition still bemoaned what they saw as a surge in sexual promiscuity and favored reforms that would make children born outside of marriage ineligible for welfare benefits. The United States Catholic Conference, by contrast, argued that the Republican plan eliminated "an essential safety net for vulnerable children" and "scapegoat[ed]" "poor women, minority families, and immigrants."[50] Wanda Franz, the president of the National Right to

Life Committee, similarly criticized the Republican plan for under-cutting needed support and thereby opening the door to more abor-tion. "Sentencing innocent children to death," Franz argued, "is not the moral equivalent of paying benefits for children in need."[51]

Franz and her colleagues were quick to note that they resolutely opposed nonmarital sex and childbearing. But the root cause of these issues, Franz claimed, was not the availability of welfare benefits but adolescents' "difficulties with rational analysis." Just as right-to-know strategies suggested that women should not be blamed for their own decisions, Franz and her colleagues stressed that young women did not fully understand the choices they made about sex. Franz argued that the government was the problem: it promoted abortion, birth control, "school-based clinics, and misguided sex 'education'" that made "sex 'risk free' in the mind of an adolescent." In opposing ille-gitimacy penalties, the United States Catholic Conference took a similar position, invoking an analogy to smoking. "Our society must discourage adolescent sexual activity," the conference explained, "with at least as much urgency and persistence as we bring to discouraging smoking." Key antiabortion groups condemned harsh welfare illegiti-macy penalties but, as with right-to-know laws, portrayed women as victims only insofar as they did not understand or want the things they chose.[52]

Partial-Birth Abortion

Some within the antiabortion movement worried that a right-to-know strategy focused too much on women. A perfect opportunity to shift the emphasis back to fetal protection came when a paper was leaked from the annual conference of the National Abortion Federa-tion, describing a technique known as intact dilation and extraction, or intact dilation and evacuation (D&X). Used later in pregnancy,

D&X involved removing an intact fetus from the uterus. Dr. Martin Haskell, the author of the paper, did not invent the method but believed it would be safer for certain patients because it involved fewer passes with a sharp instrument inside the uterus. Members of a Minnesota antiabortion group got a copy of Haskell's paper and immediately circulated a line drawing of the procedure. Leaders of the National Right to Life Committee saw broader possibilities: by spotlighting D&X and seeking to criminalize it, they could turn the procedure into a symbol of what abortion providers did. And by criminalizing D&X, antiabortion activists could highlight the reasoning used to defend fetal rights.[53]

The man who launched this effort was Doug Johnson, a veteran leader of the National Right to Life Committee. Contrary to the usual image of a lobbyist, Johnson had neither flash nor cash. He was a familiar figure on Capitol Hill, having worked for the organization since 1981 out of a dumpy office to which he commuted from the suburbs. He took the idea of a D&X ban to Charles Canady, a second-term Florida Republican congressman leading the charge against same-sex marriage.[54]

In 1995, the two men worked with Keri Folmar, a conservative Christian lawyer, to coin a term for the procedure: "partial-birth abortion." If Americans found the procedure disgusting, it would be easier to argue that all abortions were problematic because the unborn child was human and as such had rights. A model letter to Congress told politicians that the nation must ban dilation and extraction in the name of equality "for the most helpless and defenseless of its citizens."[55]

While proponents of the bill told a story about the "abortion industry," groups like the National Abortion Federation insisted that doctors performed relatively few such procedures a year nationwide, and only in tragic situations, such as when a fetus had a condition incompatible with life. Prohibiting all dilations and extractions, they argued, might pose an unnecessary risk to patients whose future fertility or health could be better protected by D&X than any alternative. Besides, abortion-rights advocates contended, the proposed ban was really just a smokescreen for an effort to stop all legal abortions. "The vote" on the bill, NARAL argued, "is a direct attack on *Roe v. Wade*."[56]

Johnson first disputed the opposition's characterization of D&X, claiming that the procedure was common and elective. But more important, he and his allies also stressed that D&X involved "the killing of a helpless baby." As Johnson explained, the arguments against partial-birth abortion could be extended to all abortions: any such procedure was "a senseless act of violence against an innocent person."[57]

Judie Brown ridiculed the idea that bans on partial-birth abortion would advance the fight for fetal personhood. "Some are working to ban a particular abortion procedure that accounts for less than 1 percent of all child-killings in the nation," she stated of partial-birth abortion, while "the proponents of abortion are busy refining other ways to kill those same children." How, Brown asked, could a ban on partial-birth abortion advance the fight for fetal personhood when such a law permitted the lives of those very same persons to be taken?[58]

Brown's criticism notwithstanding, the partial-birth abortion campaign was effective partly because it echoed an escalating campaign against the tobacco industry. Earlier in the decade, California had become the first state to launch an anti-smoking media campaign, funded by a cigarette tax approved by voters in 1988. Over time, however, the anti-tobacco campaign focused on very graphic ads, including images of the cancerous lungs of smokers or the ravages of chemotherapy. The partial-birth abortion campaign drew on this strategy. Johnson, for example, argued on behalf of the National Right to Life Committee that the procedure killed innocent persons when "their brains are vacuumed out."[59]

The debate over partial-birth abortion also echoed ideas that set the terms of debate about welfare reform. By 1996, Clinton went into negotiations with Gingrich that culminated in the Personal Responsibility and Work Opportunity Reconciliation Act, which converted AFDC into Temporary Assistance for Needy Families, a program of federal grants to the states that included work requirements and stricter eligibility criteria. Clinton's welfare reform reflected an idea of victimhood that had gained increasing currency in the antiabortion movement: victims deserved sympathy only when their indefensible choices were not truly their own. Even in its campaign for the partial-birth abortion ban, the National Right to Life Committee and its allies insisted that women were harmed by choices they did not understand. The Physicians Ad Hoc Coalition for Truth, a group of antiabortion doctors that also called for a federal ban, argued in 1996 that the procedure was "dangerous and potentially life threatening to women."[60]

Demonizing abortion providers also helped salvage the public reputation of the antiabortion movement. By elevating women like Paige Cunningham, Americans United for Life wanted to tell one kind of story about the people who belonged to the antiabortion movement: young mothers and urban professionals like her who argued that legal abortion had set back the women's movement. Reporters often focused on a very different kind of antiabortion activist: men who resembled those in increasingly visible anti-government groups. These organizations first captured attention in 1992 when Randy Weaver, a veteran and self-described white separatist, faced federal firearm charges for selling an illegal weapon to an undercover agent. When Weaver failed to appear in court, federal agents brought an arrest warrant to his property in Ruby Ridge, Idaho, and while they were surveying the compound, someone began shooting. The firefight that followed killed Weaver's son and wife and a federal agent.[61]

The next year, law enforcement tried to serve warrants on David Koresh and other leaders of the Branch Davidian sect in Waco, Texas. Koresh, who claimed to be the final prophet of Jesus Christ, was suspected of stockpiling illegal weapons and sexually abusing children. When law enforcement officers used tear gas to flush him and his followers out of their compound, a fire broke out inside, killing seventy-six Branch Davidians, including twenty-eight children (at least twenty of the dead had also been shot). The Ruby Ridge and Waco incidents radicalized Timothy McVeigh, a security guard in Oklahoma who had become a regular on the gun show circuit. In 1995, McVeigh and a co-conspirator, Terry Nichols, built a bomb, lit a two-minute fuse, and left it in a truck outside the Alfred P. Murrah Federal Building in Oklahoma City. The explosion killed 168 people, including nineteen children.[62]

For some on the right, Waco and Ruby Ridge legitimized the argument that the federal government was biased against those who supported fetal rights. At the same time, the men at the center of the Oklahoma City bombing or the Ruby Ridge siege reminded some voters of those who had killed clinic staff and other Americans in the name of defending fetal persons. Some incidents explain why the two kinds of violence might be linked in the public's mind. For instance, in 1996, Eric Rudolph, an antiabortion activist with ties to white supremacist groups, set off a nail bomb at the Atlanta summer Olympics, injuring over a hundred people and killing one (a second, a Turkish journalist, died of a heart attack while being transported from the scene of the blast). Rudolph, who was identified in 1998 as a suspect in the Olympic attack as well as the bombing of a lesbian bar and two abortion clinics, became a fugitive in the Appalachian wilderness and a folk hero to some abortion opponents. He saw the bombings as a step in the fight for fetal rights. "Because I believe that abortion is murder," he later wrote, "I also believe that force is justified in an attempt to stop it."[63]

The more the media covered violence against providers, the more the antiabortion movement's leaders framed abortion providers as part of a faceless industry intent on making money. In attacking "Big Abortion," groups like Americans United for Life insisted that abortion providers were not ordinary medical doctors because they ignored the needs of the unborn patient, a second person entitled to care and concern. Cunningham, for example, argued that *Roe* had transformed the medical establishment, undermining the "Judeo-Christian ethic of caring for those most in need." Americans United for Life circulated materials claiming that after *Roe*, rates of illegitimate births, single parenthood, teen suicide, and violent crime had increased, while many doctors had given up on helping unborn patients to pursue profit.[64]

It was against this background in 1997 that the SisterSong Women of Color Reproductive Health Collective brought together sixteen organizations focused on questions of reproductive justice. Luz Rodriguez was one of those who got SisterSong off the ground. The daughter of Puerto Rican immigrants, Rodriguez grew up on New York's Lower East Side, studied dance, and then gravitated to community organizing. By the time she played an instrumental role in the founding of SisterSong, she was a single mother, raising five children and working as the executive director of the Latina Roundtable on Health and Reproductive Rights. SisterSong members like Rodriguez framed poverty and welfare policy as issues of reproductive justice—and contended that the fight for fetal rights erased the needs of women. Abortion opponents were arguing that protecting women from negative health outcomes mostly involved preventing abortion, but as the 1990s continued, it was increasingly evident that women of color disproportionately experienced negative health outcomes unrelated to abortion. Black women, for example, died between twice and six times more often during pregnancy in the 1990s than white women. The narrative at the center of fights about right-to-know laws assumed that women would have good health and safe pregnancies unless they were denied the truth about the fetal person, took a wrong turn, and chose abortion. But SisterSong stressed that this assumption was deeply flawed, especially when applied to communities of color.[65]

At first, members of Congress and the mainstream abortion-rights movement mostly ignored these arguments for reproductive justice. Antiabortion groups, for their part, had to contend with a renewed push for the FDA to approve mifepristone, an abortion pill. In 1988, France approved the drug, which Dr. Étienne-Émile Baulieu had imagined as an alternative to surgical abortion early in the decade. Since then, physicians in Europe had begun prescribing the pill with another drug, misoprostol, routinely for early abortions. In 1995, Clarke Forsythe and Americans United for Life filed a citizens' petition urging the FDA not to approve the drug. Forsythe complained that the FDA's approval process had been "thoroughly politicized," with regulators "disregarding the data showing the short- and long-term risks for women." But momentum seemed to be against abortion opponents. In 1996, an advisory arm of the FDA recommended approval of mifepristone as a safe and effective method of early abortion.[66]

History and Tradition

The push for mifepristone approval accelerated at a time when the conservative Christian legal movement was rapidly growing— and changing the most prominent arguments for fetal personhood. By the mid-1990s, the Rutherford Institute was raising $6.5 million a year in direct mail donations, which it used to fund a radio program, books, and John Whitehead's salary as the organization's president. Whitehead made news for hiring lawyers to represent Paula Jones, a woman who had filed a sexual harassment suit against President Bill Clinton. He promised to fight for other underdogs too, explaining that Rutherford defended the rights of "parents to opt children out of sex education programs, . . . the rights of home schoolers, and . . . the rights of voluntary prayer and religious organizations."[67]

But even as the Rutherford Institute grew, other conservative Christian groups surpassed it. By the spring of 1997, Jay Sekulow's American Center for Law and Justice was pursuing cases in courts across the country. Sekulow solicited money and doled out legal advice on a radio program that aired from his basement, and his group recruited legal talent from Pat Robertson's Regent University. As the 1990s continued, a new group, the Alliance Defense Fund (ADF) gained even more power than Sekulow's group. ADF owed its creation to a group of over 30 conservative Christian leaders, including Larry Burkett, who had grown rich from offering financial counseling from a Christian point of view; D. James Kennedy, a Florida-based mega-church pastor; James Dobson, the highly influential leader of Focus on the Family; and Bill Bright, a former California businessman who had transformed the Campus Crusade for Christ from a small evangelical outfit at the University of California, Los Angeles into an international giant that raised hundreds of millions of dollars a year. The consensus among these leaders was that conservative Christians had no equivalent of the ACLU. "Many unselfish Christian lawyers were willing to donate their time," an ADF newsletter later explained, "but they could not afford the thousands of dollars of out-of-pocket expenses . . . which many of these cases require."[68]

The idea for ADF emerged during a 1993 conference call when some of these conservative Christian activists pitched the idea of creating a "super funder." The group created a legal advisory committee to train and advise lawyers. Jay Sekulow chaired a grant committee that reviewed requests for financial support. ADF soon became a prodigious fundraiser. It advocated for fetal personhood and condemned same-sex marriage and civil-rights protections for gays and lesbians. As the 1990s continued, however, ADF leaders looked for political and legal arguments that would appeal to those outside the evangelical community. Often, in demanding personhood, they turned to a message tied to a particular vision of history and tradition.[69]

Alan Sears, an ADF leader who played a key role in these struggles, grew up in Kentucky, found God, was baptized at eighteen, and became a lawyer. In 1986, Ronald Reagan's attorney general, Edwin Meese III, tapped Sears to lead a presidential anti-pornography commission. He later converted to Catholicism and took the helm of Citizens for Decent Literature, an anti-pornography organization led by Charles Keating, the swaggering Catholic Cincinnati lawyer and businessman who soon became the face of a national savings and loan scandal.[70]

After Keating's disgrace undermined Citizens for Decent Literature, Sears moved on to ADF, becoming its founding president in 1993, around the time that several same-sex couples in Hawaii brought a lawsuit because they were refused marriage licenses. Larger progressive groups initially steered clear of demands for same-sex marriage, believing they would backfire. At first, some gay and lesbian rights advocates avoided the issue as well, some because they saw the fight as an effort to assimilate into a heterosexual institution. But the couples in Hawaii and the lawyers took their case all the way to the Hawaii Supreme Court, which ruled in 1993 in *Baehr v. Lewin* that denying same-sex couples' access to marriage raised grave concerns under the state's equal protection clause. After the court's decision, Hawaii voters approved a state constitutional amendment limiting marriage to opposite-sex couples. The *Baehr* opinion nevertheless prompted a panic among Christian conservatives.[71]

At first, ADF members denounced the campaign for same-sex marriage by linking it to what they called "the homosexual agenda." "The homosexual leadership's number one goal," Sears explained in 1997, "is to redefine the family to include distortions of the law like homosexual 'marriage' and the homosexual adoption of children." Connecting the "homosexual agenda" to same-sex marriage seemed even smarter: while the nation was roughly split down the middle in 1996 on whether "homosexual relations should be legal," only 27 percent of those surveyed thought same-sex couples should be allowed to marry.[72]

But developments in the courts soon turned claims about the "homosexual agenda" into a potential liability. In the 1996 case of *Romer v. Evans*, the Supreme Court struck down Colorado's Amendment 2, a state constitutional amendment prohibiting protections against sexual orientation discrimination. The majority opinion concluded that Colorado's "amendment seems inexplicable by anything but animus toward the class it affects." Denouncing a "homosexual agenda" in promoting legislation began to look unwise when judges might be on the lookout for evidence of animus.[73]

With the "homosexual agenda" claim now carrying legal risk, groups like ADF began stressing arguments about history and tradition. "Homophobia," read a debate manual created by the American Center for Law and Justice. "If you haven't been hit with that charge yet, and you are a concerned Christian who supports traditional marriage, then you will be soon enough." The American Center for Law and Justice would deflect this accusation by emphasizing history and tradition. "The legal and historical record is clear," the manual reasoned. "America was built on the traditional family."[74]

Tradition, on this understanding, legitimized acts of exclusion that might otherwise be seen to violate the nation's commitment to equality. Single-issue antiabortion groups like Americans United for

Life, which did not take an official position on same-sex marriage, looked to arguments about tradition for a different purpose: to suggest that it was permissible or even necessary to criminalize the conduct of a physician who harmed a vulnerable, dependent person. In aid-in-dying cases, that vulnerable person was a patient suffering a terminal medical condition. In abortion cases, the vulnerable person would be the fetus.

Aid in Dying

By 1996, the debate about aid in dying had reached a fever pitch. Americans United for Life was helping states defend their laws against aid in dying in court and lobbied for new legislative restrictions. The Supreme Court was set to hear two cases on assisted suicide. In *Washington v. Glucksberg*, the Ninth Circuit Court of Appeals ruled Washington State's ban on assisted suicide in 1995 to be unconstitutional. In *Quill v. Vacco*, the Second Circuit Court of Appeals had reached a similar conclusion about New York's law on aid in dying. The Supreme Court agreed to hear argument in the states' appeals in January 1997. In briefs before the Supreme Court, both the National Right to Life Committee and Forsythe's Americans United for Life insisted that the United States had a set of fixed traditions and values, and that the Court should recognize new rights under the Fourteenth Amendment only if they were rooted in those principles. "A right to assisted suicide is neither implicit in the concept of ordered liberty nor deeply rooted in American history and tradition," National Right to Life Committee argued in *Glucksberg*. Americans United for Life agreed that the nation's deeply rooted traditions were not fluid. "There has never been a period in English or American history," Americans United for Life stressed, "when suicide (or suicide assistance) was regarded as a 'fundamental right.' "[75]

The *Glucksberg* and *Vacco* arguments fit well with the movement's new plan of attack. Many historians believed that the idea of a right to choose abortion was consistent with the nation's history and complex past traditions regarding abortion. But looking to an unchanging national tradition, abortion foes thought, could suggest that *Roe* had been wrongly decided. In the context of aid in dying, antiabortion lawyers could argue that there was no deeply rooted right to assisted suicide—and the nation's history and tradition allowed for criminal punishment of doctors who failed to protect vulnerable patients. In a press release issued before *Glucksberg*, a spokeswoman for the National Right to Life Committee called both abortion and assisted suicide "radical departure[s] from the principles of human equality" and argued that *Glucksberg* and *Vacco* were about whether the Court would ignore American tradition and continue to "devalue—and allow others to take—the lives of those who cannot speak for themselves."[76]

In June 1997, in a unanimous opinion for the Court in *Glucksberg*, Justice William Rehnquist upheld Washington's ban on aid in dying and adopted a version of the history-and-tradition test, though not precisely the one abortion opponents had hoped for. The Court rejected a broad right to die but seemed to reaffirm a right to abortion, suggesting that abortion and contraception counted as "personal activities and decisions that this Court has identified as so deeply rooted in our history and traditions." At the same time, the Court echoed antiabortion arguments that as a matter of history and tradition, aid in dying was not protected but criminalized. "Our laws," Rehnquist wrote, "have consistently condemned, and continue to prohibit, assisting suicide."[77]

At first, Clarke Forsythe warned his colleagues that *Glucksberg* would not be a silver bullet: assisted-suicide activists would "still push for legalization." In later decades, however, antiabortion activists would try to reinvent *Glucksberg*, arguing that the nation's traditions could not change. One of the most venerable, the antiabortion movement would insist, involved the criminalization of abortion. If the Court accepted this vision, it might be possible to do more than dismantle *Roe*. The antiabortion movement might be able to argue that constitutional *protection* for the unborn—and the criminalization of abortion—were deeply rooted in the nation's history and tradition too.[78]

5

The Right to Conscience

When Preven, the first emergency contraceptive, came onto the market in 1998, supporters of legal abortion hoped for a revolution. Most contraceptives, like the birth control pill, are taken daily to prevent pregnancy. Patients took emergency drugs like Preven *after* unprotected sex to stop or delay ovulation and thereby prevent pregnancy. The formula for what Americans called the morning-after pill had been known for decades and often prescribed off label, but the FDA had held back from any formal action, fearing a backlash. After the drug was approved, Gloria Feldt, the leader of Planned Parenthood, predicted that emergency contraceptives could cut the number of abortions and unintended pregnancies in half.[1]

Emergency contraception, together with the growing influence of the conservative Christian legal movement, inspired new arguments for personhood. Under the leadership of Alan Sears, the Alliance Defense Fund had become a wealthy organization headquartered in the affluent town of Scottsdale, a desert city of golf courses and spa resorts. Sears and his colleagues insisted on the importance of respecting the religious liberty of those who supported fetal personhood. At the same time, antiabortion advocates maintained that these beliefs were grounded in fact—that life or rights did begin at fertilization, for example. Related arguments played a prominent role in fights over stem cells, in vitro fertilization, and fetal-homicide laws.[2]

Over time, these conscience claims were also pulled into conflicts about corporate rights. James Bopp found himself at the center of these efforts. After decades of work for the antiabortion movement, he had never left Terre Haute, an Indiana town of fewer than sixty thousand along the banks of the Wabash River. If Bopp loved the pleasures of small-town life, he became a fixture in the nation's capital, where he did more than most to tie the struggle for personhood to the fight for corporate rights. Not every antiabortion organization supported Bopp's interest in challenging campaign-finance regulations, including those that limited corporations. Some saw it as a distraction. Others worried about expanding corporate power—or argued that focusing on campaign finance would alienate the movement from politicians who supported personhood but disagreed on money in politics. Despite these objections, however, Bopp's National Right to Life Committee and other antiabortion groups became integral to the war against campaign-finance reform.[3]

Demands for corporate rights became entangled with questions of religious liberty. Claims about conscience were not new. Conscientious objectors to war, together with a wide range of other believers, had raised them in court for decades. After Congress passed the federal Religious Freedom Restoration Act in 1993, religious believers had raised conscience-based arguments to defend the way they dressed or worshipped. The new conscience arguments, however, covered a broader universe of objectors, some of whom had little direct involvement in the activity they found offensive. In 2011, when the Obama administration required employers and insurers to cover all FDA-approved contraceptives without a co-pay, ADF represented religious business owners who challenged the contraceptive mandate, maintaining that drugs commonly marketed as birth control were in fact abortifacients—and that they did not wish to feel complicit in helping their employees access medications that violated fetal rights.[4]

In the 1960s, abortion opponents like Robert Byrn had mocked the idea that judges were willing to guarantee corporations equal treatment while denying the same protections to innocent unborn children. By the 2000s, Sears, Bopp, and their colleagues often insisted that corporations, like fetal persons, were victims of discrimination. These ideas of equality centered less on physical vulnerability and dependence and more on the idea that ideological opponents, including the media, marginalized corporations and American Christians just as they had the unborn. When the Supreme Court recognized corporate personhood under the Religious Freedom Restoration Act in *Burwell v. Hobby Lobby Stores* (2014), antiabortion groups understood that the decision was not about constitutional rights. But like many of his colleagues, Bopp hoped that justices willing at times to treat businesses as persons might be willing to do the same for the unborn child.[5]

Multi-Issue Advocacy

In 1998, birth control was supposed to be a settled issue, but not everyone thought so. Bernard Nathanson, a former abortion provider whose deadpan delivery and thick glasses had become instantly recognizable in the antiabortion movement, was one of those for whom it was not settled at all.[6]

After co-founding the National Association for the Repeal of Abortion Laws in the 1960s, Nathanson came to regret his involvement and joined the antiabortion movement in the early 1980s. He had become a fixture at Life Forum, an antiabortion strategy summit that took place several times a year. The gatherings began in 1989 to heal rifts created by the rise of Operation Rescue and quickly grew into a safe haven for activists to share ideas that might damage the movement if they became public. For this reason, everything about Life Forum meetings—even their existence—was kept strictly secret.[7]

By 1998, antiabortion organizations privately acknowledged that FDA approval of mifepristone was imminent and that they needed to minimize the fallout. Nathanson urged his colleagues to lobby for mifepristone to be approved as a schedule 2 drug, defined as having a "high potential for abuse." He also told Life Forum attendees to press for the approval of mifepristone only for abortion. Understood as an abortion drug, mifepristone would be easier to fight.[8]

Some Life Forum attendees asked about claims that mifepristone could work as a contraceptive—an argument raised by some abortion-rights activists. Nathanson responded that it did not matter if those people were right. "Moral and ethical arguments against contraception are extremely strong," he explained. "Splitting the procreative function from sex is simply unnatural." Other Life Forum attendees argued that drugs commonly marketed as birth control were in fact abortifacients. "Contraceptives," a representative of the American Life League said at another meeting, "also abort unborn children."[9]

While larger antiabortion groups remained officially neutral on the issue—and while views on contraception among rank-and-file abortion foes varied—opposition to emergency contraception remained strong within some antiabortion groups. Pharmacists for Life, founded in the early 1980s, lobbied pharmacies not to stock emergency contraceptives and defended any pharmacists who refused to fill prescriptions. This included Preven and a competitor, Plan B, approved in 1999. Most physicians agreed with the American College of Obstetricians and Gynecologists (ACOG) that emergency contraceptives delayed or prevented ovulation rather than blocking the implantation of a fertilized egg. ACOG further defined pregnancy as beginning not when an egg is fertilized but when it implants in the uterus. None of this persuaded Pharmacists for Life. "Regarding Preven," the group's leader told the press in 1999, "it's an abortifacient."[10]

As the 1990s drew to a close, it seemed unimaginable that the law would one day recognize fetal personhood, but the stigma surrounding abortion was undeniable. For decades, more Americans had identified as "pro-choice" rather than "pro-life." But in 2002, for the first time in years, equal numbers of Americans identified as either one. What seemed to have changed, according to polls, was not how Americans saw abortion regulations or even fetal rights. But in the first three years of the 2000s, only 37 to 42 percent of Americans saw abortion as "morally acceptable." A 1999 study found that nearly half of women who chose to end their pregnancies believed they would be looked down on if anyone else knew. Young Americans who supported legal abortion rarely got politically involved in the issue. Efforts to shake the so-called "post-*Roe* generation" out of its complacency began in 1998 with a $6 million ad buy commissioned by the Pro-Choice Education Project, a coalition of more than forty groups that asked young women what they would do "when their right to a safe and legal abortion was finally taken away." It was not clear whether these efforts were working. Indeed, by 2003, NARAL renamed itself NARAL Pro-Choice America, a move intended, as historian David Garrow told the *New York Times*, to "put a greater emphasis on choice rather than abortion."[11]

The leaders of the antiabortion movement of the era still saw fetal personhood as their ultimate aim. The National Right to Life Committee, which in 1999 billed itself as the largest national antiabortion organization, boasted a $12 million annual lobbying budget, and its pro-life rating of each member of Congress was a vital tool for keeping Republican legislators in line. Americans United for Life, which had played a key role in drafting model legislation for the states, celebrated 1999 as a high-water mark for new state abortion restrictions. These restrictions, for leaders of the antiabortion movement, were still a stopgap. The movement's defining goal remained recognition of fetal personhood, whether by a constitutional amendment or a judicial decision, even if few saw that as a realistic short-term objective.[12]

But with the influx of new Christian conservative groups, it was no longer clear who in the antiabortion movement was calling the shots. Mat Staver and his wife, Anita, two of the movement's newly influential voices, had launched Liberty Counsel in Orlando in 1989. Staver had grown up poor in Charlotte Harbor, Florida, one of seven children of a single mother. When he was a senior in high school, an evangelist came to town to preach about the end of times, and Staver was captivated. He was working as a pastor in Lexington, Kentucky, when he met Anita, an undergraduate psychology major, at a church party. Then in 1983, after several fellow pastors showed him a video on abortion, he decided he could make more of a difference practicing law. He opened his own firm, Staver and Associates, and soon became a major player in the Orlando legal scene, with clients that ranged from the local NBA franchise to Hyatt hotels. But he preferred to focus on advancing conservative Christians' cause through Liberty Counsel, and by 1999, Staver had become so immersed in cause lawyering that he closed Staver and Associates. Three years later, Anita graduated from law school, and the two formed a lucrative partnership with Jerry Falwell's Liberty University. Suddenly, Liberty Counsel was a major player.[13]

Liberty Counsel had its share of competitors in an emerging Christian legal movement. The televangelist Pat Robertson was pouring money into Jay Sekulow's American Center for Law and Justice. Alan Sears's Alliance Defense Fund had also become a powerhouse, with assets totaling nearly $15 million in 2001. Single-issue groups had primarily discussed fetal personhood in the context of abortion or end-of-life issues. Like the funders who backed Sekulow's and Staver's organizations, ADF instead financed litigation that fit fetal personhood into a broader agenda that addressed questions of sexuality and the separation of church and state. To compete for support, single-issue antiabortion groups had to consider different arguments and priorities.[14]

Up to that point, the conservative Christian legal movement had achieved the most success in cases involving freedom of speech and religion. In one ADF case from 1995, the University of Virginia turned down Ronald Rosenberger, an undergraduate, who asked the university for money from a student activity fund to publish a Christian student newsletter. (Administrators had concluded that the proposal violated university guidelines on the separation of church and state.) In a 5-4 decision in *Rosenberger v. University of Virginia*, the Supreme Court held that it violated the First Amendment for a university to deny Rosenberger while continuing to fund student publications with a nonreligious perspective. Another ADF case decided that year involved a group of war veterans given the right to organize the city's St. Patrick's Day parade. The veterans' council wanted to exclude a group advocating for gay and lesbian rights. A unanimous Supreme Court in *Hurley v. Irish-American Gay, Lesbian, and Bisexual Group of Boston, Inc.* held that it would violate the First Amendment to force the parade organizers to express a message that they did not want to convey. ADF also bankrolled challenges to laws protecting access to abortion clinics and insisted that the state could offer religious schools financial support without offending the Establishment Clause.[15]

As more Americans came to think that gay sex should be legal, and as an even larger number still backed abortion rights, ADF's civil liberties claims became increasingly important. When it came to fetal personhood, ADF stressed the importance of religious liberty for those who believed in fetal rights. At the same time, however, ADF lawyers suggested that the facts backed up beliefs about personhood. Sears argued that ADF was championing a "right to refuse to participate in acts that are against one's conscience." He told the story of an Illinois nurse who refused to participate in abortions at her place of employment, arguing that she had protection not only from federal conscience statutes but from the Constitution and God's natural law. Christians, he explained, had a "grave obligation of conscience not to cooperate in practices which, even if permitted by civil legislation, are contrary to God's law."[16]

How to Advance Personhood

Rather than solely prioritizing conscience claims, Harold Cassidy thought his movement should pursue the recognition of fetal personhood right away. As much as he relished his quiet life as a lawyer in New Jersey horse country, Cassidy thought he could become a historically important figure, the man who figured out how to overrule *Roe v. Wade.* He had developed a professional interest in what he saw as the law of motherhood, the rights of birth mothers and surrogates battling for custody of the children they had carried, and he was convinced that the mother-child bond formed during pregnancy enjoyed constitutional protection.[17]

He also believed large antiabortion organizations had no plan to get rid of *Roe.* So, he proposed an alternative, the Global Project, that would litigate to "establish the fact that the child is a complete, separate, unique and irreplaceable human being" with "natural inalienable rights as well as equal protection and due process rights." Cassidy was aware of earlier personhood efforts but believed that the Supreme Court had never considered the full body of evidence supporting the biological humanity of the unborn—and thus might reconsider its position on personhood with the benefit of a complete evidentiary record.[18]

To advance this idea of personhood, Cassidy initially prioritized wrongful death suits. Karen Alexander had worked at Jersey Shore

Hospital for seventeen years when she arrived in labor. When she awoke following a Cesarean section, she learned that her child had been stillborn, an outcome she attributed to medical negligence. Cassidy filed a complaint on her behalf, claiming that it violated the state constitution for New Jersey law to deny a remedy for wrongful death when a child died before birth. In 1996, he filed a medical malpractice suit on behalf of a second client, Rosa Acuna. After consulting with her doctor, Acuna, who already had two children under three and a serious kidney condition, had chosen to terminate her pregnancy, but after being hospitalized for an incomplete abortion, she came to regret her decision. Cassidy argued that she had suffered symptoms of post-traumatic stress disorder because she was never told that the unborn "was a complete, separate, unique and irreplaceable human being." He was also working on a wrongful death class action on behalf of mothers in stillbirth cases. His claims resonated with conservative Christians across the movement. "The core principle upon which a democratic republic is based is the equality of each person under the law," explained the Family Research Council in 2000. "Legalized abortion violates the principle by denying the protection of the law to the most vulnerable in society—the unborn."[19]

When George W. Bush, the former Texas governor, took office as president in 2001, abortion opponents hoped for a federal law that would bolster the case for fetal personhood. James Bopp and his colleagues promoted the Unborn Victims of Violence Act, a national version of the state fetal-homicide laws it had championed since the late 1980s. Jay Sekulow predicted that the bill would pass because "many Americans do want to see the unborn child protected from acts of violence."[20]

An alternative proposal, the Born-Alive Infants Protection Act, was the brainchild of Hadley Arkes, a professor at Amherst College who had founded the James Wilson Institute in 2000 to promote the argument that the framers of the Constitution abided by natural law, "standards of moral judgment that had to be there before we could even conceive a Constitution." As early as the 1990s, Arkes had contended that his movement could advance the cause of personhood by introducing a federal law outlawing the killing of a child born alive after an abortion. He planned to stress the similarities between a fetus and a newborn, which, he suggested, remained the same genetically unique individual from the moment an egg was fertilized. "It is time," he told attendees of Life Forum in 1998, "for Congress to pass legislation articulating that the newborn infant is entitled to equal protection of the law."[21]

James Bopp thought that Cassidy's move would backfire: the Supreme Court was not ready to overturn *Roe* and might actually strengthen abortion rights if given a chance. Paul Linton, the former general counsel of Americans United for Life, emerged as another key skeptic. As the Supreme Court interpreted the Fourteenth Amendment, plaintiffs had to meet a "state action requirement" showing that either the government or its agents were violating relevant rights under the Equal Protection and Due Process Clauses. But that, Linton wrote, meant "no protection against private actors," and abortion providers almost never had the kind of connection to the government that the law required. If the state criminalized the homicide of other persons, however, the decision *not* to criminalize abortion could be seen as an action by the government. But if courts adopted this idea of state action, it might fundamentally change how abortion prosecutions took place. Before *Roe*, women having abortions rarely faced serious charges. If a court recognized personhood, that might require prosecutors to treat the fetus like any other homicide victim, and it was clear that women were prosecuted for other killings. Leading antiabortion groups said that they opposed the punishment of women. But Linton's questions about state action raised an issue that would reemerge later, when the thought of the judiciary recognizing fetal personhood did not seem quite so far-fetched: how could the antiabortion movement claim that personhood required equal punishment of those who harmed the fetus without calling for the prosecution of women?[22]

Lawrence

The antiabortion movement was hoping for the passage of a major federal antiabortion law when news broke that extremists affiliated with the terror group Al-Qaeda had hijacked four planes and attacked both the Pentagon and New York's World Trade Center, killing almost three thousand people. In the year following the attack, hate crimes against Muslims in the United States increased dramatically. Bible sales surged in 2001, as did purchases of American flags. A record 90 percent of Americans approved of George W. Bush's performance in the White House in the immediate aftermath of the September 11 attack. The figure among conservative Christians was almost certainly higher.[23]

Bush's presence in the White House allowed abortion opponents to hope that some personhood strategies might still work. Harold Cassidy's strategy had run into trouble: in 1997 and 2002, New Jersey courts rejected his arguments. There was more progress in Congress. Bush signed Arkes's born-alive bill into law in 2002.[24]

Opposing same-sex marriage seemed to be a sound strategy too. Christian conservatives felt so sure of Americans' hostility to same-sex marriage that they spotlighted the issue when sodomy bans returned to the Supreme Court. The facts behind *Lawrence v. Texas* remain shrouded in uncertainty, but the beginning of the story is clear enough. John Geddes Lawrence, a fifty-five-year-old medical technician, had gone for dinner and drinks with Robert Royce Eubanks and

Tyrone Garner before the trio returned to Lawrence's apartment. At some point that evening, the Houston police department received a tip that someone in the apartment was brandishing a gun. The police would later maintain that they entered the apartment and observed Lawrence and Garner having sex. Lawrence and Garner denied having sex at the time, and it strains credulity to think that they continued even after law enforcement officers forced their way into the apartment. Whatever the officers saw, they quickly realized that there was no gun in the apartment but arrested Garner and Lawrence anyway. Both men were convicted of sodomy, and the Lambda Legal Defense and Education Fund argued that the Texas law was unconstitutional.[25]

Texas's defense centered on claims about history and tradition. The nation, its attorneys contended, had a tradition of "historically prohibiting a wide variety of extramarital sexual conduct." In an amicus brief, the Family Research Council, a prominent Christian conservative group, offered a similar update of *Bowers*, contending that even "a glance at history and tradition conclusively shows that there is no fundamental right to . . . any other sexual acts apart from marriage."[26]

In his July 2003 opinion for the Court, Justice Anthony Kennedy wrote that the meaning of liberty had changed. The majority opinion focused on the intersection of due process and equal protection, and Kennedy noted "an emerging awareness that liberty gives substantial protection to adult persons in deciding how to conduct their private lives."[27]

Even after the *Lawrence* decision struck down sodomy laws nationwide, Alan Sears still insisted that defending traditional marriage would be "a strong affirmation of God's natural law." But he and his colleagues began sounding the alarm about what might happen if courts (or voters) ever recognized a right for same-sex couples to marry. Then, the November after the *Lawrence* decision, the Massachusetts Supreme Judicial Court, in *Goodridge v. Department of Public*

Health, became the first to recognize such a state constitutional liberty. Most single-issue antiabortion groups did speak out about *Goodridge* or *Lawrence*. ADF, by contrast, responded to the decision by stressing that just like legal abortion, same-sex marriage threatened Christians' right to conscience. If same-sex couples could marry, Sears argued, then some states would expect business owners to serve those couples and justices of the peace to give them marriage licenses—and might penalize those Christians who refused. Legalizing same-sex marriage, he warned, would "criminalize much opposition to homosexual behavior." He and his colleagues would increasingly stress the importance of religious liberty not only for those who opposed civil rights for gays and lesbians but also for those who believed in the personhood of the fetus.[28]

Religious Liberty

At least, Sears and his colleagues felt, they could rely on the president. Bush signed the federal Partial-Birth Abortion Ban Act into law in November 2003. Antiabortion advocates realized that the law might be struck down, since in 2000, in *Stenberg v. Carhart*, the Supreme Court had invalidated a very similar Nebraska ban, finding it too vague to guide doctors on which procedures were permitted. The Court also concluded that Nebraska had unconstitutionally excluded a health exception and "place[d] women at an unnecessary risk of tragic health consequences." The federal statute did not have a health exception either.[29]

In 2003, with his colleague Tom Marzen, James Bopp sought an ADF grant to defend the Partial-Birth Abortion Ban Act. The partial-birth abortion fight, they wrote, had "been the most effective means over at least the last decade to educate the public on the radical nature of the abortion liberty." Bopp and Marzen agreed with the vast majority of abortion opponents that a fetus was a whole, separate person with constitutional rights. But they thought that defending a ban on so-called partial-birth abortion would force the public to confront graphic images of abortion and thereby become more sympathetic to life in the womb. The more the movement could stigmatize abortion, the easier it would be to build support for fetal rights.[30]

But ADF was just as interested in getting direct recognition of constitutional personhood in the near term. It helped found a new organization, the Culture of Life Leadership Coalition, that privileged the arguments Cassidy had used in his work in the Global Project about the uniqueness of each fetus and the connection between biological status and constitutional rights. Jeffery Ventrella, the senior counsel for ADF, was on the coalition's executive committee.[31]

Ventrella was known for leading the Blackstone Legal Fellowship, a program ADF had launched in 2000 to train conservative Christian students for future positions in academia, elite law firms, and the judiciary. The Blackstone program taught interns about "the framers' original intent for the US Constitution and the Bill of Rights as it reflects God's natural law and God's higher law." After a series of meetings, Ventrella and the coalition's executive committee planned litigation and a legislative strategy centered on the ideas that "children have a right to be born" and "women deserve better than abortion." But the coalition was soon crippled by internal divisions, with members of NRLC upset that they were not even invited to tactical summits. By 2004, it had disbanded.[32]

Nor were abortion opponents certain what to do about emergency contraception. By the end of 2003, use of the morning-after pill—even access to it—remained limited. Frustrated with a lack of progress, several states had already moved to allow over-the-counter access to the morning-after pill, and groups like the American Medical Association were pressing the FDA to approve it for nonprescription use.[33]

Many antiabortion groups had spent years establishing that they took no position on any form of birth control. As soon as antiabortion lawyers began defending the idea of constitutional fetal personhood in the 1960s, supporters of abortion rights charged that their real purpose was to force Catholic theology down the throats of the American people. Opposing birth control would only make that charge more convincing. Taking a neutral position on birth control also seemed important to the movement's expansion efforts. Young antiabortion activists were not uniformly in favor of contraception; some attended Rock for Life, punk concerts launched in 1993 and taken over by Judie Brown's American Life League in 1999. Brown's group had long campaigned against birth control. But the mass emails, flash internet ads, and campus teach-ins launched by abortion opponents were intended to reach the large majority of younger Americans who favored access to contraception, including the morning-after pill.[34]

The problem was that some antiabortion activists *did* oppose emergency contraception. Pharmacists for Life promoted the claim, denied by most physicians, that the morning-after pill was "emergency abortion." Other activists distrusted the scientific experts charged with evaluating how the morning-after pill worked. Another cohort opposed any drug that would facilitate sex outside of marriage or separate sex from procreation.[35]

Even the National Right to Life Committee, the best-known incrementalist group, struggled with the issue. In May 2004, the board of directors considered a resolution stating that the organization took no position on any drug that prevented fertilization but opposed medications that took effect thereafter. The resolution was intended to placate colleagues who considered the morning-after pill an abortifacient, without officially putting the organization on the record about the drug. The effort to defuse the situation failed: a board member countered with a far more ambitious resolution, suggesting that when it came to the morning-after pill, the FDA had facilitated "promiscuity and sexual violence."[36]

But most Republicans were not ready to come out against any form of birth control. Instead, since 2002, the GOP had presented emergency contraception as a threat to parental rights. In Congress, Republicans proposed the Schoolchildren's Health Protection Act, which would deny federal funding to any public school that distributed emergency contraception to students (which only a tiny fraction of schools were doing).[37]

Rather than just talking about the rights of parents, conservative activists like Beverly LaHaye connected fetal personhood to religious liberty. It would have been hard to imagine her as a social movement leader in the 1970s when she was a mother of four in San Diego, working full-time while her husband, Tim, tried to make it as a minister. One day in 1978, feeling repulsed by what Betty Friedan said in a television appearance, LaHaye rented out a local hall to bring together women opposed to feminism. To complete the reservation, she needed an organization name, so off the top of her head she came up with Concerned Women for America.[38]

Concerned Women for America quickly became the fastest-growing organization in the country. By 2004, it had an annual budget of $11 million and five hundred thousand members. Beverly herself was an ideal symbol for the cause, always perfectly made up, the author of best-selling advice books on how Christian women could joyfully submit to their husbands. There was no shortage of conservative Protestant women who wanted to be like her, and when she told them what the nation needed, many were ready to go to war.[39]

Like Sears, LaHaye argued that allowing same-sex couples to marry would threaten Christians' fundamental right of conscience. Christians, she warned, would get in trouble if they spoke out against same-sex marriages or if their businesses refused to participate in them. "You'll be told that your Biblical beliefs are bigoted, or homophobic," she warned. "You may be fired or fined."[40]

LaHaye was also ready to link concern for religious liberty to emergency contraception and fetal personhood. "The morning-after pill not only definitely terminates the life of an unborn child," she wrote in 2004, "it leaves young girls with the false impression that they can wantonly have unprotected sex without consequence."[41]

Groups like NARAL had long framed abortion *rights* as a matter of freedom of conscience. This approach informed the early planning of the spring 2004 March for Women's Lives, conceived as a massive event that would persuade congressional Democrats to prioritize the abortion issue.[42]

But reproductive-justice organizers contended that a single-issue approach was failing—and had rarely given people of color anything real in the first place. Single-issue politics had focused on freedom *from* the government when some needed government protection from sterilization abuse or government support to raise children in a safe and healthy environment. The leaders of the abortion-rights movement, who were overwhelmingly white and unlikely to rely on government aid, sometimes struck reproductive-justice organizers as out of touch. "White women cannot claim to represent all women," the reproductive-justice activist Loretta Ross wrote in 2004, "without making very specific commitments to women of color that involve sharing resources and power."[43]

Ross was already perhaps the best-known proponent of reproductive justice. The sixth of eight children in a blended family, she won a scholarship to study at Radcliffe but then was sexually assaulted by her cousin. She got pregnant and decided to keep her son rather than giving him up for adoption, a choice that cost her the scholarship, and decided to attend Howard University instead, where she became active in anti-rape and civil-rights organizations. In 1976 a doctor implanted an IUD, the Dalkon shield, which gave her a serious pelvic infection that nearly killed her and that left her sterile. These experiences convinced her that any fight for reproductive rights had to include protection from sterilization abuse and sexual violence, as well as support for people to have the children they wanted.[44]

Ross and other activists of color successfully demanded that speakers at the march discuss a range of issues. "This is the essential definition of reproductive justice," she wrote, "the right to have, or not to have children, and the right to have the conditions that allow women to make the optimal choices for their lives."[45]

More than 1 million people attended the event, and the speakers addressed a wide variety of reproductive topics beyond abortion. The attendees were diverse too. "For years, we have heard the drum beat that young people don't care," explained reproductive-justice activist Kalpana Krishnamurthy after the march. In truth, she wrote, young people were deeply supportive of reproductive justice. The key to turning them into movement members was to "purposefully link issues of universal health care, family planning, . . . and globalization" "to issues of women's health and abortion."[46]

The gradual spread of reproductive-justice arguments added a new dimension to debates about fetal personhood. Reproductive-justice organizers insisted that honoring the humanity and needs of women, especially in communities of color, required substantive commitments from the government to reduce maternal mortality and help families bear and raise the children they wanted. But in the 2000s, even as reproductive-justice advocates increasingly argued for more support for pregnant women, leading antiabortion groups instead often prioritized laws, including abortion restrictions and fetal-homicide laws, that criminalized what their proponents considered acts of violence against the unborn. If anything, some personhood proponents argued that fetal rights could not always be reconciled with the very reproductive technologies that some were using to start their families.[47]

Stem Cells and IVF

Stem cells, which can differentiate into different cell types and replicate indefinitely, had been seen as a promising source of new therapies since the 1960s. In 1998, when American biologist James Thomson first isolated embryonic stem cells, the possibility of a therapy became more than academic.[48]

Stem-cell research relied on embryos, either created for the purpose or made available through in vitro fertilization (IVF), an assisted reproductive technology in which eggs are fertilized outside the body, the embryos then placed into the uterus to develop. Often, IVF resulted in the creation of more embryos than would be implanted in a single cycle. These extra embryos could provide peace of mind should an IVF cycle not end in a healthy pregnancy. For those considering additional children, having frozen embryos on hand could lower the financial and emotional cost of an additional IVF cycle. Patients could decide whether any extra embryos would be saved for later use, destroyed, or donated to other families or for research. If some embryos created in IVF were going to be destroyed anyway, a growing bipartisan group of lawmakers asked, what was the harm in allowing them to be used in research?[49]

For many supporters of constitutional fetal personhood, the stem-cell debate confirmed that IVF itself was a problem. Antiabortion groups argued that personhood began when an egg was fertilized, and thus that frozen embryos used in IVF qualified as rights-holding children. For this reason, some questioned the destruction, donation, or even storage of embryos. As early as 1979, a year after the birth of the first "test-tube baby," Americans United for Life mounted a massive letter-writing campaign to lobby Congress to ban federal funding for IVF research. The United States Catholic Conference also opposed IVF, arguing in 1998 that "conception should occur from the marriage act, . . . not from technicians."[50]

By the 2000s, groups like the Christian Legal Society were intervening more directly in issues related to IVF. Since 1994, when Samuel Casey took over as the group's executive director, the organization had begun to play a more important role in litigation and state legislative campaigns. Casey grew up in San Francisco, surviving, as he saw it, both his parents' divorce and Stanford University's campus unrest in 1969. In the early 2000s, he made the Christian Legal Society one of the most visible champions of the "adoption" of embryos created through IVF. The first such program, in which patients donated unused embryos to other couples, was launched in 1997 in Fullerton, California, by Nightlight Christian Adoptions. In 2004, the Christian Legal Society promoted state laws designating the donations of unused embryos "adoptions."[51]

Casey seemed to have the president on his side. In 2001, Bush had vowed to veto any bill allowing funding for stem-cell research beyond the development of stem-cell lines, or self-sustaining colonies already derived from embryos. Then, in August 2002, he announced a program of block grants facilitating embryo adoption. But Bush's actions hardly quelled the debate. In 2004, the Democratic nominee, John Kerry, used Bush's position on stem-cell research to attack him. Even some leading Republicans in the House and Senate, like Senator Bill Frist of Tennessee, a physician, called Bush's ban on the procedure unjustified.[52]

Antiabortion groups responded by going on the offensive about fetal personhood. Some seized on fetal-homicide laws, which had received new attention following the high-profile murder of Laci

Peterson. Twenty-seven-year-old Peterson had been eight months pregnant when she disappeared from her home in suburban Modesto, California. A couple discovered her remains along the shores of the San Francisco Bay; shortly later, authorities arrested her husband, Scott, at a golf course. (He had bleached his hair and stocked his car with $15,000 in cash, survival gear, and four cell phones.) In the aftermath of Laci Peterson's killing, her mother, Sharon Rocha, lobbied for fetal-homicide laws. Bopp's National Right to Life Committee argued that such statutes would increase support for personhood by securing "recognition that unborn children may be victims" and setting a precedent for the "just punishment of those who harm unborn children." Bush signed "Laci and Conner's Law," a version of the Unborn Victims of Violence Act, into law in April 2004. Several states also passed fetal-homicide laws that year.[53]

Fetal-homicide laws were much more popular than Bush's stance on stem-cell research. But discontent with Bush's position on that issue was not enough to cost him the election: the incumbent carried thirty-one states and even won the popular vote. Vindicated by his win, Americans United for Life researched a model bill in 2005 restricting IVF. A Kentucky proposal would have required a woman to create and implant no more than one embryo at a time; a Louisiana law already on the books prohibited the intentional destruction of a fertilized egg created through IVF. Views on IVF would divide rank-and-file abortion foes, some of whom approved of or even used IVF in their own lives. Nevertheless, limits on stem-cell research and IVF held symbolic importance for those fighting for constitutional fetal personhood. "In as many areas as we can, we want to put on the books that the embryo is a person," Casey explained. "That sets the stage for a jurist to acknowledge that human beings at any stage of development deserve protection."[54]

Control of the Court

While personhood proponents dug in for a battle over IVF and stem cells, Justice Sandra Day O'Connor announced in July 2005 that she would retire to help care for her husband, who was suffering from Alzheimer's disease. The following September, after a long struggle, Chief Justice William Rehnquist succumbed to cancer. O'Connor's retirement especially energized groups opposed to abortion because the Court's first female justice had often cast a deciding vote in cases on everything from religious liberty to abortion.[55]

Bush first nominated John G. Roberts for O'Connor's seat, but following Rehnquist's death, the president withdrew that nomination and tapped Roberts to replace Rehnquist as chief justice. The son of a steel executive, Roberts had been a golden boy since his years as the captain of the football team at a posh Indiana boarding school. He could be guarded, but he had the charm to make up for it, and for social conservatives, he had reassuring ties to the George H. W. Bush White House.[56]

Jay Sekulow believed nothing could do more to advance the fight for fetal personhood that if conservative Christians gained control of the courts. He instructed those on his mailing list to donate to senators who would vote to confirm Roberts, who as a Supreme Court justice would be "a strong representative of YOUR beliefs and values in decisions regarding the sanctity of life [and] religious freedom."[57]

Bush tried in 2005 to appoint his close ally Harriet Miers to the Court but was forced to withdraw her nomination before it came to a vote: his own supporters were against her. Miers, like Bush, described herself as a Texan through and through, but if the president knew how to work a room, Miers radiated anxiety. Worse, from the standpoint of abortion opponents, she had no ties to the Federalist Society, and her paper trail was nonexistent. Leonard Leo, a giant in the Federalist

Society who had worked to get both Clarence Thomas and John Roberts onto the Court, took the lead in selling Miers to social conservatives, suggesting, among other things, that she had a track record of opposing abortion.[58]

But many social conservatives thought they could do better. After he withdrew Miers's nomination, Bush selected Samuel Alito, a Federalist Society stalwart and judge on the Third Circuit Court of Appeals. If John Roberts had charm to spare, Alito was a little dour. As a nominee, he gave abortion opponents no reason for concern. As a young lawyer in the Reagan Justice Department in the mid-1980s, Alito had written a memo endorsing an incremental attack that could "advance the goals of bringing about the eventual overruling of *Roe v. Wade*." During his time on the Third Circuit, Alito had been the only one to vote to uphold the entire abortion law challenged in *Planned Parenthood v. Casey*. With enough justices like Alito, the antiabortion movement might be able score wins that would be impossible in popular politics. "This is not a civics lesson," Sekulow wrote. "This is about how it will be to live as a Christian in America in the years to come."[59]

Shifting Right

Alito was narrowly confirmed in January 2006, and Bush vetoed a law lifting limits on stem-cell research in July. Still, proponents of fetal personhood felt frustrated. South Dakota Republicans pushed an absolute abortion ban, a move even Harold Cassidy, the champion of a personhood litigation campaign, considered premature because he worried that such a law would likely be struck down by the courts. Younger activists, along with some major donors, believed that the move was overdue. By 2007, Pew Forum found that 65 percent of white evangelical Protestants thought that abortion should be illegal in most or all cases. In the late 2000s, these evangelicals were disproportionately concentrated in certain regions, especially the South: in 2007, when roughly 26 percent of the nation was evangelical, white evangelicals comprised more than 35 percent of the population in states like North Carolina, Kentucky, and Arkansas. The conservative Protestants joining the antiabortion movement in the 2000s, who often grew up surrounded by those who shared their views, were growing frustrated with the pace of change.[60]

That was true, too, of Domino's Pizza founder Tom Monaghan, who had built a reputation as a big spender (the Detroit Tigers were just his best-known purchase). He had founded the Thomas More Law Center in 1999 with the intent, as its general counsel Richard Thompson put it, to defeat "a calculated strategy to keep our Catholic faith from having any influence on the future of our country." Monaghan was happy to fund other strategies to fight abortion, but his interest in a push for an immediate ban was a sign that top donors were tired of waiting for fetal rights to be recognized.[61]

Despite his doubts about the timing of the proposal, Harold Cassidy helped to steer the South Dakota effort at Monaghan's urging, and a task force report backing the South Dakota bill, which the governor signed into law in March 2006, reflected Cassidy's argument that pregnancy helped "the mother to transfer her interest from herself to her child, and to prepare her for her unique role in the child's life." The groups that had long dictated antiabortion strategy thought South Dakota was pushing too far too fast, but a growing number of rank-and-file activists disagreed. "One of the purposes of a giant step such as South Dakota's total abortion ban," one local activist explained, "is to remind state and federal elected officials that they are duty bound to protect the inalienable rights of unborn humans."[62]

South Dakota's experiment ended just eight months later. Opponents of the state's ban mounted a successful campaign to put the issue on the ballot as a referendum that November, and more than

55 percent of voters rejected the state's abortion ban. But the South Dakota initiative was only the first of many demands for a more aggressive strategy on fetal rights. Between 2006 and 2007, a handful of states introduced trigger bans, which would criminalize abortion the moment *Roe* was overturned.[63]

The newly rebranded Students for Life would play a crucial part in pushing both Republicans and movement leaders to take a harder line on fetal personhood. Since 1988, there had been an organization representing college pro-life groups, American Collegians for Life, first launched at Georgetown University, but the organization was not very active. A far more influential version of the group took off in 2005 when Danielle Huntley, a student at Boston College, found herself sitting next to Ray Ruddy, the head of the government contracting firm Maximus, at an antiabortion event in Boston. Huntley suggested that if Ruddy wanted to spend his money effectively to fight for fetal personhood, he should invest in students. So Ruddy provided seed money for reviving Collegians for Life under the name Students for Life, and in 2006, Kristan Hawkins became its leader.[64]

Hawkins had grown up in the part of West Virginia that is overshadowed by Pittsburgh, a region known for gruff talk and the shells of buildings left behind by the steel industry. Her mother had participated in local antiabortion rallies, and as a child, Hawkins had followed the pro-life float in local parades, handing out LifeSavers from her bicycle. Yet she did not think much about abortion until she began volunteering at a crisis pregnancy center at age fifteen. That experience led her to found a chapter of Teens for Life in her high school.[65]

For a time, her path seemed to lie in Republican politics. In college, she campaigned for George W. Bush and took a job in his administration after graduation. She was bored in the job but came to the conclusion that most antiabortion groups knew very little about running a political campaign. Hawkins saw that many young conservative Catholics and evangelical Protestants took buses to the March for Life every January, but no one in the movement was helping them figure out what to do next.[66]

In her first years running Students for Life, Hawkins worked to increase the number of campus groups, identify which ones were actually active, and organize a more professional annual conference. Students for Life campus chapters hosted diaper drives, created messaging campaigns, and placed articles in student newspapers. But Hawkins had bigger aspirations. She hoped that Students for Life would push politicians to take a harder line—and move the country closer to recognizing fetal personhood.[67]

Neither the South Dakota loss nor the Supreme Court's 2007 decision in *Gonzales v. Carhart*, which upheld the federal Partial-Birth Abortion Ban Act, settled the fight about how to pursue fetal rights. In *Gonzales*, the Court distinguished the federal ban from the Nebraska ban it struck down in 2000, holding that the federal law banned only dilation and extraction rather than sweeping in more common techniques. In a 5-4 majority opinion, Justice Anthony Kennedy concluded that Congress had several justifiable purposes for passing the law, including protecting women from regret over their decision to abort. To support this conclusion, the *Gonzales* opinion cited a friend of the court brief filed by Operation Outcry, an anti-abortion group that gathered affidavits of women who regretted their abortions. The Court was not concerned that the law lacked a health exception. Given that abortion opponents had contested the need for it, the majority believed that scientific uncertainty surrounded the question, and given that uncertainty, legislators had more latitude.[68]

Gonzales was deeply satisfying for James Bopp and his colleagues at the National Right to Life Committee, who had invested a decade in claims about partial-birth abortion. (ADF, which had helped to fund litigation in the case, also took credit for the result.) Those who had presented women as victims of abortion felt vindicated too. Allan Parker, the attorney leading Operation Outcry, echoed the movement's long-standing analogy between smokers and women who chose abortion. "We're kind of in the early stages of tobacco litigation," Parker said of his own campaign in the aftermath of *Gonzales*. But other antiabortion activists thought the entire partial-birth abortion campaign was a public relations stunt that had little to do with the rights of the unborn child. "There is no doubt in my mind that the five Catholic justices who concurred in the opinion agree that partial-birth infanticide is cruel," wrote Judie Brown of *Gonzales*. "What is not clear is whether this decision is really a step toward recriminalizing surgical abortion and defining it as an act that kills a human person."[69]

In 2008, some who were fed up with antiabortion incrementalism sought to write personhood into state constitutions. That push began in the tiny town of Peyton, Colorado, a dry, flat stretch of land northeast of Colorado Springs. Twenty-year-old Kristi Burton had been homeschooled and graduated early from an online Christian university before deciding to change the fight for fetal rights. She and her parents proposed a state constitutional amendment that would recognize fetal rights and ban abortion. Burton made a perfect poster child for the personhood movement, and she had help from Keith Mason, a former Operation Rescue employee who had failed to get a personhood amendment on the ballot in Michigan. Mason set up shop in Denver and launched Personhood USA to fight for such amendments nationwide.[70]

But the Colorado measure—the only personhood proposal to make it onto the ballot that year—failed spectacularly, with more than 70 percent of Coloradans opposed. The national news in the 2008 election cycle was also bleak for the antiabortion movement. Barack Obama, the Illinois senator who had won the endorsement of

NARAL Pro-Choice America during the primary season, handily beat Republican John McCain for the presidency. A promising era for federal antiabortion legislation came to an abrupt end with relatively little accomplished. And to the extent that the Supreme Court seemed interested in expanding personhood, many thought that corporations, not fetuses, would be the ones to benefit.[71]

Corporate Personhood

In the 1960s and 1970s, when the antiabortion movement was less closely tied to the Republican Party, lawyers like Robert Byrn had mocked the idea of corporate personhood. But practical and political considerations made it natural for later generations of antiabortion activists to defend corporate rights. Since 1907, when Congress passed a statute called the Tillman Act, it had been illegal for corporations to make direct contributions to candidates or campaigns. Before the 1970s, no one had much worried about the Tillman Act or any other campaign-finance law because they were so easy to circumvent. It was not until after the Watergate scandal ended Richard Nixon's presidency that Congress passed meaningful limits, restricting contributions to candidates or campaigns, creating a system of spending caps, and establishing an agency, the Federal Election Commission, to enforce the law. In 1976, in *Buckley v. Valeo*, the Supreme Court had struck down parts of this law, ruling that some forms of political spending are protected under the First Amendment.[72]

While they might have had less to spend than many businesses and big donors, most antiabortion groups *were* corporations, and they wanted to support their favored candidates. Starting in the 1980s, in cases like *Federal Election Commission v. Massachusetts Citizens for Life* (1986), antiabortion lawyers primarily contended that their corporations were different from the ones that worried the framers of the

Tillman Act: they raised money on the strength of their ideas and thus, they claimed, posed less risk of corruption. After the 1990s, some antiabortion advocates, led by James Bopp and the National Right to Life Committee, fought hard against *any* campaign-finance reform, believing that such restrictions prevented pro-life groups from advocating for their agenda and disadvantaged Republican candidates. But not every abortion opponent believed that challenging campaign-finance restrictions would advance fetal personhood. Phyllis Schlafly, the iconic anti-feminist, was running a group called the Republican National Coalition for Life, which fought to keep a strict personhood plank in the Republican platform. She was still a consummate GOP insider, calling in favors from her headquarters in a wealthy St. Louis suburb. She criticized Bopp's focus on campaign finance, suggesting that it would undermine the fight for personhood by alienating allies who favored limits on election spending. What mattered was "a steadfast commitment in defense of life," Schlafly suggested, not anyone's take on campaign spending. After Congress passed the Bipartisan Campaign Reform Act in 2002, corporations and unions were both prohibited from directly funding "electioneering communications," a term that covered most political ads, within a certain time before elections. The Supreme Court upheld this provision a year later.[73]

Bopp sought to chip away at the new law and expand corporate speech rights, working with an unwieldy coalition that included small-government conservatives, megadonors, Republican Party operatives, and civil libertarians. But strikingly, none of those battling campaign-finance laws embraced claims about the personhood of corporations. Doing so might have been counterproductive. Those insisting on corporate personhood had often contended that personhood gave corporations *fewer* rights. In *Bank of Augusta v. Earle* (1839), for example, the Supreme Court reasoned that because corporations were persons, states could stop out-of-state businesses from operating within their borders. The case grew out of an economic crisis in 1837. Joseph Earle, an Alabama businessman hurt by the downturn, tried to get out of paying a debt to a Georgia bank by arguing that Alabama law prohibited certain out-of-state banks from doing business there. The bank responded that the Alabama law violated Article IV, Section 2 of the Constitution, the Privileges and Immunities Clause, which forbade states from discriminating against "citizens" of other states. The Court rejected the argument, treating the bank not as a collection of individuals but as a "person" in its own right, one that existed only by "the force of law," and one that, by definition, had fewer rights than "natural" persons. *Earle* and cases like it showed that establishing corporate personhood could be counterproductive. And corporate personhood did not square with one of the antiabortion movement's core claims about constitutional fetal personhood: that constitutional rights were tied to human genetics.[74]

Instead of advocating for corporate personhood, Bopp argued that "all corporations are constitutionally entitled to engage in robust issue advocacy." This claim reflected a far different perspective on equality than the one developed by antiabortion activists in the 1960s. While Robert Byrn had ridiculed the idea of corporate rights, Bopp and his colleagues argued that the government discriminated against both corporations and the unborn.[75]

These claims still divided the movement. Phyllis Schlafly argued that abortion foes would not particularly benefit if corporations had more rights, especially when it came to election spending. Megadonors and for-profit businesses had much greater spending power, she argued, and would benefit far more if campaign-finance limits fell than would the champions of fetal personhood. But by the late 2000s, however, a growing group of conservative Christians was interested in a different question of corporate rights: whether corporations had religious liberty. This was evident in the framing of the 2009 *Manhattan Declaration*, a statement of principles signed by leading conservative Protestants, Catholics, and Orthodox Christians. Princeton professor Robert George helped to spearhead the effort. The son of a West Virginia liquor broker, George had abandoned the Democratic Party over abortion. His entry into politics came with a 1992 speech he wrote for Bob Casey Sr., one of the last Democrats to oppose abortion rights. Thereafter, George became a sort of unicorn, at once a political insider and an intellectual force on the right. He also became a key advisor to the George W. Bush administration, a leading strategist in the National Organization for Marriage, a group opposed to same-sex marriage, and the leading proponent of natural-law arguments against abortion.[76]

With evangelical leader Chuck Colson and Timothy George (no relation), the dean of a seminary housed at Samford University, Robert George drafted a declaration focused on "the sanctity of human life, the dignity of marriage as a union of husband and wife, and the freedom of conscience and religion." Concern for conscience ran throughout the document. Without protection for conscience, the declaration stated, the law could "compel pro-life institutions and . . . health care professionals to refer for abortions and, in certain cases, even to perform or participate in abortions." The idea of complicity woven through the declaration was broader than others that had become familiar under the Religious Freedom Restoration Act. Rather than focusing only on those with the most direct involvement in an activity like abortion, the authors of the declaration urged a broad group of business owners and other objectors to seek out exemptions from laws recognizing same-sex marriage, protecting abortion, or laying out civil-rights protections for gays and lesbians.[77]

The declaration, and the ideas of discrimination tied to it, struck a nerve with Christian conservatives because of the nation's changing religious landscape. In 1990, more than 85 percent of

Americans identified as Christian. By 2009, that number had fallen to between 75 and 78 percent, and most of those who identified differently either did not identify with any religion or declined to answer the question. The decline in Christianity came at a time of growth for evangelical Protestantism. One in three Americans polled by Trinity College's American Religious Identification Survey identified as born-again in 2009, and a growing number of Americans belonged to one of more than thirteen hundred megachurches scattered across the country. Groups like Concerned Women for America and ADF had made religious liberty arguments for decades, arguing that secularism was displacing school prayer, undercutting parents' rights, and forcing children to learn about birth control, homosexuality, and abortion at school. But concern about the marginalization of Christians had new resonance in the late 2000s after conservative Protestants gained more influence in the GOP coalition. The rhetoric of conscience seemed tailor-made for the political moment in which the declaration appeared: it reflected both Christian conservatives' fear of marginalization and the power they had to transform the status quo.[78]

The rhetoric of conscience was also calculated to appeal to conservative Black and Latino Christians, whom the antiabortion movement was working more heavily to recruit. Lila Rose, a college student at UCLA, took inspiration from Mark Crutcher, who in 1991 hired an actor to call abortion clinics posing as a minor victim impregnated by an older man. Crutcher's organization, Life Dynamics, argued that most abortion clinics were willing to "cover up statutory rape" and offer the actor an abortion without notifying her parents. Rose and her friend James O'Keefe looked for a new way to expose what Rose called this "corruption and bloodshed" at Planned Parenthood. In 2006, she began to release a series of edited videos; in one, O'Keefe posed as a racist donor to the organization. The videos energized Crutcher, who released the documentary film *Maafa 21* that year. In it, Crutcher argued that Planned Parenthood had come into being when eugenicists needed a "frontman" for their racist agenda—and that even in the present day, Planned Parenthood deliberately targeted communities of color by locating abortion clinics nearby. These arguments oversimplified or ignored a complex historical record, and did not sway many Black Americans, who were becoming more supportive of legal abortion. Nevertheless, *Maafa 21* inspired a series of billboards and a website, TooManyAborted.com, that stressed the supposed connection between abortion and racism.[79]

It was the backlash against Barack Obama's proposed Affordable Care Act that ultimately had a greater effect on the abortion struggle. Obama had made health-care reform a signature issue in his campaign, and with Democrats in control of both houses of Congress after 2008, passage of the law seemed realistic. The Tea Party, a movement that got its start opposing Obama's law, took its name from an offhand comment made by a business news anchor calling for a "Chicago tea party" to protest Obama's mortgage relief plan. The first Tea Party rallies were small, but Fox News, the cable news broadcaster, made them into a major story. Large crowds of protestors gathered on Tax Day 2009, sporting colonial-era costumes and tea bags hung from their hats. Soon, experienced Beltway political operatives took up the Tea Party's battle cry against Washington insiders.[80]

The Tea Party benefited from a broad distrust of the government. George W. Bush had launched a war in Iraq in March 2003, and as the conflict raged on, Americans increasingly opposed it. President Bush had begun withdrawing troops in 2008, but public approval had already tanked, with more than half of Americans convinced in 2010 that the war had been a bad decision.[81]

A financial crisis that began in the fall of 2008 deepened already strong anti-government sentiment. Its causes remain contested, but its effects were undeniable. Low interest rates and lax regulation had led to a spike in risky mortgages for borrowers with less-than-ideal credit. Investment banks bundled these mortgages and sold them. But the housing market peaked in 2006, and then rising interest rates and a lack of homebuyers produced a crisis. Coming on top of a bloody, foolish, and seemingly endless war, the resulting recession had a devastating effect on voters' faith in the federal government. In February 2002, 81 percent of those asked by Gallup said they trusted the government "a fair amount" or a "great deal." By September 2010, only 57 percent of respondents felt that way.[82]

Not all fetal-personhood proponents identified with the Tea Party. For starters, many Tea Party politicians said little about abortion. And Tea Partiers' embrace of small government did not resonate with all abortion foes, who urged the government to do *more* to regulate abortion. Other activists, many of them Catholic, hoped the government would expand social safety for the poor too. In either case, the Tea Party's anti-government message dominated the 2010 elections, in which Republicans picked up sixty-three seats in the House and six in the Senate. The party's results in state legislative races were even more stunning: Democrats had majorities in fifty-two of eighty-eight legislative chambers before 2010, but afterward, Republicans controlled fifty-three and Democrats thirty-five.[83]

The Tea Party's success came at a high point for corporate rights. Bopp had represented Citizens United, a group headed by David Bossie, a former congressional investigator who was forced to resign after he was discovered doctoring tapes in an effort to incriminate Hillary Clinton. Bossie used Citizens United to continue his crusade against the Clintons, and during the 2008 presidential campaign he planned to air *Hillary*, a movie-length negative advertisement against the then Democratic frontrunner. Bossie knew that federal campaign-finance law did not allow him to broadcast the film close to the election, but he planned to do it anyway so that he could challenge the constitutionality of the federal Bipartisan Campaign Reform Act. Bopp, who worked with Bossie on the case until another attorney took over oral argument in the Supreme Court, did not focus on the personhood of corporations in challenging the electioneering provision. Instead, he portrayed corporations as collectives of rights-holding individuals—stand-ins for the rights of biological persons. As he told the lawyers gathered to discuss strategy in the case, he preferred not to highlight corporate personhood but the "importance of private associations to our democracy." At the same time, Bopp argued that corporations, too, were victims of discrimination, silenced by a government that permitted speech by large media conglomerates and its own bureaucrats. Far from juxtaposing the power of corporations and the powerlessness of the unborn, Bopp had come to view both as victims.[84]

In January 2010, when the Supreme Court handed down its 5-4 decision in *Citizens United*, Justice Anthony Kennedy's majority opinion said almost nothing about corporate personhood either. Framing a corporation as "an association that has taken on the corporate form," the Court treated the electioneering provision as a ban on corporate speech and struck it down.[85]

Citizens United immediately became deeply unpopular—and, ironically, a symbol of corporate personhood. President Obama mocked the decision by insisting that only human beings were people. Occupy Wall Street, an anarchist movement against economic inequality launched in New York in 2011, demanded a constitutional amendment to undo corporate personhood. Some Catholic antiabortion activists were ambivalent about *Citizens United* too. Stephen Kent, a Catholic columnist, called for a constitutional amendment to undo both *Roe* and *Citizens United* and establish that "corporations are not people, fetuses are people." The Franciscan Action Network, a group of Franciscan nuns, friars, and other allies, lobbied for new regulations on campaign spending. "You can't worship both God and money," the group's executive director, Patrick Carolan, explained. The idea of corporate rights was unpopular at a time when recovery from the recession was uneven, with wealthier Americans and some large corporations recuperating more of what was lost than did others. But whether or not the public hated *Citizens United*, larger antiabortion groups increasingly embraced corporate rights. They hoped to make it easier for their own organizations to influence elections. And if a court *did* recognize corporate personhood, abortion opponents hoped that fetal personhood would be next.[86]

Conscience for Corporations

The backlash to *Citizens United* aside, Personhood USA leaders felt bullish about their ability to persuade voters to adopt a state amendment. It was true that every single such proposal on the ballot in 2010 had failed, but some wondered if the movement had simply started in the wrong state. Keith Mason and his colleagues liked their odds in Mississippi, a deeply conservative state with a large evangelical Protestant community.[87]

Personhood USA was a nightmare for leading antiabortion groups. The justices on the Court in 2010 seemed unlikely to reverse *Roe*. A decision striking down a state amendment seemed inevitable; it was possible that the Court would even strengthen abortion rights. Worse, the campaign for personhood amendments had vastly complicated the messaging of leading antiabortion groups. With the rise of Personhood USA, reporters described the fight for personhood amendments as a "new tack" in the abortion wars. Strictly speaking, this was true: until after 2008, antiabortion groups had not often pursued *state* constitutional personhood amendments. But the press began describing the proponents of state amendments as the "personhood movement" and contrasting them with more established groups that sponsored incremental restrictions. This framing undermined the already flagging support for established groups among some younger activists, who saw incrementalism as immoral and counterproductive.[88]

In 2011, antiabortion absolutists suffered a major setback. Together with local activists, Planned Parenthood and the American College of Obstetricians and Gynecologists convinced Mississippians that a personhood amendment would ban IUDs, emergency contraception, in vitro fertilization, and the birth control pill. Nearly 60 percent of Mississippians rejected the amendment.[89]

Establishment antiabortion groups soon turned back to what they saw as a more promising way to bolster support for fetal personhood, one that linked fetal rights to religious liberty. In August 2011, the Obama administration mandated that all FDA-approved contraceptives must be covered by the Affordable Care Act without co-pay. The mandate covered emergency contraceptives too, including Ella, a medication approved in 2010 that seemed more effective than similar drugs for patients with high body weights. The administration included an exemption for certain religious employers, but many conservatives and Catholic leaders felt that the carve-out was far too narrow. The United States Conference of Catholic Bishops, created in 2001 by the merger of the National Conference of Catholic Bishops and the U.S. Catholic Conference, announced a Fortnight for Freedom, denouncing threats to religious liberty, including the contraceptive mandate and other policies, such as limits imposed on Catholic charities that refused to place children for adoption with same-sex or unmarried opposite-sex couples. In 2013, the administration changed the rule to require insurers, rather than employers, to cover contraceptives, but this did nothing to mollify opponents. A group of religious employers had already filed suit, arguing that the mandate violated the federal Religious Freedom Restoration Act.[90]

Steve Aden was at the forefront of these efforts. Aden attended high school on Kwajalein Atoll, a tiny loop of coral reef that the U.S. military used for missile testing. From there, he went to law school at Georgetown and began practicing law in Honolulu. Before long, Aden's résumé listed most major organizations in the conservative Christian legal movement. He worked for the Rutherford Institute, then represented chapters of the Christian Legal Society seeking exemptions from university nondiscrimination policies. Aden joined ADF in 2008 and soon began litigating conscience cases: representing nurses who objected to assisting in emergency abortions and businesses that refused to comply with the contraceptive mandate.[91]

When a challenge to the contraceptive mandate arrived at the Supreme Court, Aden and ADF represented one of the petitioners, Conestoga Wood Specialties Corporation, and the Becket Fund, which specialized in religious liberty litigation, argued the case for Hobby Lobby. The case was particularly momentous for ADF, which had renamed itself the Alliance Defending Freedom in 2012. The new name reflected a fresh mission: rather than financing and coordinating Christian attorneys, ADF would do its own litigating and court funding from major conservative donors. In a set of joint talking points, ADF and Becket stressed the importance of conscience. "In a free and diverse society, we respect the freedom to live out our convictions," the talking points explained. "That means not being forced to participate in distributing potentially life-terminating drugs and devices." At the same time, antiabortion lawyers blurred the line between fact and belief, not least when it came to fetal personhood. "The employers sincerely believe that life begins at conception," argued Monaghan's Thomas More Law Center. An amicus brief submitted by a group of Catholic theologians also painted fetal rights as both a foundational religious belief and a basic scientific truth. "From the first moment of his existence," the brief explained, "a human being must be recognized as having the rights of a person."[92]

But the case focused on corporate, not fetal, personhood. Aden and ADF argued that corporations like Hobby Lobby could challenge the contraceptive mandate because they counted as "persons" under the Religious Freedom Restoration Act. The statute, they asserted, was intended to have a broad and remedial effect, and there was no evidence that Congress intended to exclude corporations from its protections.[93]

The Supreme Court agreed that corporations could be persons for the purposes of the Religious Freedom Restoration Act. In his majority opinion, Justice Alito looked to the federal Dictionary Act, which gave default definitions for any term not otherwise defined in federal statute. That the plaintiffs were for-profit businesses, he wrote, did not change the Court's analysis, since Congress historically had used explicit language to exclude corporations when lawmakers intended to do so.[94]

Alito argued that if a corporation was a person under the act, what mattered was that its owners held sincere religious beliefs. The rest of the case struck the Court as straightforward: companies that did not comply with the mandate had to pay a $2,000 penalty per employee per day. That certainly qualified as a substantial burden, and the majority believed the government could have pursued its interest in ensuring contraceptive coverage in less onerous ways (for example, by paying for the coverage itself).[95]

The *Hobby Lobby* decision vindicated those who wished to weave ideas about fetal personhood into conscience claims. The decision came as an early triumph for a movement in the midst of a transformation, one increasingly led by conservative Christian legal organizations like ADF—and one pushed to the right by a new generation of activists expecting more sweeping social change. Antiabortion leaders like James Bopp and Steve Aden insisted on protection for the deeply held beliefs of corporations and their owners when it came to protecting fetal life. And in the aftermath of the *Hobby Lobby* decision, it was easier for both men to imagine that the same justices might eventually recognize fetal personhood too.

6

The End of *Roe*

In 2015, a year after the *Hobby Lobby* decision, the Supreme Court recognized same-sex couples' right to marry. The decision, *Obergefell v. Hodges*, was not only a major victory for the LGBTQ movement but also a significant expansion of substantive due process, the body of law to which *Roe* belonged. Kristan Hawkins had not been focused on *Obergefell.* She wanted to advance the fight for fetal personhood by targeting Planned Parenthood. By 2015, Planned Parenthood had become a financial giant, with $1.3 billion in revenue that year alone, including $500 million in federal funding. "One of the strategies the pro-life movement has been using is to decrease the supply of abortion," Hawkins explained in a 2015 memo. And the best way to do that was "by taking on the nation's largest abortion provider, Planned Parenthood."[1]

Whatever the movement's focus, it was hard for personhood proponents to see *Obergefell* as a good sign. Anthony Kennedy, the author of the opinion, had also helped to write *Planned Parenthood v. Casey*, which had preserved what the Court called the essential holding of *Roe*. So long as he controlled the balance of power on the Court, there seemed to be no future for fetal rights. And yet within a decade after the *Obergefell* decision, the Court would overturn *Roe v. Wade* and cast doubt on the constitutional future of same-sex marriage. Abortion opponents, who had denounced *Roe* as the work of an anti-democratic judiciary, would rely more than ever on the federal courts in inching toward a national ban.[2]

But the more the fight for personhood moved into the open, the more difficult questions abortion opponents like Kristan Hawkins had to answer about what it would mean for everything from IVF to contraception. The antiabortion movement remained divided about what personhood required. But with new groups ascendant, many of them tied to the conservative Christian legal movement, different equality claims had become more visible. Rather than simply comparing racism to abortion, leading advocates like Hawkins argued instead that abortion heavily contributed to other forms of discrimination. Dehumanizing unborn children because of race, sex, or disability, they argued, laid the foundation for bias later in life. At the same time, groups like Students for Life stressed that fetuses faced the most insidious form of injustice because the unborn were unable to defend themselves.[3]

As Hawkins and her colleagues developed these arguments, debates about racial violence and sexual harassment led a growing group of Americans to conclude that discrimination was systemic—not only the result of intentional acts but the byproduct of past practices and current laws, customs, and institutional arrangements. Some antiabortion activists participated in other movements denouncing systemic racism or sexism. Many leading antiabortion groups instead offered their own structural explanations, suggesting that abortion often resulted from coercion from parents, partners, friends, or employers. More than anything, leading antiabortion groups often argued that one of the best ways to address many forms of inequality in America, including racial bias, was to ban abortion.[4]

The Most Pro-Life President in History

In February 2016, nine months before the next presidential election, Antonin Scalia was on a privately funded trip, his third in a few weeks. He had recently traveled to Singapore and Hong Kong, but this one took him to a West Texas ranch to hunt big game.[5]

Even if his habit of accepting free vacations had not raised a red flag with most ethics' experts, some in the public were unsure what to make of photos of the justice on one lavish all-expenses-paid vacation after another. Of course, the public might not have learned of these gifts had Scalia not passed away during that February trip. At the time, any question about ethics on the Supreme Court, or even the appearance of impropriety, gave way to grief over his death and questions about who would replace him.[6]

At the time of Scalia's death, the movement to protect legal abortion was changing. Younger activists helped to mainstream claims about reproductive justice. On social media and in online publications, these activists popularized the abortion story, revealing deeply personal details of their own experiences. In September 2015, the day after the House passed a bill defunding Planned Parenthood, the hashtag #ShoutYourAbortion took off on social media in a campaign organized by Seattle-area feminists Lindy West and Amelia Bonow. Mainstream antiabortion groups justified their opposition to punishing women by insisting that the women involved did not understand their choices. Those telling their stories as part of #ShoutYourAbortion shattered these assumptions.[7]

In 2015, Erika Bachiochi, a young attorney and former pro-choice feminist, popularized arguments that denying legal protection for the unborn would *undermine* equality for women. Through her mother's three divorces, Bachiochi had experienced a tumultuous childhood and struggled with addiction before entering college at Middlebury. It was there that she rediscovered Catholicism, opened her mind to conservative policy solutions, and became fascinated by political philosophy. In 2011, she had written a law review article, "Embodied Equality," arguing that by opposing legal protection for the unborn, feminist backers of legal abortion fueled male sexual irresponsibility, devalued pregnancy and caretaking, and thus facilitated sex discrimination. By 2015, she was balancing scholarly work with raising six children (her seventh child would be born later). That year, Bachiochi popularized her idea of embodied equality in a piece for *CNN*. She argued that genuine feminism would reckon with the fact that women and men were intractably and biologically different. "We can pretend sex differences do not exist," she wrote, "but it is women who bear the burden when we do." Legal abortion, she argued, harmed women. "When we belittle the developing child in the womb," Bachiochi wrote, "we belittle and distort that child's mother." She called for legal and policy changes, such as better protections against pregnancy discrimination, that would honor "the beautiful, wondrous truth" about sexual difference.[8]

Like Bachiochi, Hawkins argued that mainstream feminism wrongly treated sexual differences—and the capacity to procreate—as a problem. "Fertility," explained 2015 Students for Life talking points criticizing the contraceptive mandate, "isn't a disease that should be part of 'preventative medicine.'" But while Bachiochi championed more government support for pregnancy and caretaking, Hawkins suggested that women needed nothing more than the support of their families, churches, and communities. Her own experiences informed her ideas. By 2015, she was the mother of four young children, two of whom had cystic fibrosis, a condition that increased the risk of life-threatening lung and digestive issues. The diagnoses helped to inspire her conversion to Catholicism, which, she explained, helped her to accept that "suffering wasn't for nothing." While Hawkins pursued the best care for her children, her star was rising. She began to present herself as an example of what women could achieve when balancing work and motherhood: a pro-life woman "willing to take on the feminists who reduce [women] to nothing but their ability to procreate and apparently how harmful it is." Bachiochi suggested that banning abortion itself *qualified* as a structural change supporting sex equality: when *Roe* was gone, men could not use the availability of abortion rights as an excuse for their own bad behavior. But she also called for financial assistance and workplace accommodations for caretakers and new policies to encourage paternal responsibility. As Hawkins framed it, by contrast, women primarily required information and support that the pro-life movement was already ready to supply.[9]

Democrats still thought that they had the better arguments about sex equality. But if his supporters had hoped that Obama would put another woman on the Court, they were soon disappointed. He selected Merrick Garland of the DC Circuit Court of Appeals to replace Scalia—a compromise gesture, given that Garland was older and more moderate than many of the likely alternatives. But Garland was no Antonin Scalia, and Senate Majority Leader Mitch McConnell, who had no intention of bringing the nomination up for a vote in the Senate, claimed to follow a long-standing tradition of not confirming new justices in an election year.[10]

On the GOP side, an unlikely contender was topping early primaries: the real estate mogul Donald Trump. Abortion opponents had plenty of reasons to be dismayed by Trump's rise, not least his embrace of abortion rights not many years before. When he tried to reassure antiabortion voters that he understood the importance of fetal rights, he botched the job, suggesting that women should face "some punishment" for abortion—a stance leading antiabortion groups had publicly rejected for years.[11]

But by the summer of 2016, leading groups had warmed up to Trump, especially following the Supreme Court's decision that June in *Whole Woman's Health v. Hellerstedt*. The case involved a Texas law that required physicians to have admitting privileges at a nearby hospital and mandated that clinics comply with the regulations governing ambulatory surgical centers. The antiabortion movement had high hopes for *Whole Woman's Health* because Anthony Kennedy, the swing justice, had voted to uphold the federal Partial-Birth Abortion Ban Act in the Court's last abortion case, *Gonzales v. Carhart*. Woman-protective arguments had already fueled the campaign for right-to-know laws that repackaged claims about fetal personhood. Statutes like the Texas regulations had a different aim: it was often impossible or prohibitively expensive for clinics to follow them.[12]

But in *Whole Woman's Health*, Justice Kennedy voted with his more liberal colleagues to strike down both provisions of the disputed Texas law. The decision was a major loss for antiabortion groups. Under *Casey*, the Court asked whether abortion regulations were unduly burdensome. Antiabortion groups like AUL had responded with regulations that they claimed were *beneficial* for women—by guaranteeing them better continuity of care, for example. In *Whole Woman's Health*, the Court required actual proof that woman-protective laws had health benefits. As important, the Court reasoned that poor *conditions* of access or quality of care counted as burdens under *Casey* even if states did not ban access altogether. The decision dramatically raised the stakes of the 2016 election. Hillary Clinton, the Democratic nominee, had been an outspoken champion of abortion rights since the 1990s—and her candidacy unfolded at a time when Mitch McConnell was stonewalling efforts to replace Antonin Scalia on the Court.[13]

For most pollsters and pundits, a Trump presidency remained unthinkable until the day he took office. It is more than a little ironic that someone who seemed to have no understanding of fetal personhood would come to be viewed by many in the antiabortion movement as the most pro-life president in history. Donald Trump may not have cared about the issue, but thanks to him, the fight for fetal personhood moved back into the open, and for the first time in years, antiabortion groups believed they could eventually win it.

Systemic Discrimination

In January 2017, Donald Trump's press secretary, Sean Spicer, boasted that the crowd attending his boss's inauguration ceremony had been the largest in U.S. history. That photographic evidence clearly disproved this claim seemed not to be a problem. Kellyanne Conway, a counselor to the president, helpfully explained that the administration was relying on "alternative facts."[14]

The truth was that the Women's March on Washington, a major feminist protest against Trump held on January 21, 2017, drew a much larger crowd. During the campaign, the *Washington Post* had released a video of Trump talking with Billy Bush, the host of *Access Hollywood*, before a taping of the show in 2005. On the video, Trump bragged that "when you're a star, you can do anything," including grabbing women by the genitals against their will. Many women (as well as men) denounced this as harassment and assault. Several anti-abortion groups were originally listed as official partners of the march, but their inclusion sparked an outcry from marchers who insisted that women's rights were synonymous with abortion rights.[15]

Criticizing the exclusion of antiabortion groups from the march, Erika Bachiochi reiterated that legal abortion undercut equality for women. By 2017, she was a visiting fellow at the Ethics and Public Policy Center, a think tank founded in 1976 to apply Judeo-Christian moral teachings to questions of law and policy. Bachiochi made no secret of her distaste for Trump, for whom she had not voted, but she argued that "the constitutional right to abortion has only made men like Trump worse." And women's biology gave them the wondrous ability to create life, Bachiochi explained—and as such, made them uniquely able to appreciate fetal rights. "Why would any feminist," she wrote, "think it is a moral advance for women to imitate male abandonment of the vulnerable through abortion?"[16]

Hawkins also responded to the Women's March. At the time, she had moved with her family to Minneapolis to be closer to the treatment team managing her children's cystic fibrosis. She often discussed how she had felt pressured to end her own pregnancies after hearing that diagnosis. These experiences convinced her that legal abortion did more than dehumanize rights-holding persons in the womb. The idea of a right to abortion also hurt people with disabilities, who "because of their genetic code," were told that "their lives have less value." Because of legal abortion, she argued, women like her were also stereotyped as incapable of taking on the challenge of motherhood, especially when a child had special needs. She was planning what Students for Life called the "Lies Feminists Tell" speaking tour to debunk what Hawkins thought were the foundational falsehoods of mainstream feminism: "the lie that most women support abortion, that women need free contraception to succeed, that women need abortion to achieve their career goals, and that abortion is harmless and without consequences."[17]

But while Bachiochi suggested that the government needed to do more to encourage paternal responsibility and support pregnancy and caretaking, Hawkins reasoned that women primarily needed the government to get out of the way. "Telling women that they need abortion to succeed in life is the opposite of empowerment," Hawkins explained. "It's insulting, demeaning, and deceptive."[18]

For the most part, however, arguments about fetal personhood were still not center stage in national politics. Little changed when Trump nominated Neil Gorsuch, a judge from the Tenth Circuit Court of Appeals, to fill Antonin Scalia's by then long-vacant Supreme Court seat. Abortion opponents had little doubt about who Gorsuch was. He had been a prolific conservative rabble-rouser at Columbia as an undergraduate in the 1980s; as an adult, he had been a star in the Federalist Society. Leonard Leo, who served on the board of directors for Students for Life, had played a prominent role in Gorsuch's selection. In April 2017, the Senate voted 54-45 to confirm him.[19]

Within the antiabortion movement, claims about fetal personhood became entangled with shifting debates about race. In 2017, Trump issued what many would call the Muslim ban, an executive order prohibiting entrants from six Muslim-majority countries from coming into the country for 90 days, indefinitely suspending the entry of Syrian refugees, and barring any other refugees' entry for 120 days. The ban reflected the demands of key figures in the administration, including Stephen Miller, a senior advisor to the president, and Steve Bannon, the White House chief strategist, who argued that too much racial diversity was dangerous because it undermined what Bannon called "a nation with a culture and a reason for being." When the courts put a hold on the first Muslim ban, Trump issued a second. (The Supreme Court would uphold a third version in 2018.)[20]

Then in August 2017, in Charlottesville, the home of the University of Virginia, a group of white supremacists marched to protest the planned removal of a statue of Confederate general Robert E. Lee. Carrying tiki torches and Nazi banners, the protestors provoked violent confrontations with those who opposed them. More than thirty people were injured, and one, Heather Heyer, was murdered. The Unite the Right rally—and Donald Trump's response that there were "very fine people on both sides"—brought home to many that the United States was not, as liberal commentators once claimed following Obama's election, a post-racial society.[21]

The #MeToo movement, which went viral a few months later, popularized a different understanding of discrimination. Tarana Burke, who had worked on issues of racial justice, coined the term *Me Too* in 2006 to encourage survivors of sexual assault and abuse to share their stories. In October 2017, using the hashtag #MeToo, the actress Alyssa Milano urged victims to share their stories on Twitter. Millions answered the call, and at least two hundred prominent men who were accused of wrongdoing lost their jobs. Soon, #MeToo gave rise to Time's Up, a star-powered organization founded by Hollywood celebrities and talent agents, that published an open letter declaring that it was "systemic gender inequality and imbalance of power" that facilitated "abuse and harassment."[22]

Few expected the #MeToo movement to take center stage again in June 2018, when Anthony Kennedy abruptly announced his retirement from the Court. Brett Kavanaugh, a judge with an Ivy League pedigree, deep ties to the Federalist Society, and a twelve-year record on the bench, emerged as the favorite of Leonard Leo, who took leave from the Federalist Society to advise Trump on the selection.[23]

Roughly ten days before Trump named Kavanaugh as his selection, Christine Blasey Ford, a biostatistician and research psychologist, contacted the *Washington Post* and her congresswoman, Anna Eshoo, to say that Kavanaugh had sexually assaulted her when the two were high school students in Bethesda, Maryland. Some abortion opponents, like Steve Aden, took a measured approach to Ford's accusations. Aden had left ADF in 2017 to become the general counsel of Americans United for Life.[24]

Aden joined AUL at the same time as Catherine Glenn Foster, his former ADF colleague, who became the group's president and CEO. Foster had been a nineteen-year-old student at Berry College, a conservative Christian school in the foothills of the Appalachian Mountains, when she learned she was pregnant. She had an abortion, a traumatizing experience that shaped the rest of her career. After getting a master's in French in Florida, Foster moved to the nation's capital, went to law school, and got a job at ADF, where she specialized in abortion cases. Foster and Aden showed that ADF's avowedly conservative Christian perspective was spreading—and changing the dominant movement understanding of personhood.[25]

If Ford became a symbol of the #MeToo movement, Kavanaugh became a hero to conservatives who saw #MeToo as vigilante justice run amok. The hashtag #BeersforBrett trended on Twitter, with some suggesting that Kavanaugh was being attacked for typical, not especially blameworthy male behavior. Following a perfunctory FBI investigation, the Republican-controlled Senate put him on the Court by a vote of 50-48.[26]

Heartbeats and Lawsuits

Even with Kavanaugh confirmed as a justice, some movement leaders thought it was too soon to push to have *Roe* immediately overruled, much less to campaign openly for fetal personhood. James Bopp preferred to build support for personhood more gradually, through passing bans on dilation and evacuation, the most common procedure after the first trimester of pregnancy, which the organization called "dismemberment abortion laws," or statutes banning abortion at twenty weeks based on claims of fetal pain. Such laws, Bopp promised, would convince more Americans that a fetus was a rights-holding person because they would "expose the vile and gruesome aspects of abortion practice."[27]

Students for Life, which launched a 501(c)(4) organization—a nonprofit that could endorse candidates and lobby—in 2018, offered a different vision of how to inch toward personhood: to focus more on efforts to "restrict and abolish abortion state by state." A sweeping ban in Congress seemed unlikely, whatever happened to *Roe*. More important, by 2018, a single party controlled both legislative chambers in all but one state. The sources of state legislative polarization were complex, attributed to a mix of income inequality, the decline of local news outlets, the nationalization of local elections, and gerrymandering. Regardless of how single-party state governance had become so common, Kristan Hawkins saw unprecedented opportunity in the South and Midwest, where a state law on personhood might finally be possible.[28]

It did not take long for state lawmakers and voters to start meeting Hawkins's expectations. Abortion restrictions, many of them drafted by Americans United for Life or the National Right to Life Committee, had already made the procedure inaccessible across large swaths of the country. With Kavanaugh on the Court, states became bolder, sometimes looking to different groups, even local ones, for guidance. In November 2018, for example, 59 percent of Alabama voters chose to amend the state's constitution "to recognize and support the sanctity of unborn life and the rights of unborn children, including the right to life."[29]

Janet Folger Porter saw what she called a heartbeat ban as the logical next step in the fight for fetal personhood. Porter started her career as a darling of the antiabortion establishment, raised on religious crusades and dinner table debates in the Cleveland suburbs. In the late 1980s, she came up with her own strategy: a law criminalizing abortion after six weeks of pregnancy, when regular pulsation of fetal cardiac cells could be detected. At the time, lawmakers dismissed her idea as unrealistic, and Porter went back to helping make Ohio the first state to pass a ban on partial-birth abortion. But she did not like being told what to do, so it was not hard for D. James Kennedy, an ADF co-founder, to persuade her to take over his Center for Reclaiming America, which encouraged conservative Protestants to get politically active. Even in her new post, however, Porter preferred to be the star of her own story. She had already written several best-selling books on being single for conservative evangelical women before she finally met "the one," a Christian accountant who swept her off her feet and brought her back to Ohio, where she revived the idea of a heartbeat ban.[30]

Porter strongly believed that the Fourteenth Amendment "recognizes and protects unborn life at its earliest stages," but she thought a heartbeat ban could be the perfect incremental step. Lawyers at Jay Sekulow's American Center for Law and Justice helped draft the fetal heartbeat bill and defend it against critics. But there was no shortage of skeptics. Believing that a challenge to the law would go against abortion foes in the Supreme Court, the United States Conference of Catholic Bishops opposed the bill. James Bopp testified against it for the same reason in 2011.[31]

With Kavanaugh on the court, however, the game had changed. Six states passed heartbeat laws in the first half of 2019. Mark Lee Dickson and Jonathan Mitchell proposed a strategy to ensure such laws could be enforced even before *Roe* was overturned. Raised in a family that prized academic achievement, Mitchell went from law school at the University of Chicago to a clerkship with Justice Antonin Scalia, a tenure-track job at George Mason, and a prominent position in Texas state government. He had a rare technical brilliance that allowed him to see law like a video game, which he was very good at playing. If Mitchell was comfortable in Ivy League classrooms and white-shoe law firms, Dickson, who almost always sported a baseball cap worn backwards, was at ease in small-town steakhouses and civic centers. The grandson of an icon in the Texas antiabortion movement, he had a humble upbringing, raised by a father battling a serious injury sustained on the job and a mother who first worked at his school's cafeteria and then at a dollar store.[32]

The two men crossed paths when the Supreme Court agreed to hear *June Medical Services v. Russo*, a challenge to a Louisiana law that required physicians at abortion clinics to have admitting privileges at a nearby hospital. The Court had struck down an identical Texas law just a few years before, and the justices' willingness to take up the same is-sue seemed to signal a dramatic move. If the Court were to allow Loui-siana to strictly regulate abortion, Dickson thought, clinics might move over the state border into nearby Waskom, Texas, a town of fewer than two thousand people. In helping local officials draft an ordinance to prohibit abortion in the town, Dickson, like city officials, worried that a constitutional challenge might put Waskom on the hook for hundreds of thousands of dollars in attorney's fees. He contacted his state senator, Bryan Hughes, who put him in touch with Mitchell.[33]

Mitchell thought he had a fix. He had helped to write a state law, known as the Save Chick-fil-A Bill, that prohibited the government from taking any "adverse action" based on an individual's religious affiliation. But the law assigned enforcement not to the government but to those whose rights were allegedly violated by allowing them to sue for damages. Mitchell thought the Waskom ordinance could be designed the same way: enforceable only by private citizens. This plan might deny abortion clinics standing to challenge the ordinance's constitutionality. So began Dickson's fight to create what he called sanctuary cities for the unborn. Small towns across the state of Texas could keep abortion clinics out, but that was just the start. Sanctuary cities for the unborn could acknowledge the personhood of the un-born child, Dickson thought, and create a model for guaranteeing that person equal treatment.[34]

The Rise of the Abolitionists

Within the antiabortion movement, support for fetal personhood had not wavered following Kavanaugh's nomination; if anything, it had become more public, but some self-proclaimed antiabortion abo-litionists, many of them steeped in ultra-conservative evangelical Protestantism, promoted a more punitive vision of what it required.

In 2011, T. Russell Hunter, a former history graduate student, founded Abolish Human Abortion with Toby Harmon, a graduate of Jerry Falwell's Liberty University who had done prison time for dealing drugs. By 2016, an Oklahoma state lawmaker affiliated with the group, Dan Fisher, introduced a bill recognizing fetal rights and mandating the punishment of women who had abortions. In 2019, Hunter and his colleagues began an additional group, Free the States, to carry on the campaign for bills punishing abortion seekers. (Free the States would close shop, with Hunter starting a new group, Abolitionists Rising, in 2023 to continue his work.)[35]

In 2017, the Arizona pastor Jeff Durbin began promoting abolitionist ideas about personhood more broadly through his organization, End Abortion Now, and his radio program and YouTube channel. Durbin, a former martial arts expert, had had a successful career as a Hollywood stuntman and actor, but not long after getting married, his life began falling apart. Following a battle with drug addiction and a financial crisis, Durbin found religion and then launched his own church in Tempe, Arizona, in 2010. Durbin promoted the message that "from the beginning, God has intended men to lead in the home and in the church." His media platform brought abolitionist arguments to a larger audience.[36]

If Durbin and Harmon came to antiabortion abolitionism at dark moments, Bradley Pierce, the most prominent abolitionist lawyer, had always been a success. He became the student vice president at Baylor, got a law degree, and established a practice defending Christian homeschooling parents. In 2017, Pierce and other conservative Christians in central Texas founded Abolish Abortion Texas, a loosely organized group that sent protestors to the state capitol to attack abortion restrictions for not going far enough.[37]

The most powerful groups in the movement rejected the abolitionist call to punish women for abortion. Many pro-life activists offered their own explanations for why women chose abortion—not systemic racism or sexism but, as Sharon Serratore of Feminists for Life wrote in 2018, pressure from "husbands, unmarried partners, and parents" as well as "peers, school authorities, and employers." Some connected the idea of coerced abortion to endemic domestic violence against pregnant women. In 2019, Americans United for Life sponsored laws making it a crime to coerce another person into abortion.[38]

For some antiabortion groups, however, the question of punishing women was more complicated. If fetuses were independent rights-holding persons, then why were women who chose abortion not responsible for harming them? Hawkins coached recruits to stress that in a post-*Roe* world, states would move toward recognizing the personhood of the unborn by enforcing tough criminal laws on abortion, but women would not be punished, and few women would die if abortion were outlawed. But if some *did* die, that would not change the organization's position. "Should we decriminalize crimes that have a high death rate, like bank robbery, just because the robber could die?" Students for Life asked in a strategy memo. "The bottom line here is that what's wrong is wrong."[39]

Other leading antiabortion groups embraced fetal personhood while dodging the questions posed by abolitionists, arguing that legal abortion itself was the primary expression of racism, sexism, and ableism in modern America. Since the 1980s, some states had passed bans on abortion for the purpose of sex selection, arguing that "any law that denies a mother's right to abortion, even for the most frivolous reasons, points out the personhood of the unborn child." By the 2010s, a new wave of statutes also prohibited procedures in cases of disability or "race selection." In 2019, in the case of *Box v. Planned Parenthood of Indiana and Kentucky*, the Supreme Court heard a challenge to an Indiana law regulating the disposal of fetal remains and barring abortion for reasons of fetal race, sex, or disability. ADF lawyers presented the case as an opportunity for the Court to move toward the recognition that fetuses, like other Americans, were persons: "victims of discrimination . . . worthy of protection."[40]

The Supreme Court upheld the fetal-remains provision but declined to reach a conclusion on the trait-selection regulation, leaving the lower courts more time to consider the matter. Clarence Thomas, in a concurring opinion, suggested that banning trait-selection abortions surely must be constitutional. He emphasized what he called "abortion's eugenic possibilities," seemingly accusing the abortion-rights movement—and individual women of color—of deep, intentional discrimination. "Abortion," he wrote, "has proved to be a disturbingly effective tool for implementing the discriminatory preferences that undergird eugenics."[41]

Antiabortion groups had made arguments linking abortion and eugenics before *Box*—including in briefs cited in Justice Thomas's concurrence. But after the decision, it seemed that abortion-is-eugenics arguments might allow antiabortion groups to make progress in the Supreme Court—and to address difficult questions about equality by pointing the finger at the abortion-rights movement. Groups like ADF insisted that racial discrimination began in the womb—and that racism against the unborn was especially insidious. At the same time, these arguments suggested that attacking racism required not so much uprooting the kind of systemic bias spotlighted by the MeToo movement but banning abortion.[42]

Preborn Lives Matter

In January 2020, the United States recorded its first case of the novel coronavirus COVID-19. By the end of May, one hundred thousand Americans had died of the disease. From the start, the pandemic exposed severe race-related health disparities: for much of the year, the age-adjusted COVID death rate was at least twice as high for Black, Latinx, and Indigenous Americans as for white Americans.[43]

The pandemic hit George Floyd hard. A forty-six-year-old Black man, he had been working as a nightclub security guard and delivery driver in Minneapolis when the pandemic began but lost the delivery job after a minor accident. In March, the nightclub closed due to pandemic rules. Then, in May, an employee at Cup Foods, a grocery store, suspected Floyd of passing a fraudulent $20 bill and called the police.[44]

Derek Chauvin, a white police officer who once worked security with Floyd, murdered him by kneeling on his neck for more than nine minutes. A video of the murder quickly went viral, and within days, protests had erupted in cities across the country. Protestors recalled the deaths of other unarmed Black Americans: Breonna Taylor, a twenty-six-year-old first responder killed by Louisville police the previous March while she was lying in bed, or Ahmaud Arbery, a twenty-five-year-old working in his father's business, shot to death in February by two white men while he was out jogging.[45]

Black Lives Matter, the organization associated with the protests, was founded in 2013 to protest the acquittal of George Zimmerman in the killing of Trayvon Martin, a seventeen-year-old Black teenager. Floyd's death briefly made Black Lives Matter the largest movement in U.S. history. Like #MeToo, Black Lives Matter condemned what it called systemic bias: the idea that racism was not simply a matter of individual malice but a property of institutions, laws, and social practices. Similar ideas spread online, in politics, and in corporate boardrooms. More than two-thirds of Americans in a 2020 Pew Forum poll supported the movement.[46]

Some opposed to abortion drew on the language of systemic racism in condemning Floyd's murder. The United States Conference of Catholic Bishops, which had issued educational materials on structural racism in 2019, taught that "continuing inequalities in education, housing, employment, wealth, and representation in leadership positions are rooted in our country's shameful history of slavery and systemic racism."[47]

Many antiabortion groups, however, sought to redefine the protests by identifying abortion as the most dangerous form of racial discrimination. Some explicitly rejected the idea of systemic racism. Kay James, a prominent Black Republican who had long worked for the National Right to Life Committee, had become the president of the Heritage Foundation in 2018. In the wake of Floyd's killing, she stressed that there was no need for systemic change or even new laws to address racism. "What we're left with are not systemic problems," she explained in June 2020. "We're left with people who still harbor ill will." Ryan Bomberger, a Black pro-life activist who led his own organization, the Radiance Foundation, argued that the antiabortion movement already addressed systemic problems like racism and poverty every day at crisis pregnancy centers. Rejecting Black Lives Matter as "radically pro-abortion," Bomberger insisted that abortion itself was the ultimate issue of inequality in America, especially for people of color. "A dead child doesn't need an education," he explained in 2020. "A dead child doesn't need a safe environment. . . . Without life, nothing else matters."[48]

In September 2020, Students for Life held a rally to proclaim that "Black Preborn Lives Matter." Kristan Hawkins pointed out that abortion rates were higher in communities of color: evidence, she argued, that Black Americans began to be devalued and targeted while they were in the womb. Skeptics of abortion-is-eugenics arguments stressed that many women of color wanted access to abortion, and that disproportionately high abortion rates in Black communities reflected a variety of structural factors, including a lack of access to contraception or health care, or the effects of racism and poverty. But antiabortion groups like Students for Life foregrounded claims that Planned Parenthood was racist, drawing on movement narratives about the organization's founder, Margaret Sanger. As a 2020 report to its board of directors put it, Students for Life sought to draw a "connection between Margaret Sanger's eugenics roots and the current racist practices of Planned Parenthood."⁴⁹

A month after Floyd's murder, abortion was back in the news. The Supreme Court announced its decision in *June Medical*, addressing the Louisiana law requiring abortion clinics to have admitting privileges at a nearby hospital. Less than five years earlier, the Court had struck down an identical Texas provision in *Whole Woman's Health*, but with a newly minted conservative majority on the Court, antiabortion lawyers expected a different outcome. Chief Justice Roberts dashed those hopes, joining his more liberal colleagues to rule Louisiana's law unconstitutional.⁵⁰

Social conservatives publicly excoriated the conservative legal movement to which Roberts belonged, especially when, that same June, the Court ruled in *Bostock v. Clayton County* that sex discrimination under Title VII included discrimination on the basis of sexual orientation or gender identity. This time, the author of the opinion was not Roberts, who had disappointed conservatives before. Instead, it was Neil Gorsuch, one of Donald Trump's nominees.⁵¹

Together, *Bostock* and *June Medical* exposed divisions between the conservative legal movement and many champions of fetal personhood. In March, before the release of the decisions, Harvard law professor Adrian Vermeule had written in the *Atlantic* magazine that originalism had outlived its usefulness. He proposed an alternative, common-good constitutionalism, that required judges to use reason to discern what would serve the public good—a process that involved what Vermeule called "a candid willingness to 'legislate morality.'"

Many believed that common-good constitutionalism could lead to the recognition of fetal personhood. Even the possibility of a loss in *Bostock* convinced Josh Hammer, a conservative *Newsweek* columnist and online provocateur, that Vermeule was on to something. He proposed a fusion of Vermeule's idea and originalism that he called "common good originalism": "a substantively conservative" approach to originalism. Hammer, too, stressed that his approach could lead to the recognition of fetal rights.[52]

Advocates like Hammer gave conventional conservative originalism a second chance in the fall of 2020 when Justice Ruth Bader Ginsburg, the Supreme Court's most eloquent defender of abortion rights, died of cancer. Trump selected Amy Coney Barrett, a recent appellate court nominee, to take her place. The appointment of Barrett, who had deep ties to the Alliance Defending Freedom and once belonged to an Indiana antiabortion group, caused great excitement among abortion foes. Because she was raising seven children, two of them adopted and one with Down syndrome, Barrett embodied Students for Life's claim that "a new generation of women . . . do not believe that there is a Civil War in their lives between Career and Family." But Barrett's importance to abortion opponents was more practical than symbolic. She was an insurance policy: if John Roberts would not vote to reverse *Roe*, Barrett probably would.[53]

Having pledged never to confirm a Supreme Court nominee in an election year, Mitch McConnell, the Republican majority leader, promptly made a new promise: to push through Donald Trump's nominees as quickly as possible. Republicans confirmed Barrett, 52-48, six weeks after the death of Justice Ginsburg and less than a month before the election.[54]

The antiabortion movement had high hopes for whatever remained of Donald Trump's time in office when it came to fetal personhood. In November 2020, Americans United for Life, long the symbol of movement pragmatism, issued what it called the Lincoln Proposal, which argued that the president could "faithfully execute the guarantees of the Fourteenth Amendment" by issuing an executive order "recognizing preborn persons as constitutional persons entitled to the fundamental rights of due process and equal protection under the laws." In earlier years, the antiabortion movement had prioritized a constitutional fetal-personhood amendment and set out to win over voters to support it. Some, like the antiabortion attorney Harold Cassidy, had later worked to secure recognition of fetal rights in the courts. The authors of the Lincoln Proposal explored ways that the executive branch could enforce fetal rights. Catherine Glenn Foster, the group's leader, teamed up with Chad Pecknold, a theology professor, to write the proposal. Its third author, Josh Craddock, had grown up praying outside of abortion clinics, and by the time he got to high school, he had serious doubts about the incremental strategy pursued by larger antiabortion organizations.[55]

Craddock and his family had gathered signatures for Colorado's 2008 personhood amendment, and as a student at The King's College, a now-defunct Christian school in New York, he wrote his senior thesis on the claim that as a matter of original public meaning, the word *person* in the Fourteenth Amendment applied to the unborn child. After college, he went to work for Personhood USA, coordinating its activities with VIFAC, a Mexican network of crisis pregnancy centers. He soon became the Personhood USA's vice president, a strategy leader on a tiny staff of six, and then left for Harvard Law School. In 2017, while still a student, he published a version of his senior thesis, "Protecting Prenatal Persons," that proved to be highly influential in the antiabortion movement. After graduating that year, Craddock did not become a professional activist, instead working for law firms in Washington, DC, and Colorado. But he became a sought-after speaker on how to better advocate for fetal personhood.[56]

Craddock's idea of an originalist case for personhood was not new. The antiabortion legal scholar Joseph P. Witherspoon had made a related claim before *Roe v. Wade* was decided, and others had done so in the years since. For the most part, however, personhood proponents had not consistently embraced originalism or stressed claims that the framers of the Fourteenth Amendment understood it to ban abortion. Craddock picked an opportune time to yoke personhood to originalism. Abortion foes were now better integrated into the broader conservative legal movement, and the Supreme Court was embracing originalist ideas. Donald Trump was in the White House and depended more than many of his predecessors on support from conservative Christian voters.[57]

The Lincoln Proposal outlined a number of concrete steps that Trump could take toward the recognition of fetal personhood: the Department of Justice could investigate state and local laws that deprived "preborn persons of due process of law or the equal protection of the laws." The Department of Health and Human Services could condition access to federal health-care dollars on states' willingness to defund providers who offered abortions. The Food and Drug Administration could suspend its approval of mifepristone; and the Department of Education could withhold federal funds from any school that advocated for or provided abortion services.[58]

Craddock and his colleagues did not ultimately have the opportunity to sell Donald Trump on the Lincoln Proposal. The result of the 2020 election was hardly extraordinary: Joe Biden received 306 Electoral College votes and slightly more than 51 percent of the popular vote. The vote was close, as it often is, but clear enough. The aftermath, however, was anything but routine. Trump refused to concede. His attorneys contested the result in several key states, and Trump and his aides pressured state election officials in Georgia to "find" more votes to ensure his victory. In seven states, Trump's team found officials willing to cast fraudulent Electoral College votes in the hope that Vice President Mike Pence would keep Trump in office. On the day the election certification was scheduled to take place, Trump called his supporters to Washington, DC, to "stop the steal."[59]

The images from that day—rioters carrying zip ties to bind politicians, the gallows waiting for Mike Pence—suggest that something in the United States had fundamentally changed. But with Trump at least temporarily in the rearview mirror, personhood proponents were ready to move on. The movement seemed to have found a more reliable savior in the new conservative majority on the Supreme Court.

The Enforcement of Personhood

Texas lawmakers had been reluctant to follow other conservative states in passing a heartbeat ban, especially after losing the *Whole Woman's Health* case in 2016 and having to pay more than $2 million in attorneys' fees. Bryan Hughes and Jonathan Mitchell persuaded the legislature that the ordinances Mark Dickson promoted in small towns could serve as a model for the whole state and drafted a bill, SB8, that prohibited abortion six weeks after a patient's last menstrual period. But rather than authorizing the state to enforce the laws itself, SB8 permitted only private citizens—indeed, *any* private citizen, regardless of whether they had any connection to a case—to sue abortion providers or anyone aiding them for at least $10,000. By assigning enforcement to private citizens, Texas could invoke a doctrine called state sovereign immunity, which established that states could not generally be sued in state or federal court without their consent. An exception created by a 1908 decision, *Ex parte Young*, applied when state officials enforced unconstitutional laws. In such cases, plaintiffs could seek an injunction in federal court to stop further violations. But if *no* government official enforced the law, that might make a federal court challenge impossible. That strategy, Mitchell promised, would allow the state to shut down abortion while insulating its law from constitutional challenge. Soon after, in May 2021, Texas passed SB8.[60]

In December 2021, the Court gave the abortion provider challenging SB8 in *Whole Woman's Health v. Jackson* a pyrrhic victory. In his majority opinion for the Court, Justice Gorsuch concluded that language in SB8 implied that the state health department could still enforce the law. Jonathan Mitchell's argument hinged on the government's inability to enforce the law. But if some health officials *could* enforce the law, then maybe some narrow version of the suit could survive. If Whole Woman's Health could still sue in federal court, it might be possible to raise an effective challenge to the constitutionality of SB8.[61]

In practice, however, the majority opinion in *Whole Woman's Health v. Jackson* read like a roadmap for lawmakers who wanted to create a more airtight version of SB8. And if the Court was suggesting that abortion providers could sue certain state officials, that opening vanished quickly: in less than a year, the Texas Supreme Court held that the statute did not allow state officials to enforce the law after all.[62]

It was not all good news for the antiabortion movement. Since the FDA approved mifepristone in 2000, the drug had been subject to serious restrictions—and more so, after the introduction of a Risk Evaluation and Mitigation Strategy (REMS) in 2011. The FDA created the REMS program for drugs with serious potential side effects to make sure that their benefits outweighed their dangers. Mifepristone, which had a very low reported complication rate, did not fit the classic profile of a REMS drug, but the FDA gave it that classification anyway. In 2016, regulators modified some of the restrictions, and then in early 2021, the FDA made mifepristone available via telehealth for the remainder of the COVID-19 pandemic. The pandemic itself accelerated a shift toward telehealth in health care more broadly.[63]

Telehealth abortions proceeded quite differently from the clinic procedures that had been the norm for decades. Physicians screened patients online and often sent them mifepristone and misoprostol in the mail. With drugs like mifepristone widely available, the antiabortion movement had to confront a harsh new reality. Once *Roe* was gone, passing an abortion ban or even a personhood law might be relatively easy. Enforcing one could be another thing entirely.[64]

Conversations about mifepristone took place against the backdrop of a sharp decrease in support for Black Lives Matter, from 67 percent in June 2020 to 55 percent—and only 17 percent of Republicans—by September 2021, according to Pew Forum. (This decline would continue, with only 51 percent of those surveyed in 2023 supporting Black Lives Matter.) One cause was a conservative outcry against critical race theory (CRT) that would shape leading abortion opponents' arguments about fetal personhood. The term *CRT*, most often applied to academic scholarship from the 1990s, gained a second life after conservative activist Chris Rufo wrote a piece on a leaked antiracism training for certain Seattle city employees. The spread of ideas arguing that racism was "a matter of structured disadvantages," Rufo argued, was merely an excuse for "race essentialism." Rufo's ideas became a staple of Trump's press conferences, and states began drafting bills, often with Rufo's assistance, banning the discussion of CRT in schools.[65]

Arguments about systemic racism had been increasingly visible since George Floyd's murder, and these now became the target of the anti-CRT campaign. Critics began claiming that lessons about systemic racism were themselves racist because they blamed white Americans for wrongs they had nothing to do with. Florida governor Ron DeSantis argued that CRT—and arguments about systemic racism in particular—were "basically teaching kids to hate our country and to hate each other."[66]

Some in the pro-life movement discussed the connection between poverty, racism, sexism, and abortion. In a 2021 book, for example, Erika Bachiochi argued for an "embodied equality" (the title of her earlier law review article) that would require better workplace accommodations, paid family leave, and child tax credits. The United States Conference of Catholic Bishops also at times linked the fight against abortion to battling poverty, racism, and sexism. Invoking Pope Francis's 2020 encyclical, *Fratelli Tutti*, Archbishop Paul Coakley of Oklahoma City, the chairman of the United States Conference of Catholic Bishops' Committee on Justice and Development, explained in 2021 that the pope decried "the reality that women are not yet recognized as having the same dignity as men, that racism shamefully continues, and that those who are poor, disabled, unborn, or elderly are often considered dispensable." But even those who sympathized with Bachiochi generally saw criminal bans protecting the unborn as an indispensable step toward equality under the law.[67]

But exactly who should be punished under these criminal laws remained unsettled. Leading antiabortion groups opposed punishing women for abortion. The United States Conference of Catholic Bishops had staked out a similar position, pointing to a 1995 encyclical, *Evangelium Vitae*, in which Pope John Paul II described abortion as "an unspeakable crime," but promised women that they could seek forgiveness from their aborted children. *Evangelium Vitae* also blamed many abortions on pressure from partners, friends, family and "the spread of an attitude of sexual permissiveness and a lack of esteem for motherhood." In the early 2020s, Pope Francis made this perspective on mercy for women who chose abortion even more visible.[68]

In ultraconservative evangelical circles, by contrast, abolitionist ideas were gaining support. At its June 2021 annual convention, the

Southern Baptist Convention passed a resolution declaring that "the murder of preborn children" was "a crime against humanity that must be punished equally under the law." Because it did not call directly for the punishment of women, this resolution did not go far enough for antiabortion abolitionists. Still, the 2021 convention showed that support was growing, in the denomination and the antiabortion movement as a whole, for the idea that recognizing fetal personhood meant punishing abortion seekers.[69]

Internally, Students for Life circulated talking points stressing that mainstream groups endorsed fetal personhood but opposed the punishment of women, for both practical and principled reasons. "It would be mixed messaging," Students for Life explained, "to say that we care about you when you are pregnant but want to put you in jail." But the more plausible the push for fetal personhood became, the harder it was for groups to explain how, if a fetal person was truly identical to any other, abortion seekers should be exempt from punishment.[70]

Another divide emerged surrounding IVF, at a time, according to a 2023 Pew Forum study, when more than 40 percent of Americans had pursued infertility treatment themselves or knew someone who had. Nevertheless, Students for Life issued talking points criticizing IVF for "creating Disposable People." The talking points did not spell out how IVF should be regulated but made clear that the organization considered the status quo untenable because a fetus or embryo was a person. "Since we know that life begins at conception," the talking points explained, "setting up a business and taking actions that deliberately kill preborn humans is a violation of that truth."[71]

Students for Life also suggested that some drugs and devices commonly viewed as contraceptives were abortifacients, designed not to prevent fertilization but to end a pregnancy. If protecting unborn persons required punishment for those who would take their lives,

Students for Life argued, the law should do more to limit access to drugs often thought of as contraceptives, such as the morning-after pill, IUDs, and the birth control pill. "Some drugs and devices that end preborn life," it explained, "are mislabeled as contraception."[72]

Dobbs

Meanwhile, another case, *Dobbs v. Jackson Women's Health Organization*, was proceeding through the federal courts. *Dobbs* began in 2018, at a time when abortion opponents were experimenting with a variety of fetal-pain laws. Such laws could bolster support for personhood by emphasizing a critical way in which the fetus was argued to resemble any other individual: the experience of pain. Most research concluded that fetal pain was not possible until at least the twenty-fourth week of pregnancy, but ADF drafted its own model fetal-pain law, the Gestational Age Act, to apply at fifteen weeks. After Mississippi passed such a law in 2018, both the district court and the Fifth Circuit Court of Appeals struck it down under *Roe*. That was no surprise. Mississippi's law, like others, was designed to test how far a reconfigured Court would go toward destroying the right to choose abortion. The Supreme Court's very decision to take the case was seen as the foreshock of some massive tectonic event. Then, in May 2022, *Politico* magazine announced that it had obtained a leaked copy of the full majority opinion. In it, the Court overturned *Roe v. Wade*.[73]

When the Court released its final 5-4 decision at the end of June, it was virtually identical to the version circulated in May (Chief Justice John Roberts also concluded that Mississippi's law was constitutional but did not vote to reverse the 1973 decision, portraying that move as unnecessary). The author of the majority, Justice Alito, began by declaring that the Court honored unenumerated rights under the Fourteenth Amendment only if they were deeply rooted in the nation's history and tradition. That notion itself was controversial—in cases like *Obergefell*, the Court had presented history as only one of the relevant constitutional considerations. Alito, however, suggested that only an approach rooted in history and tradition could constrain the Court—and that under such an approach, *Roe* was egregiously wrong.[74]

When describing the nation's past, the Court relied on the accounts of scholars like Joseph Dellapenna, the expert on water law who had attended AUL's Reversing *Roe* conference in 1984 and whose writing on the subject, which broke from the scholarly consensus, argued that abortion had always been viewed as immoral, if not criminal, throughout pregnancy. Far from showing any recognition of a right to abortion, Alito wrote, the nation's history bore witness to "an unbroken tradition of prohibiting abortion on pain of criminal punishment." The majority also shot down the claim that a right to abortion naturally followed from decisions honoring other privacy rights, such as contraception or the right to marry. Abortion was different: it "destroys . . . what the law at issue in this case regards as the life of an 'unborn human being.'"[75]

In Alito's view, deference to precedent was not enough to save *Roe*. He described the reasoning in both the *Roe* and *Casey* decisions as exceedingly weak: on par with the racist, discredited *Plessy v. Ferguson*, which had upheld laws segregating Americans by race. In response to the objection that many Americans relied on the legality of abortion in organizing their reproductive lives, Alito explained that there was no principled way for the Court to measure whether anyone had relied on legal abortion. The voters in each state could settle the matter for themselves once an abortion right was gone. "Women," Alito wrote tartly, "are not without electoral or political power."[76]

The Court seemed divided on how far the decision would reach. Kavanaugh echoed Alito's claims that *Dobbs* would not change the

Court's jurisprudence on same-sex marriage or contraception, even if neither of those rights seemed, on the Court's account, deeply rooted in the nation's history and tradition. The dissenting justices were not buying it. Clarence Thomas wrote a separate concurring opinion calling for the Court to overrule many of its decisions involving unenumerated rights, including those on birth control and same-sex marriage. Remarkably, however, no opinion explicitly mentioned fetal personhood.[77]

Kavanaugh's comment that the Constitution was "neutral" on abortion suggested that for him, the door was closed to fetal personhood, at least for the moment. Yet personhood proponents could still find hopeful signs. The Court had echoed the antiabortion movement's language in places, and it had argued that a right to abortion differed from other liberties because abortion was the taking of a human life. The version of history the majority adopted—in which Americans had always opposed or criminalized abortion—bore a striking resemblance to the account offered by personhood advocates. While the Court seemed unlikely to recognize fetal personhood in the short term, personhood proponents reading the *Dobbs* decision felt they had plenty to work with.[78]

Personhood After *Dobbs*

Dobbs was instantly unpopular. Americans, a majority of whom had supported *Roe* in years of polls, were unsurprisingly angry that the Court had overturned it. Many scholars exposed what they saw as glaring historical flaws in Justice Alito's opinion. In the decision's aftermath, a little over a dozen bans went into effect automatically after *Roe* was overturned, mostly in the South and Midwest. Abortion was then newly criminalized in states like North Carolina, Nebraska, West Virginia, and Florida. Many of the new bans were initially tied up in court as judges sorted through various challenges, but those that were in effect seemed to make an immediate difference. Travel to and the mailing of pills from jurisdictions where abortion was legal ensured that bans did not have their desired effect. Research by the Society of Family Planning and the Guttmacher Institute established that nationwide, the number of abortions *increased* in the first years after *Dobbs.* But the bans also had profound and perhaps unintended consequences later in pregnancy: patients with life-threatening pregnancy complications found themselves turned away by physicians fearful of violating state bans.[79]

Antiabortion leaders generally agreed that the movement needed a new "north star," as a major group of movement leaders would later write—a rallying cry to replace demands for the overruling of *Roe.* Naturally, most in the movement turned to the fight for fetal personhood—a struggle on which most in the movement had never given up. Most movement leaders, including Kristan Hawkins, argued that the Constitution *already* recognized the fetus as a rights-holding person and urged the Supreme Court to declare that to be true. By contrast, Clarke Forsythe, who had done more than anyone to advance fetal-homicide laws, argued that the Supreme Court would not realistically embrace personhood without "irrefutable" evidence of fetal personhood. No such proof existed, Forsythe wrote, and "in *Dobbs*, constitutional personhood had reached a dead end." He and others like him preferred that the movement continue fighting for a constitutional personhood amendment. Erika Bachiochi supported "constitutional protection of unborn children as equal 'persons' under the law" but worried that in adopting the language of personhood, her allies now sometimes wrongly painted the fetus and mother as autonomous when in truth, "unborn children are, like the rest of us, dependent and needy persons." Recognizing this, she reasoned, made clear that women needed not punishment but "society's utmost assistance."[80]

In either case, most in the movement saw an open fight for fetal rights as the movement's next chapter: a battle to guarantee "the end of abortion through ensuring the equal protection of the laws." What did most leading groups mean by equality? The "New North Star Letter" identified several ways that the law would recognize personhood: the appointment of guardians ad litem to provide "legal representation and due process," "prenatal child support laws" that would force "men [to] take responsibility for the children they father," and prenatal tax deductions. The plan further proposed undoing policies that treated embryos created through IVF as property.[81]

Most simply, the "New North Star Letter" insisted that recognizing personhood would require criminalizing abortion and other conduct related to pregnancy. The letter further called for the vigorous enforcement of fetal homicide, chemical and child endangerment laws, and wrongful death statutes. Criminalization, the letter's authors maintained, was needed to ensure that "preborn babies and their families can obtain justice against the criminals who harm them." The letter closed with a reference to the Civil War. Just as it had been intolerable for the nation to be "half slave and half free," as Abraham Lincoln famously put it, nothing less than the national recognition of personhood—and the banning of abortion "throughout our land"—would be "acceptable."[82]

Members of the antiabortion movement disagreed about what to prioritize while laying the groundwork for fetal personhood. Activists aligned with the United States Conference of Catholic Bishops fought for the passage of the Pregnant Workers Fairness Act, a federal law that required employers to accommodate pregnant workers. A Better Balance, a group founded in 2005 to advocate for laws facilitating a healthy work-life balance, had led the fight for the bill since 2012. Other activists argued that the government should respond to *Dobbs* by expanding the nation's social safety net. In 2023, Catherine Glenn Foster, Kristen Day, the executive director of Democrats for Life, and

Americans United for Life created a plan to "make birth free" by exempting co-pays and deductibles in certain insurance plans, reforming Medicare and Medicaid, and creating a monthly stipend for the first two years of a child's life. In many cases, however, antiabortion groups and Republican politicians assigned the job of helping pregnant Americans to private religious charities, crisis pregnancy centers, and maternity homes—in 2023, for example, twelve states passed bills providing $250 million in funding or tax credits for crisis pregnancy centers.[83]

A growing group of abolitionists focused on establishing that the recognition of fetal personhood would require the punishment of women. The groups that had grown out of the clinic-blockade movement led this charge. Following the passage of the FACE Act in 1994, blockaders had veered from crisis to crisis. First came the 2009 murder of George Tiller, the Nebraska doctor whom blockaders had often targeted. The same year, Troy Newman, the head of Operation Rescue West, got into trouble with the Internal Revenue Service, which stripped the group of tax-exempt status. Newman then launched a new group he called "Operation Rescue," which triggered a lawsuit from Randall Terry, who believed that Newman had violated his trademark.[84]

Abolitionism gave the blockade movement a new lease on life. Jason Storms, a construction company owner who had often protested outside a Milwaukee Planned Parenthood with his wife and ten children, played a central role in this shift. After taking the helm in 2022, Storms reinvented Operation Save America, the successor of Operation Rescue, as a champion of abolitionist bills and a defender of what Storms thought of as biblical manhood. The group began hosting a Manhood Restored Bootcamp in Indiana, where men were schooled in hand-to-hand combat, shooting, and ending abortion. "Abortion will end in America," explained Operation Save America's Facebook page, "when Men learn to be Men again."[85]

Operation Save America lobbied for bills drawn up by Bradley Pierce, the Texas abolitionist lawyer who had founded the Foundation to Abolish Abortion in 2019, that recognized the personhood of the fetus and called for the punishment of women. In early 2022, Louisiana became the first state that pushed such a bill out of committee (following an outcry from larger antiabortion groups, the bill failed to become law). But abolitionism certainly had a broader platform. Working closely with Jeff Durbin and Jason Storms, Pierce stressed that if the fetus was a person, the Constitution required the punishment of women. "I hold the supposedly extreme position," Pierce quipped, "that murdering anyone should be illegal for everyone."[86]

Other short-term solutions gained the attention of antiabortion activists and donors. James Bopp and the National Right to Life Committee promoted an "abortion trafficking law" that would criminalize "recruiting, harboring, or transporting" a pregnant minor out of the state to have an abortion without parental consent. The law applied even if a minor traveled to a state where abortion was legal. Idaho passed such a law in April 2023; others began considering similar bills in early 2024. In several Texas counties and cities, Mark Lee Dickson and Jonathan Mitchell lobbied for ordinances that allowed SB8-style suits against anyone who helped transport someone seeking an abortion within county or city limits, even if their destination was a state where abortion was legal. Dickson, a minister, had made the ordinances his full-time job, spending weeks on the road in hotels strategizing about how to win over holdouts on city councils. Dickson had personhood in mind. Even if abortion seekers were voluntarily traveling, he insisted, unborn children were being transported against their will.[87]

Other antiabortion groups focused on limiting access to abortion pills. The Alliance Defending Freedom filed a lawsuit on behalf of a group of antiabortion physicians, *Alliance for Hippocratic Medicine v. Food and Drug Administration.* The suit argued that the FDA had never had the authority to approve mifepristone under relevant laws and regulations because pregnancy was not a disease, and because medical abortion was less safe than surgical abortion. ADF's suit also echoed an idea developed by Jonathan Mitchell about a nineteenth-century obscenity law, the Comstock Act. The FDA, ADF argued, lacked the authority to allow telehealth abortion (a decision made permanent in 2023) because the Comstock Act prohibited mailing or receiving any abortion-related information, drugs, or devices. Mitchell and Dickson stressed that every abortion in the United States, including surgical procedures, required an item sent in the mail. For that reason, they contended that the Comstock Act was a de facto prohibition on all abortions.[88]

Their plan ignored the statute's historical context and presented an ambiguous text as clear and straightforward. Their strategy also hinged on the political resurrection of Donald Trump. In the winter of 2024, Trump faced a total of ninety-one felony charges, related to everything from hoarding classified documents to interfering with the 2020 election. But these charges only seemed to have strengthened his hold on the party, with Republicans viewing Trump as the victim of a deeply biased system. Mitchell and Dickson hoped that if Trump won a second presidential term, his Department of Justice would seek to enforce the Comstock Act as an abortion ban across the United States. Other antiabortion groups picked up on this strategy. The Heritage Foundation organized more than one hundred conservative groups, known as Project 2025, to write a transition plan for Republican presidential candidates that made the Comstock law the centerpiece of a new abortion policy.[89]

Kristan Hawkins felt optimistic about the Comstock Act too. By 2023, she had moved her family into an RV that followed her as she worked to abolish abortion across the United States. She knew that Donald Trump had a good shot at another four years in the White

House. With the right people in the Department of Justice, she explained, the federal government would be willing to enforce Comstock and "uphold the rule of law." But for Hawkins, as for most in the movement, strategies built around the Comstock Act were at most a stopgap. On the first anniversary of *Dobbs*, she joined a rally that included almost every major antiabortion group. Those present celebrated *Dobbs* and demanded that the Supreme Court recognize fetal personhood under the Fourteenth Amendment. "The very idea of a human being who is relegated to the status of a non-person is a moral atrocity," the leaders of key groups from Americans United for Life to Students for Life wrote in July 2023. The time had come "to secure equal protection for the child in the womb."[90]

Decades ago, skeptics had argued that a judicial decision recognizing personhood under the Fourteenth Amendment would not do much. That amendment applied only to state actors, and most abortions took place in private clinics. But Josh Craddock and Robert George did not see the state action requirement as a problem. If states enforced homicide laws against those who killed other persons but not those who killed fetuses through abortion, the two argued, that would be an action by the state. Did that mean that the Constitution *required* the state to punish women seeking abortions? Since 2016, George had maintained there were sound reasons for not punishing abortion seekers. Women who had abortions did so without understanding "the truth about abortion and unborn children," he argued, and it made sense to show mercy to women in "difficult and sometimes . . . desperate circumstances." Besides, as a practical matter, George wrote at the time with his co-author, Ramesh Ponnuru, prosecutors would want to cut a deal with patients to more effectively prosecute their doctors.[91]

Craddock argued that homicide law permissibly treated some killings, such as the murder of a police officer, as worse than others.

That might make it acceptable to impose lighter penalties on those who chose abortion than on other homicide offenders. Even if states exempted *all* abortion seekers, Craddock believed, it might be constitutional as long as the laws did not reflect discrimination against the unborn person, and as long as the state had a sufficient reason to exempt women from punishment.[92]

In the wake of *Dobbs*, antiabortion lawyers proposed an incremental approach to promoting fetal personhood. When possible, signers of the "New North Star Letter" championed state measures treating fetuses as "legal and constitutional persons entitled to . . . equal protection." When such laws remained politically out of reach, the movement could promote laws recognizing a fetus as a person for more limited purposes, such as "prenatal child support laws" or "fetal-homicide, wrongful-death, and child-endangerment laws." For the most part, though, antiabortion groups preferred to be in federal court. The Supreme Court had a conservative supermajority, and Donald Trump had shaped the lower courts. Federal judges had lifetime appointments and would be insulated from the political backlash that might follow unpopular decisions.[93]

In ADF's challenge to mifepristone access, Matthew Kacsmaryk, a district judge with long-standing ties to the antiabortion movement, not only called for mifepristone to be removed from the market but also favorably cited a fetal-personhood brief co-authored by Robert George. The Fifth Circuit Court of Appeals issued a somewhat narrower ruling, reasoning that the plaintiffs had waited too long to challenge the FDA's initial decision on mifepristone but that the FDA's 2016 and 2021 decisions to loosen restrictions on the drug were arbitrary and capricious. In the spring of 2024, the Supreme Court agreed to hear the government's appeal.[94]

Abortion-rights supporters began experimenting with strategies to expand abortion access or reverse *Dobbs*. Some looked to state constitutions, arguing that bans were impermissibly vague or violated state guarantees involving privacy, equality, or the right to life. The Center for Reproductive Rights, a leading reproductive-rights litigator, also represented clients with wanted pregnancies whose health and future fertility were threatened by continuing a pregnancy. Their stories only reinforced public opposition to *Dobbs*.[95]

Those opposed to *Dobbs* also had major success at the ballot box. Every state to consider a ballot initiative in 2022 favored abortion rights, including conservative states like Kentucky and Kansas and swing states like Michigan. The trend continued in 2023, when Ohio, a state where Republicans controlled every branch of government, embraced a ballot initiative creating a state right to reproductive freedom. Abortion-rights supporters pushed for ballot initiatives in 2024 in states from Florida and Arizona to North Dakota and Missouri.[96]

Abortion opponents were more optimistic about the race for the White House. For much of the summer of 2024, Donald Trump seemed unstoppable. He enjoyed a steady lead in the polls over the incumbent, Joe Biden. While Trump faced criminal charges stemming from the effort to overturn the 2020 election, his attorneys argued that presidents had sweeping immunity from prosecution for actions taken while in office. In June 2024, in a 6-3 ruling, the Supreme Court agreed that Trump had "at least presumptive immunity from prosecution for all his official actions." Precisely what counted as an "official action" was unclear, but almost any interaction within the executive branch—such as Trump's efforts to press Pence not to certify the election—could plausibly qualify under the Court's definition. The decision in *Trump v. United States*—and the return of action to the lower courts—ensured that the election interference trial would not take place until after the 2024 election, and that if Trump prevailed, he could attempt to pardon himself or select an attorney general who would dismiss the charges. Then in July, Trump survived an assassination attempt, convincing some supporters that God had special plans for the former president. Trump was so confident about his chances that he selected J. D. Vance, an untested ultraconservative senator from Ohio, as his running mate. Vance, who had close ties to the authors of Project 2025, had called on the Justice Department to enforce the Comstock Act as an abortion ban and expressed sympathy for federal limits on abortion-related travel.[97]

Even after Biden dropped out and the Democratic Party rallied around the presidential candidacy of Kamala Harris, the vice president, many abortion opponents believed that Trump would win and advance their personhood agenda. The polls remained tight, and even while Trump tried at times to distance himself from the antiabortion movement, his position was ambiguous enough for many abortion foes to make big plans for a second Trump term. While no longer mentioning a fetal-personhood amendment, for example, the GOP platform nodded to the idea that the Fourteenth Amendment *already* recognized fetal personhood. Ed Martin, the head of the Phyllis Schlafly Eagles and prominent member of the platform committee, stressed that the platform spelled out that as far as the fetus was concerned, "there was protection under the Constitution." Kristan Hawkins certainly understood the platform that way. She praised the GOP for recognizing that "the Fourteenth Amendment 'guarantees' legal protection for the preborn."[98]

Perhaps the most promising path for fetal personhood ran through state and federal courts. In February 2024, the Alabama Supreme Court decided a case involving three couples who had pursued IVF at a clinic in the city of Mobile. A patient from a hospital connected to the fertility clinic had entered a storage facility and accidentally destroyed several embryos. The couples sued for wrongful death, and the state supreme court held that the state wrongful-death law applied "to all children, born and unborn, without limitation." "Even before birth," wrote Chief Justice Tom Parker in a concurring opinion, "all human beings bear the image of God, and their lives cannot be destroyed without effacing his glory." Most clinics in the state paused IVF services because of the fear of legal liability. Realizing that the ruling was deeply unpopular, Republican lawmakers in Alabama pushed through a bill creating civil and criminal immunity for IVF providers and administrators (but not challenging the state court's conclusion that embryos were persons). Two of the families who brought the original IVF lawsuit soon went back to court, arguing that the IVF shield law violated the state constitution's protections for the "rights of unborn children."[99]

Members of the antiabortion movement saw an opening to push restrictions or even prohibitions of IVF. Hawkins and Students for Life put out talking points stating that the "IVF industry is poorly regulated and too rarely monitored"—and that it was time to rethink the practice of "creating disposable children." Americans United for Life described the ruling as "a step in the right direction toward ensuring that all preborn children are equally protected under the law." Recognizing fetal personhood, argued Steve Aden, meant understanding that "our nation's children should not be stored in liquid nitrogen for undetermined amounts of time." The fight to restrict or even ban IVF quickly gained the support of the Southern Baptist Convention, which passed a resolution in 2024 arguing that IVF violated the rights of embryonic persons and calling on the government to "restrain actions inconsistent with the dignity and value of every human being, which necessarily includes frozen embryonic human beings."[100]

Questions related to personhood even made their way to the U.S. Supreme Court. ADF's challenge to the FDA approval of mifepristone failed when the Supreme Court unanimously held that the challengers in the case, the Alliance for Hippocratic Medicine, did not have standing to sue. The Court also punted in a second case about emergency access to abortion. The Biden administration had argued that the federal Emergency Medical Treatment and Labor Act (EM-TALA), a statute passed in 1986 to stop hospitals from turning away uninsured emergency patients, required abortion access for patients facing critical risks to life or health. The Biden administration took Idaho to court, contending that EMTALA preempted the state's ban, and won an injunction blocking its enforcement. Idaho then asked the Supreme Court to intervene early in the case. After initially agreeing to do so, the justices later had second thoughts and dismissed Idaho's petition as improvidently granted in *Moyle v. United States.* Three of the justices, Samuel Alito, Neil Gorsuch, and Clarence Thomas, dissented, complaining that the statute's references to the "unborn child" meant that EMTALA could not be read to require emergency access to abortion, even for pregnant patients at risk of dying or losing an organ. The framers of EMTALA had expressed concern that hospitals were turning away laboring pregnant patients who lacked insurance, including some women whose babies were stillborn as a result of delays in care. Alito saw this history—and an apparent statutory distinction between labor and non-labor emergency conditions—as irrelevant. While Alito and his colleagues said nothing about *constitutional* fetal rights, they seemed to think that at least under EMTALA, fetuses were rights holders. The mere mention of the term "unborn child," they reasoned, indicated that Congress intended to create "express protection for the unborn child," even at the expense of the health or life of the pregnant patient.[101]

The question of what personhood meant—and how it should be enforced—continued to divide the antiabortion movement. For example, some commentators, like the pro-life *New York Times* columnist David French, criticized Alito's take on personhood in *Moyle.* Nevertheless, the groups leading the antiabortion movement itself had changed, and Christian legal groups like ADF had gained more financial pull and strategic influence than many of the single-issue groups that had once dominated the movement. With the recognition of fetal rights now a practical possibility, more activists had become willing to shoot for legal changes, like those involving IVF, beyond the abortion context.[102]

Many of those who embrace personhood have long believed that Americans disagreed with them because they misunderstood abortion. Americans *should* oppose abortion, they thought, and most would if they knew what the termination of a pregnancy—or the destruction or storage of an embryo—really involved.

But even if majority support for abortion or IVF were genuine, few members of the movement intend to change course. That is true of Kristan Hawkins. Winning, she believes, requires confidence and, at times, patience. For half a century, she and her allies have seen themselves as fighting an era-defining human rights battle. It might take another generation or more to secure judicial recognition of fetal personhood, but that does not trouble the activists who had successfully destroyed *Roe v. Wade.* They have played the long game before.[103]

Conclusion

In June 2022, when Americans awaited a decision in *Dobbs v. Jackson Women's Health Organization*, some still hoped that the justices would give *Roe* a last-minute reprieve. There was no reason to doubt the outcome, and yet it seemed unthinkable to some that the Supreme Court would do something so unpopular, and so quickly, when there was no disagreement in the lower courts to resolve. For others, it was hard to credit that with a single opinion, abortion could once again be made a crime in large swaths of the United States.

As I write this, the Court's decision is less than two years old, but its effects have already been breathtaking. For the Supreme Court, *Dobbs* undermined public faith in the institution's legitimacy and served as the precursor to a series of judicial ethics scandals and sweeping decisions on everything from guns to affirmative action and the separation of church and state. For the Republican Party, *Dobbs* has posed a deep danger, forcing the GOP to balance the demands of base voters and the need to appeal to the majority opposed to sweeping restrictions. For patients in ban states, *Dobbs* has changed the experience of pregnancy, making abortion less accessible and raising the possibility that pregnant patients with dangerous complications will be turned away unless they are close enough to death. For any American, *Dobbs* stands for the principle that constitutional rights can be wiped away. This is the story of *Dobbs* we can tell less than two years after the decision came down.

But if *Dobbs* has produced once-unthinkable shifts in American life, it is not the end of the story. Some legal scholars, political scientists, and historians have long argued that the Supreme Court was to blame for much of the polarization of the abortion issue. *Roe*, the argument went, ruled out compromises that might have cooled off the debate. This argument had a certain logic, and it especially commended itself to conservative judges and politicians, many of whom maintained that *Roe* had even politicized judicial confirmations themselves. The Court in *Dobbs* picked up on this claim too, suggesting that overturning *Roe*—and restoring abortion decision-making to voters and their elected representatives—might make the conflict less ugly.[1]

Today, the federal right to choose abortion is gone. States are free to set their own abortion policies. In some instances, voters can bypass politicians and approve ballot initiatives. And yet with *Roe* a thing of the past, the nation's abortion divide only seems deeper.

States have eschewed compromise measures and passed sweeping bans. Penalties under these laws are sometimes more severe than those in place before *Roe*. Physicians are refusing to treat patients with potentially life-threatening pregnancy complications because they worry about inadvertently violating the law. States are launching a new war about travel, with jurisdictions passing shield laws that claim to protect residents from criminal prosecution and conservative states experimenting with the idea that they can punish their own citizens for facilitating an abortion in places where the procedure is legal. Rather than allowing voters to express preferences about abortion through ballot initiatives, some Republicans are experimenting with strategies that make it harder for voters to have a say. And ironically, it is abortion opponents who spent decades railing against the anti-democratic federal courts who have invested the most in the federal judiciary, litigating about the fate of the Comstock Act, access to abortion pills, and much more.[2]

Overturning *Roe* has polarized the debate partly because most Americans deeply oppose the *Dobbs* decision. But the end of *Roe* did little to demobilize the *antiabortion* movement. Many abortion foes rallied to the fight for fetal personhood before the Supreme Court intervened and saw constitutional protection for the unborn, not the mere elimination of an abortion right, as the endpoint of their struggle.

To understand the past and future of the American war over reproduction, then, we must tell the story of the fetal-personhood movement. It may be tempting for supporters of abortion rights to see fetal personhood as nothing more than a tactic for activists whose real ambition is simply to ban abortion or control sexuality and reproduction. There is no denying that some personhood arguments emerged and changed for strategic reasons—not least in the 1960s, when what was at the time a Catholic movement looked for a way to avoid faith-based arguments and broaden its base.

But for more than half a century, the fight for fetal personhood was a singular point of agreement in a fractious movement. Personhood arguments came and went in Congress, the Supreme Court, and the front page of the nation's newspapers. But within the antiabortion movement, claims for fetal rights never went anywhere. Ideas about personhood remained a constant in the strategy sessions and private correspondence of those who define themselves as pro-life.

That personhood arguments had an emotional pull for their proponents does not mean that nothing lies below the surface of beliefs about the fetus. Nor does it mean that personhood had a stable definition. Indeed, personhood partly captivated so many conservatives because its meaning could and did change. Arguments around fetal personhood reflected other convictions about race, sex, motherhood, religion, and the possession of a soul. Within the antiabortion movement, sharp disagreements emerged about what personhood meant and how to enforce it. But we will fail to understand conflicts over reproduction in the United States if we dismiss the antiabortion movement's personhood arguments as nothing but a strategic ploy, or see personhood as nothing more than an argument for banning abortion.

Personhood today is shorthand for fetal rights, and fetal rights are synonymous with the criminalization of abortion. The history of struggles over fetal personhood suggests that there was nothing inevitable about this carceral turn. In Germany in 1993, the Federal Constitutional Court reiterated that the nation's constitution obligated the state to protect the life of the unborn. Nevertheless, the court suggested that the nation did not have to criminalize all abortions to safeguard fetal rights—and instead had to make a good-faith effort to "reconcile" women's rights to autonomy, dignity, and life with the unborn child's right to life by addressing the reasons some women ended pregnancies, such as "an unfavorable housing situation, the impossibility of looking after a child parallel to vocational training or working, economic hardship and other material reasons, and in the case of single women, fear of discrimination by the community." In 2019, the South Korean Supreme Court stopped short of recognizing a right to life but stressed the importance of the government's interest in "protecting life." Nevertheless, the court invalidated a law criminalizing abortion. Criminal abortion bans, the court reasoned, did not protect life because they had "only a limited effect on a pregnant woman's decision whether to terminate her pregnancy"—and because criminal bans awarded "absolute and unilateral superiority" to fetal life rather than also accounting for the rights of women.[3]

Within the antiabortion movement, there are and have been disagreements about what personhood means. What does personhood require when a pregnant woman faces a life-threatening emergency? How should the law honor and enforce personhood? Even today, it is possible to imagine a vision of fetal rights less focused on criminalization.

Perhaps personhood could even accommodate those who think abortion should be legal—or even a protected right. Fully sketching this vision is beyond the scope of this book. But de-emphasizing criminalization would be a good starting point. Stronger protections against domestic violence during pregnancy, better sex-discrimination laws, paid family leave policies—and more support from the government for women and children, including those whose families have few resources—might be ways to express respect for fetal life while honoring the equality, dignity, and autonomy of pregnant patients.

Fetal personhood has been a fluid concept, one that reflected and reinforced changing ideas of liberty and equality in other areas of the law. In advocating for personhood, abortion foes insisted that a fetus was a unique, separate individual and as such, had fundamental rights. In other ways, however, personhood arguments changed. Those advocating for personhood drew on ideas about desegregation, consumer protection, sex discrimination, affirmative action, sex and pregnancy outside of marriage, civil rights, corporate power, religious liberty, criminal punishment, the rights of civilians in wartime, and the shape of the welfare state. Arguments for personhood thus offer a window into how socially conservative Americans understood discrimination across issues and decades.

Telling the story of personhood, too, allows us to trace the arc of conservative constitutionalism. Key studies in the field focus on the lawyers and organizations, like the Federalist Society, that have brought important cases, or the jurisprudential approaches, such as natural-law theory, or some versions of originalism and textualism, that have been most central to it. Scholars have shown how conservatives redefined themselves as champions of freedom of speech and religious liberty.[4]

To date, personhood arguments have not been as directly successful as originalism or textualism. Nor, for the most part, have personhood proponents yet convinced courts to adopt their arguments about constitutional fetal rights as often as they have in the case of speech or religious liberty.

Often, fetal-personhood arguments were resonant because they were aspirational. Imagining a world where the rights of the unborn were protected was, for many social conservatives, a way to rethink the interpretation of the Constitution and the future of the nation. Personhood arguments first took shape in response to a push for abortion reform in the 1960s. Changing sexual mores and concern about the discriminatory effects of criminal bans had fueled a push to loosen existing restrictions. Abortion opponents sought to defeat reform and eventually insisted that more liberal laws were themselves unconstitutional. But personhood became much more than a reaction to reform. By the 1960s, personhood proponents challenged the idea that those who had suffered past injustice had the most urgent claim to constitutional redress. Equality, personhood proponents stressed, was less about lifting up those at the margins than it was about restoring longstanding protection for the weak. The ultimate victim of discrimination in America, abortion opponents maintained, was the fetus.

By the 1980s, many in the movement insisted the unborn was a victim of violent crime. To treat the victims of violence as equal to the rest of us required the criminalization of abortion—and perhaps other acts that harmed fetuses. Some antiabortion advocates insisted on mercy for some, women first among them. But they agreed that there could be no equality, no justice in America, until abortion was a crime.

Proponents of personhood also joined an effort to transform the role played by history or tradition in constitutional interpretation. They resisted the argument that the nation's traditions were fluid, even as the idea of fetal personhood itself had consistently changed. Like other conservative allies, personhood champions insisted that the Court should recognize rights that were deeply rooted in a fixed tradition—and that Americans should look back to past eras that were more moral.

None of this is to say that most personhood proponents were distracted from their quest for fetal rights. But if abortion opponents wanted protections for the fetus, what they proposed would have had deeper consequences. Personhood arguments have already changed how the Court approaches the recognition of rights under the Due Process Clause. If abortion opponents are successful, they will also change how the Court understands equality under the law in the context of race, sex, and sexual orientation.

More than anything, the story of fetal personhood is a searing reminder of where Americans find themselves in the war over reproduction. Everyone understands that the effects of the *Dobbs* decision will take years to fully grasp, but *Dobbs* may feel like a final conclusion. It appears to be the result that Americans opposed to abortion yearned, marched, and voted for.

It is true that *Dobbs* is the end of one story, one about what it means to lose a constitutional right. But the antiabortion movement has never been just a fight to eliminate the right to choose abortion. It has always been a fetal-personhood movement. History tells us that personhood has had different meanings, but one thing has remained constant: if fetal personhood became a part of our constitutional law, the meaning of equality would change for everyone, and in contexts well beyond abortion itself. Once, *Dobbs* struck many as unimaginable. But if history teaches us anything, it is that *Dobbs* is just the beginning.

Notes

CCR	Catholic Charities USA Records, American Catholic History Research Center and University Archives, Catholic University of America, Washington, DC
CCTA	California Committee on Therapeutic Abortion Records, Charles E. Young Research Library, University of California, Los Angeles, Los Angeles, California
CRP	Charles Rice Papers, on file with the author
DRP	David Reardon Papers, on file with the author
EHP	Elizabeth Holtzman Papers, Schlesinger Library, Radcliffe Institute, Harvard University, Cambridge, Massachusetts
FFL	Feminists for Life Records, Schlesinger Library, Radcliffe Institute, Harvard University, Cambridge, Massachusetts
FKP	Florynce Kennedy Papers, Schlesinger Library, Radcliffe Institute, Harvard University, Cambridge, Massachusetts
FSP	Frederick T. Steeper Papers, Gerald R. Ford Presidential Library and Museum, University of Michigan, Ann Arbor, Michigan
FWHC	Feminist Women's Health Center Records, David M. Rubenstein Rare Book and Manuscript Library, Duke University, Durham, North Carolina
GHW	George Huntston Williams Papers, Andover-Harvard Theological Library, Harvard Divinity School, Cambridge, Massachusetts
HMP	Hugh Moore Papers, Seeley Mudd Manuscript Library, Princeton University, Princeton, New Jersey
JBP	James Bopp Jr. Papers, Terre Haute, Indiana
JRS	Joseph R. Stanton Papers, Schlesinger Library, Radcliffe Institute, Harvard University, Cambridge, Massachusetts
JWC	John Willke Collection, Cincinnati History Library and Archives, Cincinnati, Ohio
LMP	NOW Legal Momentum Collection, Schlesinger Library, Radcliffe Institute, Harvard University, Cambridge, Massachusetts
MBP	Morton Blackwell Papers, Ronald Reagan Presidential Library, Simi Valley, California
MCP	Mary Calderone Papers, Schlesinger Library, Radcliffe Institute, Harvard University, Cambridge, Massachusetts
MFJ	Mildred F. Jefferson Papers, Schlesinger Library, Radcliffe Institute, Harvard University, Cambridge, Massachusetts
MGP	Myrna Gutiérrez Papers, on file with the author

MHP	Merle Hoffman Papers, David M. Rubenstein Rare Book and Manuscript Library, Duke University, Durham, North Carolina
MRX	Father Paul Marx Papers, University of Notre Dame Archives, Notre Dame, Indiana
NAPAW	National Asian Pacific American Women's Forum Records, Sophia Smith Collection of Women's History, Smith College, Northampton, Massachusetts
NARAL	National Abortion Rights Action League Papers, Schlesinger Library, Radcliffe Institute, Harvard University, Cambridge, Massachusetts
NARALMA	National Abortion Rights Action League of Massachusetts Papers, Schlesinger Library, Radcliffe Institute, Harvard University, Cambridge, Massachusetts
NCAP	National Coalition of Abortion Providers Papers, David M. Rubenstein Rare Book and Manuscript Library, Duke University, Durham, North Carolina
NOW	National Organization for Women Papers, Schlesinger Library, Radcliffe Institute, Harvard University, Cambridge, Massachusetts
NOWLDEF	National Organization for Women Legal Defense and Education Fund, Schlesinger Library, Radcliffe Institute, Harvard University, Cambridge, Massachusetts
PAW	People for the American Way Collection of Conservative Political Ephemera, Bancroft Library, University of California, Berkeley, Berkeley, California
PCSW	President's Committee on the Status of Women Records, Schlesinger Library, Radcliffe Institute, Harvard University, Cambridge, Massachusetts
PLN	Pro-Life Newsletter Collection, Schlesinger Library, Radcliffe Institute, Harvard University, Cambridge, Massachusetts
PMC	Pauli Murray Collection, Schlesinger Library, Radcliffe Institute, Harvard University, Cambridge, Massachusetts
PPFA	Planned Parenthood Federation of America Records, Sophia Smith Collection of Women's History, Smith College, Northampton, Massachusetts
PRP	Paul Ramsey Papers, David M. Rubenstein Rare Book and Manuscript Library, Duke University, Durham, North Carolina
PSR	*Phyllis Schlafly Review* Collection, Schlesinger Library, Radcliffe Institute, Harvard University, Cambridge, Massachusetts

PWP	Paul Weyrich Papers, American Heritage Center, University of Wyoming, Laramie, Wyoming
RHS	Reproductive Health Services Records, University of Missouri, St. Louis, Missouri
RJN	Richard John Neuhaus Papers, American Catholic History Research Center and University Archives, Catholic University of America, Washington, DC
RNCL	Republican National Coalition for Life Collection, Phyllis Schlafly Center Archives, Clayton, Missouri
RNP	Ron Nessen Papers, Gerald R. Ford Presidential Library and Museum, University of Michigan, Ann Arbor, Michigan
RPS	Ruth Proskauer Smith Papers, Schlesinger Library, Radcliffe Institute, Harvard University, Cambridge, Massachusetts
SBL	Southern Baptists for Life Records, Southern Baptist Historical Library and Archives, Nashville, Tennessee
SCFU	Sanctuary City for the Unborn Records, on file with the author
SFL	Students for Life of America Papers, on file with the author
SSW	SisterSong Women of Color Reproductive Justice Records, Sophia Smith Collection of Women's History, Smith College, Northampton, Massachusetts
THV	Therese Hester Vaughn Papers, Schlesinger Library, Radcliffe Institute, Harvard University, Cambridge, Massachusetts
WCX	Wilcox Collection of Contemporary Political Movements, Kenneth Spencer Research Library, University of Kansas, Lawrence, Kansas
WKP	William J. Kenealy, SJ, Papers, Boston College Libraries, Boston, Massachusetts
WPP	Senator William Proxmire Papers, Wisconsin Historical Society, Madison, Wisconsin

Preface

1. For the Court's decision in *Dobbs*, see *Dobbs v. Jackson Women's Health Organization*, 597 U.S. 215 (2022). For coverage of what *Dobbs* signaled, see Charles Savage, "For Conservative Legal Movement, a Long-Sought Triumph Appears at Hand," *New York Times*, May 3, 2022, https://www.nytimes.com/2022/05/03/us/conservative-legal-movement-roe-v-wade.html; Emma Green, "How the Federalist Society Won," *New Yorker*, July 24, 2022, https://www.newyorker.com/news/annals-of-education/how-the-federalist-society-won.

2. A note on terminology is warranted here. Some individuals who experience abortion, pregnancy, and childbirth do not identify as women. As such, when writing about abortion seekers, I sometimes use gender-inclusive terms, such as "patients" or "pregnant people." In the history of the abortion conflict, however, the terms "woman" or "women" carry special meaning, particularly when used by proponents of fetal personhood. At other points, the use of gender-neutral terms may be anachronistic. Therefore, I primarily use gendered terms, such as "women," to capture the ideas attached to those terms by particular movements at specific moments in time.

Relatedly, controversy surrounds the language used to describe the movements contesting the abortion wars. For the most part, I follow the Associated Press style guide in describing the opposing sides as "antiabortion" and "abortion-rights" movements. See Associated Press, "Abortion," *Stylebook: 2024–2026*, 57th ed. (New York: Basic Books, 2024), vii, 2. On occasion, I also use the language movements use to identify themselves, such as "pro-choice," "pro-life," and "right to life." Probing this language—and why it has appealed to a broad cross-section of activists—can be illuminating.

Finally, there is the question of how to refer to life in the womb. Those opposed to abortion use the terms "preborn" or "unborn" child or human. Those who support abortion rights instead use the terms "zygote," "fertilized egg," "embryo," or "fetus." Medically, these terms may refer to particular gestational stages—for example, "fetus" applies only after eight weeks' gestation. American College of Obstetricians and Gynecologists, "How Your Fetus Grows during Pregnancy," https://www.acog.org/womens -health/faqs/how-your-fetus-grows-during-pregnancy. In following the AP style guide, I most often use the term "fetus." On occasion, when other medical uses prevail, I follow them—such as using "embryo" in the context of assisted reproduction. At times, I also use "unborn child"—especially when discussing the work of the personhood movement—to capture the beliefs and arguments of those advocating for fetal rights.

3. Contemporary scholarship continues this debate. For a sample of philosophical work on the meaning of personhood, see Richard Eldridge, *On Moral Personhood: Philosophy, Literature, Criticism, and Self-Understanding*, 2nd ed. (Chicago: University of Chicago Press, 1989), 3–27; Harry G. Frankfurt, "Freedom of Will and the Concept of a Person," *Journal of Philosophy* 68 (1971): 5–7; Francis J. Beckwith, "The Explanatory Power of the Substance View of Persons," *Christian Bioethics* 10 (2004): 33–54. On the application of the term "person" to corporations, see Adam Winkler, *We the Corporations: How American Businesses Won Their Civil Rights* (New York: Liveright, 2018). For a view of bioethical debate about personhood, see Martha Farah and

Andrea S. Eberlein, "Personhood and Neuroscience: Naturalizing or Nihilating?" *American Journal of Bioethics* 7 (2007): 37–46; R. M. Green, "Part III: Determining Moral Status," *American Journal of Bioethics* 2 (2002): 20–30; Jennifer Blumenthal-Barby, "The End of Personhood," *American Journal of Bioethics*, January 2023, https://www.tandfonline.com/doi/full/10.1080/15265161.2022.2160515; Steve Clarke and Julian Savulescu, "Rethinking Our Assumptions about Moral Status," in *Rethinking Moral Status* (New York: Oxford University Press, 2021). Other historians have sometimes used personhood in different ways. Sara Dubow, for example, often uses personhood to signal individual human existence rather than a legal status, although her study also touches on the fight for legal fetal rights. See *Ourselves Unborn: A History of the Fetus in Modern America* (New York: Oxford University Press, 2010), 16–17, 78–108. Daniel K. Williams, by contrast, at times frames personhood convictions as centering on human rather than constitutional rights. See *Defenders of the Unborn: The Pro-Life Movement Before Roe v. Wade* (New York: Oxford University Press, 2016), 18, 123–152. Jennifer Holland's *Tiny You* examines both biological and legal arguments while focusing on Western anti-abortion mobilizations and their approach to race. See *Tiny You: A Western History of the Anti-Abortion Movement* (Berkeley: University of California Press, 2020), 6, 220. Other scholars have discussed legal arguments for personhood while not focusing primarily on the subject. See David J. Garrow, *Liberty and Sexuality: The Right to Privacy and the Making of* Roe v. Wade (Berkeley: University of California Press, 1998), 371–394. His earlier chapters discuss the terms of debate about personhood in the first decades of the struggle over abortion.

4. See "America's Abortion Quandary," *Pew Research Center*, May 6, 2022, https://www.pewresearch.org/religion/2022/05/06/americas-abortion-quandary/. In a 2019 survey by NPR, PBS, and Marist, a majority concluded that life began at some point after fertilization. See NPR/PBS/Marist Poll, June 7, 2019, https://maristpoll.marist.edu/npr-pbs-newshour-marist-poll-results-6/. For polls on fetal rights, see "Majority of Americans Oppose Alabama Supreme Court Ruling around IVF," *Axios-Ipsos Poll*, February 28, 2024, https://www.ipsos.com/en-us/majority-americans-oppose-alabama-supreme-court-ruling-around-ivf; 538/Ipsos Poll, December 12, 2022, https://www.ipsos.com/en-us/news-polls/FiveThirtyEight-2022-midterm-election. A poll by Americans United for Life and YouGov found majority support for fetal rights and majority *opposition* to abortion bans. See YouGov, "Abortion," May 6–13, 2022, https://aul.org/wp-content/uploads/2022/06/2022–05-AUL-YouGov-National-Survey.pdf.

5. Chapter 1 studies the reform movement and the response of abortion opponents to it.

6. Chapters 1 and 2 consider the evolution of the early fetal-personhood movement.

7. Chapters 4, 5, and 6 chronicle these developments in the personhood movement.

8. On polls suggesting belief that life begins at conception or support for protecting fetal life and opposition to criminalizing abortion, see "America's Abortion Quandary"; YouGov, "Abortion."

9. Pauli Murray, "A Proposal to Reexamine the Applicability of the Fourteenth Amendment to State Laws and Practices Which Discriminate on the Basis of Sex Per Se" (December 1962), 10, PCSW, Box 8, Folder 62.

10. National Organization for Women, Statement of Purpose (1966), BFP, Carton 126, Folder 1544; Betty Friedan, "Abortion: A Woman's Civil Right: Keynote Speech before the First National Conference on the Repeal of Abortion Laws" (February 14, 1969), 1, BFP, Box 121, Folder 1467.

11. On competing ideas of equality in the period, see, for example, Tomiko Brown-Nagin, *Courage to Dissent: Atlanta and the Long History of the Civil Rights Movement* (New York: Oxford University Press, 2011), 3–22, 123–167, 400–439; Serena Mayeri, *Reasoning from Race: Feminism, Law, and the Civil Rights Revolution,* 2nd ed. (Cambridge, MA: Harvard University Press, 2014), 7, 45–62; Mark Brilliant, *The Color of America Has Changed: How Racial Diversity Shaped Civil Rights Reform in California, 1941–1978* (New York: Oxford University Press, 2010); Risa Goluboff, *The Lost Promise of Civil Rights* (Cambridge, MA: Harvard University Press, 2007); Risa Goluboff, *Vagrant Nation: Police Power, Constitutional Change, and the Making of the 1960s* (New York: Oxford University Press, 2016).

1. Before Personhood

1. Scholars of originalism distinguish between what they call "old originalism," which looked at "the subjective intentions of the founders," and "new originalism," which centers on the "public meaning of the text when adopted." Keith E. Whittington, "The New Originalism," *Georgetown Journal of Law and Public Policy* 2 (2004): 601–612; see also Thomas Colby, "The Sacrifice of the New Originalism," *Georgetown Law Journal* 99 (2011): 720–731. For discussion of contemporary approaches to originalism, see John McGinnis and Michael Rappaport, "Unifying Original Intent and Original Public Meaning," *Northwestern Law Review* 113 (2019): 1373–1374; Randy Barnett, *Restoring the Lost Constitution: The Presumption of Liberty* (Princeton: Princeton University Press, 2014), 389–407. There are a wide variety of approaches to originalism, of course, some of them espoused by progressive scholars and justices,

including Justice Ketanji Brown Jackson. See, for example, Jack Balkin, *Living Originalism* (Cambridge, MA: Harvard University Press, 2014); Evan Turiano, "Justice Jackson's Progressive Originalism Isn't New," *Washington Post*, October 10, 2022, https://www.washingtonpost.com/made-by-history/2022/10/10/originalism-ketanji-brown-jackson-supreme-court/. A younger generation of originalist scholars have taken other approaches, seeking to establish that originalism better accounts for the present-day workings of our legal system, for example, or to show that the founders sought to confer rights that were part of general law, a set of customary principles that spanned jurisdictions. See, for example, William Baude, Jud Campbell, and Stephen E. Sachs, "General Law and the Fourteenth Amendment," *Stanford Law Review* 76 (2024): 1195–1212; William Baude and Stephen E. Sachs, "Grounding Originalism," *Northwestern University Law Review* 113 (2019): 1457–1462.

For a sample of contemporary arguments for personhood, see John Finnis, "Abortion Is Unconstitutional," *First Things*, April 2021, https://www.firstthings.com/article/2021/04/abortion-is-unconstitutional; Joshua Craddock, "Protecting Prenatal Persons: Does the Fourteenth Amendment Prohibit Abortions?" *Harvard Journal of Law and Public Policy* 40 (2017): 539–552; Michael Stokes Paulsen, "The Plausibility of Personhood," *Ohio State Law Journal* 74 (2012): 14–68; Josh Craddock, "Our Pro-Life Constitution," *National Review*, December 21, 2023, https://www.nationalreview.com/magazine/2024/02/our-pro-life-constitution/; Brief Amici Curiae of Scholars of Jurisprudence John Finnis and Robert George, 1–33, *Dobbs v. Jackson Women's Health Organization*, 597 U.S. 215 (2022) (No. 19-1392).

2. See Finnis, "Abortion Is Unconstitutional"; Craddock, "Protecting Prenatal Persons," 539–552; Paulsen, "The Plausibility of Personhood," 14–68; Craddock, "Our Pro-Life Constitution"; Brief Amici Curiae of Scholars of Jurisprudence John Finnis and Robert George, 1–33.

3. For the use of "person" in Article I, Section 2, see U.S. Const. art. 1 § 2.

4. On Storer's concerns about contemporary attitudes about abortion, see Horatio Storer, *On Criminal Abortion in America* (Philadelphia: L. P. Lippincott, 1860), 9 ("We turn now to public opinion. It, too, both in theory and in practice, fails to recognize the crime [of abortion]"); Horatio Storer and Franklin Fiske Heard, *Criminal Abortion: Its Nature, Its Evidence, and Its Law* (Boston: Little, Brown, 1868), 7 ("We shall soon perceive how extensive and high-reaching is its frequency; we must therefore conclude that the public do not know, or knowing deny, the criminal character of the action performed"). For more critiques of original public meaning arguments for personhood, see Evan Bernick and Jill Wieber Lens, "Abortion, Original Public Meaning, and the Ambiguities of Pregnancy," *Michigan Law Review* 122 (forthcoming 2024);

Aaron Tang, "After *Dobbs:* History, Tradition, and the Uncertain Future of a National Abortion Ban," *Stanford Law Review* 75 (2023): 1150–1156; Reva B. Siegel, "Memory Games: *Dobbs*'s Originalism as Anti-Democratic Living Constitutionalism—and Some Pathways for Resistance," *Texas Law Review* 101 (2024): 1129–1204; Clarke Forsythe, "The Fourteenth Amendment's Personhood Mistake," *National ReviewPlus*, February 2024, https://www.nationalreview.com/magazine/2024/02/the-14th-amendments-personhood-myth/. Scholars of the Thirteenth and Fourteenth Amendments have also stressed that the amendment's framers were concerned about forced childbearing and the destruction of Black families. See Peggy Cooper Davis, *Neglected Stories: The Constitution and Family Values* (New York: Hill and Wang, 1997); Michele Goodwin, "Opportunistic Originalism: *Dobbs v. Jackson Women's Health Organization,*" *Supreme Court Review* (2022): 157–188. Jack Balkin has also argued that a right to abortion is supported by the original meaning of the Fourteenth Amendment. "Abortion and Original Meaning," *Constitutional Commentary* 24 (2007): 292–315.

5. *Dobbs v. Jackson Women's Health Organization,* 597 U.S. 215, 231-233 (2022).

6. See Leslie J. Reagan, *When Abortion Was a Crime: Women, Medicine, and Law in the United States, 1867–1973,* 2nd ed. (Berkeley: University of California Press, 2022), 53–65, 99–108; Linda Gordon, *The Moral Property of Women: A History of Birth Control Politics in America* (Urbana: University of Illinois Press, 2002), 28–32; James C. Mohr, *Abortion in America: The Origins and Evolution of National Policy* (New York: Oxford University Press, 1979), 156–183. For discussion of unblocking menses from the colonial period to the nineteenth century, see Reagan, *When Abortion Was a Crime,* 42–55; Kristin Luker, *Abortion and the Politics of Motherhood* (Berkeley: University of California Press, 1984), x, 19–20. States that introduced laws of this kind included Missouri (1825), Illinois (1827), Indiana (1835), Alabama (1841), Massachusetts (1845), Vermont (1846), New Jersey (1849), and Texas (1854). See *Dobbs v. Jackson Women's Health Organization,* 597 U.S. 215, 302–310 (2022) (Appendix A).

7. "The Case of Caroline A. Clark: Seduction and Death," *Boston Post*, June 28, 1843, 2; "Coroner's Inquest: Seduction, Abortion, and Death," *Livingston Democrat*, July 5, 1843, 5 (Geneseo, NY). On the role played by newspapers in the era, see Lawrence M. Friedman and Hutchinson Fann, "High and Low: Abortion in the Press in the Late 19th Century and Early 20th Century," *Cleveland State Law Review* 72 (2024): 866–868; Patricia Cline Cohen, "Married Women and Induced Abortion in the United States, 1820–1860" (July 22, 2022) (unpublished manuscript), 4, https://ssrn.com/abstract=4197554.

8. For the Massachusetts law, see Eugene Quay, "Justifiable Abortion—Medical and Legal Foundations," *Georgetown Law Journal* 49 (1961): 481. On the New York law,

see ibid., 478. On the expansion of the abortion business and Restell, see Nicholas L. Syrett, *The Trials of Madame Restell: Nineteenth-Century America's Most Infamous Female Physician and the Campaign to Make Abortion a Crime* (New York: New Press, 2023), 1–9, 34–54; Jennifer Wright, *Madame Restell: The Life, Death, and Resurrection of New York's Most Fabulous, Fearless, and Infamous Abortionist* (New York: Hachette, 2023), 3–25, 167–202. Examples of such laws include those in New York (1828), Michigan (1846), and Wisconsin (1858), which made it manslaughter to administer "any medicine, drug or substance whatever, or . . . use or employ any instrument or other means" with criminal intent if doing so resulted in the death of the mother. *Dobbs v. Jackson Women's Health Organization*, 597 U.S. 215, 302–317 (2022) (Appendix A).

9. On the struggles of the early AMA, see William G. Rothstein, *American Medical Schools and the Practice of Medicine: A History* (Baltimore: Johns Hopkins University Press, 1987), 42–96; Paul Starr, *The Social Transformation of American Medicine: The Rise of a Sovereign Profession and the Making of a Vast Industry* (New York: Basic Books, 1982), 90–112. On the nation's experience with abortion in the nineteenth century, see generally R. E. Fulton, *The Abortionist of Howard Street: Medicine and Crime in Nineteenth-Century New York* (Ithaca: Cornell University Press, 2024), ix–xiii.

10. For the edited, original Storer Sr.'s lecture, see David Humphreys Storer, "Duties, Trials, and Rewards of the Student of Midwifery," November 7, 1855, reprinted as "Dr. Storer's Introductory," *Boston Medical and Surgical Journal* 53 (1856): 410–412. The full lecture was not published until 1872. See "Editorial Notes," *Journal of the Obstetrical Society of Boston* 6 (1872): 393–400. On the initial response to Storer's lecture, see Janet Farrell Brodie, *Contraception and Abortion in Nineteenth-Century America* (Ithaca: Cornell University Press, 1994), 266–268.

11. Nathan Smith Davis, *A History of the American Medical Association from Its Organization up to January 1855* (Philadelphia: Lippincott, Grambo, 1855), 189.

12. "Report of a Committee on the Subject of Medical Legislation, to the Monroe County Medical Society, Rochester, New York" (November 9, 1842), cited in Douglas Haynes, "Policing the Social Boundaries of the American Medical Association, 1847–70," *Journal of the History of Medicine and Allied Sciences* 60 (2005): 175. On the demographic composition of the AMA, see ibid., 174–178.

13. "American Medical Association: Twelfth Annual Meeting, Held at Louisville, Kentucky," *Louisville Journal* (May 1859): 503.

14. Horatio Storer, *Why Not? A Book for Every Woman* (Boston: Lee and Shepherd, 1867), 64, 83, 85.

For more on Storer's arguments, see Siegel, "Memory Games," 1129–1185; see also Reva B. Siegel, "Reasoning from the Body: A Historical Perspective on Abortion and Questions of Equal Protection," *Stanford Law Review* 44 (1992): 261–381.

15. *Corfield v. Coryell*, 6 F. Cas. 546 (C.C.E.D. 1823). For more on the idea of rights in the antebellum Constitution, see G. Edward White, *Law in American History, vol. 1: From the Colonial Years through the Civil War* (New York: Oxford University Press, 2012), 7–17, 121–186; Baude, Campbell, and Sachs, "General Law," 1–64; Randy E. Barnett and Evan D. Bernick, *The Original Meaning of the Fourteenth Amendment: Its Letter and Spirit* (Cambridge, MA: Harvard University Press, 2021), 59–80. On the influence of *Corfield*, see Barnett and Bernick, *The Original Meaning of the Fourteenth Amendment*, 141–162, 216–235; Gerard N. Magliocca, "Rediscovering *Corfield v. Coryell*," *Notre Dame Law Review* 95 (2019): 708–726 (reconstructing the thinking of Justice Washington and tracing *Corfield*'s legacy); Jud Campbell, "General Citizenship Rights," *Yale Law Journal* 132 (2023): 615, 644–650 (arguing that *Corfield* reflected a vision of general citizenship rights, "a status conferring reciprocal protection of general citizenship rights across state lines").

16. For Jones's statement: Martha S. Jones, *Birthright Citizens: A History of Race and Rights in Antebellum America* (New York: Cambridge University Press, 2018), 12. For more on pre–Civil War rights-claiming, see ibid., 10–25; Corinne T. Field, *The Struggle for Equal Adulthood: Gender, Race, Age and the Fight for Citizenship in Antebellum America* (Chapel Hill: University of North Carolina Press, 2014), 3–14; Kate Masur, *Until Justice Be Done: America's First Civil Rights Movement, from the Revolution to Reconstruction* (New York: Norton, 2021), 99–208.

17. *Dred Scott v. Sandford*, 60 U.S. 393 (1857). For more on the case's historical significance, see Eric Foner, *The Second Founding: How the Civil War and Reconstruction Remade the Constitution* (New York: Norton, 2019), 152–163; Jones, *Birthright Citizens*, 155–158. For examples of arguments comparing the fetus to enslaved persons, see Family Research Council, *Washington Watch*, September 27, 2000, PAW, Carton 39, Folder 4 ("Lincoln's debate about slavery then is a lot like America's abortion debate today"); Robert G. Morrison, Family Research Council, "Only Tyrants Shed Innocent Blood" (2000), PAW, Carton 39, Folder 4.

18. Abraham Lincoln, "The *Dred Scott* Decision and Slavery, June 26, 1857," in *Voices of the African-American Experience*, ed. Lionel C. Bascom (Westport, CT: Greenwood, 2009), 76. For discussion of the distinction between social equality and civil rights, see Pamela Brandwein, *Rethinking the Judicial Settlement of Reconstruction* (New York: Cambridge University Press, 2003), 70, 73–85; Eric Foner, *The Fiery Trial: Abraham Lincoln and American Slavery* (New York: Norton, 2010), 110–118.

19. Frederick Douglass, *Selected Speeches and Writings*, ed. Philip S. Foner (Chicago: Chicago Review Press, 1999), 334; see also Abraham Lincoln, "Cooper Union Address" (February 27, 1860), http://www.abrahamlincolnonline.org/lincoln/speeches/cooper.htm. For more on the distinction between "political," "social," and "civil" rights in the nineteenth century, see Saidiya Hartman, *Scenes of Subjugation: Terror, Slavery, and Self-Making in Nineteenth-Century America* (New York: Norton, 2022), 53–100.

20. "Minutes of the American Medical Association for 1863," *Transactions of the American Medical Association* 14 (1864): 14, 51.

21. Storer, *Why Not?* 41, 80–81; see also Storer, *Criminal Abortion in America*, 41; Horatio Storer et al., "Suffolk District Medical Society, Report of the Committee on Criminal Abortion," *Boston Medical and Surgical Journal* 56 (1857): 386–387.

22. New York Society for the Suppression of Vice, *Second Annual Report of the New York Society for the Suppression of Vice* (New York: New York Society for the Suppression of Vice, 1876), 9; see also Anthony Comstock, *Frauds Exposed; or, How the People Are Deceived and Robbed, and Youth Corrupted* (New York: J. Howard Brown 1880), 427 (Comstock describing abortion, contraception, and erotica as "incentives to crime to young girls and women"); Heywood Broun and Margaret Leech, *Anthony Comstock: Roundsman of the Lord* (New York: A. and C. Boni, 1927), 192 (quoting Comstock's diary denouncing "obscene publications, abortion implements, and other incentives to crime").

23. Rev. James Buckley, "The Suppression of Vice," *North American Review* 135 (1883): 500. On Comstock's use of the term "abortionist," see Broun and Leech, *Roundsman*, 178. For more on Comstock, see Donna Dennis, *Licentious Gotham: Erotic Publishing and Its Prosecution in Nineteenth-Century New York* (Cambridge, MA: Harvard University Press, 2009), 190–225; Amy Werbel, *Lust on Trial: Censorship and the Rise of American Obscenity in the Age of Anthony Comstock* (New York: Columbia University Press, 2018); Amy Sohn, *The Man Who Hated Women: Sex, Censorship, and Civil Liberties in the Gilded Age* (New York: Farrar, Straus and Giroux, 2021). For the text of the original statute: An Act for the Suppression of Trade in, and Circulation of, Obscene Literature and Articles of Immoral Use, Ch. 258, § 1, 17 Stat. 598, 598–99 (1873). On anti-vice activism, see Geoffrey R. Stone, *Sex and the Constitution: Sex, Religion, and Law from America's Origins to the Twenty-First Century* (New York: Liveright, 2017), 161–167; Nicola K. Beisel, *Imperiled Innocents: Anthony Comstock and Family Reproduction in Victorian America* (Princeton: Princeton University Press, 1997), 20–27, 120–198. On the legal history of the statute's enforcement, see Reva B. Siegel and Mary Ziegler, "Comstockery: How Government Censorship

Gave Birth to the Law of Reproductive Freedom, and May Again Threaten It," *Yale Law Journal* 134 (forthcoming 2025). On enforcement of the Comstock Act in cases of abortion, see Elizabeth Bainum Hovey, "Stamping out Smut: The Enforcement of Obscenity Laws, 1872–1915" (PhD diss., Columbia University, 1998), 213, 437–451; Shirley J. Burton, "Obscenity in Victorian America: Struggles over Definition and Concomitant Prosecutions in Chicago's Federal Court, 1873–1913" (PhD diss., University of Illinois–Chicago, 1991), 172–189.

24. See *Dobbs v. Jackson Women's Health Organization*, 597 U.S. 215, 302–317 (2022) (Appendix A); Quay, "Justifiable Abortion," 454–507; Mohr, *Abortion in America*, 200–230; Joseph Dellapenna, *Dispelling the Myths of Abortion History* (Durham: Carolina Academic Press, 2006), 319–326 (chronicling development of state laws and disputing the accepted account of criminalization).

25. On prosecutorial patterns at the time, see Reagan, *When Abortion Was a Crime*, 120-122, 171–177; Hovey, "Stamping out Smut," 437–451; Burton, "Obscenity in Victorian America," 172–189; Reva B. Siegel and Mary Ziegler, *Abortion's New Criminalization: A History-and-Tradition Right to Access After* Dobbs *and the 2023 Term*, Virginia Law Review (forthcoming 2025). On Storer's later life, see Frederick N. Dyer, *Horatio Storer: Champion of Women and the Unborn* (New York: Science History, 1999), 256; Malcolm Storer, "Horatio Storer, '50," *Harvard Graduates' Magazine* 31 (1923): 362–367. On the spread of the term "Comstockery," see "Comstockery," *Google Books Ngram Viewer*, https://books.google.com/ngrams/graph?content=Comstockery&year_start=1800&year_end=2019&case_insensitive=on&corpus=en-2019&smoothing=3, accessed July 2, 2024.

26. For more on Sanger and the varying arguments she made for birth control access, see Ellen Chesler, *Woman of Valor: Margaret Sanger and the Birth Control Movement in America*, 2nd ed. (New York: Simon and Schuster, 2007); Jean H. Baker, *Margaret Sanger: A Life of Passion* (New York: Farrar, Straus and Giroux, 2011). For Sanger's statement about breaking the law, see Margaret Sanger, "Shall We Break the Law?" *Birth Control Review* 1 (1917): 4.

27. For more on the history of eugenics and its early targets, see Alexandra Minna Stern, *Eugenic Nation: Faults and Frontiers of Better Breeding in Modern America*, 2nd ed. (Berkeley: University of California Press, 2016), 1–28; Wendy Kline, *Building a Better Race: Gender, Sexuality, and Eugenics from the Turn of the Century to the Baby Boom* (Berkeley: University of California Press, 2001); Daniel J. Kevles, *In the Name of Eugenics: Genetics and the Uses of Human Heredity*, 2nd ed. (Cambridge, MA: Harvard University Press, 1998). On Dennett's position: Lauren MacIvor Thompson, "The Politics of Female Pain: Women's Citizenship, Twilight Sleep, and the Early

Birth Control Movement," *British Medical Journal* 45 (2017): 67–73. For Roosevelt's statement about the duty of women: "Motherhood: The Duty of Women," *New York Times*, March 14, 1905, A1. For Roosevelt's statement about the dangers of race suicide: Baker, *Margaret Sanger*, 159–160.

28. On Sanger's alliances with doctors and the mainstreaming of birth control, see Gordon, *The Moral Property of Women*, 182-186; David M. Kennedy, *Birth Control in America: The Career of Margaret Sanger* (New York: Yale University Press, 2009, 1970), 180–211. For cases interpreting the Comstock Act to protect health, see *Burton v. United States*, 142 F. 57, 63 (8th Cir. 1906) (reasoning that the act would not apply to "a communication from a doctor to his patient" or "a work designed for the use of medical practitioners only"); *United States v. Clarke*, 38 F. 732, 735 (E.D. Mo. 1889) (holding that the statute did not criminalize the mailing of "standard medical works" and direct physician-patient communications about "physical ailments, habits, and practices"); *United States v. Smith*, 45 F. 476, 478 (E.D. Wis. 1891) ("proper and necessary communication between physician and patient touching any disease may properly be deposited in the mail"). For the 1930s cases broadening the understanding of health, see *United States v. One Package of Japanese Pessaries*, 86 F.2d 737, 740–753 (2d Cir. 1936); *Youngs Rubber Corp. v. C.I. Lee & Co.*, 45 F.2d 103, 105–108 (2d Cir. 1930); *United States v. Nicholas*, 97 F.2d 510, 512 (2d Cir. 1938).

29. Pius XI, *Casti Connubii* (1930), https://www.vatican.va/content/pius-xi/en/encyclicals/documents/hf_p-xi_enc_19301231_casti-connubii.html. For Coughlin's statement: "Birth Control Would Exterminate Anglo-Saxons, Priest Tells House," *Salt Lake Tribune*, January 19, 1934, 9; see also "Birth Control 'Race Suicide,'" *Atlantic City Press*, December 19, 1935, 2 (NJ) (Archbishop Patrick Hayes of New York arguing that "use of birth control involves the risk of race suicide").

30. On pronatalism in the 1940s and 1950s, see Reagan, *When Abortion Was a Crime*, 163, 195; Kline, *Building a Better Race*, 12–127. On the rate of complications in the era, see Regine Stix, "A Study of Pregnancy Wastage," *Millbank Quarterly* 11 (1935): 362–363. On increasing abortion rates in the 1930s, see Reagan, *When Abortion Was a Crime*, 133-135, 177–192; Luker, *The Politics of Motherhood*, 41–50.

31. On the rise of mental-health justifications in therapeutic abortion committees, see C. Lee Buxton, "One Doctor's Opinion of Abortion," *American Journal of Nursing* 68 (1968): 1026–1028; Herbert L. Packer and Ralph J. Gampell, "Therapeutic Abortion: A Problem in Law and Medicine," *Stanford Law Review* 11 (1959): 417–455.

32. "Unnecessary to Choose between Mother and Baby," *Catholic Union and Echo*, December 30, 1951, 11. On the decline in maternal mortality in the era, see *Vital*

Statistics of the United States: 1947 (Washington, DC: Government Printing Office, 1949), 38. On growing skepticism among antiabortion physicians about the need for abortion in medical emergencies, see Daniel K. Williams, *Defenders of the Unborn: The Pro-Life Movement Before* Roe v. Wade (New York: Oxford University Press, 2016), 48.

33. On mortality rates caused by illegal abortion, see Edwin Gold et al., "Therapeutic Abortions in New York City: A Twenty-Year Review," *American Journal of Public Health* 55 (July 1965): 965; Christopher Tietze, "Mortality with Contraception and Induced Abortion," *Studies in Family Planning* 1 (1969): 6–8; Russell S. Fisher, "Criminal Abortion," in *Abortion in America: Medical, Psychiatric, Legal, Anthropological, and Religious Considerations*, ed. Harold Rosen (Boston: Beacon, 1967), 9.

34. Mary Steichen Calderone, "Illegal Abortion as a Public Health Problem," *American Journal of Public Health* 50 (1960): 748–752. For more on Calderone's work, see Ellen S. More, *The Transformation of Sexual Education: Mary Calderone and the Fight for Sexual Health* (New York: New York University Press, 2022). For Calderone's book on the subject, see Mary Steichen Calderone, *Abortion in the United States* (New York: Paul Hoeber, 1958). For Guttmacher's book, see Alan Guttmacher, *Babies by Choice or by Chance* (New York: Doubleday, 1959), 197–199. For Guttmacher's statement about the general health: Alan Guttmacher, "The Law That Doctors Often Break," *Redbook*, August 1959, 25, 95–98. On internal discussions within the American Law Institute: "Continuation of the Discussion of the Model Penal Code," *American Law Institute Proceedings* 36 (1959): 265–266. For Vogt's statement: William Vogt, "William Vogt on Abortion," December 5, 1955, MCP, Box 2, Folder 11.

35. Clipping, Alice Rossi, "Abortion Laws and Their Victims" (1966), PMC, Box 114, Folder 2043; see also Pamphlet, Allen J. Moore, "Abortion: A Human Choice" (n.d., ca. 1962), PMC, Box 114, Folder 2043 ("The question of abortion is closely related to the theological understanding of the nature and purpose of the sexual act"); Clipping, Herman Schwartz, "Abortion and the Law" (n.d., ca. 1966), PMC, Box 114, Folder 2043 (equating opposition to abortion to opposition to promiscuity). On the changing sexual politics that shaped the ALI's Model Penal Code, see David Allyn, "Private Acts/Public Policy: Alfred Kinsey, the American Law Institute and the Privatization of American Sexual Morality," *Journal of American Studies* 30 (1996): 407–428; Leigh Ann Wheeler, *How Sex Became a Civil Liberty* (New York: Oxford University Press, 2013), 106–114.

36. In 1969, a majority of Catholics in some polls favored a health exception. See Judith Blake, "Abortion and Public Opinion: The 1960 to 1970 Decade," *Science* 171 (1971): 543. In 1962, one-third of Catholics supported the decision of a woman to

terminate her pregnancy because of the risk of severe birth defects. See Megan Brenan, "Gallup Vault: Majority Supported Therapeutic Abortion in 1962," *Gallup*, June 12, 2018, https://news.gallup.com/vault/235496/gallup-vault-public-supported-therapeutic-abortion-1962.aspx. On anti-Catholic sentiment in the 1960s and its role in the presidential election, see Shaun Casey, *The Making of a Catholic President: Kennedy v. Nixon 1960* (New York: Oxford University Press, 2009), 129–184.

37. On Gampell's statement and the *Catholic Standard and Times*'s response, see "Medical Practice and God's Law," *Catholic Standard and Times*, October 21, 1960, 7 (Philadelphia); see also "Panelists at Medical Meeting Urge 'Liberalizing' Laws on Therapeutic Abortions," *Catholic News Service*, October 17, 1960, 8.

38. "Anti-Abortion Movement Pioneer, Newspaperwoman," *Chicago Tribune*, May 1, 1994, C8; "Effie Quay, Pro-Life Pioneer, Celebrates Ninetieth Birthday," 2013, http://www.canonlaw.info/a_tribute.htm.

39. "Anti-Abortion Movement Pioneer," C8; "Effie Quay, Pioneer."

40. Quay, "Justifiable Abortion," 178, 234–238.

41. Ibid. This argument would continue to carry weight within the movement. See Richard P. Vaughn, SJ, "Respect for the Unborn" (1965), CCR, Box 9, Folder 15 ("Respect for human life is part of human culture"); Pamphlet, "In Defense of the Unborn Child" (1965), CCR, Box 9, Folder 15 ("The laws preventing such cruelty [abortion] are not 'archaic' or 'antiquated' rather they are time-tested and time-honored and have their origins in the common conscience of humanity throughout the centuries"); Pamphlet, "Abortion and the Law" (n.d., ca. 1965), CCR, Box 9, Folder 16. For more on arguments about women dishonestly using abortion exceptions in the ALI model, see Robert Byrn, "Critique and Commentary on the Pertinent Sections of the American Law Institute Model Penal Code" (1965), CCR, Box 94, Folder 16 (stressing "the acknowledged likelihood of fraud on the part of the mother").

42. "Bishop Assails Measure to Ease New Hampshire Therapeutic Abortion Law," *Catholic News Service*, February 13, 1961, 3. For more on the New Hampshire struggle, see David J. Garrow, *Liberty and Sexuality: The Right to Privacy and the Making of* Roe v. Wade (Berkeley: University of California Press, 1998), 172. On the doctrine of double effect in the period, see Peter Knauer, "The Hermeneutic Function of the Principle of Double Effect," *Natural Law Forum* 12 (1967); Philippa Foot, "The Problem of Abortion and the Doctrine of Double Effect," *Oxford Review* 5 (1967): 5–15.

43. On Finkbine's story, see Leslie J. Reagan, *Dangerous Pregnancies: Mothers, Disabilities, and Abortion in Modern America* (Berkeley: University of California Press, 2012), 59–87; Garrow, *Liberty and Sexuality*, 174–179; Williams, *Defenders of the Unborn*, 55–59. For more contemporary criticism of life exceptions among Catholics, see

Father Daniel H. Brennan, "Question Box: Prefer Mother or Child?" *Pittsburgh Catholic*, April 7, 1960, 5 (disapproving "the direct taking of the life of the child to ensure the mother's living"); "Vatican Says, Nothing Can Justify, Authorize Abortion," *Catholic Transcript*, August 9, 1962, 1 (Hartford, CT) ("From the very moment of conception, every human being has all the rights inherent in a human being. There is nothing that can justify his direct and voluntary suppression, not even the purpose of saving the life of the mother"). Later generations of advocates would sometimes take different positions on exceptions for the life of the patient.

44. On the response to Finkbine and the rubella outbreak, see Sara Dubow, *Ourselves Unborn: A History of the Fetus in Modern America* (New York: Oxford University, 2010), 64–66, 75–82; Jennifer Holland, *Tiny You: A Western History of the Anti-Abortion Movement* (Berkeley: University of California Press, 2020), 49–52. For the poll on Finkbine, see Brenan, "Gallup Vault."

45. "Direct Abortion Always Immoral, Priest Reminds," *Catholic Standard and Times*, August 3, 1962, 2 (Philadelphia); see also Mrs. G. J. Gunning, "Letter to the Editor," *Atlanta Journal-Constitution*, August 15, 1962, 4; "Catholic Abortion Stand Clarified by Spokesman," *Tucson Daily Citizen*, July 28, 1962, 1 (AZ). For Filas's argument on life exception, see "Direct Abortion Always Immoral," 2 (Filas arguing that "direct abortion is never permitted, even when the ultimate purpose is to save the life of the mother").

46. "Unborn Child Has a Right to Life, Priest Tells Legislators Studying Bill to Relax State Abortion Bill," *Catholic News Service*, December 31, 1962, 2. For more arguments of this kind made in the era, "Changes in Abortion Law Lauded, Censored," *Los Angeles Times*, December 18, 1962, C8; "Bill for Abortions Opposed," *San Francisco Chronicle*, December 19, 1962, 28. On shifting opinion among Catholics, see Blake, "Abortion and Public Opinion," 546.

47. "Rights of Unborn Stressed at Abortion Law Hearing," *Catholic Transcript*, January 3, 1963, 5 (Hartford, CT).

48. For the declaration, see *Universal Declaration of Human Rights* (Washington, DC: Government Printing Office, 1949). For more on the declaration's influence on abortion politics, see Williams, *Defenders of the Unborn*, 37–40, 89.

49. On the civil-rights history of the 1950s, see Mary L. Dudziak, *Cold War Civil Rights: Race and the Image of American Democracy* (Princeton: Princeton University Press, 2000), 2–24; Andrew B. Lewis, *The Shadows of Youth: The Remarkable Journey of the Civil Rights Generation* (New York: Macmillan, 2009), 17–63; Tomiko Brown-Nagin, *Courage to Dissent: Atlanta and the Long History of the Civil Rights Movement* (New York: Oxford University Press, 2011), 83–133. On the backlash to *Brown* and its

importance, see Michael J. Klarman, *From Jim Crow to Civil Rights: The Supreme Court and the Struggle for Racial Equality* (New York: Oxford University Press, 2004), 3–24, 143–205.

50. The Court created important new protections for criminal defendants in the era, including *Griffin v. Illinois*, 351 U.S. 12 (1956) and *Mapp v. Ohio*, 367 U.S. 643 (1961). The Court also incorporated the Eighth Amendment against the states in 1962. See *Robinson v. California*, 370 U.S. 660 (1962). On the Court's "Due Process revolution," see Fred P. Graham, *The Due Process Revolution: The Warren Court's Impact on Criminal Law* (Ann Arbor: University of Michigan Press, 1970); Sarah Seo, *Policing the Open Road: How Cars Transformed American Freedom* (Cambridge, MA: Harvard University Press, 2019), 62–108. For the text of the Due Process Clause: U.S. Const. amend. XIV.

51. "Proposal to Relax Kansas Abortion Law Dies in Committee," *Catholic News Service,* March 25, 1963, 8. For an example of a similar claim, see Mr. and Mrs. Eugene Forney to Anthony Beilenson (May 28, 1967), ABP, Box 520, Folder 3 ("We strive to give even the hardened criminal a just trial and every chance for this right to life, and yet you would deny this basic right to the innocent baby?").

52. *Gideon v. Wainwright*, 372 U.S. 335, 342 (1963). On the growth of public defenders' offices, see Sara Mayeux, "What *Gideon* Did," *Columbia Law Review* 116 (2016): 15–45; Jonathan Rapping, *Gideon's Promise: A Public Defender Movement to Transform Criminal Justice* (Boston: Beacon, 2020), 20–45. For the Court's decisions on protection from self-incrimination, see *Malloy v. Hogan*, 378 U.S. 1 (1964); *Miranda v. Arizona*, 384 U.S. 436 (1966).

53. June Peters, "Episcopalian Pleads for Legal Abortion," *Sacramento Bee*, October 14, 1966, B1 (CA); "Local Vicar Raps 'Cynical Disposal' of Abortion Law," *Salinas Californian*, June 5, 1965, 18 (Salinas, California); see also Transcript of Hearings on the Humane Abortion Act, Assembly Interim Committee on Criminal Procedure (September 29, 1964), ABP, Box 509, Abortion Interim Assembly Folder.

54. Anthony Beilenson to Dorothy Zoller (November 16, 1965), ABP, Box 514, Folder 1. For Kinsolving's statement: Lester Kinsolving to California Committee on Therapeutic Abortion Board of Directors (September 28, 1966), CCTA, Box 1, Folder 9. For similar arguments, see Mrs. M. S. Engen to Anthony Beilenson (February 15, 1967), ABP, Box 580, Folder 3 (complaining that criminal abortion laws were founded on "basically religious premises"). For a later version of this argument, see Rossi, "Abortion Laws," 1 (arguing that the Catholic Church should "be free to characterize abortion as a sin if it sees fit" but should not be able to stop the "rest of society" from choosing to "enjoy the right to control their own reproductive lives").

55. On the growing support of mainline Protestants, see Williams, *Defenders of the Unborn*, 79–80; Kerry N. Jacoby, *Souls, Bodies, Spirits: The Drive to Abolish Abortion since 1973* (Westport, CT: Praeger, 1998), 3. On the support for reform among liberal Jewish clergy, see Williams, *Defenders of the Unborn*, 67-69; "Jewish Women Urge Eased Moral Laws," *New York Times*, November 19, 1965, 15; Dorothy Townsend, "Needs of Times Called Aim of Reform Jewry," *Los Angeles Times*, December 4, 1965, B8.

56. William J. Kenealy, "Law and Morals," *Catholic Lawyer* 9 (1963): 201–202, 207–209. For earlier drafts of the piece, see Typescript, "Law and Morals," WKP, Box 7, Folder 1.

57. Kenealy, "Law and Morals," 209.

58. For the Court's decisions in *Meyer* and *Pierce*, see *Meyer v. Nebraska*, 262 U.S. 390 (1923); *Pierce v. Society of Sisters*, 268 U.S. 510 (1925). For the Court's decision in *Lochner*, see *Lochner v. New York,* 198 U.S. 45 (1905). On shifting opinion on *Lochner*, see Victoria Nourse, "A Tale of Two *Lochners:* The Untold History of Substantive Due Process and the Idea of Fundamental Rights," *California Law Review* 97 (2009): 751–773; David Bernstein, *Rehabilitating* Lochner: *Defending Individual Rights against Progressive Reform* (Chicago: University of Chicago Press, 2011), 8–18.

59. On Jaffa and declarationism, Kenneth I. Kersch, *Conservatives and the Constitution: Imagining Constitutional Restoration in the Heyday of American Liberalism* (New York: Cambridge University Press, 2019), 55–70; Jefferson Decker, *The Other Rights Revolution: Conservative Lawyers and the Remaking of the American Government* (New York: Oxford University Press, 2016), 87. For Murray's analysis, see John Courtney Murray, *We Hold These Truths: Catholic Reflections on the American Proposition* (Lanham, MD: Rowman and Littlefield, 2005), 28, 31–32, 36, 96, 106–107 (originally published by Sheed and Ward in 1960). For Kenealy's statement: Kenealy, "Law and Morals," 209.

60. Norman St. John-Stevas, "The Right to Life—The Abortion Dilemma," *Gonzaga Law Review* 4 (1968): 5. For Stevas's book, see Norman St. John-Stevas, *The Right to Life* (Ann Arbor: University of Michigan Press, 1964).

61. On Stevas's quirks and accomplishments, see Michael White, "Lord St. John of Fawsley, a 'One-Off' Character," *Guardian*, March 5, 2012, https://www.theguardian.com/politics/2012/mar/05/lord-st-john-fawsley-character. For examples of right-to-life arguments from the period: Esther Boyer to Anthony Beilenson (May 9, 1967), ABP, Box 380, Folder 3 ("These as yet unborn children have rights, the most important, the right to life"); Leo Landry to Anthony Beilenson (May 7, 1967), ABP, Box 520, Folder 3 ("Every unborn child has a right to life"); Mr. and Mrs. Donald Burke to Anthony Beilenson (May 7, 1967), ABP, Box 520, Folder 3 ("The Bill of Rights . . . guarantees the right to life").

62. On spending on contraception, see Carole Ruth McCann, *Birth Control Politics in the United States, 1916–1945* (Ithaca: Cornell University Press, 1999), 71. On FDA approval of the birth control pill and its influence, see Elaine Tyler May, *America and the Pill: A History of Promise, Peril, and Liberation* (New York: Basic Books, 2011), 1–32; Gordon, *The Moral Property of Women*, 286–324. For the Court's decision in *Poe*, see *Poe v. Ullman*, 367 U.S. 497 (1961).

63. Brief for the Catholic Council on Civil Liberties as Amicus Curie at 7–19, *Griswold v. Connecticut*, 381 U.S. 479 (1965) (No. 64-496); see also "Catholic Group Raises Right to Privacy Issue," *Transcript-Telegram*, February 16, 1965, 16 (Holyoke, MA). On the history of *Griswold*, see Reva B. Siegel, "*Griswold* at 50: How Conflict Entrenched a Right to Privacy," *Yale Law Journal Forum* 124 (2015): 318–322; Garrow, *Liberty and Sexuality*, 132–172; Stone, *Sex and the Constitution*, 338–352.

64. *Griswold v. Connecticut*, 389 U.S. 479, 481–486 (1965).

65. Chapter 2 discusses the formation of a secular, state-by-state grassroots anti-abortion movement.

66. See Gold et al., "Therapeutic Abortions," 965; Tietze, "Mortality," 6; Fisher, "Criminal Abortion," 9. For arguments made by the ASA, see Association for the Study of Abortion, Press Release (March 31, 1966), RPS, Carton 1, Folder 10; "Medical Societies Call for Reform," *ASA Newsletter*, 8, PMC, Box 114, Folder 2044. For ASA's statement on its purpose: Press Release, "Association for Humane Abortion Launches Program" (February 18, 1965), RPS, Carton 1, Folder 10.

67. Rossi, "Abortion Laws," 3. For more on Rossi's life, see Margalit Fox, "Alice Rossi, Sociologist and Feminist Scholar, Dies at 87," *New York Times*, November 7, 2009, https://www.nytimes.com/2009/11/08/us/08rossi.html; Elaine Woo, "Obituary: Alice Rossi, 1922–2009," *Los Angeles Times*, November 15, 2009, https://www.latimes.com/archives/la-xpm-2009-nov-15-me-alice-rossi15-story.html. For Guttmacher's comment: Alan Guttmacher, Speech on Race and Abortion (April 21, 1965), AGP, Box 1, Folder 17; see also Murial Dobbin, "2 Ask Action on Abortion," *Baltimore Sun*, August 11, 1965, 8.

68. Pat Maginnis, President of the Citizens Committee for Humane Abortion Laws, "Testimony," Citizens Committee for Humane Abortion Laws Newsletter (January 1963), 1, CCHA, Box 1, Folder 1.

69. Citizens Committee for Humane Abortion Laws Resolution, Citizens Committee for Humane Abortion Laws Newsletter (December 1964), CCHA, Box 1, Folder 1.

70. On Robert Byrn and his family, see "Lawyer Fights Abortions, Calls for 'Fetal Power,'" *Hartford Courant*, November 7, 1968, 17 (CT); "Irishman Leads Anti-Abortion Campaign in New York," *Irish Times*, December 21, 1970, 13 (Dublin); Judy

Klemesrud, "He's the Legal Guardian for the Fetuses about to Be Aborted," *New York Times*, December 17, 1971, 48; Joseph Sweeney, "Professor Robert Byrn: A Remembrance," *Fordham Law Review* 85 (2017): 2549–2550.

71. Robert Byrn, "Abortion in Perspective," *Duquesne Law Review* 5 (1966): 132; see also John T. Noonan, "An Almost Absolute Value in History," in *The Morality of Abortion: Legal and Historical Perspectives,* ed. John T. Noonan (Cambridge, MA: Harvard University Press, 1970), 51–59.

72. On the changing politics of race in the mid-1960s, see Gary May, *Bending toward Justice: The Voting Rights Act and the Transformation of American Democracy* (New York: Basic Books, 2013), 3–25; Brown-Nagin, *Courage to Dissent*, 135, 230–247; Risa Goluboff, *The Lost Promise of Civil Rights* (Cambridge, MA: Harvard University Press, 2009), 250–264. On the centrality of "like race" arguments for the early women's movement, see Serena Mayeri, *Reasoning from Race: Feminism, Law, and the Civil Rights Revolution* (Cambridge, MA: Harvard University Press, 2011). Chapter 2 further discusses these developments. For the Court's decision in *McLaughlin*, see *McLaughlin v. Florida*, 379 U.S. 184, 191–192 (1964).

73. Byrn, "Abortion in Perspective," 132–134.

74. The Court later explained that the justices interpreted the Equal Protection Clause as a "direction that all persons similarly situated should be treated alike." *City of Cleburne v. Cleburne Living Center*, 473 U.S. 432, 439 (1985) (citation omitted).

75. Byrn, "Abortion in Perspective," 133. For similar arguments of this kind, see Pamphlet, "The Right of the Fetus to Be Born" (n.d., ca. 1965), PMC, Box 114, Folder 2045 (arguing that legalizing abortion would "create a revolutionary hierarchy of rights in which the rights of the living to happiness transcend the rights of the unborn to existence").

2. Individualizing the Fetus

1. On Tomshany's political career and work with Reagan, see "Teague Given Little Chance to Beat Hanna," *Los Angeles Times*, October 11, 1968, 3; "GOP Couples Hear Work Outlined," *Chino Companion*, October 15, 1964, 11 (CA); Karen Tumulty, *The Triumph of Nancy Reagan* (New York: Simon and Schuster, 2022), 140. On Tomshany's involvement in the Right to Life League, see Dave Tomshany, Letter to Potential Member (1967), ABP, Box 510, Folder 16; Dave Tomshany, Right to Life League of Southern California Press Release (1967), ABP, Box 510, Folder 16.

2. On the early operations of the Right to Life League, see "Right to Life," *Tidings*, March 3, 1967, 1 (Los Angeles); "Anti-Abortion Group Readies State Campaign," *San Francisco Examiner*, April 18, 1967, 3; "League Asks Legislature to Ban

Abortion," *Tidings*, March 24, 1967, 1 (Los Angeles). For further analysis of the Right to Life League, see Daniel K. Williams, *Defenders of the Unborn: The Pro-Life Movement Before* Roe v. Wade (New York: Oxford University Press, 2016), 79–84, 179–183.

3. For Reagan's statement: "Obey or Get Out: Reagan," *San Francisco Chronicle*, December 3, 1966, 3.

4. For a sample of equality arguments from this period, see Robert Byrn, "Abortion on Demand: Whose Morality?" *Notre Dame Lawyer* 26 (1970): 28; Pamphlet, "His Right to Life" (n.d., ca. 1967), ABP, Box 510, Folder 16; Pamphlet, Mary Ann Williams, "Abortion: A Collision of Rights" (1972), NARAL, Box 49, Folder 5. For a later version of this argument, see Pro-Life Model Letter to Congress (March 22, 1973), NARAL, Box 49, Folder 6 (arguing that *Roe* had created a "classification based on the quality, stage of development, or the 'meaningfulness'" of the life of the fetus).

5. For an example of the campaigns mounted by the league, consider the letters sent to the California legislature. See Anne Brillz to Anthony Beilenson (March 30, 1967), ABP, Box 510, Folder 16; Margaret Gallagher to Anthony Beilenson (March 30, 1967), ABP, Box 510, Folder 16; Maria White to Anthony Beilenson (March 30, 1967), ABP, Box 510, Folder 16.

6. "Catholic Group Opposes Change in Abortion Law," *Danville Register,* October 21, 1967, 3 (VA); "Trojan Defends Abortion Law, Heads Right to Life," *Troy Record,* January 26, 1967, 1 (NY); "Two Abortion Bill Foes," *San Francisco Examiner*, April 20, 1967, 30.

7. On illegal abortions and mortality in the period, see Willard Cates Jr. and Roger Rochat, "Illegal Abortions in the United States, 1972–1974," *Family Planning Perspectives* 8 (1976): 87. On the limits of reform laws, Keith Monroe, "How California's Abortion Law Isn't Working," *New York Times*, December 29, 1968, SM12; Robert McFadden, "Flaws in Abortion Reform Found in an 8-State Study," *New York Times*, April 13, 1970, 1.

8. Katherine Turk, *The Women of NOW: How Feminists Built an Organization That Transformed America* (New York: Farrar, Straus and Giroux, 2023), 4–21. For more on NOW, see Maryann Barasko, *Governing NOW: Grassroots Activism in the National Organization for Women* (Ithaca: Cornell University Press, 2004), 11–39; Sara Evans, *Tidal Wave: How Women Changed America at Century's End* (New York: Free Press, 2004). For Friedan's book, see Betty Friedan, *The Feminine Mystique* (New York: Norton, 1963). For the resolution debated, see NOW Proposed Resolution, "The Right of a Woman to Determine Her Own Reproductive Process" (1967), BFP, Carton 127, Folder 1553. For more discussion of the NOW debate and early feminist arguments for legal abortion, see Reva B. Siegel and Linda Greenhouse, eds., *Before*

Roe v. Wade: Voices That Shaped the Abortion Debate before the Supreme Court's Ruling (New York: Kaplan, 2010), 36, 42–56.

9. Ti-Grace Atkinson, "Refutation of Catholic Position on Abortion" (1967), NOW, Box 3, Folder 23. For the statement of Abolish All Abortion Laws: Abolish All Abortion Laws (September 18, 1973), CCTA, Box 1, Folder 4; see also Clipping, Herman Schwartz, "Abortion and the Law," (n.d., ca. 1966), PMC, Box 114, Folder 2043 (arguing that the fetus was not a person because personhood required an entity "to be a rational creature, with emotions, feelings, intellect, and a personality").

10. John Kaplan, "Segregation Litigation and the Schools—Part II: The General Northern Problem," *Northwestern University Law Review* 58 (1964): 173–188. For Wisdom's statement: *United States v. Jefferson County Board of Education*, 372 F.2d 836, 875 (5th Cir. 1966). For more on the emergence of this anti-classification view of equality, see Reva B. Siegel, "Equality Talk: Antisubordination and Anticlassification Principles in Struggles over *Brown*," *Harvard Law Review* 117 (2004): 1470–1532. For the Court's decisions in *Brown and Loving*, see *Loving v. Virginia*, 388 U.S. 1, 12 (1967); *Brown v. Board of Education*, 347 U.S. 483 (1954).

11. Pamphlet, "His Right to Life" (n.d., ca. 1967), ABP, Box 510, Folder 16. For more equal protection arguments of this kind, see "Liberalized Abortions Hit by Prof," *Los Angeles Evening Citizen News*, July 8, 1969, 11 (Professor David Louisell arguing that legal abortion conflicted with "the legal norms crystallized in the constitutional mandates of equal protection and due process of law"); Gerard Weidmann, "The Case against Abortion: Life Not Expendable," *Boston Globe*, February 26, 1970, 14.

12. Right to Life League of Southern California, "Strategies, Cruxes, and Main Persuasions for Defeating Beilenson-Type Bills for Liberalizing Abortion Bills," 1–3 (n.d., ca. 1967), ABP, Box 510, Folder 16. For the statement about marriage: Paul and Catherine Beals to Anthony Beilenson (March 28, 1967), ABP, Box 520, Folder 3. For more on the personhood arguments of the era, see Right to Life League of Southern California, Press Release (April 1967), ABP, Box 510, Folder 16; Pamphlet, "The Right to Life League Believes . . ." (n.d., ca. 1967), ABP, Box 510, Folder 16; Walter Trinkaus to Whom It May Concern (November 7, 1966), ABP, Box 510, Folder 16. On the patient population seeking abortion, see Centers for Disease Control, *Abortion Surveillance: Annual Summary 1972* (Washington, DC: Department of Health, Education, and Welfare, 1974), 4; "Legal Abortions: Morbidity and Mortality—1970," *Morbidity and Mortality* 20 (1971): 412–413, 418.

13. Rev. John S. McLaughlin, SJ, "Abortion, the Law, and Society," *Tampa Times*, April 6, 1968, 6 (FL); see also Jo-Ann Albers, "Couple Considers Abortion Killing," *Cincinnati Enquirer*, March 19, 1971, 25 (OH); Ed Scherer, "Why Committee Members Voted 'No' on Abortion, *Tallahassee Democrat*, April 28, 1970, 5 (FL). For the

statement on "modern scientific evidence": Right to Life League of Southern California, "Strategies," 2.

14. Strategy Meeting on Abortion (June 23, 1966), CCR, Box 94, Folder 15; see also Meeting of the Standing Committee of Directors of the Catholic Charities (June 28, 1966), CCR, Box 94, Folder 15 ("We must stress the absolute value of human life").

15. "Catholic Lawyers Urged to Fight Abortion," *Catholic News Services*, April 25, 1967, 2. For McHugh's statement about dignity and equality: James McHugh, "Report on Abortion Questionnaire" (n.d., ca. 1966), CCR, Box 94, Folder 15.

16. On the formation and early operation of the NRLC, see Williams, *Defenders of the Unborn*, 94–99, 176–182; Mary Ziegler, *After Roe: The Lost History of the Abortion Debate* (Cambridge, MA: Harvard University Press, 2015), 76-82; Patricia Miller, *Good Catholics: The Battle over Abortion in the Catholic Church* (Berkeley: University of California Press, 2011), 46–83. On Ryan: "Obstructing Officer Brings Pair Fines," *Courier News*, August 8, 1963, 4 (Bridgewater, NJ); see also "Traffic No Hazard, Says Apartment Planner," *Chatham Press*, December 22, 1966, 1 (NJ).

17. On Marjory and Fred Mecklenburg's background, see "4-Hers Spend Most of Evening on Their Feet," *Star Tribune*, August 29, 1952, 11 (Minneapolis); "Fair Plays Host to Editors, Legislators," *Minneapolis Star*, August 29, 1952, 17; "South St. Paul Wins High School Debate Tourney," *Star Tribune*, March 8, 1953, 33 (Minneapolis).

18. "Priest, Attorney Split on Abortion," *Fort Lauderdale News*, August 8, 1967, 8 (FL); see also Robert Riley, "Key Abortion Question: Who Decides?" *Honolulu Advertiser*, February 13, 1969, 3 (HI). For other arguments from the period about rape, see Rev. Gerald Niklas to Dr. John Willke (March 15, 1963), JWC, Sex Education Folders (Willke taking the position that "if a girl was raped, she could not do anything to remove the male semen").

19. "Lawyer Fights Abortions, Calls for 'Fetal Power,'" *Hartford Courant*, November 7, 1968, 17 (CT). On the formation of right-to-life leagues in various states, "Non-Sectarian 'Right to Life' Committee Formed in Casper," *Casper Star-Tribune*, August 16, 1970, 3 (WY); "'Right to Life' Stressed," *Birmingham Post-Herald*, December 3, 1971, 6 (AL); "Abortion Issue Draws Church into Politics," *Daily Journal*, September 10, 1971, 4 (Vineland, NJ); "Salt Lakers Debate Sterilization, Abortion," *Daily Herald*, January 24, 1969, 12 (Salt Lake City). For discussion of Byrn's reputation at Fordham, see "Faculty Profile: Professor Robert A. Byrn," *Fordham Law School Advocate*, November 6, 1968, 3.

20. Gene Roberts, "Mississippi Reduces Police Protection for Marchers," *New York Times*, June 17, 1966, https://www.nytimes.com/1966/06/17/archives/mississippi-reduces-police-protection-for-marchers-mississippi-cuts.html.

21. "Black Supremacists," *Washington Post*, May 29, 1966, E6. On persistent poverty in the Black community, see Drew Desilver, "Who's Poor in America? 50 Years into the 'War on Poverty,' a Data Portrait," *Pew Forum*, January 13, 2014, https://www.pewresearch.org/short-reads/2014/01/13/whos-poor-in-america-50-years-into-the-war-on-poverty-a-data-portrait/#:~:text=Poverty%20among%20blacks%20has%20fallen,%25)%20of%20all%20poor%20Americans.

22. Martin Luther King Jr., "Beyond Vietnam—A Time to Break the Silence," in *A Time to Break the Silence: The Essential Works of Martin Luther King Jr., for Students* (Boston: Beacon, 2013), 79–99.

23. On the Poor People's Campaign, see Sylvie Laurent, *King and the Other America: The Poor People's Campaign and the Quest for Economic Equality* (Berkeley: University of California Press, 2019); Gary Dorrien, *Breaking White Supremacy: Martin Luther King Jr. and the Black Social Gospel* (New Haven: Yale University Press, 2018), 267–268. On the divide between local civil-rights activists and the NAACP, see Tomiko Brown-Nagin, *Courage to Dissent: Atlanta and the Long History of the Civil Rights Movement* (New York: Oxford University Press, 2011), 447. On debates about race and equality in the courts and among scholars, see Siegel, "Equality Talk," 1469–1483. For King's statement: Martin Luther King Jr., "The American Negro: A Bill of Rights for the Disadvantaged," *New York Times*, November 12, 1967, E11.

24. On the causes and impact of the uprisings of the 1960s, see Elizabeth Hinton, *America on Fire: The Untold History of Police Violence and Black Rebellion since the 1960s* (New York: Liveright, 2021), 5–31; Michael Flamm, *In the Heat of the Summer: The New York Riots of 1964 and the War on Crime* (Philadelphia: University of Pennsylvania Press, 2017), 1–29, 287–297; Patricia Sullivan, *Justice Rising: Robert Kennedy's America in Black and White* (Cambridge, MA: Harvard University Press, 2021), 2–19. On polls about the uprisings, see Hazel Erskine, "The Polls: Demonstrations and Race Riots," *Public Opinion Quarterly* 31 (1968): 655–677.

25. Florynce Kennedy, Rough Draft, "Black Genocide? Black Community and Third World People Shun the Struggle" (n.d., ca. 1969), FKP, Box 17, Folder 9; National Lawyers Guild, "Abortion Rap" (1969), FKP, Box 17, Folder 9; see also Frances Beal, "Double Jeopardy: To Be Black and Female," in *The Black Woman,* ed. Toni Cade Bambara (New York: Signet, 1970), 93–99. For more on the role of feminists of color in the early movement to legalize abortion, see Melissa Murray, "Race-ing *Roe*: Reproductive Justice, Racial Justice, and the Battle for *Roe v. Wade*," *Harvard Law Review* 124 (2021): 2027–2101; Loretta Ross, "African-Americans and Abortion," in *Abortion Wars: A Half-Century of Struggle, 1950–2000*, ed. Rickie Solinger (Berkeley:

University of California Press, 1998), 180–182; Jennifer Nelson, *Women of Color and the Reproductive Rights Movement* (New York: New York University Press, 2003), 77–90. For an overview of polls in the Black community in the early 1970s, see Michael Coombs and Susan Welch, "Blacks, Whites, and Attitudes toward Abortion," *Public Opinion Quarterly* 46 (1982): 510–520; see also William Darity and Castellano Turner, "Fears of Genocide among Black Americans as Related to Age, Sex, and Region," *American Journal of Public Health* 63 (1973): 1029.

26. Hugh Moore to Ruth Proskauer Smith (October 19, 1962), HMP, Box 16, Folder 6. For more on AVS and its eugenic connections, see Wendy Kline, *Building a Better Race: Gender, Sexuality, and Eugenics from the Turn of the Century to the Baby Boom* (Berkeley: University of California Press, 2005), 176–192; Rebecca Kluchin, *Fit to Be Tied: Sterilization and Reproductive Rights in America, 1950–1980* (New Brunswick: Rutgers University Press, 2009), 35–42, 92–134, 142–160. On the decline of open discussion of eugenics, see Daniel J. Kevles, *In the Name of Eugenics: Genetics and the Uses of Human Heredity* (New York: Knopf, 1985), 164, 168; Celeste Michelle Condit, *The Meanings of the Gene: Public Debates about Human Heredity* (Madison: University of Wisconsin Press, 1998), 64–69. For a copy of the charter of the Population Council: John D. Rockefeller III, "On the Origins of the Population Council," *Population and Development Review* 3 (1977): 496, 502. For more on Osborn's role in both the eugenics and population control movements, see Frederick Osborn, "A History of the American Eugenics Society" (1971), AESR, Box 17, History of the American Eugenics Society Folder 1; Frederick Osborn, "Major Aspects of Eugenic Selection" (1936), AESR, Box 17, Frederick Osborn Folder 4.

27. Edith Evans Asbury, "Women Break Up Abortion Hearing," *New York Times*, February 14, 1969, 42. For more on radical feminists and their advocacy for legalization, see Flora Davis, *Moving the Mountain: The Women's Movement in America since the 1960s* (Champaign: University of Illinois Press, 1999), 134–165; Felicia Kornbluh, *A Woman's Life Is a Human Life: My Mother, Our Neighbor, and the Journey from Reproductive Rights to Reproductive Justice* (New York: Grove, 2023), 23–54, 101–145. On the population control movement, see Donald Critchlow, *Intended Consequences: Birth Control, Abortion, and the Federal Government in Modern America* (New York: Oxford University Press, 1999), 3–19; Matthew Connelly, *Fatal Misconception: The Struggle to Control World Population* (Cambridge, MA: Harvard University Press, 2008), 134–151; Kluchin, *Fit to Be Tied*, 79–87.

28. Planned Parenthood, Pamphlet, "Facts and Figures on Abortion of Interest to All Americans" (1972), PPFA II, Box 93, Folder 84; see also NARAL Speaker and Debater's Notebook Excerpt (n.d., ca. 1972), NARAL, Carton 7, Debating the

Opposition Folder. On debates about abortion in the Black community, see Murray, "Race-ing *Roe*," 2041–2070; Nelson, *Women of Color*, 79–89.

29. For the statement about "'rights' to a few": "November 5, 1968 Election: Vote for James Buckley," *Journal News*, November 4, 1968, 19 (Westchester, NY). Buckley nevertheless urged his party not to back George Wallace's presidential bid, calling Wallace "a symbol of racism." Edward Benes, "Step Aside for Minorities, O'Dwyer Urges Delegates," *New York Daily News*, July 8, 1968, 22. On Buckley's statement about "condescending": Pam Bishop, "Scrap HEW, Return Authority to Localities," *Star Gazette*, September 28, 1968, 16 (Elmira, NY). On Rice's involvement with the Conservative Party, see Patrick Allitt, *Catholic Intellectuals and Conservative Politics in America, 1950–1985* (Ithaca: Cornell University Press, 2019), 183–190. On the role of whiteness in the antiabortion movement, see Jennifer Holland, *Tiny You: A Western History of the Anti-Abortion Movement* (Berkeley: University of California Press, 2020), 3–33. For more on the Conservative Party's positions on race and civil rights, see Timothy Sullivan, *New York State and the Rise of Modern Conservatism* (Buffalo: State University of New York Press, 2009), 58–64, 112–115. For Buckley's statement about civil disorders: Tom Cawley, "Conservative Buckley Visits City, Hits Javits," *Press and Sun Bulletin*, September 3, 1968, 2 (Binghamton, NY).

30. See "Fulton County Democratic Women Accelerate Pace of Campaigning," *Atlanta Constitution*, October 22, 1960, 17; Mrs. Ferdinand Buckley, "Write in Arnall," *Atlanta Constitution*, October 21, 1966, 4; "House Seat Is Sought by Buckley," *Atlanta Constitution*, March 29, 1965, 7; "Lawyers Club Bars Negro Attorneys," *Atlanta Constitution*, May 9, 1969, 6.

31. "State MDs Back Wide Abortion Reform," *Newsday*, February 13, 1969, 3 (New York). On the pamphlet: Pamphlet, Abortion and the Law (n.d., ca. 1967), CCR, Box 94, Folder 16; see also Pamphlet, "The Humanness of the Fetus: A Question of Fact or Morality?" (n.d., ca. 1967), NARAL, Box 49, Folder 5 (describing every abortion as the "decision to kill an individual, unique human baby"); "Time Has Come to Recall the Sacredness of Life," *Southwest Kansas Register*, March 9, 1967, 4 (Dodge City) (Minnesota bishops stressing equality claims based on the argument that the fetus was an "individual, a unique personality"); "Letter to the Editor," *Newsday*, March 4, 1969, 5B (New York) (describing the abortion issue as a struggle pitting the equality of the individual against the state).

32. See Michael Grossberg, *Governing the Hearth: Law and the Family in Nineteenth-Century America* (Chapel Hill: University of North Carolina Press, 1985), 169–200.

33. On the wide variety of arguments against illegitimacy discrimination, see Serena Mayeri, "Marital Supremacy and the Constitution of the Nonmarital Family,"

California Law Review 103 (2015): 1286–1300, 1310–1323. For the polls: George Gallup, "Illegitimacy Support Opposed by Majority," *Washington Post*, January 27, 1965, 2; see also "Would Curb Aid to Unwed Mothers Who Repeat," *Des Moines Register*, January 27, 1965, 5 (IA).

34. See Petition for Damages Due to Malpractice on Behalf of Levy (La. Civ. Dist. Ct. for Orleans, Dec. 16, 1964), reprinted in Appendix at 5, *Levy v. Louisiana*, 391 U.S. 68 (1968) (No. 508); Mayeri, "Marital Supremacy," 1290–1291. On the 1960 Louisiana law, see Ellen Reese, *Backlash against Welfare Mothers: Past and Present* (Berkeley: University of California Press, 2005), 32–44, 45-47.

35. *Levy v. Louisiana*, 391 U.S. 68, 71–72 (1968). For the Court's decision in *Glona*, see *Glona v. American Guarantee & Liability Insurance Company*, 391 U.S. 73 (1968).

36. Robert Byrn, "Demythologizing Abortion Reform," *Catholic Lawyer* 14 (1968): 183.

37. See Ziegler, *After* Roe, 285–296; Karissa Haugeberg, *Women against Abortion: Inside the Largest Moral Reform Movement of the Twentieth Century* (Urbana: University of Illinois Press, 2017), 25–33. For an example of Mecklenburg's early work on illegitimacy, see Resolution #4 (June 1974), ACCL, Box 8, 1974 NRLC Executive Committee Folder.

38. Charles Rice, *The Vanishing Right to Live: An Appeal for a Renewed Reverence for Life* (New York: Doubleday, 1969), 120–130; see also Frank Ayd Jr., "Liberal Abortion Laws," *America*, February 1, 1969, 130–132; "Respect for Life," *Thousand Oaks Star,* June 2, 1970, 10 (CA) ("What better way to destroy the home as a basic unit of a healthy society than further to promote promiscuity, with abortion as the panacea to correct 'mistakes'?"); John T. Noonan Jr., "The Family and the Supreme Court," *Catholic University Law Review* 23 (1973): 258.

39. Daniel K. Williams, "The GOP's Abortion Strategy: Why Pro-Choice Republicans Became Pro-Life in the 1970s," *Journal of Policy History* 23 (2011): 515–520; William Prendergast, *The Catholic Voter in American Politics: The Passing of the Democratic Monolith* (Washington, DC: Georgetown University Press, 1999), 155–159, 177–194.

40. On divisions within the Democratic Party about abortion, see Mary Ziegler, *Dollars for Life: The Anti-Abortion Movement and the Fall of the Republican Establishment* (New Haven: Yale University Press, 2022), 40–42; Williams, *Defenders of the Unborn*, 8, 129–132, 151–153, 221–239; Stacie Taranto, *Kitchen Table Politics: Conservative Women and Family Values in New York* (Philadelphia: University of Pennsylvania Press, 2017), 129–152.

41. *People v. Belous*, 458 P.2d 194, 199 (Cal. 1969). On reaction to *Belous*, see Williams, *Defenders of the Unborn*, 116–119, 195; David Garrow, *Liberty and Sexuality: The*

Right to Privacy and the Making of Roe v. Wade (Berkeley: University of California Press, 1998), 232–239. For contemporary discussion of *Belous*, see Howard Hassard and David Willett, "Abortion Supreme Court Decision under Former Law Sheds Some Light on Conduct under Amended Act," *California Medicine* (1969), CCTA, Box 1, Folder 1; California Committee on Therapeutic Abortion, Memo re. *People v. Belous* (1969), CCTA, Box 1, Folder 1.

42. On repeal in Hawaii, see George Zucker, "Hawaii Governor Says Abortion Is 'Grave Sin' but Refuses to Veto Law," *Palo Alto Times*, March 12, 1970, 3 (CA); "Hawaii Near Legalized Abortion," *Press Democrat*, February 12, 1970, 8 (Santa Rosa, CA). On the New York commission and repeal push, see "Right to Life Group Chides Liberal Abortion Commission," *Record*, December 23, 1968, 3 (Hackensack, NJ). For the commission's report, see Majority Report and Recommendations of the Governor's Commission Appointed to Study the State's Abortion Law (March 25, 1968), AMR Box 3, Folder 1; Minority Report of Robert M. Byrn, John Grant Harrison, and Monsignor William F. McManus (March 25, 1968), AMR Box 3, Folder 1. For the statement of the California advocate: Keith Russell to Signers of the Physicians Brief, *People v. Belous* (October 28, 1969), CCTA, Box 1, Folder 1.

43. See "Dennis Horan: Lawyer and Author," *New York Times*, May 3, 1988, D29; Eugene Diamond, "Eulogy Given at the Funeral of Dennis Horan," *Linacre Quarterly* 55 (1988): 4–5; Clarke Forsythe, "The Legacy of Dennis Horan, Jr. for Protecting Human Life," Americans United for Life, May 2, 2013, https://aul.org/2013/05/02/the-legal-legacy-of-dennis-horan/. For Horan's argument: Brief and Appendices in Support of Dr. Bart Heffernan in Support of Appellant, 7–27, *United States v. Vuitch*, 402 U.S. 62 (1971) (No. 84).

44. Motion for Leave to File a Brief and Brief Amicus Curiae of Ferdinand Buckley, iii, *Roe v. Wade*, 410 U.S. 113 (1973) (Nos. 70-18, 70-40); see also Martin McKernan, NRLC Legal Counsel, "Legal Report: Court Cases" (July 1970), 3–4, ACCL, Box 4, 1970 National Right to Life Meeting Folder. For the district court's decision in *Vuitch*, see *United States v. Vuitch*, 305 F. Supp. 1032, 1033–1036 (D.D.C. 1969). For Horan's statement: Brief and Appendices, 10.

45. Motion of Appellant Bart Heffernan to Consolidate and Brief in Support, 9–10, *Heffernan v. Doe*, 321 F. Supp. 1385 (N.D. Ill. 1971) (No. 70-106); see also Women for Life, "Slavery and Abortion" (n.d., ca. 1970), NARAL, Box 49, Folder 5 ("Will the unborn baby be the next *Dred Scott?* Or will our country use its great resources to protect every life, black and white, rich and poor, woman and man, unborn and octogenarian?"). For more on Horan's work in the era, see "Anti-Abortion Seminar Held," *Stickney Life and Forest View*, February 7, 1971, 14 (Berwyn, IL);

"Expect High Court to Overturn Abortion Ruling," *Elk Grove Herald*, February 5, 1971, 5 (IL).

46. On Horan's guardianship bid, see "Unborn Appeal to Supreme Court," *Belleville News-Democrat*, September 18, 1970, 4 (IL); Glen Elsasser, "Court May Act on Stay of Abortions," *Chicago Tribune*, February 17, 1971, 17; "Guardian of Unborn Tells How He Attained Unique Court Role," *Chicago Tribune*, February 15, 1971, 22. On the spread of ultrasound images, see Dr. John Willke to Whom It May Concern (n.d., ca. 1972), NARAL, Box 49, Folder 5 (describing the use of a "pic pack" in anti-abortion litigation).

47. See "Outcome of N.Y. Abortion Showdown May Affect Entire U.S.," *Montreal Star*, January 10, 1973, 10; Jim Murray, "Edward J. Golden: A Determined Man," *Troy Record*, December 26, 1972, 11 (NY); Thomas Poster, "Set Abortion Debate Tomorrow," *New York Daily News*, May 4, 1972, 34.

48. "2,000 Rally for Abort Repeal," *New York Daily News*, April 28, 1971, 9; see also Fred C. Shapiro, " 'Right to Life' Has Message for New York Legislators," *New York Times*, August 20, 1972, SM10.

49. "Priest Says Abortion Foe Is Guilty of 'Smear,' " *Minneapolis Star*, April 3, 1971, 19.

50. Byrn, "Abortion on Demand," 28. For Byrn's statement that a fetus was a client: "Lawyer Fights Abortions," 17. For examples of related arguments, Pamphlet, Manhattan Right to Life, Abortion and Morality (n.d., ca. 1970), NARAL, Box 49, Folder 5 ("The concepts of equality and freedom, so basic to our way of life, are fundamentally incompatible with the new morality of pro-abortionism"). For Kirk's statement: Russell Kirk, "Abortions Arousing Public," *Palladium-Item*, June 9, 1971, 14 (Richmond, IN).

51. For McCabe's statement: "Busing Protestors Don't Like District," *Weirton Daily Times*, April 4, 1972, 1 (Steubenville, OH). For Nixon's statement: "Text of Nixon Statement," *New York Times*, August 4, 1971, 15. For more on opposition to busing, see Matthew Delmont, *Why Busing Failed: Race, Media, and the National Resistance to School Desegregation* (Berkeley: University of California Press, 2016), 3–18; Ronald P. Formisano, *Boston against Busing: Race, Class, and Ethnicity in the 1960s and 1970s,* 2nd ed. (Chapel Hill: University of North Carolina Press, 2004), 3–15.

52. Nathan Glazer, " 'Reverse Racism': Leaning over Backwards," *New York Times*, March 12, 1972, E3; Richard M. Nixon, "Remarks on Accepting the Presidential Nomination of the Republican National Convention," August 23, 1972, *The American Presidency Project*, https://www.presidency.ucsb.edu/documents/remarks-

accepting-the-presidential-nomination-the-republican-national-convention. For more on resistance to affirmative action in the 1970s, see Dennis Deslippe, *Protesting Affirmative Action: The Struggle over Equality After the Civil Rights Revolution* (Baltimore: Johns Hopkins University Press, 2012), 89–126; Terry H. Anderson, *The Pursuit of Fairness: A History of Affirmative Action* (New York: Oxford University Press, 2004), 164–217.

53. Byrn, "Abortion on Demand," 27. For related arguments in the period, see Terrance Cardinal Cooke, Letter to Friend in Christ, December 2, 1970, NARAL, Box 49, Folder 5 ("Once the destruction of innocent life at any stage is placed at the mercy of others, . . . a simple majority may decide that life is to be denied to the defective, the aged, [and] the incorrigible").

54. *United States v. Vuitch*, 402 U.S. 62, 71–72 (1971). For more on the significance of *Vuitch*, see Garrow, *Liberty and Sexuality*, 238–239, 256–283.

55. Dennis Horan to Paul Ramsey (September 30, 1970), PRP, Box 12, Dennis Horan Folder. For the lower court's decision in *Doe v. Scott*, see *Doe v. Scott*, 321 F. Supp. 1385, 1389–1393 (N.D. Ill. 1971).

56. *Roe v. Wade*, 314 F. Supp. 1217, 1222 (N.D. Tex. 1970). For more on *Roe* and McCorvey, see Joshua Prager, *The Family Roe: An American Story* (New York: Norton, 2021), 123–178. For the lower court's decision in *Doe*, see *Doe v. Bolton*, 319 F. Supp. 1048, 1050–1056 (N.D. 1970).

57. Declaration of Purpose from Americans United for Life (1971), AUL, Executive File Box, Folder 91. On the diverse membership of AUL, see Arthur Dyck to George Huntston Williams (February 14, 1972), GHW, Box 6, Folder 4; Germain Grisez to George Huntston Williams (February 1, 1972), GHW, Box 6, Folder 4; Charles Rice to George Huntston Williams (February 10, 1972), GHW, Box 6, Folder 4. For more on Bozell, see Daniel Kelly, *Living on Fire: The Life of L. Brent Bozell Jr.* (Wilmington, DE: Intercollegiate Research Institute, 2014).

58. On Baird, see Garrow, *Liberty and Sexuality*, 183–197, 200-233; Davis, *Moving the Mountain*, 176–177; Geoffrey Stone, *Sex and the Constitution: Sex, Religion, and Law from America's Origins to the Twentieth Century* (New York: Norton, 2017), 511–543.

59. Garrow, *Liberty and Sexuality*, 183–197; Davis, *Moving the Mountain*, 176–177. On Horan's view, see Ziegler, *After* Roe, 32–35.

60. Affidavit of Jesse Levine, *Byrn v. New York City Health and Hospitals Corporation*, Index No. 13113-71 (December 13, 1971), AMR Box 3, Folder 1. For more on Byrn's complaint, see Complaint, 1–13, *Byrn v. New York City Health and Hospitals Corporation*, Index No. 13113-71 (November 29, 1971), AMR, Box 2, Folder 61;

see also Robert Byrn, Affidavit in Support of Motion for Preliminary Injunction, 3–8, Index No. 13113-71 (December 2, 1971), AMR, Box 2, Folder 61.

61. Affidavit of Dennis Procaccini, Assistant Professor of Biology at Emmanuel College, *Byrn v. New York City Health and Hospitals Corporation*, Index No. 13113-71 (December 9, 1971), AMR, Box 3, Folder 1.

62. For the statements from Byrn's complaint: Complaint, 7, 9. For the court's decision, see Memorandum, Index No. 13113-71 (December 3, 1971), AMR, Box 2, Folder 61.

63. Bernard Rabin, "Judge Orders Abortions Halted in City," *New York Daily News*, January 6, 1972, 5; see also Judy Klemesrud, "He's the Legal Guardian for the Fetuses about to Be Aborted," *New York Times*, December 17, 1971, 48; "Bachelor Guardian of the Unborn Babies Takes Gibes with a Smile," *Des Moines Register*, December 18, 1971, 5 (IA). For views of Byrn at Fordham, see "Byrn v. Women's Rights," *Fordham Law School Advocate*, December 17, 1971, 2; Allen P. Karen, "Byrn: Abortions Are Illegal," *Fordham Law School Advocate*, December 17, 1971, 1.

64. For the court's January order in *Byrn*, see Memorandum Decision, Index No. 13113-71 (January 4, 1972), AMR, Box 3, Folder 1. For the decision in *Steinberg: Steinberg v. Brown*, 321 F. Supp. 741, 746–747 (N.D. Ohio). For other decisions in the antiabortion movement's favor, see *Cheaney v. State*, 285 N.E.2d 265 (Ind. 1972); *Rodgers v. Danforth*, 486 S.W.2d 258 (Mo. 1972); *State v. Scott*, 255 So.2d 736 (La. 1971); *Sasaki v. Com.*, 485 S.W.2d 487 (Ky. 1972). For the appellate division's opinion, see *Byrn v. New York City Health and Hospitals Corporation*, 38 A.2d 316, 322–355 (N.Y. App. Div. 1972). The abortion-rights movement scored significant victories of its own.

65. See Rice to Williams, 2–3; John Archibald to George Huntston Williams (February 4, 1972), CRP; Brent Bozell to George Huntston Williams (January 4, 1972), GHW, Box 6, Folder 4.

66. Bozell to Williams, 2; Brent Bozell to George Huntston Williams (January 31, 1972), GHW, Box 6, Folder 4.

67. Rice to Williams, 3.

68. Americans United for Life, Board of Directors Meeting Minutes (March 10–11, 1972), AUL, Executive File Box, Folder 91. Rice and his faction would join another organization, the United States Coalition for Life, that opposed contraception as well as abortion. Charles Rice to L. Brent Bozell (March 15, 1972), CRP.

69. *Population and the American Future: The Report of the Commission on Population Growth and the American Future* (March 1972), https://www.population-security .org/rockefeller/001_population_growth_and_the_american_future.htm.

70. George Huntston Williams to Richard Nixon (March 17, 1972), GHW, Box 6, Folder 5.

71. See Richard Nixon, Statement on Abortion (April 3, 1972), CCF, Box 7, John Ehrlichman Folder 2; Charles Colson to Henry Cashen (July 19, 1972), CCF, Box 132, July 1972 Folder. For Muskie's statement: James Reston, "Nixon and Muskie on Abortion," *New York Times*, April 7, 1971, 43. On the push to get Nixon to take a position on abortion, see Williams, "The GOP's Abortion Strategy," 515–520; Linda Greenhouse and Reva B. Siegel, "Before (and After) *Roe v. Wade:* New Questions about Backlash," *Yale Law Journal* 128 (2011): 2053–2072.

72. *Eisenstadt v. Baird*, 405 U.S. 438, 453 (1972). For more on response to *Eisenstadt*, see Garrow, *Liberty and Sexuality*, 336–345; Williams, *Defenders of the Unborn*, 229–230. Justices Powell and Rehnquist did not take part in the decision of the case.

73. On the growing support for the ERA in the late 1960s and early 1970s, see Julie Suk, *We the Women: The Unstoppable Women of the Equal Rights Amendment* (New York: Skyhorse, 2020), 82–103; Jane Mansbridge, *Why We Lost the ERA* (Chicago: University of Chicago Press, 1986), 201–219; Reva Siegel, "Constitutional Culture, Social Movement Conflict, and Constitutional Change: The Case of the De Facto ERA," *California Law Review* 94 (2006): 1394–1423.

74. Mary Alice Duffy, "The Case against Abortion: A Plea for the Unborn Child," *Women Lawyers' Journal* 56 (1970). On Goltz and early antiabortion feminism, see Feminists for Life Task Force on Consumer Credit, *Feminists for Life Journal* (1972): 2, FFL; Pat Goltz, "The Equal Rights Amendment," *Feminists for Life Journal* (1973): 8, FFL.

75. Marie MacDonald, "Women for Women Kansas Born," *Wichita Eagle*, June 27, 1971, 1E (KS). For Schlafly's statement: Phyllis Schlafly, "What's Wrong with Equal Rights for Women?" *Schlafly Report* (January 1, 1972), PSR. For more on Schlafly's influence, see Donald Critchlow, *Phyllis Schlafly and Grassroots Conservatism: A Woman's Crusade* (Princeton: Princeton University Press, 2005); Donald G. Mathews and Jane De Hart, *Sex, Gender, and the Politics of ERA: A State and the Nation* (New York: Oxford University Press, 1990), 50–92, 154–159; Marjorie J. Spruill, *Divided We Stand: The Battle over Women's Rights and Family Values That Polarized American Politics* (London: Bloomsbury, 2018), 79–96.

76. On Nixon's letter to the New York archdiocese and the fallout from it, see Robert B. Semple, "Nixon Aides Explain Aims of Letter on Abortion Law," *New York Times*, May 11, 1972, 1. On the Rockefeller veto, see "Governor Vetoes Abortion Repeal as Not Justified," *New York Times*, May 14, 1972, 1. On the Michigan vote, see Karen Aldag, "Abortion Defeat Nags 'Pros,'" *Lansing State Journal*, November 10, 1972, D3 (MI).

77. *Byrn v. New York City Health and Hospitals Corporation*, 286 N.E.2d 887, 888 (N.Y. 1972). For the Connecticut district court's decision in *Abele*, see *Abele v. Markle*, 351 F. Supp. 224, 231 (D. Conn. 1972). For the statement of Byrn's attorney: "Now Abortion Law Battle Goes to Highest Tribunal," *Democrat and Chronicle*, May 31, 1972, 8C (Rochester, NY); see also "Rights of Unborn Get More Support in Court Battle," *Catholic News Service*, June 5, 1972, 7 (Byrn explaining that his case offered an opportunity for a "clear and complete presentation of the issues of the unborn"). For Byrn's promise to appeal to the Supreme Court, see "New York Court Upholds State's Abortion Law," *Catholic Transcript*, July 14, 1972, 3 (Hartford, CT).

3. Victims' Rights

1. Second Inaugural Address of Richard Milhous Nixon, January 20, 1973, in *The Avalon Project*, https://avalon.law.yale.edu/20th_century/nixon2.asp.

2. On Byrn's appeal to the Supreme Court, see "Abortion Battle Shapes Up in New York Legislature," *Cincinnati Enquirer*, January 14, 1973, 4K (OH).

3. Transcript of Oral Argument, *Roe v. Wade*, October 11, 1972, 20, 40. *Roe* was argued twice before the court, in 1971 and 1972, because the Court had held over the case for reargument. For more on the oral arguments in the case, David J. Garrow, *Liberty and Sexuality: The Right to Privacy and the Making of* Roe v. Wade (Berkeley: University of California Press, 1998), 300–335.

4. *Frontiero v. Richardson*, 411 U.S. 677, 685 (1973) (plurality opinion). For discussion of the importance of *Frontiero*, see Serena Mayeri, *Reasoning from Race: Feminism, Law, and the Civil Rights Revolution* (Cambridge, MA: Harvard University Press, 2011), 73–94; Serena Mayeri, "The Story of *Frontiero v. Richardson*," in *Women and the Law Stories*, ed. Elizabeth M. Schneider and Stephanie M. Wildman (New York: Foundation, 2011), 67.

5. *Roe v. Wade*, 410 U.S. 113, 132–133 (1973).

6. Ibid., 153; see also Reva B. Siegel and Linda Greenhouse, "The Unfinished Story of *Roe v. Wade*," in *Reproductive Rights and Justice Stories,* ed. Melissa Murray, Katherine Shaw, and Reva B. Siegel (New York: Foundation, 2019).

7. *Roe v. Wade*, 410 U.S. 113, 174–175, 177 (1973) (Rehnquist, J., dissenting). The Supreme Court would later adopt a state-counting method like the one used by Rehnquist in justifying the reversal of *Roe*. See Reva B. Siegel, "The History of History and Tradition: The Roots of *Dobbs*'s Method (and Originalism) in the Defense of Segregation," *Yale Law Journal Forum* 133 (2023): 101–125.

8. On the abortion rate in 1974 and 1975, see Edward Weinstock, Christopher Tietze, Frederick Jaffe, and Joy Dryfoos, "Abortion Need and Services in the United

States, 1974–1975," *Family Planning Perspectives* 8 (1976): 58. On McCorvey's reaction to the *Roe* decision, see Joshua Prager, *The Family Roe: An American Story* (New York: Norton, 2021), 145, 202–230. On the number of hospitals offering abortions, see Edward Weinstock et al., "Legal Abortions in the United States since the 1973 Supreme Court Decisions," *Family Planning Perspectives* 17 (1974–1975): 24–31. On the decline of abortion-related mortality, see Council on Scientific Affairs, American Medical Association, "Induced Termination of Pregnancy Before and After *Roe v. Wade:* Trends in the Mortality and Morbidity of Women," *Journal of the American Medical Association* 22 (1992): 3231–3239.

9. For the statement about an entire class and the Constitution's framers: Barry Schweid, "Catholic Prof Asks Abortion Ruling Review," *Statesman Journal*, February 15, 1973, 52 (Salem, Oregon). On the fate of Byrn's appeal, see *Byrn v. New York City Health and Hospitals Corporation,* 410 U.S. 949 (1973) (dismissing Byrn's appeal for want of a substantial federal question); see also "Professor Asks High Court to Weigh Rights of Unborn," *Portland Evening Express*, February 15, 1973, 11 (ME).

10. See National Right to Life Committee Ad Hoc Strategy Meeting Minutes (February 11, 1973), ACCL, Box 4, 1973 NRLC Folder; see also Edward Golden to Members of New York State Right to Life (1973), NARAL, Box 49, Folder 5; Young Americans for Freedom, "The Right to Life" (August 18, 1973), NARAL, Box 49, Folder 6 ("Any remedy short of equal protection of life from the moment of conception is philosophically, morally, and medically untenable"); National Right to Life Committee, Resolution on Human Life Constitutional Amendment (June 30, 1973), ACCL, Box 4, 1973 NRLC Folder. On Hyde's work in the Illinois state legislature, see "House Passes Abortions Bill," *Herald and Review*, July 2, 1973, 16 (Decatur, IL); "Illinois Gets Abortion Bill," *Winona Daily News*, January 25, 1973, 5 (MN).

11. Alan Cranston, "Involvement Is Futile, Immoral," *Los Angeles Times*, March 9, 1975, H5; David Zierler, *The Invention of Ecocide: Agent Orange, Vietnam, and the Scientists Who Changed the Way We Think about the Environment* (Athens: University of Georgia Press, 2011), 1–13; Hannibal Travis, *Genocide, Ethnonationalism, and the United Nations: Exploring the Causes of Mass Killing since 1945* (New York: Taylor and Francis, 2013), 102.

12. Press Release, National Youth Pro-Life Coalition (December 8, 1973), NARAL, Box 49, Folder 5; Pamphlet, Committee of the Ten Million (n.d., ca. 1974), NARAL, Carton 49, Folder 5 ("If you are concerned about the war, you should be more concerned about abortion"); Pamphlet, "The Facts of Death" (n.d., ca. 1973), EHP, Box 196, Folder 28 ("The #1 killer is not war. The #1 killer is abortion!"). For Hilgers's statement: Abortion Part II: Senate Judiciary Subcommittee on Constitutional

Amendments, 93d Congress, 2d Session (1974), 850 (copy of Thomas W. Hilgers, "Induced Abortion: A Documented Report" [2d ed. 1973]). For Chamblee's statement: Abortion Part II: Senate Judiciary Subcommittee on Constitutional Amendments, 93d Congress, 2d Session (1974), 449 (Statement of Roland Chamblee).

13. On Whitehurst and his amendment, see Proposed Constitutional Amendments on Abortion, Part I: Testimony before the House Judiciary Subcommittee on Civil and Constitutional Rights, 94th Congress, 2d Session (1976), 366–367 (Statement of G. William Whitehurst); Philip Walzer, "Whitehurst Looks Back at Life in the Classroom, Congress," *Old Dominion University*, October 15, 2020, https://www.odu.edu/article/whitehurst-looks-back-at-life-the-classroom-congress.

14. National Right to Life Committee Resolution #4 (July 10, 1973), ACCL, Box 4, 1973 NRLC Folder 2. For Byrn's statement: Abortion Part IV: Testimony on S. 119 and S. 130 before the Senate Judiciary Subcommittee on Constitutional Amendments, 94th Congress, 1st Session (1974) (Statement of Robert Byrn), 108. For more criticism of the Whitehurst Amendment, see Albert Dingman to Elizabeth Holtzman (March 4, 1974), EHP, Box 196, Folder 28.

15. Nellie Gray to Members of the Right-to-Life Movement, 3 (December 1, 1973), ACCL, Box 6, Constitutional Amendment 1973 Folder. For more on disagreement about amendment details, see Dennis Horan to NRLC Board of Directors (January 19, 1974), ACCL, Box 8, 1974 Board and Executive Committee Folder 3.

16. For Rice's argument: Charles Rice to Joseph Witherspoon, September 5, 1973, ACCL, Box 6, Constitutional Amendment 1973 Folder.

17. Dennis Horan to NRLC Policy Committee (September 5, 1973), 1, ACCL, Box 6, Constitutional Amendment 1973 Folder. On the Thirteenth Amendment model, see Joseph Witherspoon to NRLC Executive Committee (August 14, 1973), 5, ACCL, Box 6, Constitutional Amendment 1973 Folder.

18. Witherspoon to NRLC Executive Committee, 2–5. On Witherspoon's background, see "Committee to Act as Safety Valve for Racial Tensions," *Corpus Christi Caller-Times*, December 29, 1963, 15 (TX); Jackie Madigan, "National Rights Groups Proposed," *The Austin-American*, December 17, 1965, 6 (TX); "Textbook Hearing Views Divergent," *Corsicana Daily Sun*, February 10, 1962, 1 (TX); Chris Whitcraft, "Wilkins: Says Oppression Easing Is Too Slow," *Austin Statesman*, February 16, 1966, 10 (TX).

19. Witherspoon to NRLC Executive Committee, 1. For Witherspoon's argument in *Roe:* Brief on Behalf of Texas Diocesan Attorneys, in Support of Appellee, 15, *Roe v. Wade*, 410 U.S. 113 (1973) (Nos. 70-10, 70-18).

20. Robert Byrn to Joseph Witherspoon, September 4, 1973, ACCL, Box 6, Constitutional Amendment 1973 Folder; see also Rice to Witherspoon, 1–2.

21. Gray to Members of the Right-to-Life Movement, 8–10. On Gray, see Barbara Gamarekian, "Leader of 'March for Life' Sees Issue as Apocalyptic," *New York Times*, March 13, 1981, A18; Timothy S. Goeglein, "Nellie Gray: A Portrait of Perseverance in the Quest for Civil Rights," *Epoch Times*, July 8, 2022, https://www.theepochtimes .com/opinion/nellie-gray-a-portrait-of-perseverance-in-the-quest-for-civil-rights-4585480?welcomeuser=1 (New York).

22. On ACCL and Mecklenburg's work, see Mary Ziegler, *After* Roe: *The Lost History of the Abortion Debate* (Cambridge, MA: Harvard University Press, 2015), 223–256, 289–298.

23. Abortion Part 3: Senate Judiciary Subcommittee on Constitutional Amendments, 93d Congress, 2d Session (1974), 166 (Statement of Warren Schaller). On Schaller's civil-rights involvement, see "More Outsiders at Selma Urged," *Minneapolis Star*, March 20, 1965, 5. For Schaller's views on ERA: Warren Schaller, interview with Mary Ziegler, February 11, 2011, quoted in Ziegler, *After* Roe, 288–289.

24. For Pilpel's argument: Harriet Pilpel, "The Fetus as Person: Possible Legal Consequences of the Hogan-Helms Amendment," *Family Planning Perspectives* 6 (1974): 6–7. For more on Pilpel's work on abortion within the ACLU, see Meeting of the ACLU Due Process Committee (November 18, 1965), ACLUMF, Reel 317; Leigh Ann Wheeler, *How Sex Became a Civil Liberty* (New York: Oxford University Press, 2013), 115–135.

25. JGC, Memorandum: Abortion, November 29, 1974, RNP, Box 117, Abortion Folder. For more on Ford's position, see Memorandum to Ron Nessen (September 9, 1976), RNP, Box 117, Abortion Folder.

26. Jules Witcover, "Carter Finds His Words Are Watched," *Washington Post*, January 27, 1976, A4. For the poll: Robert Reinhold, "Poll Finds Voters Judging '76 Rivals on Personality," *New York Times*, February 13, 1976, 1.

27. On Reagan's campaign rhetoric about welfare, see Ian Haney-López, *Dog Whistle Politics: How Coded Racial Appeals Have Reinvented Racism and Wrecked the Middle Class* (New York: Oxford University Press, 2014), 55–61. For Reagan's story about the "welfare queen," see " 'Welfare Queen' Becomes Issue in Reagan Campaign," *New York Times*, February 15, 1976, 51. On the story about a "young buck," see Robert Kaiser, "On Welfare: Democrats Bullish, Republicans Bearish (but Less Now)," *Washington Post*, October 22, 1980, https://www.washingtonpost.com /archive/politics/1980/10/23/on-welfare-democrat-bullish-republican-bearish-but-less-now/d3c7899e-cd6b-461f-911d-718c86c2c6a9/. On Reagan's statement about the HLA: "Ronald Reagan Supports HLA," *National Right to Life News* (September 1975), 4, JRS, 1976 National Right to Life News Box.

28. *Planned Parenthood of Central Missouri v. Danforth*, 428 U.S. 52 (1976). On the Hyde Amendment and its significance, see Mary Ziegler, *Abortion and the Law in America: Roe v. Wade to the Present* (New York: Cambridge University Press, 2020), 60–74.

29. On the results of the 1976 presidential election, see Daniel K. Williams, *The Election of the Evangelical: Jimmy Carter, Gerald Ford, and the Presidential Contest of 1976* (Lawrence: University of Kansas Press, 2020), 102–143; Rick Perlstein, *Reaganland: America's Right Turn, 1976–1980* (New York: Simon and Schuster, 2020), 3–7, 143–165.

30. Laura Foreman, "President Defends Court's Action Curbing Federal Aid for Abortion," *New York Times*, July 13, 1977, A1; Myra McPherson, "Carter's Abortion-Aid Stance Assailed," *Washington Post*, July 16, 1977, A1. On Carter's opposition to a fetal-protective amendment, see David E. Rosenbaum, "Carter's Position on Issues Designed for Wide Appeal," *New York Times*, June 11, 1976, 1. On the stalling of the amendment, see Ziegler, *Abortion and the Law*, 43–88, 90–95. For the court's decisions in *Maher*, *Beal*, and *Poelker*, see *Maher v. Roe*, 432 U.S. 464 (1977); *Beal v. Doe*, 432 U.S. 438 (1977); *Poelker v. Doe*, 432 U.S. 519 (1977).

31. "NRLC Legal Project Formed," *National Right to Life News* (July 1977), 6, JRS, 1977 National Right to Life News Box. For more on the project, see Mary Reilly Hunt to NRLC Board of Directors (September 21, 1978), JBP, Matter Box 143; James Bopp to Mildred Jefferson (March 2, 1978), JBP, Matter Box 143.

32. Talking Points, "Informed Consent" (n.d., ca. 1978), JBP, Matter Box 143; see also Citizens for Informed Consent, "Summary of Proposed Abortion Ordinance for Akron, Ohio" (1978), JBP, Matter Box 301; Press Release, "Akron Abortion Ordinance Set to Become National Model" (March 4, 1978), JBP, Matter Box 301.

33. See W. F. Spicer, Assistant Director of Law City of Akron, to Robert Goehler, Akron City Council (1978), JBP, Matter Box 301; James Bopp to NRLC Executive Committee (March 16, 1978), JBP, Matter Box 301.

34. On the 1980 election, see Donald Granburg and James Burlison, "The Abortion Issue in the 1980 Election," *Family Planning Perspectives* 15 (1983): 231–238; Douglas L. Koopman, *Hostile Takeover: The House Republican Party, 1980–1995* (Lanham, MD: Rowman and Littlefield, 1996), 34–44, 52–61.

35. On Wattleton, see Judy Klemesrud, "Planned Parenthood's New Head Takes a Fighting Stand," *New York Times*, February 3, 1978, A14; "Family Planning's Top Advocate," *Ebony Magazine*, September 1978, 87–88. Wattleton also wrote a book about her own life. See Faye Wattleton, *Life on the Line* (New York: Ballantine, 1998). On the transition from Mulhauser to Falkenberg, see Mary Ziegler, *Roe: The History of a National Obsession* (New Haven: Yale University Press, 2023), 52–54.

36. American Civil Liberties Union, "Abortion: A Fundamental Right under Attack" (n.d., ca. 1979), PMC, Box 119, Folder 2045; For the plaintiffs' argument in *McRae:* Brief of Appellees, 96–100, 167–178, *Harris v. McRae*, 448 U.S. 297 (1980) (No. 79-1268). For more on the use of arguments connecting fetal personhood to the establishment of religion, see The Religious Coalition for Abortion Rights, "It's Hyde Again" (1979), RHS, Box 1, Folder 19. For a history of these claims, see Rhonda Copelon and Sylvia Law, " 'Nearly Allied to Her Right to Be'—Medicaid Funding for Abortion: The Story of *Harris v. McRae*," in Schneider and Wildman, *Women and the Law Stories*, 220–221.

37. *Harris v. McRae*, 448 U.S. 297, 316–322 (1980).

38. For discussion of the poll: Joe R. Feagin, "Affirmative Action in an Era of Reaction," *Consultations on the Affirmative Action Statement of the U.S. Commission on Civil Rights*, February–March 1981, 45–46. For the decisions in *Feeney* and *Davis*, see *Personnel Administrator of Massachusetts v. Feeney*, 442 U.S. 256 (1979); *Washington v. Davis*, 426 U.S. 229 (1976). For the Court's decision in *Milliken*, see *Milliken v. Bradley*, 418 U.S. 717, 747 (1974). For more on the Court's shifting ideas of equal protection and race, see Reva B. Siegel, "Foreword: Equality Divided," *Harvard Law Review* 127 (2013): 20–23; Katie R. Eyer, "Ideological Drift and the Forgotten History of Intent," *Harvard Civil Rights–Civil Liberties Review* 51 (2016): 34–65.

39. On the emergence of the disability-rights movement in the late 1970s and early 1980s, see Doris Zames Fleischer and Frieda Zames, *The Disability Rights Movement: From Charity to Confrontation* (Philadelphia: Temple University Press, 2001); Karen Tani, "The Pennhurst Doctrines and the Lost Disability History of the 'New Federalism,' " *California Law Review* 110 (2022): 1157–1187. For an example of contemporary layoffs, see Isadore Barmash, "Xerox to 'Restructure' and Cut Staff," *New York Times*, September 24, 1981, D1.

40. On the Human Life Bill, see T. R. Reid, "Hill Abortion Opponents Seek New Law to Nullify '73 Supreme Court Decision," *Washington Post*, February 7, 1981, A2; Joan Beck, "The Pro-Life Groups Turn to Congress on Abortion," *Chicago Tribune*, January 30, 1981, B2.

41. Human Life Bill: Testimony before the Senate Judiciary Subcommittee on Separation of Powers, 97th Congress, 1st Session (June 18, 1981), 1066 (Statement of John Willke). For more on Willke's earlier work: John Willke to Dino Lorenzetti (March 4, 1966), JWC, Family Planning Folders; Pamphlet, "Something Is Happening in Cincinnati" (n.d., ca. 1966), JWC, Family Planning Folders. For the Willkes' account of their journey to the antiabortion movement, see John Willke and Barbara Willke, "Throwing Bread upon the Waters," *ACT: The Voice of the Christian Family Movement*, January 1977, 1–3, JWC, Family Planning Folders.

42. On the American Life League and absolutism, see Carol Mason, *Killing for Life: The Apocalyptic Narrative of Pro-Life Politics* (Ithaca: Cornell University Press, 2002), 45, 109–153; Ziegler, *After Roe*, 142–150. On Brown's life and background, see "Top Catholics of the Century Number 49: Judie Brown," *Daily Catholic* 10 (1999); Judie Brown, *Not My Will but Thine: An Autobiography* (Stafford, VA: American Life League, 2002).

43. For Willke's statement: John Willke, "The HLA: Unity," *National Right to Life News* (October 13, 1981), 7, JRS, 1981 National Right to Life News Box. On the unity amendment, see "NRLC Board Reaches Historic Consensus on HLA Wording," *National Right to Life News* (October 13, 1981), 1, JRS, 1981 National Right to Life News Box; James Bopp Jr., "NRLC's Human Life Amendment," *National Right to Life News* (October 26, 1981), 1, JRS, 1981 National Right to Life News Box. NRLC still described a personhood amendment as the "purpose of its legislative project." National Right to Life Committee, "Three-Year Plan: Introduction and General Recommendation" (1980), JWC, National Right to Life Committee Materials. For the text of the paramount amendment, see National Right to Life Committee, "Text of Draft Human Life Amendment" (1980), JWC, National Right to Life Committee Folders.

44. Testimony on S. 158, a Bill to Provide That Human Life Shall Exist from Conception, before the Senate Judiciary Subcommittee on Separation of Powers, 97th Congress, 1st Session (June 1, 1981), 310 (Statement of Robert Bork). For more on this view in the period, see Ziegler, *Abortion and the Law*, 81–84.

45. See Elizabeth Hinton, *From the War on Poverty to the War on Crime: The Making of Mass Incarceration in America* (Cambridge, MA: Harvard University Press, 2016), 3–21.

46. See Lee Lescaze, "President May Leave Hospital This Weekend," *Washington Post*, April 9, 1981, A1; "Reagan's Lung Clearing," *Austin American-Statesman*, April 9, 1981, 5 (TX); Darrow Tully, "Let Lawmakers Hear the Public's Demand for Victims' Rights," *Arizona Republic*, June 27, 1982, 6 (Phoenix).

47. "Don't Forget the Victim's Rights," *Christian Science Monitor*, April 22, 1981, 24. For more on the victim rights' movement in the era, see Carrie A. Rentschler, *Second Wounds: Victims' Rights and the Media in the U.S.* (Durham: Duke University Press, 2011), 35–70; Markus Dirk Dubber, *Victims in the War on Crime: The Use and Abuse of Victims' Rights* (New York: New York University Press, 2006), 171–190.

48. "Reagan Praises 'Thin Blue Line,'" *Los Angeles Times*, September 28, 1981, A2. For more on the task force and its proposals, see William J. Eaton, "Crime Panel

Proposes Limits on Basic Rights," *Los Angeles Times*, August 18, 1981, B1; "Legal Changes in Bail, Evidence, Appeals Are Advocated by U.S. Crime Task Force," *Wall Street Journal*, August 6, 1981, 33.

49. Robert W. Rardin, "Letter to the Editor," *Chicago Tribune*, September 1, 1981, 10. For the NRLC debate manual: National Right to Life Committee, "Some Questions and Answers About Abortion" (n.d., ca. 1981), JWC, Talking Points Folder.

50. On the vote and the fallout from it, see John Willke, "The Healing Commences," *National Right to Life News* (April 11, 1981), 3, JRS, 1981 National Right to Life News Box; Judie Brown to John Willke (February 19, 1982), JBP, Matter Box 300; Helen DeWitt to Friend of Life (August 23, 1981), 1–3, JBP, Matter Box 300. For Roach's statement: Steven V. Roberts, "Catholic Bishops for Amendment Allowing States to Ban Abortion," *New York Times*, November 6, 1981, A1.

51. "Senate Kills Abortion, School Prayer," in *Congressional Quarterly Almanac*, 38th ed. (Washington, DC: Congressional Quarterly Press, 1983), 403–405.

52. For Bork's comments: Marcia Chambers, "Yale Is a Host to 2 Meetings about Politics," *New York Times*, May 2, 1982, A53; see also "Conservative Forum," *Human Events*, April 3, 1982, 18; "Federal Judge Assails Supreme Court Rulings," *New York Times*, April 27, 1982, A17. On the early conservative legal movement, see Steven Teles, *The Rise of the Conservative Legal Movement: The Battle for Control of the Law* (Princeton: Princeton University Press, 2010), 32–54, 111–135; Amanda Hollis-Brusky, *Ideas with Consequences: The Federalist Society and the Conservative Counterrevolution* (New York: Oxford University Press, 2015), 12–32.

53. On the early work of the Christian Legal Society, see Christian Legal Society, Pamphlet, "Bringing the Profession Together" (n.d., ca. 1987), AUS, Box 12, Folder 37; "Turning Crises into Opportunity," Christian Legal Society's *Briefly* (August 1988), AUS, Box 12, Folder 37; Christian Legal Society, Fundraising Letter (August 1989), AUS, Box 12, Folder 37.

54. On the Baby Doe cases, see Martha Minow, *Making All the Difference: Inclusion, Exclusion, and American Law* (Ithaca: Cornell University Press, 1990), 310–345; Sam Bagenstos, *Law and the Contradictions of the Disability Rights Movement* (New Haven: Yale University Press, 2009), 92–102.

55. The Reagan administration promulgated the final version of the Baby Doe Rules in 1984 and pushed for federal legislation. Later that year, Congress passed the Child Abuse Amendments of 1984, which reflected many of the requirements of the administration's rules. Meanwhile, the American Hospital Association filed a court challenge to the new federal regulations, culminating in the Supreme Court's 1986 decision in *Bowen v. American Hospital Association*, which held that the regulations

were not authorized by the Rehabilitation Act. See *Bowen v. American Hospital Association*, 476 U.S. 610, 640–648 (1986).

56. "AUL Lawyers Work on Infant Doe Infanticide Appeal," *AUL Newsletter* (November 1982), 1, PAW, Carton 9, Folder 2; see also James Bopp to Maura Quinlan (October 19, 1983), JBP, Matter Box 374; National Right to Life Committee, "Pro-Life Legislation in Congress" (January 21, 1987), JWC, National Right to Life Committee Folders (describing the importance of the Baby Doe cases to the movement).

57. On Biden's vote on the Hatch Amendment, see Lisa Lerer, "When Joe Biden Voted to Let States Ban Abortion," *New York Times*, March 29, 2019, https://www.nytimes.com/2019/03/29/us/politics/biden-abortion-rights.html; see also Steven Roberts, "Senate Kills Plan to Curb Abortion by a Vote of 47-46," *New York Times*, September 16, 1982, A1. On debates within the Reagan administration, see Dee Jepsen, Memorandum to Elizabeth Dole (January 12, 1983), MBP, Box 14, National Right to Life Folder 2; see also Ziegler, *Abortion and the Law*, 254–256.

58. *City of Akron v. Akron Center for Reproductive Health*, 462 U.S. 416, 443–451 (1983).

59. Ibid., 459 (O'Connor, J., dissenting).

60. "AUL Announces National Conference on Reversing *Roe v. Wade*," *AUL Newsletter* (December 1983), 1, PAW, Carton 9, Folder 1; see also AUL Fundraising Letter (May 21, 1984), MFJ, Box 13, Folder 6; Brochure, "Reversing *Roe* through the Courts" (1984), MRX, Box 38, Folder 68. Dellapenna went on to write the book he envisaged. See Joseph Dellapenna, *Dispelling the Myths of Abortion History* (Durham, NC: Carolina Academic Press, 2006).

61. " 'Reversing *Roe* through the Courts': An Absolute Success," *AUL Newsletter* (Summer 1984), 3, GHW, Box 4, Folder 5; see also "Experts Set for 'Reversing *Roe v. Wade* through the Courts,' " *AUL Newsletter* (Spring 1984), 1, GHW, Box 4, Folder 5. For more on Rosenblum, see Ziegler, Roe, 56–77.

62. See Thomas S. Kidd, *Who Is an Evangelical? The History of a Movement in Crisis* (New Haven: Yale University Press, 2019), 2–12, 55–105, 116–125; Francis FitzGerald, *The Evangelicals: The Struggle to Shape America* (New York: Simon and Schuster, 2017), 289–353; Daniel K. Williams, *God's Own Party: The Making of the Christian Right* (New York: Oxford University Press, 2010), 124–135; Andrew K. Lewis, *The Rights Turn in Conservative Christian Politics: How Abortion Transformed the Culture Wars* (New York: Cambridge University Press, 2017), 18–38, 89–101.

63. On Francis Schaeffer and his influence, see Frank Schaeffer, *Crazy for God: How I Grew Up as One of the Elect, Helped Found the Religious Right, and Lived to Take It All (or Almost All) of It Back* (New York: Hachette, 2008), 260–265, 270–288;

Williams, *God's Own Party*, 138–155. On Falwell's tour and influence, see Williams, *God's Own Party*, 45, 172–199; Perlstein, *Reaganland*, 160–215. For the convention's resolution, see Southern Baptist Convention, Resolution on Abortion, June 1980, https://www.sbc.net/resource-library/resolutions/resolution-on-abortion-6/. Schaeffer's views of the United States as a necessarily Christian nation, with a Christian constitutional tradition, reflected what some scholars describe as Christian nationalism. For discussion of the history, evolution, and present-day ideology of Christian nationalism, see Kevin Kruse, *One Nation under God: How Corporate America Invented Christian America* (New York: Hachette, 2015), 52–76, 242–258; Kristin Kobes Du Mez, *Jesus and John Wayne: How White Evangelicals Corrupted a Faith and Fractured a Nation* (New York: Liveright, 2020), 25–38. For a study of contemporary Christian nationalist beliefs, see Andrew Whitehead and Samuel L. Perry, *Taking Back America for God: Christian Nationalism in the United States* (New York: Oxford University Press, 2020).

64. *Thornburgh v. American College of Obstetricians and Gynecologists*, 476 U.S. 747 (1986). For more on *Thornburgh*, see Ziegler, *Abortion and the Law*, 61–66.

65. On the Federalist Society's power in the mid-1980s, see "Judge Scalia's Cheerleaders," *New York Times*, July 23, 1986, B6; Stuart Taylor Jr., "Conservatives Assert Legal Presence," *New York Times*, February 1, 1987, 1; Al Kamen, "Federalist Society Quickly Comes of Age," *Washington Post*, February 1, 1987, A3. For more on the Federalist Society's arguments at the time: Eugene Meyer to Gabrielle Caselle (September 4, 1986), 1, PAW, Carton 39, Folder 26; see also Federalist Society Fundraising Letter (August 31, 1987), PAW, Carton 39, Folder 26; Clipping, Charley Roberts, "Conservative Lawyer Lobby Grows," *St. Louis Daily Record* (September 2, 1986), PAW, Carton 39, Folder 27; The Federalist Society for Law and Policy Studies Proposal (August 1988), 1–6, PAW, Carton 39, Folder 27. For Meese's speech, see Edwin Meese III, Speech to the American Bar Association, July 9, 1985, /https://www.justice.gov/sites/default/files/ag/legacy/2011/08/23/07-09-1985.pdf .

66. On the background and impact of *Bowers*, see William Eskridge, *Dishonorable Passions: Sodomy Laws in America, 1861–2003* (New York: Viking, 2008), 278–318; Michael Klarman, *From the Closet to the Altar: Courts, Backlash, and the Struggle for Same-Sex Marriage* (New York: Oxford University Press, 2013), 37–42; Dudley Clendinen and Adam Nagourney, *Out for Good: The Struggle to Build a Gay Rights Movement in America* (New York: Touchstone, 1999), 531–548. For the Court's 1976 decision, see *Doe v. Commonwealth's Attorney of Richmond*, 425 U.S. 901 (1976).

67. John W. Whitehead, *The Separation Illusion: A Lawyer Examines the First Amendment* (Ridgewood, NJ: Mott Media, 1977), 18, 22, 25; see also Pamphlet, The Rutherford Institute (n.d., ca. 1988), THV, Box 18, Folder 1; Fundraising Letter,

Rutherford Institute (n.d., ca. 1990), THV, Box 18, Folder 1. For Lindsey's book, see Hal Lindsey, *The Late Great Planet Earth* (New York: Bantam, 1973).

68. The Rutherford Institute Newsletter (July/August 1986), 1, PAW, Carton 65, Folder 25. For Rutherford's claim to be doing all it could: Rutherford Institute, Fundraising Pamphlet (n.d., ca. 1986), PAW, Carton 65, Folder 25. For Rutherford's cases, see Rutherford Institute, Pamphlet (1985), PAW, Carton 65, Folder 25.

69. Brief of the Rutherford Institute et al., 2, 10–28, *Bowers v. Hardwick*, 478 U.S. 186 (1986) (No. 85-140). For Powell's opinion in *Moore*, see *Moore v. City of East Cleveland*, 431 U.S. 494, 503 (1977). On the lead-up to *Bowers*, see Klarman, *From the Closet to the Altar*, 37–42. For a sample of the arguments in *Bowers*, see Brief for Respondent, 5–19, *Bowers v. Hardwick*, 478 U.S. 186 (1986) (No. 85-140) (explaining that "when relationships are intimate in kind and insulated in the home, there is double reason to demand special justification from any government that would root them out there"); Amicus Brief of Lambda Legal Defense and Education Fund et al., 4–12, *Bowers v. Hardwick*, 478 U.S. 186 (1986) (No. 85-140) (arguing that "privacy rights protect the individual's decision to engage in private sexual activity and to choose a consenting adult partner, including an individual of the same sex").

70. For Harlan's dissent in Ullman: *Poe v. Ullman*, 367 U.S. 497, 542–543 (1961) (Harlan, J., dissenting). For Rutherford's argument, see Brief of the Rutherford Institute, 12–18; see also Brief of the Presbyterian Church U.S.A. et al., 14–15, *Bowers v. Hardwick*, 478 U.S. 186 (1986) (No. 85-140).

71. Nebraska Coalition for Life, "When Is Human Life Not Sacred?" (n.d., ca. 1986), JWC, National Right to Life Committee Folders. For the statement about Western civilization: Thomas J. Marzen et al., "Suicide: A Constitutional Right?" *Duquesne Law Review* 24 (1985): 17–100.

72. For the Court's decision in *Bowers*: *Bowers v. Hardwick*, 478 U.S. 186, 191–192 (1986). For Burger's statement: ibid., 196 (Burger, J., concurring). For the argument in Rutherford's brief: Brief of the Rutherford Institute, 13.

73. On Forsythe's background and influence, Clarke Forsythe, interview with Mary Ziegler, July 18, 2023. For Forsythe's statement: Deanna Silberman, "They're in It for Life," *Student Lawyer* 18 (1989): 30–35. For examples of Forsythe's work in the period, see Clarke Forsythe, "Precedent?" *Chicago Tribune*, March 28, 1987, 10; Ethan Bronner, "Abortion Foes Lose Suit under Racketeering Law," *Boston Globe*, March 3, 1989, 1.

74. Joe Kimball, "Bill Making It a Crime to Harm Pregnant Women Advances in Senate," *Star Tribune*, February 6, 1986, 1B (Minneapolis). For more on the debate about feticide in Minnesota, see Stephanie Salter, "Feticide Bill," *San Francisco*

Chronicle, January 20, 1986, 43. For Forsythe's argument on the born-alive rule, see Clarke D. Forsythe, "Homicide of the Unborn Child: The Born-Alive Rule and Other Legal Anachronisms," *Valparaiso Law Review* 21 (1987): 563–585.

75. On the law that Forsythe helped to write, see Marney Rich, "A Question of Rights," *Chicago Tribune*, September 18, 1988, F1. For more on the organization's work on the issue, see "Rights of the Unborn (Non-Abortion Context)," *Lex Vitae* (Spring 1986), 4–6, WCX, AUL Folder; "Rights of the Unborn (Non-Abortion Context)," *Lex Vitae* (Spring 1988), 5, WCX, AUL Folder. For Forsythe's article, see Forsythe, "Homicide of the Unborn Child," 563–585.

76. For AUL's statement: "Special Issue," *Life Docket* (February 1989), 1, SBL, Box 1, Folder 5001.

77. See Federalist Society for Law and Policy Studies Proposal, 1–8. On Bork's nomination and significance to the Federalist Society, see Teles, *The Conservative Legal Movement*, 186–190; Damon Root, *Overruled: The Long War for Control of the U.S. Supreme Court* (New York: St. Martin's, 2014), 79–109.

78. For Meese's speech: Edwin Meese III, "Speech before the American Bar Association," July 9, 1985, 1–5, reprinted in *The Great Debate: Interpreting Our Written Constitution*, ed. Paul G. Cassell (Washington, DC: Federalist Society, 1986). For Bork's statement: Robert H. Bork, "The Constitution, Original Intent, and Economic Rights," *San Diego Law Review* 23 (1986): 826. For Scalia's argument: Antonin Scalia, "Originalism: The Lesser Evil," *University of Cincinnati Law Review* 57 (1988–1989): 864. On the degree of change pursued by the Federalist Society, see Teles, *The Conservative Legal Movement*, 283; Mary Ziegler, "The History of Neutrality: *Dobbs* and the Social-Movement Politics of History and Tradition," *Yale Law Journal Forum* 133 (2023): 175–176. Early originalist scholars called for an approach based on original intent. See Raoul Berger, *Government by Judiciary: The Transformation of the Fourteenth Amendment* (New York: Liberty Fund, 1977), 250–251, 390–396; William Rehnquist, "The Notion of a Living Constitution," *Texas Law Review* 54 (1976): 595. Later, beginning in the late 1980s and 1990s, scholars began to develop originalist theories that sought to identify the Constitution's original public meaning. See Keith E. Whittington, "The New Originalism," *Georgetown Journal of Law and Public Policy* 2 (2004): 601–612; see also Thomas Colby, "The Sacrifice of the New Originalism," *Georgetown Law Journal* 99 (2011): 720–731.

79. Chapter 1 discusses the arguments and counterarguments involving an original public meaning argument for fetal personhood.

80. For the *Webster* decision and reactions to it, see *Webster v. Reproductive Health Services*, 492 U.S. 419, 517–523 (1989); Family Research Council, "An Analysis of the

Supreme Court's Landmark Decision in *Webster v. Reproductive Health Services*" (1989), PAW, Carton 32, Folder 1; James Bopp Jr. and Richard Coleson, "What Does *Webster* Mean?" *University of Pennsylvania Law Review* 138 (1989): 157–176.

81. On Terry and the early years of Operation Rescue, see James Risen and Judy Thomas, *Wrath of Angels: The American Abortion War* (New York: Basic Books, 1998), 239–261. On antiabortion work on the right to die, see National Right to Life Committee Board of Directors, "Resolution on Death Legislation" (July 5–6, 1983), JWC, National Right to Life Committee Folders.

82. Brochure, National Day of Rescue II (April 1989), FWHC, Carton 9, Operation Rescue Folder 2; see also Project Rescue, Fundraising Letter (June 7, 1990), NOWLDEF, Box 564, Folder 2.

83. National Day of Rescue Brochure, 2; see also "Repentance and Rescue: Atlanta" (1989), FWHC, Operation Rescue Folder. For more on Operation Rescue's arguments about fetal life and personhood from the period, see Brochure, "National Days of Rescue" (1991), FWHC, Operation Rescue Folder; "A Pro-Se Defense," *Rescue Newsbrief* (August 1989), 3, FWHC, Operation Rescue Folder; Brochure, "Operation Rescue Continues" (1989), FWHC, Carton 9, Operation Rescue Folder 2.

84. On Mecklenburg's work in the Reagan administration, see "Parental Notice Requirements Applicable to Projects for Family Planning Services," *Federal Register* 48 (1983): 3600, MBP, Box 22, Pro-Life Folder 3; "The Department's Response" (1983), MBP, Box 22, Pro-Life Folder 3 ("Parental notification is justifiable on health grounds. . . . Some teens may be persuaded by parents to abstain from sexual activity"); "Writer of U.S. 'Squeal Rule' Resigns After Travel Probe," *Los Angeles Times*, February 27, 1985, 6. On Schaller's exit from the movement: Warren Schaller, interview with Mary Ziegler, February 11, 2011, quoted in Ziegler, *After* Roe, 332–333.

85. Carol McGraw, "Abortion Protest Cases May Swamp Courts," *Los Angeles Times,* October 3, 1989, A1; see also Eric Malnic and Tracy Wilkinson, "Abortion Protest Arrestees Force Slowdown in Court," *Los Angeles Times*, March 28, 1989, 3. For more on blockaders' legal approach, see "A Pro-Se Defense," 3; "Tar Babies Still in Jail," *Rescue Newsbrief* (March 1989), 3, FWHC, Operation Rescue Folder.

86. On the police violence mortality rate, see GBD 2019 Police Violence Collaborators, "Fatal Police Violence by Race and State in the USA, 1980–2019: A Network Mega-Regression," *Lancet* 398 (2021): 1239–1255. On the percentage of Black drug arrestees in the period, see Human Rights Watch, "Decades of Disparity: Drug Arrests and Race in the United States," (March 2, 2009), https://www.hrw.org/report /2009/03/02/decades-disparity/drug-arrests-and-race-united states#:~:text=In%20 the%20years%20with%20the,ranged%20between%203.5%20and%203.9. For

Operation Rescue's arguments about police brutality, see "Nation's Politicians Awake to Police Abuse," *Rescue Newsbrief* (August 1989), 4, FWHC, Operation Rescue Folder; "Non-Violent Rescuers Draw Police Brutality," *Catholic League Newsletter* (June 1989), THV, Box 16, Folder 6; Linda Davis to Frank DeBot (December 8, 1989), THV, Box 16, Folder 6 (responding to "concern regarding allegations of police brutality against antiabortion protestors").

87. On the history behind *Cruzan* and its significance, see Mary Ziegler, *Beyond Abortion:* Roe v. Wade *and the Battle for Privacy* (Cambridge, MA: Harvard University Press, 2018), 166–184; Ian Dowbiggin, *A Merciful End: The Euthanasia Movement in Modern America* (New York: Oxford University Press, 2003), 164–165.

88. Brief Amicus Curiae of the National Right to Life Committee, 27, *Cruzan by Cruzan v. Director, Missouri Department of Public Health*, 497 U.S. 261 (1990) (No. 88-1503). For the AUL/Focus on the Family argument: Brief Amicus Curiae of Focus on the Family and the Family Research Council, 3, *Cruzan by Cruzan v. Director, Missouri Department of Public Health*, 497 U.S. 261 (1990) (No. 88-1503). For more on the advantages of a history-and-tradition approach, see John Willke, Draft, "President's Column: Reversing *Roe v. Wade*" (1987), JWC, National Right to Life Committee Folders (acknowledging that it was not until the later nineteenth century that "states, one by one, moved the felony punishment back to conception").

89. For the Court's decision in *Cruzan,* see *Cruzan by Cruzan v. Director, Missouri Department of Public Health*, 497 U.S. 261, 274–287 (1990). For more on struggles over a right to die, see Ziegler, *Beyond Abortion*, 168–180; Dowbiggin, *A Merciful End*, 165–183.

90. For the Anti–Drug Abuse Act of 1986, see 21 U.S.C. § 801 et seq. (1986). On racialized anxieties about crack in the 1980s and related media coverage, see Craig Reinarman and Henry Levine, "Crack in Context: America's Latest Demon Drug," in *Crack in America: Demon Drugs and Social Justice*, ed. Craig Reinarman and Henry Levine (Berkeley: University of California Press, 1997), 1–17; David Farber, *Crack: Rock Cocaine, Street Capitalism, and the Decade of Greed* (New York: Cambridge University Press, 2019), 8–18, 33–82.

91. Rich, "A Question of Rights," F1. For more on concern about "crack babies" in the era, see Sara Dubow, *Ourselves Unborn: A History of the Fetus in Modern America* (New York: Oxford University Press, 2010), 148–158; Laura Briggs, *Taking Children: A History of American Terror* (Berkeley: University of California Press, 2020), 109–123. On the statistics on fetal abuse and related prosecutions, see Dorris Massardo McGinnis, "Prosecution of Mothers of Drug-Exposed Babies: Constitutional and Criminal Theory," *University of Pennsylvania Law Review* 139 (1990): 505. For the Catholic

Conference's pastoral statement, see United States Catholic Conference, *Putting Children and Families First: A Challenge for Our Church, Nation, and World* (Washington, DC: United States Conference of Catholic Bishops, 1992).

92. On Hardy's case, see Stephanie Wood, "Pregnant, Addicted—and Guilty?" *New York Times*, August 19, 1990, A34; Tamar Lewin, "Drug Use in Pregnancy: New Issue for the Courts," *New York Times*, February 5, 1990, A14; "Charges Filed against Cocaine Baby's Mother," *Chicago Tribune*, November 14, 1989, A1.

93. "Drug Mom Case Pits Rights against Right," *St. Cloud Times*, January 4, 1990, 9A (MN). On the collateral consequences faced by pregnant drug users, see Michele Goodwin, *Policing the Womb: Invisible Women and the Criminalization of Motherhood* (New York: Cambridge University Press, 2020), 118–134; Dorothy Roberts, *Killing the Black Body: Race, Reproduction, and the Meaning of Liberty* (New York: Penguin, 1997), 155–188. On racial disparities in such prosecutions, see Gina Kolata, "Bias Seen against Pregnant Addicts," *New York Times*, July 20, 1990, A13. On the conclusion of Hardy's case, see Isabelle Wilkerson, "Woman Cleared After Drug Use in Pregnancy," *New York Times*, April 3, 1991, A15. For the ruling, see *People v. Hardy*, 469 N.W. 2d 50, 53 (Mich. App. 1991).

4. Abortion's Second Victim

1. For the Court's decision in *Casey*, see *Planned Parenthood of Southeastern Pennsylvania v. Casey*, 505 U.S. 833 (1992) (plurality decision).

2. Nomination of Ruth Bader Ginsburg to Be an Associate Justice of the Supreme Court of the U.S., 103d Congress, 1st Session (1993), 411, 413 (Statement of Paige Comstock Cunningham); see also Impact of the Equal Rights Amendment Part II: Testimony before the Senate Judiciary Subcommittee on the Constitution, 98th Congress, 2d Session (1993), 378–380 (Statement of Paige Comstock Cunningham). For more on Cunningham, see Mary Ziegler, *Abortion and the Law in America:* Roe v. Wade *to the Present* (New York: Cambridge University Press, 2020), 73–75.

3. For examples of arguments of this kind, see AUL Fundraising Letter (August 8, 1994), PAW, Carton 9, Folder 8; NRLC Model Informed Consent for 1995 (December 15, 1994), JBP, Matter Boxes, File 1203; Paige Comstock Cunningham, "Can We Love Women Who Abort?" *AUL Forum* (March 1993), PAW, Carton 9, Folder 7; MCFL Fact Sheet, "A Woman's Right to Know: Informed Consent for Abortion" (n.d., ca. 1995), NARALMA, Box 14, Folder 12.

4. Paige Comstock Cunningham, "Looking Forward to Life," *AUL Forum* (April 1994), 1, PAW, Carton 9, Folder 7; John Welsh, " 'Women's Right to Know Act' Stirs Tough Debate in Legislature," *St. Cloud Times*, February 24, 1995, 1 (MN).

5. *Planned Parenthood of Southeastern Pennsylvania v. Casey*, 505 U.S. 833, 846 (1992) (plurality decision). On both movements' strategic decisions in the lead-up to *Casey*, see Ziegler, *Abortion and the Law*, 134–136; Serena Mayeri, "Un-Dueing *Roe*: Constitutional Conflict and Political Polarization in *Planned Parenthood v. Casey*," in *Reproductive Rights and Justice Stories,* ed. Melissa Murray, Katherine Shaw, and Reva B. Siegel (New York: Foundation, 2019).

6. *Planned Parenthood of Southeastern Pennsylvania v. Casey*, 505 U.S. 833, 857–879 (1992) (plurality decision). For antiabortion optimism about these parts of the decision at the time, see Clarke D. Forsythe, "AUL Briefing Memo: The Good News about *Planned Parenthood v. Casey*," *AUL Briefing Memo* (July 1992), PLN, AUL Folder.

7. On the history and import of the Court's constitutional sex discrimination jurisprudence, see Cary Franklin, "Inventing the 'Traditional Concept' of Sex Discrimination," *Harvard Law Review* 125 (2012): 1207–1234; Serena Mayeri, *Reasoning from Race: Feminism, Law, and the Civil Rights Revolution* (Cambridge, MA: Harvard University Press, 2011), 110–188; Reva B. Siegel, "Constitutional Culture, Social Movement Conflict, and Constitutional Change: The Case of the De Facto ERA," *California Law Review* 94 (2006): 1323–1356.

8. For an overview of equality-based arguments for abortion rights, see Ruth Bader Ginsburg, "Some Thoughts on Autonomy and Equality in Relation to *Roe v. Wade*," *North Carolina Law Review* 63 (1985): 375–394; Reva B. Siegel, Serena Mayeri, and Melissa Murray, "Equal Protection in *Dobbs* and Beyond: How States Protect Life Inside and Outside of the Abortion Context," *Columbia Journal of Law and Gender* 43 (2023): 67–95. For a sample of key scholarship of the era on equality and abortion, see Sylvia Law, "Rethinking Sex and the Constitution," *University of Pennsylvania Law Review* 32 (1984): 955–1020; Catharine A. MacKinnon, "Reflections on Sex Equality under the Law," *Yale Law Journal* 100 (1991): 1281–1328; Reva B. Siegel, "Reasoning from the Body: A Historical Perspective on Abortion Regulation and Questions of Equal Protection," *Stanford Law Review* 44 (1992): 262–380; Peggy Cooper Davis, *Neglected Stories: The Constitution and Family Values* (New York: Hill and Wang, 1997).

9. *Planned Parenthood of Southeastern Pennsylvania v. Casey*, 505 U.S. 833, 856 (1992) (plurality decision).

10. Edward Walsh, "Anomalies of the Abortion Fight," *Washington Post*, May 21, 1994, A3. On the culture and politics of the "Year of the Woman," see Lisa Young, *Feminists and Party Politics* (Vancouver: University of British Columbia Press, 2000), 49–55; Richard Logan Fox, "Congressional Elections: Where Are We on the Road to

Gender Parity?" in *Gender and Elections: Shaping the Future of American Politics*, ed. Susan J. Carroll and Richard Logan Fox (New York: Cambridge University Press, 2005), 191–200. On NARAL's new approach, see Charles Babington, "Abortion-Rights Group Broadens Focus," *Washington Post*, December 24, 1992, A1.

11. For the study on the impact of abortion, see Alan I. Abramowitz, "It's Abortion, Stupid: Policy Voting in the 1992 Presidential Election," *Journal of Politics* 57 (1995): 176–186. For GOP internal polling, see Market Strategies, "Post-Election Report for RNC" (January 10, 1993), FSP, Box 36, Post-Election Folder 1; Hansen Post-Election Report 1992 (1992), FSP, Box 36, Post-Election Folder 1. On the 1992 poll, see "Abortion," *Gallup In-Depth Topics*, https://news.gallup.com/poll/1576/abortion.aspx.

12. Pamphlet, National Days of Rescue 3 (1991), FWHC, Carton 8, Operation Rescue Folder 1; see also Pamphlet, Brochure, Operation Rescue Los Angeles (n.d., ca. 1991), FWHC, Carton 9, Operation Rescue Folder 2; Carol J.C. Maxwell, *Pro-Life Activists in America: Meaning, Motivation, and Direct Action* (New York: Cambridge University Press, 2002), 99–100. On the debt and Operation Rescue's other troubles, see Charles Shepherd, "Operation Rescue's Mission to Save Itself," *Washington Post*, November 23, 1991, A1.

13. For the pamphlet: Brochure, The American Center for Law and Justice (n.d., ca. 1993), THV, Box 18, Folder 1; see also Clipping, Keith Fournier, "Religion, the Right Wing, and Political Morality," (1997), PAW, Carton 88, Folder 2. On the attorneys who represented blockaders in the period, see "Atlanta's Baby Does Rescued," *Free Speech Advocates* (December 1988), LMP, Box 82, Folder 11 (detailing the work of Free Speech Advocates, a group that litigated on behalf of antiabortion protestors); see also Free Speech Advocates, Fundraising Letter (December 21, 1988), LMP, Box 82, Folder 11. For more on ACLJ's claims of persecution, see ACLJ, "IRS Documents Reveal Attacks on Christians" (March 1998), PAW, Carton 88, Folder 3; ACLJ, "U.S. Post Office Delays and Censors Christian Mail" (May 1998), PAW, Carton 88, Folder 3. On Sekulow's background: Elizabeth Williamson, "Trump's Other Lawyer: Close to the Right, but Far from Giuliani," *New York Times*, December 1, 2019, https://www.nytimes.com/2019/12/01/us/politics/trump-sekulow-impeachment.html.

14. For an example of these suits, see Memorandum of Law in Support of Plaintiffs' Motion for Civil Contempt, *Roe v. Operation Rescue*, Civil Action No. 88-5157 (E.D. Pa. 1988), NOWLDEF, Box 564, Folder 2. On these strategies, see Mary Ziegler, *Roe: The History of a National Obsession* (New Haven: Yale University Press, 2023), 92–101. The original Ku Klux Klan Act included both criminal and civil penalties, but the criminal provisions were invalidated by the Supreme Court and later

repealed by Congress. The portions permitting civil liability remained, authorizing lawsuits against people who conspired to strip marginalized groups of their rights. On Clayton's story: "Now Is She a Household Name?" *Chicago Tribune*, January 31, 1994, https://www.chicagotribune.com/1994/01/31/now-is-she-a-household-name/. AUL lawyers argued that the use of the RICO statute was "legal warfare with those who are simply trying to protect innocent unborn children from abortion." "Pro-Life Activists Win Civil Rights Victory," *Life Docket* (June/July 1991), 3, SBL, Box 1, Folder 5001.

15. Statement of Merle Hoffman (July 6, 1992), 1, MHP, Box 1, Folder 3; Operation Rescue Strategy Meeting (May 13, 1989), FWHC, Box 1, Operation Rescue Folder 1. For the statement that blockaders sought to take away patients' health care: Pamphlet, "Your Body, Their Choice" (n.d., ca. 1992), MHP, Box 1, Folder 3. For more arguments of this kind, see Bebe Verdery to Planned Parenthood Public Affairs Offices Re Proactive Clinic Legislation (n.d., ca. 1993), MHP, Box 1, Folder 3 (advising advocates to expose "the broader agenda of the anti-choice movement: to deny individuals not only access to abortion but also to the full range of reproductive health services"); Clinic Defense Task Force, Statement of Purpose (June 3, 1994), MHP, Box 1, Folder 3 (vowing to ensure that "no woman is denied access to health-care because of illegal tactics by anti-abortion terrorists").

16. "High Court Declines to Reinstate Louisiana Penalties for Abortion," *Honolulu Star Advertiser*, March 9, 1993, 6 (HI). For the Court's decision in *Bray*, see *Bray v. Alexandria Women's Health Clinic*, 506 U.S. 263, 270 (1993). For AUL's statement: "Court Says Rescuers Aren't Anti-Woman," *AUL Forum* (March 1993), 1, PAW, Carton 9, Folder 7; see also "Operation Rescue and the Rule of Law: The Story from Wichita," *Life Docket* (August 1991), SBL, Box 1, Folder 5001.

17. On Griffin, Gunn, and the fallout from his murder, see Johanna Schoen, *Abortion After* Roe (Chapel Hill: University of North Carolina Press, 2015), 210–219; David S. Cohen and Krysten Connon, *Living in the Crosshairs: The Untold Stories of Anti-Abortion Terrorism* (New York: Oxford University Press, 2015), 58, 76, 98. For Burt's conviction, see Bill Kaczor, "Abortion Foe Gets 18 Years in Abuse Case," *Lakeland Ledger*, May 13, 2004, https://www.theledger.com/story/news/2004/05/13/abortion-foe-gets-18-years-in-abuse-case/26113878007/ (FL).

18. Molly Ivins, "If Michael Griffin Was Culpable, So Are Others," *Detroit Free Press*, March 18, 1993, 14. For the defensive action statement, see First Defensive Action Statement (March 10, 1993), on file with the author. For discussion of Hill's "defensive action statement," see Carol Mason, *Killing for Life: The Apocalyptic Narrative of Pro-Life Politics* (Ithaca: Cornell University Press, 2002), 46–49, 70–72.

19. For arguments of this kind, see Pamphlet, National Days of Rescue 3, 1–3; Pamphlet, Operation Rescue Los Angeles, 1–2.

20. Strategy Proposal, Guy Condon to Richard John Neuhaus (February 11, 1991), RJN, Box 2, Folder 34; see also Americans United for Life Conceptual Meeting (March 21, 1990), RJN, Box 2, Folder 33; RJN Memo on August 22, 1991, Roundtable Convened by the Secretariat of Pro-Life Activities, RJN, Box 2, Folder 33. For more on Women Exploited by Abortion, see Women Exploited by Abortion, "Memorial to the Unborn Child" (July 15, 1987), JWC, National Right to Life Committee Folders ("Millions of unborn children . . . have lost their lives in a war against the family"). For more on Women Exploited by Abortion and Rachel's Vineyard, see Sara Dubow, *Ourselves Unborn: A History of the Fetus in Modern America* (New York: Oxford University Press, 2010), 161–163, 172; Jennifer Holland, *Tiny You: A Western History of the Anti-Abortion Movement* (Berkeley: University of California Press, 2020), 139.

21. Cunningham, "Can We Love Women Who Abort?"

22. AUL Fundraising Letter (August 8, 1994), 1; NRLC Model Informed Consent for 1995, 1. For an example of literature from the right-to-know campaign, see Pamphlet, "Abortion: Some Medical Facts" (n.d., ca. 1996), MFJ, Box 8, Folder 4 (explaining that "Americans . . . have a right to be informed about things that might affect our health"—and that "abortion ends a pregnancy by destroying and removing the developing child").

23. On the litigation against the tobacco industry and its challenges, see Alan M. Brandt, *The Cigarette Century: The Rise, Fall, and Deadly Persistence of the Product That Defined America* (New York: Basic Books, 2009), 323–345; Peter Pringle, *Cornered: Big Tobacco at the Bar of Justice* (New York: Henry Holt, 2014), 3–15; Sarah Milov, *The Cigarette: A Political History* (Cambridge, MA: Harvard University Press, 2019), 280–305.

24. See *Inside the Tobacco Deal, PBS Frontline*, https://www.pbs.org/wgbh/pages /frontline/shows/settlement/timelines/fullindex.html; Brandt, *The Cigarette Century*, 323–345; Milov, *The Cigarette*, 288–305.

25. Clarke Forsythe, "The Enduring Solution to Abortion?" *AUL Forum* (July/ August 1995), PAW, Carton 9, Folder 8. For the statement about constitutional protection: "The Pro-Life Plank: Luxury or Necessity in the Republican Platform?" *AUL Forum* (Spring 1996), 2, PAW, Carton 9, Folder 8.

26. Paige Comstock Cunningham, "A Compassionate—and Caring—Agenda for the Next Four Years," *AUL Forum* (May 1993), 1, PAW, Carton 9, Folder 7. For more on the development of this strategy, see Americans United for Life Meeting Minutes (April 24, 1993), MFJ, Box 13, Folder 8; Talking Points, "Abortion and Women's

Equality" (n.d., ca. 1994), MGP; Americans United for Life, Press Release (June 30, 1994), MGP; Americans United for Life, Media Guide (n.d., ca. 1994), MGP. For Operation Rescue's position on the exploitation of women, see Keith Tucci to Members of Operation Rescue National (February 8, 1991), FWHC, Carton 9, Operation Rescue National Folder 2 (describing women as engaging in child killing while arguing that legal abortion allowed women "to be exploited"). For the statement on restoring justice: Operation Rescue, Pamphlet: Atlanta 1988, FWHC, Carton 9, Operation Rescue National Folder 2; see also Operation Rescue, National Day of Rescue II (1989), FWHC, Carton 9, Operation Rescue National Folder 2.

27. On the health-care reform debate in the period, see Theda Skocpol, *Boomerang: Health Care Reform and the Turn against Government* (New York: Norton, 1996), 3–24; Paul Starr, *Remedy and Reaction: The Peculiar American Struggle over Health Care Reform* (New Haven: Yale University Press, 2013), 4–18, 106–122.

28. For Radford's statement, see Gina Kolata, "Under Pressure and Stigma, More Doctors Shun Abortion," *New York Times*, January 8, 1990, A1. On the lack of abortion training, see Susan Gilbert, "Clinic Violence Sets off Push for Wider Abortion Training," *New York Times*, January 11, 1995, C11. For more on concern within the movement about a lack of trained providers, see National Abortion Federation, "Who Will Provide Abortions?" (1990), NCAP, Box 1, Folder 1.

29. "Choices, Debate Manual" (n.d., ca. 1994), NCAP, Box 1, Folder 2; NARAL Foundation, "Talking about the Freedom to Choose" (n.d., ca. 1996), NARALMA, Box 14, Folder 12.

30. MCFL Fact Sheet, 1; see also National Right to Life Committee, "Marked Draft of Wisconsin Informed Consent Bill" (n.d., ca. 1994), JBP, Matter Boxes, File 1203; Barbara Listing, "Women Should Know Abortion Alternatives," *Lansing State Journal*, June 24, 1993, 7 (MI). For more on opposition to the health-care reform, see Burke Balch, "Medicare Rationing: The Calm Before the Storm," *National Right to Life News* (August 22, 1995), 1, JRS, 1995 National Right to Life News Box.

31. Brown had been skeptical of such laws as early as 1992. See "Bush Cheers Anti-Abortion Demonstrators," *Atlanta Journal*, January 22, 1992, 6 (GA). For Brown's statement: Judy Brown and Brian Young, "Exceptions: Abandoning the 'Least of These My Brethren,'" *The Eternal Word Network* (*ETWN*) (1994), https://www.ewtn.com/catholicism/library/exceptions-abandoning-the-least-of-these-my-brethren-11972 (Irondale, AL). For her later statements: Judie Brown, "Consent for What?" *American Life League*, June 6, 2006. For Cunningham's statement: Paige Comstock Cunningham, "Looking Forward to Life," *AUL Forum* (April 1994), 1, PAW, Carton 9, Folder 7. For more on woman-protective arguments, see Reva B. Siegel, "The

Right's Reasons: Constitutional Conflict and the Spread of Woman-Protective Anti-Abortion Argument," *Duke Law Journal* 57 (2008): 1641–1692.

32. U.S. Women of Color Coalition for Reproductive Rights, "Statement on Poverty, Development, and Population Activities," prepared for the International Conference on Population and Development, Cairo (1994), 2, on file with the author. For Saika's statement: Jael Silliman, Loretta Ross, Elena Gutiérrez, and Marlene Gerber Fried, *Undivided Rights: Women of Color Organize for Reproductive Justice*, 2nd ed. (New York: Haymarket, 2016), 199–200. For more on Saika's story: "Excerpts from the Voices of Feminism Oral History Project Interview with Peggy Saika by Loretta Ross," *Meridians: Feminism, Race, and Transnationalism* 10 (2010): 163–197.

33. See Silliman et al., *Undivided Rights*, 65–66; Zakiya Luna, *Reproductive Rights as Human Rights: Women of Color and the Fight for Reproductive Justice* (New York: New York University Press, 2020), 23–65.

34. On Crutcher's time as a car salesman, see "America's #1 Selling Car: The 1976 Monte Carlo," *Denton Record Chronicle*, February 22, 1976, 32 (TX); "Salesman Named to Honor Club," *Denton Record Chronicle*, March 20, 1977, 21 (TX). On Crutcher's role in North Texas Right to Life, see Mark Crutcher, "Rights Are Relative, but None Outweighs the Right to Life," *Fort Worth Star-Telegram*, May 11, 1989, 25 (TX); Mark Crutcher, Letter to the Editor, "Two Wrongs Don't Make a Right," *Fort Worth Star-Telegram*, April 3, 1989, 14 (TX). On "Bottom Feeder," see Terri Langford, "AMA Looking into Whether Abortion Foes Have Its Mailing List," *Fort Worth Star-Telegram*, March 18, 1993, A24 (TX).

35. On Britton's murder, see Cohen and Connon, *Living in the Crosshairs*, 76–80; Johanna Schoen, "Introduction: Providing Abortion Care," in *Abortion Care as Moral Work: Ethical Considerations of Maternal and Fetal Bodies*, ed. Johanna Schoen (New Brunswick: Rutgers University Press, 2022), 8.

36. "Principle and Prudence," *AUL Forum* (October 1994), 2, PAW, Carton 9, Folder 8. For Cunningham's statement: Paige Comstock Cunningham, "No Room for Violence," *AUL Forum* (October 1994), 1, PAW, Carton 9, Folder 8.

37. On the divide about violence within the blockade movement, see Tamar Lewin, "Death of a Doctor: The Moral Debate," *New York Times*, July 30, 1994, A1; Laurie Goodstein, "Life and Death Choices: Antiabortion Faction Tries to Justify Homicide," *Washington Post*, August 13, 1994, A1; Gustav Niebuhr, "Anti-Abortion Tactics Debated by Nation's Christian Leaders," *New York Times*, January 9, 1995, A1. For Hill's argument: "In Defense of Another: The Paul Hill Brief," *Regent University Law Review* 5 (1995): 34.

38. On the FACE Act and its impact, see 18 U.S.C. § 248 (1994); see also David S. Cohen and Carol Joffe, *Obstacle Course: The Everyday Struggle to Get Abortion in America* (New York: Oxford University Press, 2020), 136–137. On movement reaction to the bill: Concerned Women for America, Fundraising Letter (May 1995), PAW, Carton 28, Folder 7 (describing FACE "as a way to restrict the freedom of speech and religion rights of Christians").

39. On Crutcher's strategy, see Mark Crutcher, "Firestorm: A Guerilla Strategy for a Pro-Life America" (1992), 1–11, JBP, Matter Boxes, File 1067; Tamar Lewin, "Latest Tactic against Abortion: Accusing Doctors of Malpractice," *New York Times*, April 9, 1995, A1. For an earlier effort like Crutcher's, see "Cash Awards in Abortion Complication Litigation" (n.d., ca. 1984), LMP, Box 82, Folder 11.

40. For Rue's arguments: Vincent Rue, "Mourning Responses, Reconciliation, and Abortion" (n.d., ca. 1994), PAW, Carton 32, Folder 2; Pamphlet, "Forgotten Fathers" (n.d., ca. 1988), LMP, Box 82, Folder 11. For Rue's testimony: Constitutional Amendments relating to Abortion: Hearings on SJ Res 18, SJ Res 19, and SJ Res 110 before the Subcommittee on the Constitution of the Committee on the Judiciary, 97th Congress, 1st Session (1981), 330–331 (testimony of Vincent Rue). For more on Rue's work, see Dubow, *Ourselves Unborn*, 161; Siegel, "The Right's Reasons," 1658–1664.

41. David Reardon to C. Everett Koop (September 30, 1989), DRP. For examples of Reardon's work: Pamphlet, the Elliot Institute, "Post-Abortion Trauma: Learning the Truth, Telling the Truth" (n.d., ca. 1993), NCAP, Box 3, Elliot Institute Folder; David C. Reardon, "The Abortion-Suicide Connection," *The Post-Abortion Review* (Summer 1993), 1, NCAP, Box 3, Elliot Institute Folder.

42. On Reardon's background, see Ziegler, *Abortion and the Law*, 138–139; Edmund L. Andrews, "Patents: Fingerprinting to Detect Fraud," *New York Times*, January 18, 1992, 18. For Reardon's statements: Reardon to Koop, 2.

43. RAND, "Backlash against HMOs Caused Few People to Bolt from Health Plans," March 24, 2005, https://www.rand.org/news/press/2005/03/24.html; see also M. Susan Marquis et al., "The Managed Care Backlash: Did Consumers Vote with Their Feet?" *Inquiry* 41 (2005): 376–390. On the increasing importance of HMOs in the 1990s, see Bradford H. Gray, "The Rise and Decline of the HMO: A Chapter in U.S. Health-Policy History," in *History and Health Policy in the United States: Putting the Past Back In*, ed. Rosemary Stevens, Charles Rosenberg, and Lawton Burns (New Brunswick: Rutgers University Press, 2006), 309–341; Jan Gregoire Coombs, *The Rise and Fall of HMOs: An American Health Care Revolution* (Madison: University of Wisconsin Press, 2005), 195–236.

44. See Amy Goldstein, "How HMOs Became the Enemy, from Nonprofit Ideals to Corporate Horror Stories," *Washington Post*, October 10, 1999, A1; Robert J. Samuelson, "HMO Backlash," *Washington Post*, March 4, 1998, A21.

45. "Health Care Reform and You," *AUL Forum* (September 1994), 3, PAW, Carton 9, Folder 8.

46. *Quill v. Koppell*, 870 F. Supp. 78, 82 (S.D.N.Y. 1994); *Compassion in Dying v. State of Washington*, 850 F. Supp. 1454, 1459 (W.D. Wash. 1994). For Bopp's case: Joan Biskupic, "Oregon's Assisted Suicide Law Lives On," *Washington Post*, October 15, 1997, A3. For more on the movement's work on the issue in the period, see Burke Balch, "Court Rulings on Suicide 'Right' Goes Far Beyond Voluntary Killing of Terminally Ill," *National Right to Life News* (March 15, 1996), 1, JRS, 1996 National Right to Life News Box; "Supreme Court to Decide Whether Aged or Disabled May Be Killed without Their Consent," *National Right to Life Committee* (October 9, 1996), 8, JRS, 1996 National Right to Life News Box.

47. Clarke D. Forsythe, "The Enduring Solution to Abortion," *AUL Forum* (July/August 1995), 1, PAW, Carton 9, Folder 8. For more on AUL's new vision, see Paige Cunningham to AUL Forum Readers (May 1, 1995), PAW, Carton 9, Folder 8; Clarke D. Forsythe, "The America We Seek," *AUL Forum* (Summer 1996), 1, PAW, Carton 9, Folder 8.

48. For AFDC numbers from 1993, see Bureau of Statistics, "Mothers Who Receive AFDC Payments: Fertility and Socioeconomic Characteristics," *Bureau of the Census Statistical Brief* (1995), https://www2.census.gov/library/publications/1995/demographics/sb95–02.pdf. For Clinton's 1991 speech: Bill Clinton, "The New Covenant: Responsibility and Rebuilding the American Community," October 23, 1991, https://digital.tcl.sc.edu/digital/collection/p17173coll40/id/480/. On the intersection of welfare policy and race in the decades that preceded Clinton's proposals, see Jill Quadagno, *The Color of Welfare: How Racism Undermined the War on Poverty* (New York: Oxford University Press, 1994), 2–33, 123–156; Daniel Geary, *Beyond Civil Rights: The Moynihan Report and Its Legacy* (Philadelphia: University of Pennsylvania Press, 2015), 172–205.

49. "Clinton Criticizes Illegitimacy Rate," *Hartford Courant*, September 10, 1994, A8 (CT); see also Bill Clinton, "Address before a Joint Session of the Congress on the State of the Union" (January 24, 1995), https://www.presidency.ucsb.edu/documents/address-before-joint-session-the-congress-the-state-the-union-11. For Rector's statement: Hilary Stout, "GOP's Welfare Stance Owes a Lot to Prodding from Robert Rector," *Wall Street Journal*, January 23, 1995, A1. For more on Republicans' proposals: John MacDonald, "Reforms of Welfare Debated," *Hartford Courant*,

December 8, 1995, A1 (CT); see also Mary Reintsma, *The Political Economy of Welfare Reform in the United States* (New York: Elgar, 2007), 158–162.

50. United States Catholic Conference, *Children and Families First: Moral Principles and Policy Priorities for Welfare Reform* (Washington, DC: United States Conference of Catholic Bishops, 1995), 1–2. On the views of the Heritage Foundation and Christian Coalition, see Stout, "GOP's Welfare Stance," A1; Megan Rosenfeld, "Faith, Politics, and Charity," *Washington Post*, August 9, 1995, D1.

51. Wanda Franz, "Pro-Lifers Must Reject Welfare 'Reforms' That Increase Abortion Rates," *National Right to Life News* (February 22, 1995), 3, JRS, 1996 National Right to Life News Box.

52. Franz, "Pro-Lifers Must Reject." For Franz's March statement: Wanda Franz, "Welfare 'Reforms' Must Not Increase Abortion Rates," *National Right to Life News* (March 16, 1995), 3, JRS, 1996 National Right to Life News Box. For more on early opposition to welfare reform within the movement, see "Pro-Lifers Air Concern over Welfare Reform and Abortion," *National Right to Life News* (February 3, 1995), 1, JRS, 1995 National Right to Life News Box. For the conference's statement: "Children and Families First," 6.

53. Martin Haskell, "Dilation and Extraction for Second-Trimester Abortion" (September 23, 1992), on file with the author. For more on the early strategy regarding partial-birth abortion, see Ziegler, *Abortion and the Law*, 166–184; Dubow, *Ourselves Unborn*, 164–180; Schoen, *Abortion after Roe*, 253–273.

54. On Doug Johnson, see Ziegler, *Abortion and the Law*, 156–188; Patricia Miller, *Good Catholics: The Battle over Abortion in the Catholic Church* (Berkeley: University of California Press, 2015), 108, 176.

55. Petition to the Following 10 U.S. Senators (n.d., ca. 1998), THV, Carton 15, Folder 2. For more on NRLC's strategy around dilation and extraction: National Right to Life Committee Meeting Minutes (April 13–14, 1996), JBP, Matter Boxes, File 1327; see also National Right to Life Committee (June 19, 1995), JBP, Matter Boxes, File 1275; National Right to Life Committee Executive Committee (October 13, 1995), JBP, Matter Boxes, File 1275.

56. NARAL, "Talking about Freedom of Choice," (n.d., ca. 1997), NARALMA, Box 42, Folder 12; see also NARAL Pro-Choice Massachusetts, "Defending against Attacks" (n.d., ca. 1997), NARALMA, Box 42, Folder 12; Bob to NOW Action Mailing List (April 29, 1997), LMP, Box 82, Folder 11 (arguing that women "do not want congressmen dictating how their doctors should practice medicine when their lives and health are at risk"). On NAF's argument, see Ziegler, *Abortion and the Law*, 169, 178, 187.

57. National Right to Life Committee (July 10, 1996), JBP, Matter Boxes, File 1327; see also Board of Directors Meeting Minutes (June 18–19, 1996), JBP, Matter Boxes, File 1327; National Right to Life Committee (February 26, 1996), JBP, Matter Boxes, File 1327.

58. Concerned Women for America, Fundraising Letter (July 1996), 2, PAW, Carton 28, Folder 8. For Brown's position: Judie Brown, "Letter to the Editor," *First Things*, March 1996, on file with the author.

59. NLRC, Memo: Misinformation (June 15, 1995), JBP, Matter Box 1395; Partial-Birth Abortion: The Painful Truth (n.d., ca. 1996), JBP, Matter Box 1395; National Right to Life Committee, "Partial-Birth Abortion: A Look behind the Misinformation" (October 25, 1995), JBP, Matter Box 1395. On anti-tobacco campaigns in the period, see Milov, *The Cigarette*, 136–152.

60. NRLC Fundraising Letter (June 10, 1996), JBP, Matter Box 1395. For the PHACT statement: "The Activists Have Spoken, The Politicians Have Spoken. May We Say Something?" (n.d., ca. 1996), JBP, Matter Box 1395. For the welfare reform law, see 42 U.S.C. §§ 604a, 608a (1996). For more on the history and consequences of the law, see Gwendolyn Mink and Felicia Kornbluh, *Ensuring Poverty: Welfare Reform in Feminist Perspective* (Philadelphia: University of Pennsylvania Press, 2019), 2–17, 87–99.

61. See Kathleen Belew, *Bring the War Home: The White Power Movement and Paramilitary America* (Cambridge, MA: Harvard University Press, 2019), 24, 196–199; Robert H. Churchill, *To Shake Their Guns in the Tyrant's Face: Libertarian Political Violence and the Origins of the Militia Movement* (Ann Arbor: University of Michigan Press, 2009), 23, 190–199. For Cunningham's statement: Walsh, "Anomalies," A3.

62. See Belew, *Bring the War Home*, 214–227; Churchill, *To Shake Their Guns*, 7–8, 206, 256–257.

63. On Rudolph, see Mason, *Killing for Life*, 87, 204; Belew, *Bring the War Home*, 223. For Rudolph's statement: "Full Text of Eric Rudolph's Confession," *NPR*, April 14, 2005, https://www.npr.org/templates/story/story.php?storyId=4600480. In 1994, John Salvi, another antiabortion extremist, attacked two Massachusetts clinics, killing two people and injuring others.

64. For Cunningham's statement: Paige Comstock Cunningham, " 'Solving' the Problem of Death," *AUL Forum* (March 1995), 1, PAW, Carton 9, Folder 8. For AUL's argument: "America Pre- and Post-*Roe*," *AUL Forum* (January 1995), 2, PAW, Carton 9, Folder 8.

65. On the founding of SisterSong, see Luna, *Reproductive Rights as Human Rights*, 113–209; Loretta Ross and Rickie Solinger, *Reproductive Justice: An Introduction*

(Berkeley: University of California Press, 2020), 54–67. On disparities in maternal mortality, see American Medical Association, "State-Specific Maternal Mortality among Black and White Women: United States, 1987–1996," *Journal of the American Medical Association* 282 (1999): 1220–1222; American Medical Association, "Differences in Maternal Mortality among Black and White Women, United States," *Journal of the American Medical Association* 273 (1995): 370–371. For Rodriguez's story: Luz Rodriguez, interview with Joyce Follett, June 16–17, 2006, https://www.smith.edu /libraries/libs/ssc/vof/transcripts/Rodriguez.pdf.

66. On the history of early struggles over mifepristone, or RU 486, see Greer Donley, "Medication Abortion Exceptionalism," *Cornell Law Review* 107 (2022): 627–654; Carrie N. Baker, "History and Politics of Medication Abortion in the United States and the Rise of Telemedicine and Self-Managed Abortion," *Journal of Health, Politics, Policy and Law* (2023): 485–510. For Forsythe's statement: "Conservative Spotlight: Americans United for Life," *AUL Forum* (Spring 1996), 3, PAW, Carton 9, Folder 8. On the citizens' petition: "RU 486 Petition Draws Strong Response from Abortion Advocates, Media," *AUL Forum* (May/June 1995), 1, PAW, Carton 9, Folder 8; see also "RU 486 Consumer Boycott List of Copley and Hoechst-Roussel Products," *National Right to Life News* (January 1996), 11, JRS, 1996 National Right to Life News Box.

67. Clipping, "Conservative Spotlight: The Rutherford Institute," *Human Events* (1995), PAW, Carton 66, Folder 4; see also Rutherford Institute, Parental Rights Petition (October 1995), PAW, Carton 66, Folder 13; Rutherford Institute, Fundraising Letter (September 1995), PAW, Carton 66, Folder 12; Rutherford Institute, Fundraising Letter (July 1995), PAW, Carton 66, Folder 12. For Rutherford's involvement in the Jones case, see Robert L. Jackson, "Conservatives Rally to Paula Jones," *Los Angeles Times*, December 13, 1997, 23. On Rutherford's fundraising, see Mark Curriden, "Defenders of the Faith," *American Bar Association*, December 1994, 89.

68. Clipping, Michael Whitehead, "Alliance Defense Fund" (n.d., ca. 1997), PAW, Carton 2, Folder 12. For more on the founding of ADF, see Joshua C. Wilson, *The New States of Abortion Politics* (Palo Alto: Stanford University Press, 2016), 39–43; Amanda Hollis-Brusky and Joshua Wilson, *Separate but Faithful: The Christian Right's Radical Struggle to Transform Law and Legal Culture* (New York: Oxford University Press, 2020), 34–53, 53–60.

69. Alliance Defense Fund, Fundraising Letter (September 1995), PAW, Carton 2, Folder 11; see also ADF Fundraising Letter (n.d., ca. 1994), AUS, Box 1, Folder 12; "ADF Answers" (n.d. ca. 1996), AUS, Box 1, Folder 16 (arguing that the principles of "religious freedom, the sanctity of human life, and family values" were given to

Americans "by God through the Founding Fathers"). For more on ADF's founding and vision of the Constitution, see Clipping, "Making the Streets Safe from the Legal Left" (n.d., ca. 2000), PAW, Carton 2, Folder 11; Clipping, "The ADF's Reconstructionist Ties: Enforcing God's Law," (n.d., ca. 2000), PAW, Carton 2, Folder 11. On the number of cases ACLJ was pursuing, see "God Is My Co-Counsel," *New York Times*, March 23, 1997, SM25. On ACLJ's budget and influence, see Marc Fischer, "Unlikely Crusaders: Jay Sekulow, 'Messianic Jew' of the Christian Right," *Washington Post*, October 21, 1997, D1.

70. On Sears's career, see Carrie Labriola, "Porn Could Be Wiped out within Two Years, Official Says," *Dayton Daily News*, August 31, 1986, 12 (OH); Clarence Smith, "Louisville's Alan Sears Shapes Ideas into Southern Baptist Resolutions," *Courier-Journal*, June 12, 1986, B4 (Louisville, KY); Jonathan Roos, "Obscenity Law Too Weak, Lawyer Says," *Des Moines Register*, September 29, 1988, 2 (IA). On Keating's connection to CDL, see Francie Noes, "The Keating Way of Doing Business," *Arizona Republic*, April 13, 1987, C1 (Phoenix).

71. On the early conflict over same-sex marriage, see Michael Klarman, *From the Closet to the Altar: Courts, Backlash, and the Struggle for Same-Sex Marriage* (New York: Oxford University Press, 2013), 48–75; Lillian Faderman, *The Gay Revolution: The Story of the Struggle* (New York: Simon and Schuster, 2016), 586–765; William N. Eskridge and Christopher Riano, *Marriage Equality: From Outlaws to In-Laws* (New Haven: Yale University Press, 2020), 92–120; George Chauncey, *Why Marriage? The History Shaping Today's Debate over Same-Sex Marriage* (New York: Basic Books, 2004), 124–140. For the court's ruling in *Baehr*, see *Baehr v. Lewin*, 852 P.2d 44 (Haw. 1993).

72. For Sears's arguments: ADF, Fundraising Letter (April 1997), PAW, Carton 2, Folder 11; see also "The ACLU Finally Meets Its Match," *ADF Quarterly Briefing* (April 1998), PAW, Carton 2, Folder 9; Steven A. Schwalm, "Conservative Spotlight: The American Center for Law and Justice," *Human Events*, December 20, 1996, 20; Concerned Women for America, Fundraising Letter (June 1996), PAW, Carton 28, Folder 8. For the poll: "LGBTQ+ Rights," *Gallup*, https://news.gallup.com/poll/1651/gay-lesbian-rights.aspx.

73. *Romer v. Evans*, 517 U.S. 620, 632 (1996). For more on growing (but limited) tolerance, see Klarman, *From the Closet to the Altar*, 180–213; Eskridge and Riano, *Marriage Equality*, 226–385.

74. Peter Montgomery to ACLJ Legal (September 14, 1997), PAW, Carton 88, Folder 2. For ADF's statement: ADF Fundraising Letter (September 1995), PAW, Carton 2, Folder 19. ACLJ and ADF both stressed that the United States was and must remain a Christian nation, and that the nation's Constitution reflected (and

should be interpreted in line with) Christian teachings. For more on the groups' ties to Christian nationalism, see Sara Posner, *Unholy: How White Christian Nationalists Powered the Trump Presidency, and the Devastating Legacy They Left Behind* (New York: Random House, 2020), 161–173; Katherine Stewart, *The Power Worshippers: Inside the Dangerous Rise of Religious Nationalism* (New York: Bloomsbury, 2020), 215–266.

75. Brief Amicus Curiae of the National Right to Life Committee, 23, *Washington v. Glucksberg*, 521 U.S. 702 (1997) (No. 96-110). For AUL's argument: Brief of Focus on the Family et al., 5–10, *Washington v. Glucksberg*, 521 U.S. 702 (1997) (No. 96-110). For more on AUL's work in this area: Clarke D. Forsythe, "Holding the Line against Assisted Suicide," *AUL Forum* (Spring 1996), PAW, Carton 9, Folder 8; see also "Assisted Suicide in the Courts," *AUL Forum* (Spring 1996), 1, PAW, Carton 9, Folder 8.

76. For the NRLC press release: National Right to Life Committee, "Upcoming Supreme Court Decision on Physician-Assisted Suicide"(May 27, 1997), MFJ, Box 9, Folder 3. On antiabortion work on aid in dying in the period, see "Assisted Suicide in the Courts," 1; "Legal News Update," *AUL Forum* (May/June 1995), 1, PAW, Carton 9, Folder 8; "Assisted Suicide Defeated in Michigan, New York," *AUL Forum* (April 1995), 1, PAW, Carton 9, Folder 8. For more arguments about the duties of guardians and doctors toward those with illnesses, see "Illinois Court Reverses 'Right to Die' Ruling," *Life Docket* (June/July 1988), 2, SBL, Box 1, Folder 5001 (Clarke Forsythe arguing that a guardian had "no authority to cut off food and water from an incompetent ward").

77. See *Washington v. Glucksberg*, 521 U.S. 702, 727, 733 (1997). Three justices concurred only in the judgment, disagreeing with the majority's approach to identifying unenumerated rights.

78. For Forsythe's statement: Judy Peres, "Assisted Suicide Bans Upheld," *Chicago Tribune*, June 27, 1997, 1.

5. The Right to Conscience

1. See Sandra Boodman, "The 'Morning-After' Kit," *Washington Post*, September 22, 1998, 13. For Feldt's prediction: Steve Proffitt, "Gloria Feldt: Advocate Wins Hearts and Minds, but Not the War," *Los Angeles Times*, December 13, 1998, M3. On the differences between emergency contraception and birth control, see "Birth Control Pills v. Plan B: What's the Difference?" *Medicine.Net*, https://www.medicinenet.com/birth_control_pills_vs_plan_b_levonorgestrel/drug-vs.htm.

2. For examples of these arguments, see "Consumer Reports Must Get the Facts Straight on Birth Control Pills: They Cause Abortion," American Life League Press Release (January 5, 2005), MFJ, Box 12, Folder 7; American Life League, Press

Release, "Plan B Up for Over-the-Counter Review Again" (January 13, 2005), MFJ, Box 12, Folder 7 (arguing that emergency contraceptives "can take the life of a newly conceived baby").

3. For Bopp's story, see generally Mary Ziegler, *Dollars for Life: The Anti-Abortion Movement and the Fall of the Republican Establishment* (New Haven: Yale University Press, 2022).

4. See ADF and Becket Fund, "Top Line Coalition Talking Points" (n.d., ca. 2014), SFL, 2014–2015 Talking Points Folder. For ADF's briefs in the case, see Petitioners' Reply Brief, 10–11, *Conestoga Wood Specialties Corporation v. Sebelius*, 573 U.S. 682 (2014) (Nos. 13-354, 13-356) (contending that "families can exercise religion in business and are not denied that right simply because they operate through a corporation"); Brief of Petitioners, 20–25, *Conestoga Wood Specialties Corporation v. Sebelius*, 573 U.S. 682 (2014) (Nos. 13-354, 13-356). On the history of earlier conscience claims, see Sara Dubow, "'A Constitutional Right Rendered Utterly Meaningless:' Religious Exemptions and Reproductive Politics," *Journal of Policy History* 27 (2015): 1–35; Jerry Elmer, *Conscription, Conscientious Objection, and Draft Resistance in American History* (Leiden: Brill, 2023).

5. *Burwell v. Hobby Lobby Stores*, 573 U.S. 682 (2014).

6. On the approval of emergency contraception and its impact, see Heather Munro Prescott, *The Morning After: A History of Emergency Contraception in the United States* (New Brunswick: Rutgers University Press, 2011), 101–115; Elaine Tyler May, *America and the Pill: A History of Promise, Peril, and Liberation* (New York: Basic Books, 2010), 148–190. On the role played by Nathanson, see William Grimes, "B. N. Nathanson, 84, Dies; Changed Sides on Abortion," *New York Times*, February 22, 2011, https://www.nytimes.com/2011/02/22/us/22nathanson.html.

7. On the background of Life Forum, see Life Forum Meeting Minutes (October 4, 1996), PWP, Box 80, Folder 2. For more on Life Forum, see Life Forum Meeting Minutes (September 26, 1996), PWP, Box 80, Folder 3; Life Forum Meeting Minutes (October 24, 1997), PWP, Box 80, Folder 7. In earlier years, Life Forum was known as the Fieldstead Forum, after the donor funding it. Frank Pavone, interview with Mary Ziegler, September 12, 2023. Since the early 2000s, the forum has been called 115 Forum, after Psalm 115.

8. Life Forum Meeting Minutes (October 24, 1997), 3–8.

9. Life Forum Meeting Minutes, January 24, 1997, 2–3, PWP, Box 80, Folder 2. For Nathanson's statement: Life Forum Meeting Minutes (October 24, 1997), 3.

10. Dana Canedy, "Wal-Mart Decides against Selling a Contraceptive," *New York Times*, May 14, 1999, C1; see also Kimberlee Roth, "Pharmacists, Doctors Refuse to

Dispense Pill on Moral Grounds," *Chicago Tribune*, November 17, 2004, 8; Suz Redfearn, "Preparing for a Mistake: For Emergency Birth Control, Plan Ahead," *Washington Post*, May 21, 2002, F1.

11. For the 1998 ad campaign: Paula Span, "'Choice' Ads Target Young and Listless," *Washington Post*, December 3, 1998, D1. For Garrow's statement: Jennifer Lee, "Abortion Rights Group Plans a New Focus and a New Name," *New York Times*, January 5, 2003, 1. On shifting perspectives on the morality of abortion, see Megan Brenan, "Record-High 47 % in U.S. Think Abortion Is Morally Acceptable," *Gallup*, June 9, 2021, https://news.gallup.com/poll/350756/record-high-think-abortion-morally-acceptable.aspx. On the stigma experienced by abortion patients in the period, see Brenda Major and Richard H. Gramzow, "Abortion as Stigma: Cognitive and Emotional Implications of Concealment," *Journal of Personality and Social Psychology* 77 (1999): 735–745; M. A. Ellisson, "Authoritative Knowledge and Single Women's Unintentional Pregnancies, Abortion, and Single Motherhood," *Medical Anthropology Quarterly* 17 (2003): 322–347. On the relative number of Americans who identified as pro-life versus pro-choice, see Lydia Saad, "Broader Support for Abortion Rights Continues Post-*Dobbs*," *Gallup*, June 14, 2023, https://news.gallup.com/poll/506759/broader-support-abortion-rights-continues-post-dobbs.aspx.

12. On NRLC's budget, see Michael Grunwald, "Campaign Finance Issue Divides Abortion Foes," *Washington Post*, September 14, 1999, A1. For more on NRLC's activities in the period, see Doug Johnson to Jim Bopp (April 18, 2001), JBP, Matter Box 2264; NRLC Letter to Member of Congress (June 13, 2001), JBP, Matter Box 2264; Doug Johnson to National Right to Life Committee Board of Directors (September 21, 2001), JBP, Matter Box 2264. On the then record number of restrictions passed, see Julie Rovner, "New Restrictions on Abortion Almost Tied Record Last Year," *NPR*, January 19, 2012, https://www.npr.org/sections/health-shots/2012/01/19/145465011/new-restrictions-on-abortion-almost-tied-record-last-year (reporting on 1999 as record year).

13. On Liberty Counsel's early work, see Liberty Counsel, "Faith and Freedom: A Complete Handbook to Defend Your Religious Liberty Rights" (n.d., ca. 1999), AUS, Box 29, Folder 15; Liberty Counsel, "Same-Sex Marriage Petition" (n.d., ca. 2000), AUS, Box 29, Folder 15. On Staver's background, see Lynn Vincent, "Religious Liberty Lawyer Ready for First Case at High Court," *Baptist Press*, March 1, 2005, https://www.baptistpress.com/resource-library/news/religious-liberty-lawyer-ready-for-1st-case-before-high-court/; Jamie Thompson, "Christian Soldier, Legal Battlefield," *Tampa Bay Times,* November 15, 2004, https://www.tampabay.com/archive/2004/11/15/christian-soldier-legal-battlefield/.

14. On ADF's financial situation, see Alliance Defense Fund, Form 990 (2001), https://projects.propublica.org/nonprofits/display_990/541660459/2002_03_ EO%2F54–1660459_990_200106. On ADF's funding plans, see Clipping, Michael Whitehead, "Alliance Defense Fund" (n.d., ca. 2000), PAW, Carton 2, Folder 13.

15. U.S. Const. amend. I. On ADF's cases from the era, see ADF, "The ACLU Meets Its Match," *ADF Quarterly Briefing* (2000), 1–2, PAW, Carton 2, Folder 13. For the Court's decision in *Rosenberger*, see *Rosenberger v. University of Virginia*, 515 U.S. 819 (1995). For the decision in *Hurley*, see *Hurley v. Irish-American Gay, Lesbian, and Bisexual Group of Boston, Inc.*, 515 U.S. 557 (1995). For the Court's decisions in ADF's cases on funding for religious schools, see *Agostini v. Felton*, 521 U.S. 203 (1997); *Mitchell v. Helms*, 530 U.S. 793 (2000). For the Court's decisions on antiabortion protests, see *Madsen v. Women's Health Center, Inc.*, 512 U.S. 753 (1994); *Schenck v. Pro-Choice Network of Western New York*, 519 U.S. 357 (1997). For ADF's own analysis of its early wins, see ADF Fundraising Letter (May 15, 1995), AUS, Box 1, Folder 16.

16. Alliance Defense Fund, Fundraising Letter (September 1995), PAW, Carton 2, Folder 13; see also Family Research Council, "Pro-Family Vision for the New Millenium" (July 2000), PAW, Carton 39, Folder 4 ("All federal laws should provide for conscience exceptions").

17. On Cassidy and his strategy, see Life Forum Meeting Minutes (July 10, 1998), 4, PWP, Box 80, Folder 10; "Trial to Determine Fate of Abortion Ban," *New York Times*, September 9, 1998, B6; Patrick Mullaney, "A Father's Trial and the Case for Personhood," *Human Life Review* 27 (2001): 87–96; Mary Ziegler, *Abortion and the Law in America: Roe v. Wade to the Present* (New York: Cambridge University Press, 2020), 123–124, 189–195.

18. Life Forum Meeting Minutes (July 27, 1998), PAW, Carton 80, Folder 10; see also National Foundation for Life, Brochure, "The Global Project" (n.d., ca. 1998), PAW, Carton 80, Folder 8.

19. Family Research Council, "Pro-Family Vision for the New Millennium" (July 2000), PAW, Carton 39, Folder 4. For Cassidy's argument in *Alexander*, see Reply Brief for Plaintiffs-Appellants, 22–24, *Alexander v. Whitman*, 114 F. 3d 1392 (3d Cir. 1997) (No. 95-5414). For Cassidy's argument in *Acuna*, see Brief Submitted by Plaintiff-Appellant Rosa Acuna in Her Capacity as Administratrix Ad Prosequendum of the Estate of Andres Acuna, *Acuna v. Turkish*, 930 A.2d 416 (N.J. 2007) (No. 59-643); Petitioner's Brief for a Writ of Certiorari, 17–19, *Acuna v. Turkish*, 552 U.S. 825 (2007) (No. 07-1328). For Cassidy's argument in the class action *Donna Santa Marie*, see Brief and Appendix Volume I on Brief of Appellants, *Donna Santa Marie v. Whitman*, 15–21, 314 F.3d 136 (3d Cir. 2002) (Nos. 01-1068, 01-1461).

20. Gil Donovan, "Abortion Foes Applaud New Bill," *National Catholic Reporter*, May 11, 2001, 9. For more on the Unborn Victims of Violence Act, see NRLC, Letter to Senator (May 8, 2001), JBP, Matter Box 2264; Strategy Memo, "Pain of the Unborn" (November 19, 2004), JBP, Matter Box 2565.

21. Life Forum Meeting Minutes (July 27, 1998), RJN, Box 80, Folder 10. For Arkes's published argument: Hadley Arkes, "Life Watch: The Adventures of Summer Continued," *Crisis*, September 1, 1998, https://crisismagazine.com/vault/life-watch-the-adventures-of-summer-continued. For more on Arkes's strategy, see Hadley Arkes to Richard John Neuhaus (September 11, 1998), RJN, Box 3, Folder 27; Hadley Arkes to Richard John Neuhaus (June 11, 1998), RJN, Box 3, Folder 27.

22. Paul Benjamin Linton, "Thoughts on the Global Project and Personhood Litigation" (n.d., ca. 2001), JBP, Digital Files, Harold Cassidy Folder. For more on the state action requirement, see Erwin Chemerinsky, "Rethinking State Action," *Northwestern University Law Review* 80 (1986): 503–557. On Linton's earlier work, see "Guam Case Forces Tough Questions on Abortion's Constitutionality," *Life Docket* (June 1990), 1, SBL, Box 1, Folder 5001; "Human Life Protection," *Life Docket* (August 1991), SBL, Box 1, Folder 5001. For more on Linton's view, see also Paul Linton to Harold Cassidy (July 15, 2004), JBP, Digital Files, Harold Cassidy Folder. On pre-*Roe* prosecutions, see Leslie Reagan, *When Abortion Was a Crime: Women, Medicine, and Law in the United States, 1867–1973*, 2nd ed. (Berkeley: University of California Press, 2022), 120–125, 158–237.

23. Dana Milbank, "Religious Right Finds Its Center in Oval Office," *Washington Post*, December 24, 2001, A2. On the surge in anti-Muslim hate crimes, see Human Rights Watch, "The September 11 Backlash" (2002), https://www.hrw.org/reports/2002/usahate/usa1102-04.htm. On Bush's approval, see David Moore, "Bush Approval Highest in Gallup History," *Gallup*, September 24, 2001, https://news.gallup.com/poll/4924/bush-job-approval-highest-gallup-history.aspx. On the increased sales of flags and Bibles, see Dana Heller, "Introduction: Consuming 9/11," in *The Selling of 9/11: How a National Tragedy Became a Commodity*, ed. Dana Heller (London: Palgrave-Macmillan, 2016), 2–16.

24. For the text of the Born-Alive Act, see 1 U.S.C. § 8 (2002). For contemporary discussion of the law, see Mike Allen, "President Signs Bill on Abortion Procedures," *Washington Post*, August 6, 2002, A2. For Cassidy's losses, see *Alexander v. Whitman*, 114 F.3d 1392 (3d Cir. 1997); *Acuna v. Turkish*, 808 A.2d 149 (N.J. Super. 2002); *Marie v. McGreevy*, 314 F.3d 136 (3d Cir. 2002).

25. On the backstory of *Lawrence*, see Dale Carpenter, *Flagrant Conduct: The Story of* Lawrence v. Texas (New York: Norton, 2012), 102–187; William N. Eskridge,

Dishonorable Passions: Sodomy Laws in America, 1861–2003 (New York: Viking, 2008), 360–398.

26. Brief of the Family Research Council, 19, *Lawrence v. Texas*, 539 U.S. 558 (2003) (No. 02-102). For Texas's argument: Brief of Respondent, 4, *Lawrence v. Texas*, 539 U.S. 558 (2003) (No. 02-102).

27. *Lawrence v. Texas*, 539 U.S. 558, 572 (2003).

28. Alliance Defense Fund, "Stopping Same-Sex Marriage" (n.d., ca. 2005), PAW, Carton 2, Folder 15; see also Alliance Defense Fund, Press Release, "ADF Launches DOMA Watch" (September 7, 2004), PAW, Carton 2, Folder 15; "We Can Win," *Washington Briefing: Focus on Family Action* (2004), PAW, Carton 2, Folder 15. For the court's decision in *Goodridge*, see *Goodridge v. Department of Public Health*, 798 N.E.2d 941, 955–963 (Mass. 2003).

29. *Stenberg v. Carhart*, 530 U.S. 914, 937–938 (2000). For movement advocacy around the federal ban on partial-birth abortion, see Gracie Hsu, "Ban Partial-Birth Abortions" (n.d., ca. 2002), PAW, Carton 37, Folder 13; "Partial-Birth Abortion: Dispelling the Myths" (n.d., ca. 2000), PAW, Carton 32, Folder 15. Meanwhile, Harold Cassidy failed to convince the New Jersey courts of his personhood strategy. See *Alexander v. Whitman*, 114 F.3d 1392, 1400 (3d Cir. 1997); *Acuna v. Turkish*, 808 A.2d 149, 153–160 (N.J. Super. 2002). Cassidy's appeal in *Acuna* would ultimately fail in the New Jersey Supreme Court in 2007. See *Acuna v. Turkish*, 930 A.2d 416 (N.J. 2007).

30. James Bopp and Tom Marzen et al., Alliance Defense Fund Funding Request (May 2, 2003), JBP, Digital Files. ADF ultimately decided to fund litigation in the case. See Alliance Defending Freedom, "*Gonzales v. Carhart*," https://adflegal.org/case/gonzales-v-carhart.

31. On the coalition, see Letter to Culture of Life Leadership Coalition (2003), JBP, Matter Boxes, File 2343; Presentation of the Public Relations Working Group (April 29, 2003), JBP, Matter Boxes, File 2343; Culture of Life Legal Working Group Preliminary Report (2003), 1–12, JBP, Matter Boxes, File 2343.

32. On the Blackstone Fellowship, see Amanda Hollis-Brusky and Joshua Wilson, *Separate but Faithful: The Christian Right's Radical Struggle to Transform Law and Legal Culture* (New York: Oxford University, 2020), 4, 60–63, 133–135; Anne Southworth, *Lawyers on the Right: Professionalizing the Conservative Coalition* (Chicago: University of Chicago Press, 2008), 33; Blackstone Fellowship, History, https://web.archive.org/web/20100221015510/http://www.blackstonelegalfellowship.org/About/History, accessed July 6, 2024. For the commission's conclusions: Letter to Culture of Life Leadership Coalition, 1; Presentation of the Public Relations Working Group, 2. On the demise of the coalition, see Ziegler, *Abortion and the Law*, 192–193.

33. Marc Kaufman, "Nonprescription Sale Sought for Contraceptive," *Washington Post*, April 21, 2003, A2; Kate Zernike, "Use of Morning-After Pill Rising, and It May Go over the Counter," *New York Times*, May 19, 2003, A1.

34. On efforts within the movement to distance itself from opposition to contraception, see Daniel K. Williams, *Defenders of the Unborn: The Pro-Life Movement Before* Roe v. Wade (New York: Oxford University Press, 2016), 18–20. On Rock for Life and efforts to recruit younger Americans to the antiabortion movement, see American Life League, "*Rock for Life* Message to President Bush: Protect Unborn Babies" (January 18, 2005), MFJ, Box 12, Folder 7; "Rock for Life News" (n.d., ca. 2006), MFJ, Box 12, Folder 7. On support for emergency contraception, see Heather Boonstra, "Emergency Contraception: The Need to Increase Public Awareness," *Guttmacher Institute*, October 2002, https://www.guttmacher.org/gpr/2002/10/emergency-contraception-need-increase-public-awareness.

35. For the Pharmacists for Life statement: Karen Brandon, "Clash over Emergency Contraception," *Chicago Tribune*, May 10, 2022, 1. For more on opposition to emergency contraception, see "Life Issues Today with Dr. John Willke: Emergency Contraception It Is Not," *Life Issues Today* (October 1998), 2, PAW, Carton 52, Folders 18–19; Concerned Women for America, Fundraising Letter (2004), PAW, Carton 28, Folder 11.

36. National Right to Life Committee, Board of Directors Meeting Minutes (May 2004), MFJ, Box 4, Board of Directors Folder; see also Board of Directors of Cincinnati Right to Life to James Bopp (May 21, 2004), JBP, Matter Box 2436.

37. On the strategy around minors and the Schoolchildren's Health Protection Act, see Life Forum Meeting Minutes (January 21, 2004), PWP, Box 81, Folder 4; Anna Wilde Matthews and Barbara Martinez, "Plan B Shift Threatens to Deepen Rift," *Wall Street Journal*, August 25, 2006, A3.

38. On LaHaye's background, see Janet Cawley, " 'Boss Lady' Beverly LaHaye Leads Her 600,000 Concerned Women for America Down the Right Path," *Chicago Tribune*, May 26, 1992, E1; Megan Rosenfeld, "Not NOW, Dear: The Conservative Alternative of Concerned Women for America," *Washington Post*, September 26, 1991, A1.

39. On the organization's strength in 2004, see Richard Cooper and Johanna Neuman, "They Won't Stand on Common Ground: Concerned Women for America Even Takes on Allies on the Right When They're Seen as Soft," *Los Angeles Times*, December 27, 2004, A1. For more on Concerned Women for America, see Sarah Barringer Gordon, *The Spirit of the Law: Religious Voices and the Constitution in Modern America* (Cambridge, MA: Harvard University Press, 2010), 132–141, 157–168.

40. Concerned Women for America, Fundraising Letter (2004), 1; see also Concerned Women for America, Fundraising Letter (November 25, 2004), PAW, Carton 28, Folder 15; Concerned Women for America, Fundraising Letter (March 18, 2002), PAW, Carton 28, Folder 16.

41. Concerned Women for America, Fundraising Letter (2004), 4. For more conscience arguments in the period, see Alliance Defense Fund, Press Release, "Supreme Court Should Review California Contraception Case" (August 12, 2004), PAW, Carton 2, Folder 15; Alliance Defense Fund, Press Release (February 15, 2005), PAW, Carton 2, Folder 15; Reva B. Siegel and Douglas NeJaime, "Conscience Wars: Complicity-Based Conscience Claims in Religion and Politics," *Yale Law Journal* 124 (2015): 2516–2535.

42. On the March for Women's Lives, see Zakiya Luna, *Reproductive Rights as Human Rights: Women of Color and the Fight for Reproductive Justice* (New York: New York University Press, 2020), 111–126; Loretta Ross and Rickie Solinger, *Reproductive Justice: An Introduction* (Berkeley: University of California Press, 2020), 67.

43. Loretta Ross, "Notes on Analytical Perspectives" (February 4, 2004), SSW, Box 10, March for Women's Lives Folder; see also Strategy Notes, "The Color of Choice: Women of Color and the March for Reproductive Rights" (2004), SSW, Box 10, March for Women Lives Folder; Email Memo to Loretta Ross on March for Women's Lives (March 26, 2004), SSW, Box 10, March for Women's Lives Folder.

44. On Ross's background, see Voices of Oral History Project, Loretta Ross, Interviewed by Joyce Follett, Nov. 3, 2004–February 4, 2005, https://www.smith.edu/libraries/libs/ssc/vof/transcripts/Ross.pdf.

45. On the unfolding of the march, see Hank Stuever, "Body Politics: Today's Feminist, It Turns Out, Looks Like a Lot of People—Maybe a Million," *Washington Post*, April 26, 2004, C1.

46. Third Wave Foundation, Grant Proposal (January 2005–2007), NAPAW, Box 4, Third Wave Grant Folder.

47. Some Catholics still continued advocating for a broader social safety net in this period, even when larger antiabortion groups did not. See "Dominican Sisters Take Public Stand," *Catholic Commentator* 39 (2001): 5 (Baton Rouge, LA); "Bishops Ask Senate to Avoid Partisan Politics," *Pittsburgh Catholic* 157 (August 2001): 9 (PA).

48. On the evolution of stem-cell research, see Sara Dubow, *Ourselves Unborn: A History of the Fetus in Modern America* (New York: Oxford University Press, 2010), 80–81, 195; Williams, *Defenders of the Unborn*, 266.

49. Sheryl Gay Stolberg, "Limits on Stem-Cell Research Re-emerge as a Political Issue," *New York Times*, May 6, 2004, A1; "Republicans for Stem Cell Research," *New York Times*, May 11, 2004, A22.

50. John M. Hass, "Begotten, Not Made: A Catholic View of Reproductive Technology," United States Conference of Catholic Bishops (1998), https://www.usccb .org/issues-and-action/human-life-and-dignity/reproductive-technology/begotten-not-made-a-catholic-view-of-reproductive-technology. On early opposition within the movement to IVF, see Constitutional Amendments related to Abortion, Hearings before the Senate Judiciary Subcommittee on the Constitution, 97th Congress, 1st Session (1981), 1182 (Statement of Nellie Gray); National Right to Life Committee, "Three-Year Plan: Introduction and General Recommendations," (1980), 2–3, JWC, National Right to Life Folders (explaining that "in vitro fertilization" "dramatize the need for a Human Life Amendment"); Michael Budde, "Test-Tube Life a Serious Issue," *Chicago Defender*, August 14, 1979, 9 (detailing AUL's campaign against IVF funding); Joseph Stanton to Ethicians et al. (June 3, 1983), JRS, Box 336, Folder 5 (Stanton, a prominent activist, arguing that IVF illustrated "the paradox of a nation destroying 1,500,000 normal, but unwanted, unborn and the unseeming frenzy by, in many instances, the destroyers of new life to create 'wanted' pregnancies (for a price)"). For examples of the letters solicited by AUL, see Anthony Young to William Proxmire (March 12, 1979), 1, WPP, Box 90, Folder 33 (objecting to "tax dollars being used to finance the murder of helpless little people"); Mrs. William Kaun to William Proxmire (March 19, 1979), 1, WPP, Box 90, Folder 33 (complaining about being the federal government's "money supplier" for harming fetal persons); Edith Hofrichter to William Proxmire (March 15, 1979), 1, WPP, Box 90, Folder 33 (arguing that IVF exposed "newly conceived human life to destruction, abandonment, or unnatural risks"); Kathleen Shelvik to William Proxmire (March 14, 1979), 1, WPP, Box 90, Folder 33 (opposing IVF because it would not offer "young lives the same respect and care we show newborn babies").

51. Aaron Zitner, "The Nation: Abortion Foes Attack *Roe* on New Research," *Los Angeles Times*, January 19, 2003, A1; see also Christian Legal Society, Fundraising Letter (January 1990), AUS, Box 12, Folder 34; Christian Legal Society, Transcript Excerpt, *Davis v. Davis*, E-14496 (1990), AUS, Box 12, Folder 34; Susan B. Anthony List, "Dear Pro-Life Friend" (March 7, 2007), PAW, Carton 68, Folder 9 (condemning "experimentation with the tiniest of human beings"); Traditional Values Coalition, Mailer (August 28, 2000), PAW, Carton 69, Folder 1 (arguing that the Clinton administration planned to skirt the rules "preventing the use of tax dollars to destroy human life"); Traditional Values Coalition (September 22, 2000), PAW, Carton 69, Folder 1. On the expansion of CLS, see "Faith Events," *Kansas City Star*, October 28, 1995, E13 (MO); Richard Ostling, "Pope Makes Antidivorce Appeal to Lawyers," *Herald*, January 31, 2002, 23 (Jasper, IN). For more on embryo adoption, see Laura

Meckler, " 'Embryo Adoption' Getting Push from $1 Million Awareness Drive," *Chicago Tribune*, August 21, 2002, 9.

52. For Bush's 2001 decision, see Katharine Q. Seelye, "Bush Gives His Backing to Limited Research on Existing Stem Cells," *New York Times*, August 10, 2001, A1; "Bush's Address on Federal Financing for Research on Embryonic Stem Cells," *New York Times*, August 10, 2001, A16. On Bush's support for embryo adoption, see Meckler, " 'Embryo Adoption,' " 9. On the rise of stem-cell research as a political issue, see Stolberg, "Limits on Stem-Cell Research," A1.

53. National Right to Life Committee, "Key Facts on the Unborn Victims of Violence Act" (April 1, 2004), https://nrlc.org/federal/unbornvictims/keypointsuvva/. On Peterson's death and its influence on fetal-homicide laws and the broader personhood debate, see Helen Dewar, "Senate Passes Bill on Harm to Fetuses," *Washington Post*, March 26, 2004, A1; Kirk Johnson and Adam Liptak, "Harm to Fetuses Becomes Issue in Utah and Elsewhere," *New York Times*, March 27, 2004, A9. For the statute: 18 U.S.C. § 1841 (2004).

54. Zitner, "Abortion Foes," A1. On legal proposals to restrict IVF in the states, see ibid.; Judy Peres, "In Vitro New Front in Embryo War," *Chicago Tribune*, July 6, 2005, 1. For more on the struggle over stem cells, see Doug Johnson to National Right to Life Committee Board of Directors (September 21, 2001), JBP, Matter Box 2264; Amber Matchen to Mildred Jefferson et al., Media Meeting Minutes (February 7, 2005), MFJ, Box 12, Folder 7 (American Life League running ads criticizing stem-cell research). On Bush's reelection, see James E. Campbell, "Why Bush Won the Presidential Election of 2004: Incumbency, Ideology, Terrorism, and Turnout," *Political Science Quarterly* 120 (2005): 219–245.

55. On the reshaping of the Court, see Peter Baker, "Bush Nominates Roberts as Chief Justice," *Washington Post*, September 6, 2005, A1; Adam Liptak, "Alito Vote May Be Decisive in Marquee Cases This Term," *New York Times*, February 1, 2006, A1.

56. On Roberts's background, see Joan Biskupic, *The Chief: The Life and Turbulent Times of Chief Justice John G. Roberts* (New York: Basic Books, 2019), 3–12, 43–87. On abortion opponents' response to Roberts's nomination, see Jay Sekulow to Carol Keyes (July 26, 2005), PAW, Carton 2, Folder 32; Jay Sekulow to Kyle Mantyla (April 19, 2005), PAW, Carton 2, Folder 32; Jay Sekulow to Carol Keyes (June 1, 2005), PAW, Carton 2, Folder 32.

57. Sekulow to Keyes (June 1), 1; see also Susan B. Anthony List, "Pro-Life Judicial Nominations Still Stalled in the Senate" (May 19, 2004), PAW, Carton 68, Folder 19.

58. On Miers and Leo's role in her confirmation battle, see Leonard Leo, Memo to Interested Parties (October 3, 2005), JBP, Matter Box 2411; see also Jeanne

Cummings, "Point Man on Miers Juggles Allegiances," *Wall Street Journal*, October 26, 2005, A4. For more on Leo, see Jeffrey Toobin, "The Conservative Pipeline to the Supreme Court," *New Yorker*, April 17, 2017, https://www.newyorker.com/magazine/2017/04/17/the-conservative-pipeline-to-the-supreme-court.

59. Jay Sekulow to Claire Keyes, Fundraising Letter (April 2005), PAW, Carton 2, Folder 32. For more on Alito and perceptions of him among conservatives, see Jeanne Cummings and Jess Bravin, "New Round: Choice of Alito for High Court Sets Stage for Ideological Battle," *Wall Street Journal*, November 1, 2005, https://www.wsj.com/articles/SB113075736648684085; Rebecca Traister, "Conservative Women's Groups React to Alito Pick," *Salon*, October 31, 2005, https://www.salon.com/2005/10/31/conservative_women/. On Alito's previous record on abortion, see Samuel Alito, Memorandum to the Solicitor General (May 30, 1985), CCP, Record Group 60, Box 20; Charles Savage, "Decades Ago, Alito Laid Methodical Strategy to Eventually Overrule *Roe v. Wade*," *New York Times*, June 25, 2022, https://www.nytimes.com/2022/06/25/us/politics/samuel-alito-abortion.html.

60. For the 2007 Pew poll: "Clinton and Giuliani Not Seen as Highly Religious; Romney's Religion Raises Concerns," *Pew Forum*, September 6, 2007, https://www.pewresearch.org/religion/2007/09/06/clinton-and-giuliani-seen-as-not-highly-religious-romneys-religion-raises-concerns/#abortion. On evangelicals' concentration in the South, see "U.S. Religious Landscape Survey," *Pew Forum*, June 1, 2008, https://www.pewresearch.org/religion/2008/06/01/u-s-religious-landscape-survey-religious-beliefs-and-practices/; Robert P. Jones, "Southern Evangelicals: Dwindling, and Taking the GOP's Edge with Them," *Atlantic*, October 2014, https://www.theatlantic.com/politics/archive/2014/10/the-shriking-evangelical-voter-pool/381560/. For more on shifting evangelical attitudes toward abortion, see Andrew Lewis, *The Rights Turn in Conservative Christian Politics: How Abortion Transformed the Culture Wars* (New York: Cambridge University Press, 2017); Brian Robert Calfano, "Bringing the Faithful Back In: The Influence of Catholics and White Evangelical Protestants on Polarization in State Abortion Politics," *American Review of Politics* 126 (2006): 129–143.

61. Thomas More Law Center, Fundraising Letter (n.d., ca. 2006), AUS, Box 14, Folder 42; see also Thomas More Law Center, Fundraising Letter (n.d., ca. 2007), AUS, Box 14, Folder 42. For more on Monaghan, see Ted Sylvester, "Tom Monaghan/Word of God Connection," *American Atheist*, January 1990, 1, AUS, Box 29, Folder 34; Clipping, John Nehman, "A Gift from God," *Detroit News* (June 22, 1990), AUS, Box 29, Folder 34. For more on the South Dakota vote, see J. S. Adams, Traditional Values Coalition, "South Dakota IS Major Political Background This November 7" (October 23, 2006), PAW, Carton 69, Folder 16.

62. Roger Rieger to Pro-Life Colleagues (December 21, 2004), JBP, Digital Files, Harold Cassidy Folder; see also American Life League, Press Release, "South Dakota Abortion Ban Right on Target" (January 14, 2005), MFJ, Box 12, Folder 7 (arguing that the South Dakota bill "represents the rights of the preborn child" and that opposing it, for abortion opponents, was a "crime"). For the South Dakota report, see Report of the South Dakota Commission to Study Abortion (December 2005), JBP, Digital Files, Harold Cassidy Folder. On the signing of the bill, see Monica Davey, "South Dakota Bans Abortion, Setting Up a Battle," *New York Times*, March 7, 2006, https://www.nytimes.com/2006/03/07/us/south-dakota-bans-abortion-setting-up-a-battle.html.

63. On the South Dakota vote, see Monica Davey, "South Dakotans Reject Sweeping Abortion Ban," *New York Times*, November 8, 2006, https://www.nytimes.com/2006/11/08/us/politics/08issues.html. On the proposal of trigger laws in the period, see Elizabeth Nash and Isabel Guarnieri, "13 States Have Abortion Trigger Laws—Here's What Happens if *Roe* Is Overturned," *Guttmacher Institute*, June 6, 2022, https://www.guttmacher.org/article/2022/06/13-states-have-abortion-trigger-bans-heres-what-happens-when-roe-overturned.

64. On the founding of Students for Life: Kristan Hawkins, interview with Mary Ziegler, April 17, 2023; Kristan Hawkins, interview with Mary Ziegler, December 21, 2022.

65. Hawkins, April 2023 interview; Hawkins, December 2022 interview; see also Holly Honderich, "She Helped Kill *Roe v. Wade*. Now, She Wants to End Abortion in America," *BBC*, June 23, 2023, https://www.bbc.com/news/world-us-canada-65923956; Elaine Godfrey, "The New Pro-Life Movement Has a Plan to End Abortion. And It Doesn't Care if American Voters Agree with It," *Atlantic*, April 2023, https://www.theatlantic.com/politics/archive/2023/04/pro-life-anti-abortion-roe-mifepristone-pill-ban/673763/.

66. See Students for Life, "Five Steps to Plan a Successful Diaper Drive" (2007), SFL; Students for Life, "Five Steps to Write a Letter to the Editor" (2007), SFL.

67. Hawkins, April 2023 interview; Hawkins, December 2022 interview; Students for Life, "Diaper Drive"; Students for Life, "Letter to the Editor."

68. *Gonzales v. Carhart*, 550 U.S. 124, 134–150 (2007). For the Operation Outcry brief, see Brief for Sandra Cano et al., 22–24, *Gonzales v. Carhart*, 550 U.S. 124 (2007) (Nos. 05-380, 05-1382).

69. On responses to *Gonzales*, see Alan Cooperman, "Supreme Court Ruling Brings Split in Antiabortion Movement," *Washington Post*, June 4, 2007, A3; Judie Brown, "Partial-Birth Abortion Ruling: Where Is the Victory?" *American Life League*,

April 26, 2007, https://all.org/judie-brown-commentary/partial-birth-abortion-ruling-where-is-the-victory. For Parker's comments: Robin Toner, "Abortion Foes See Validation for New Tactic," *New York Times*, May 22, 2007, A1.

70. On the Colorado personhood struggle, see Judith Graham and Judy Peres, "Rights for Embryos Proposed," *Chicago Tribune*, December 3, 2007, 1; Nicholas Riccardi, "Foes of Abortion Shift to States," *Los Angeles Times*, November 23, 2007, A1; T. W. Farnam, "Antiabortion Initiatives Divide Movement," *Wall Street Journal*, April 21, 2008, A4.

71. On the failure of the Colorado amendment, see Tim Hoover, "Angling for a Rematch on Personhood," *Denver Post*, July 3, 2009, Bl. On Obama's election, see Mike Dorning, "Democrats Weigh How Hard to Hit Agenda," *Chicago Tribune*, November 16, 2008, A1. Chapter 2 further discusses Byrn's view of corporate personhood.

72. For the relevant decisions at the intersection of campaign finance, corporate rights, and abortion, see *Buckley v. Valeo*, 424 U.S. 1, 41–49 (1976); *First National Bank v. Bellotti*, 435 U.S. 765, 790–813 (1978); *Federal Election Commission v. Massachusetts Citizens for Life*, 479 U.S. 238, 248–252 (1986). On the connection between abortion and campaign finance, see Ziegler, *Dollars for Life*, 98–142; see also Ann Southworth, *Big Money Unleashed: The Campaign to Deregulate Campaign Spending* (Chicago: University of Chicago Press, 2024).

73. On antiabortion support for corporate rights, see Ziegler, *Dollars for Life*, 178–190. For examples of evolving arguments for corporate rights, see James Bopp Jr. and Richard Coleson to Amici in *Wisconsin Right to Life* and *Randell v. Sorrell* (October 10, 2005), JBP, Digital Files, Citizens United Folder; Amicus Conference, *Wisconsin Right to Life* and *Randall v. Sorrell* (2005), JBP, Digital Files, Citizens United Folder. On Schlafly's position, see Republican National Coalition for Life, Press Release (August 11, 1998), JBP, Matter Boxes, File 1931; see also Phyllis Schlafly to Republican National Coalition for Life (December 1996), RNCL, Box 1, Folder 7.

74. See *Bank of Augusta v. Earle*, 38 U.S. 519, 537–545 (1839). On the nature of corporate rights, see Adam Winkler, *We the Corporations: How American Businesses Won Their Civil Rights* (New York: Liveright, 2018), 1–11, 392–410; see also Gregory A. Mark, "The Personification of the Business Corporation in American Law," *Chicago Law Review* 54 (1987): 1441–1483; Mark Tushnet, "Corporations and Free Speech," in *The Politics of Law: A Progressive Critique*, ed. David Kairys (New York: Pantheon, 1982), 253; Nikolas Bowie, "Corporate Personhood versus Corporate Statehood," *Harvard Law Review* 132 (2019): 2010–2020.

75. Bopp and Coleson to Amici, 1–3.

76. On George, see Alexandra Mitchell, "Review—Weekend Confidential: Robert George, the Conservative Scholar, Is Having an 'I Told You So' Moment," *Wall Street Journal*, February 25, 2017, C11; David D. Kirkpatrick, "The Conservative-Christian Big Thinker," *New York Times*, December 16, 2009, https://www.nytimes.com/2009/12/20/magazine/20george-t.html.

77. *The Manhattan Declaration: A Call of Christian Conscience* (November 20, 2009), https://www.manhattandeclaration.org/. For more on the declaration and its impact, see Neil J. Young, *We Gather Together: The Religious Right and the Problem of Interfaith Politics* (New York: Oxford University Press, 2016), 190–223; Katherine Stewart, *The Power Worshippers: Inside the Dangerous Rise of Religious Nationalism* (London: Bloomsbury, 2019), 187–190. For more on the politics of conscience in the era, see NeJaime and Siegel, "Conscience Wars"; Nomi Maya Stolzenberg, "It's about Money: The Fundamental Contradiction of *Hobby Lobby*," *Southern California Law Review* 88 (2015): 727–767.

78. "America Becoming Less Christian, Survey Finds," *CNN*, March 2009, https://www.cnn.com/2009/LIVING/wayoflife/03/09/us.religion.less.christian/index.html; Frank Newport, "This Christmas, 78 Percent of Americans Identify as Christian," *Gallup*, December 24, 2009, https://news.gallup.com/poll/124793/this-christmas-78-americans-identify-christian.aspx. On the growth of megachurches, see "America's Biggest Mega-Churches," *Forbes*, January 6, 2009, https://www.forbes.com/2009/06/26/americas-biggest-megachurches-business-megachurches.html?sh=2f8f33b440ec.

79. The Internet Movie Data Base (IMDb) describes *Maafa 21* as a documentary. See "Maafa 21: Black Genocide in 21st Century America," *Internet Movie Database*, https://www.imdb.com/title/tt1500818. For more on the significance of *Maafa 21*, see Karen Maroney, "*Maafa 21:* Ten Years Later," *American Life League*, April 13, 2020, https://www.all.org/guest-commentary/maafa21-ten-years-later; Anthea Butler, "African American Religious Conservatives in the New Millennium," in *Faith in the New Millennium: The Future of Religion and American Politics*, ed. Darren Dochuk and Matthew Avery Sutton (New York: Oxford University Press, 2016), 65; Reva B. Siegel and Mary Ziegler, "Abortion-Eugenic Discourse in *Dobbs:* A Social Movement History," *Journal of American Constitutional History* 2 (2024): 72–98. On growing support for abortion rights in Black communities, see Frank Newport, "Black Americans and Abortion," *Gallup*, September 3, 2020, https://news.gallup.com/opinion/polling-matters/318932/black-americans-abortion.aspx. For Rose's statement: Lila Rose, "Fighting for Life," *First Things*, October 2010, https://www.firstthings.com/article/2010/10/fighting-for-life.

80. See Theda Skocpol and Vanessa Williamson, *The Tea Party and the Remaking of American Conservatism* (New York: Oxford University Press, 2012), 10–31; Ronald P. Formisano, *The Tea Party: A Brief History* (Baltimore: Johns Hopkins University Press, 2012), 3–14; Kate Zernike, *Boiling Mad: Behind the Lines in Tea Party America* (New York: Henry Holt, 2010), 3–24.

81. "Topics in Depth: Iraq," *Gallup*, https://news.gallup.com/poll/1633/iraq.aspx. On the start of troop withdrawals, see Jackie Northam, "Bush to Withdraw Troops from Iraq," *NPR*, September 10, 2008, https://www.npr.org/2008/09/10/94449431 /bush-to-withdraw-troops-from-iraq.

82. Robert L. Hetzel, *The Great Recession: Market Failure or Policy Failure?* (New York: Cambridge University Press, 2012); James H. Stock and Mark W. Watson, "Disentangling the Channels of the 2007–2009 Recession" (National Bureau of Economic Research Paper, 2012), https://www.nber.org/system/files/working_papers /w18094/w18094.pdf. For the Gallup poll, see "Trust in Government," *Gallup*, https://news.gallup.com/poll/5392/trust-government.aspx.

83. Tyler Millhouse and Geoff Pallay, "A Look Back at the 2010 State Legislative Elections," *Ballotpedia*, January 11, 2011, https://ballotpedia.org/A_look_back_at_ the_2010_state_legislative_elections; see also Rachel M. Blum, *How the Tea Party Captured the GOP: Insurgent Factions in American Politics* (Chicago: University of Chicago Press, 2020), 4–26; Christopher S. Parker and Matt A. Barreto, *Change They Can't Believe In: The Tea Party and Reactionary Politics in America* (Princeton: Princeton University Press, 2013), 165–167, 220–240.

84. James Bopp Jr. et al. to Potential Amici in Citizens United (November 19, 2008), JBP, Digital Records, Citizens United Folder; see also James Bopp Jr. et al. to Potential Amici in Citizens United Re: Briefing Recommendations (November 19, 2008), JBP, Digital Records, Citizens United Folder; Memo, "Citizens United: What Is This Case About?" (November 2008), JBP, Digital Records, Citizens United Folder; Kaylan Lytle Phillips to Potential Amici (July 24, 2008), JBP, Digital Records, Citizens United Folder.

85. *Citizens United v. Federal Election Commission*, 558 U.S. 310, 348 (2010).

86. On backlash to *Citizens United*, see Glenn Thrush, "Obama Launches Reelection Campaign," *Politico*, May 5, 2012, https://www.politico.com/story/2012/05/its-official-obama-launches-2012-campaign-075948; Greg Stohr, "Bloomberg Poll: Americans Want Supreme Court to Turn Off Spending Spigot," *Bloomberg News*, September 28, 2015, https://www.bloomberg.com/politics/articles/2015–09–28 /bloomberg-poll-americans-want-supreme-court-to-turn-off-political-spending-spigot; Erica W. Morrison, "Occupiers Wag Fingers at High Court," *Washington Post*,

January 21, 2012, A4. On the recession recovery and economic inequality, see Timothy Sneeding, "Income, Wealth, Debt and the Great Recession," *The Stanford Center for Inequality*, October 2012, https://inequality.stanford.edu/sites/default/files/IncomeWealthDebt_fact_sheet.pdf; David Johnson, "Income Gap: Is It Widening?" *United States Census Bureau Random Samplings*, September 15, 2011, https://www.census.gov/newsroom/blogs/random-samplings/2011/09/income-gap-is-it-widening.html. For Kent's comment: Stephen Kent, "Coalition of the Willing," *Catholic Commentator* 5 (April 4, 2012): 18 (Baton Rouge). For Carolan and his group, Mark Pattison, "A New Constitutional Amendment? Even if It Fails, It May Work," *Catholic Commentator* 51 (2013): 11 (Baton Rouge).

87. Ashton Pittman, "Ten Years After Mississippi Rejected 'Personhood,' Federal 'Life at Conception' Efforts Underway," *Mississippi Free Press*, November 12, 2021, https://www.mississippifreepress.org/18093/10-years-after-mississippians-rejected-personhood-new-national-efforts-target-abortion. For more on the early work of Personhood USA, see Personhood USA, Press Release, "Personhood Passes by Supermajority in Georgia" (August 1, 2012), on file with the author; Personhood USA, Press Release, "Alabama Supreme Court Recognizes Unborn as Persons in Landmark Ruling" (January 12, 2013), on file with the author.

88. Erik Eckholm, "Push for 'Personhood' Amendment Represents New Tack in Abortion Fight," *New York Times*, October 25, 2011, https://www.nytimes.com/2011/10/26/us/politics/personhood-amendments-would-ban-nearly-all-abortions.html; Cameron McWhirter, "'Personhood' Backers Target Abortion," *Wall Street Journal*, October 29, 2011, A2.

89. On the defeat of the Mississippi law, see Frank James, "Mississippi Voters Reject Personhood Amendment by Wide Margin," *NPR*, November 8, 2011, https://www.npr.org/sections/itsallpolitics/2011/11/08/142159280/mississippi-voters-reject-personhood-amendment; Katharine Q. Seelye, "Mississippi Voters Reject Anti-Abortion Amendment," *New York Times*, November 9, 2011, https://www.nytimes.com/2011/11/09/us/politics/votes-across-the-nation-could-serve-as-a-political-barometer.html.

90. See Louise Radnofsky et al., "Obama Retreats on Contraception," *Wall Street Journal*, February 11, 2012, A1; David Savage, "Bishops Dismiss Obama's Birth Control Revision," *Los Angeles Times*, February 12, 2012, A13. On the Fortnight for Freedom: "Fortnight for Freedom," *National Catholic Register*, May 5, 2012, https://www.ncregister.com/blog/fortnight-for-freedom (Irondale, AL).

91. On Aden's background, see "Marriages," *Marion Star*, February 21, 1993, 20 (OH). On Aden's work, see John Dart, "Religious Objections to DMV Upheld," *Los*

Angeles Times, October 25, 1997, 25; "A Tribute to the Bible Splits a Community in New Mexico," *Philadelphia Inquirer,* February 28, 1998, 12; Paul Davenport, "U.S. Court Blocks Arizona 20-Week Abortion Plan," *Brownsville Herald,* August 2, 2012, A6 (TX). For examples of cases Aden litigated at ADF, see *Cenzon-DeCarlo v. Mt. Sinai Hospital,* 626 F.3d 695 (2d Cir. 2010) (a nurse alleging retaliation for a conscience-based refusal to assist in an abortion); *Rock for Life–UMBC v. Hrabowski,* 594 F.Supp.2d 598 (D. Md. 2009) (Rock for Life arguing that university sexual harassment rules, code of conduct, and facilities policies violated members' rights to freedom of speech); *Stuart v. Huff,* 834 F.Supp.2d 424 (M.D. N.C. 2014) (defending a right-to-know abortion restriction). Aden also worked with plaintiffs in challenges to the contraceptive mandate, as the chapter later discusses. For Aden's earlier work, see *Jones v. Clinton,* 57 F.Supp.2d 719 (E.D. Ark. 1999) (Aden working on Paula Jones case); *Sons of Confederate Veterans v. Holcomb,* 288 F.3d 610 (4th Cir. 2002) (Aden challenging constitutionality of license plate depicting Confederate flag); *In re LePage,* 18 P.3d 1177 (Wyo. 2001) (Aden representing a parent seeking a religious exemption to a state-mandated hepatitis vaccine).

92. Brief of 67 Catholic Theologians and Ethicists, 10, *Burwell v. Hobby Lobby Stores,* 573 U.S. 682 (2014) (Nos. 13-354, 13-356). For the Thomas More Law Center argument: Brief of Thomas More Law Center, 8, *Burwell v. Hobby Lobby Stores,* 573 U.S. 682 (2014) (Nos. 13-354, 13-356). For the talking points, ADF and Becket Fund, "Top Line Coalition Talking Points," 1.

93. Brief Amicus Curiae of the Pacific Legal Foundation et al., 3, *Burwell v. Hobby Lobby Stores,* 573 U.S. 682 (2014) (Nos. 13-354, 13-356); see also Brief Amici Curiae of Massachusetts Citizens for Life et al., 3–22, *Burwell v. Hobby Lobby Stores,* 573 U.S. 682 (2014) (Nos. 13-354, 13-356).

94. *Burwell v. Hobby Lobby Stores,* 573 U.S. 682, 710–715 (2014).

95. Ibid., 720–736.

6. The End of *Roe*

1. Students for Life, "Planned Parenthood Campus Training Guide 2015" (2015), SFL, Training Guide Folders; see also Students for Life, "Planned Parenthood Talking Points" (2015), SFL, 2015–2016 Talking Points Folder (arguing that Planned Parenthood "cares about abortions and profits, not women's health"); Alliance Defending Freedom, Talking Points, "Pretty Ugly: Main Points" (2015), SFL, 2015–2016 Talking Points Folder (arguing that Planned Parenthood "promotes sexual promiscuity to children" and "enforces abortion quotas"). On Planned Parenthood's revenue, see Planned Parenthood Federation of America, *2014–2015 Annual Report* (Washington,

DC: Planned Parenthood Federation of America, 2015), 33. For more on Planned Parenthood's entry into abortion provision, see Joanna Schoen, *Abortion After* Roe (Chapel Hill: University of North Carolina Press, 2015), 89–130.

2. This chapter later discusses several of the key federal cases litigated in 2024.

3. For examples, see Students for Life, *Students for Life 2020–2021 Board Report* (2021), 22, 28, SFL, Board Report Folders; Catherine Glenn Foster, Chad Pecknold, and Joshua Craddock, "The Lincoln Proposal: Pro-Life Presidents Must Take Bold and Ambitious Action to Protect the Constitutional Rights of Preborn Children," *Public Discourse*, November 8, 2020, https://www.thepublicdiscourse. com/2020/11/72631/; "The New North Star Coalition Letter" (June 2023), on file with the author.

4. For examples of related arguments: Brief of Alliance Defending Freedom and the Radiance Foundation, 14–15, *Box v. Planned Parenthood of Indiana and Kentucky*, 139 S. Ct. 1780 (2019) (No. 17-3163); Americans United for Life, *Defending Life 2021* (Washington, DC: Americans United for Life, 2021), 10–11; Students for Life, *Students for Life 2020–2021 Board Report,* 22, 28. For examples of pro-life groups embracing the arguments of Black Lives Matter, see Meg Bowerman, "As the Body of Christ Is Hurting, Do We Hear God's Voice?" *Catholic Voice*, June 22, 2020, 8 (Oakland, CA); "Injustice of Racism Perpetuated by Indifference," *Catholic Commentator* 8 (June 2020): 4 (Baton Rouge, LA) (stressing that "racism is a sinful act that results in prejudice, injustice, and lack of respect for human dignity"). For antiabortion arguments about the forces shaping women's abortion decisions, including coercion, see Sharon Serratore, "Coerced into Unwanted Abortion," *American Feminist*, December 2018. For AUL's model law: "Coercive Abuse against Mothers Prevention Act," in *Defending Life 2019* (Washington, DC: Americans United for Life, 2020), 416–424.

5. Eric Lipton, "Scalia Took Dozens of Trips Funded by Private Sponsors," *New York Times*, February 26, 2016, https://www.nytimes.com/2016/02/27/us/politics/scalia-led-court-in-taking-trips-funded-by-private-sponsors.html.

6. Carl Hulse and Mark Landler, "After Antonin Scalia's Death, Fierce Battle Lines Emerge," *New York Times*, February 14, 2016, https://www.nytimes.com/2016/02/15/us/politics/antonin-scalias-death-cuts-fierce-battle-lines-in-washington. html; Emily Bazelon, "Antonin Scalia's Supreme Court Seat and the Next Frontier in Political Hardball," *New York Times*, February 13, 2016, https://www.nytimes. com/2016/02/14/magazine/scalias-supreme-court-seat-and-the-next-frontier-in-political -hardball.html.

7. On abortion storytelling and #ShoutYourAbortion, see Jill Filipovic, "Reclaiming Abortion," *Washington Post*, June 14, 2015, 1; Caitlin Gibson, "I Didn't Feel

Angry. I Didn't Feel Sad. And I Didn't Look Back," *Washington Post*, November 16, 2015, C1.

8. For Bachiochi's law review article, see Erika Bachiochi, "Embodied Equality: Debunking Equal Protection Arguments for Abortion Rights," *Harvard Journal of Law and Public Policy* 34 (2011): 934–949. For more on Bachiochi's life, see Charlotte Hays, "Reclaiming a Lost Feminism: Erika Bachiochi," Independent Women's Forum, August 29, 2022, https://www.iwf.org/people/erika-bachiochi-2/. For more discussion of this vision of feminism, see Reva B. Siegel, "Why Restrict Abortion? Expanding the Frame on *June Medical*," *Supreme Court Review* 2020 (2020): 304–305, 325–336. For Bachiochi's 2015 article, see Erika Bachiochi, "I'm a Feminist, and I'm Against Abortion," *CNN*, January 22, 2015, https://www.cnn.com/2015/01/22/opinion/bachiochi-abortion-roe-v-wade/index.html.

9. Students for Life, "Talking Points: War on Women" (2015), SFL, 2015–2016 Talking Points Folder. For Bachiochi's 2015 editorial, see Bachiochi, "I'm a Feminist." For more on Hawkins's background, see Sean Salai, "Q&A with Kristan Hawkins of Students for Life of America," *America*, January 30, 2016, https://www.americamagazine.org/content/all-things/students-life-25-questions-kristan-hawkins; Jessica Weinberger, "Leading the Pro-Life Generation," *Catholic Spirit*, January 11, 2018, https://thecatholicspirit.com/news/local-news/leading-pro-life-generation (Minneapolis, MN). For more on her perspective, see "Pregnant on Campus Talking Points" (2015), SFL, 2015–2016 Talking Points Folder; "Women Betrayed Tour Talking Points" (2015), SFL, 2015–2016 Talking Points Folder (arguing that "Planned Parenthood uses women and their prenatal children for profit" and that women "facing unplanned pregnancies need support and empowerment," including from "pregnancy resource centers").

10. Amita Kelly, "McConnell: Supreme Court Nomination about 'a Principle, Not a Person,'" *NPR*, March 16, 2016, https://www.npr.org/2016/03/16/470664561/mcconnell-blocking-supreme-court-nomination-about-a-principle-not-a-person; Ariane De Vogue, "How Obama Lost, and McConnell Won, the Merrick Garland Fight," *CNN*, November 9, 2016, https://www.cnn.com/2016/11/09/politics/merrick-garland-supreme-court/index.html.

11. On early antiabortion opposition to Trump, see Susan B. Anthony List, "Pro-Life Women Sound the Alarm: Donald Trump Is Unacceptable," January 26, 2016, https://sbaprolife.org/home/pro-life-women-sound-the-alarmdonald-trump-is-unacceptable; Jennifer Haberkorn, "Anti-Abortion Groups Say They Distrust Trump," *Politico*, January 26, 2016, https://www.politico.com/story/2016/01/donald-trump-anti-abortion-group-distrust-218258.

12. For criticisms that the law was useless, see Brief for Petitioners, 31, *Whole Woman's Health v. Hellerstedt*, 579 U.S. 582 (2016) (No. 15-274); Brief Amicus Curiae of the American Civil Liberties Union et al., 28–36, *Whole Woman's Health v. Hellerstedt*, 579 U.S. 582 (2016) (No. 15-274). For more on the strategy behind these targeted regulations and the importance of *Whole Woman's Health*, see Linda Greenhouse and Reva B. Siegel, "The Difference a Whole Woman Makes: Protection for the Abortion Right after *Whole Woman's Health*," *Yale Law Journal Forum* 126 (2016); Reva Siegel, "The Right's Reasons: Constitutional Conflict and the Spread of Woman-Protective Antiabortion Argument," *Duke Law Journal* 57 (2008): 1641–1692.

13. See Mary Ziegler, *Dollars for Life: The Anti-Abortion Movement and the Fall of the Republican Establishment* (New Haven: Yale University Press, 2022), 214, 220–230. For the Court's decision in *Hellerstedt*, see *Whole Woman's Health v. Hellerstedt*, 579 U.S. 582, 590–610 (2016).

14. On Spicer's and Conway's comments: Kevin Liptak, "Reality Check: Sean Spicer Hits Media over Crowds," *CNN*, January 21, 2017, https://www.cnn.com/2017/01/21/politics/sean-spicer-fact-check/index.html; Nicholas Fandos, "White House Pushes 'Alternative Facts.' Here Are the Real Ones," *New York Times*, January 22, 2017, https://www.nytimes.com/2017/01/22/us/politics/president-trump-inauguration-crowd-white-house.html.

15. On Trump's comment and the Women's March, see "Full Transcript of Donald Trump's Obscene Video Tape," *BBC*, October 9, 2016, https://www.bbc.com/news/election-us-2016–37595321; Anemona Hartocollis and Yamiche Alcindor, "Women's March Highlights as Huge Crowd Protests Trump," *New York Times*, January 21, 2017, https://www.nytimes.com/2017/01/21/us/womens-march.html.

16. Erika Bachiochi, "I'm a Feminist against Abortion. Why Should I Be Excluded from a March for Women?" *CNN*, January 17, 2017, https://www.cnn.com/2017/01/17/opinions/prolife-and-feminist-under-trump-bachiochi-opinion/index.html. Bachiochi continued to develop her ideas in scholarly work. For an example, see Erika Bachiochi, "A Putative Right in Search of a Constitutional Justification: Understanding *Planned Parenthood v. Casey*'s Equality Rationale and How It Undermines Women's Equality," *Quinnipiac Law Review* 3 (2017): 593–610.

17. Students for Life, "Talking Points: Women's March" (2017), SFL, 2017–2018 Talking Points Folder. On the conflict about abortion in the women's march, see Sheryl Gay Stolberg, "Views on Abortion Strain Calls for Unity at Women's March on Washington," *New York Times*, January 18, 2017, https://www.nytimes.com/2017/01/18/us/womens-march-abortion.html. On the Lies Feminist Tell Tour, see Students for Life America, Board of Directors Report, 2017–2018 (2018), 19, SFL,

Board Reports Folder. On Hawkins's story in this period, "When Living Pro-Life Is Deeply Personal," *Focus on the Family*, March 26, 2018.

18. Students for Life, "Talking Points: Women's March," 1.

19. On Gorsuch's background and confirmation, see Corey Brettschneider, "Gorsuch, Abortion, and the Concept of Personhood," *New York Times*, March 21, 2017, https://www.nytimes.com/2017/03/21/opinion/gorsuch-abortion-and-the-concept-of-personhood.html; Thomas Vinciguerra, "The Education of Neil Gorsuch," *Columbia Magazine*, Fall 2017, https://magazine.columbia.edu/article/education-neil-gorsuch. For Gorsuch's book, see Neil Gorsuch, *The Future of Assisted Suicide and Euthanasia* (Princeton: Princeton University Press, 2006). For the confirmation vote: Audrey Carlsen et al., "How Senators Voted on the Gorsuch Confirmation," *New York Times*, April 7, 2017, https://www.nytimes.com/interactive/2017/04/07/us/politics/gorsuch-confirmation-vote.html.

20. On Bannon's and Miller's view of immigration, see Amanda Holpuch, "Trump Aide Stephen Miller Told Bannon That Immigration Would 'Decimate' America," *Guardian*, November 22, 2019, https://www.theguardian.com/us-news/2019/nov/22/stephen-miller-bannon-interview-immigration-america; John Walcott et al., "Trump's Go-To Man Bannon Takes Hardline View on Immigration," *Reuters*, January 30, 2017, https://www.reuters.com/article/us-usa-trump-immigration-bannon/trumps-go-to-man-bannon-takes-hardline-view-on-immigration-idUSKBN15E2TG. For the Supreme Court's decision in the case, see *Trump v. Hawaii*, 588 U.S. 667 (2018).

21. On the realizations prompted by the Charlottesville violence, see Claudia Rankine, "Was Charlottesville the Exception or the Rule?" *New York Times*, September 13, 2017, https://www.nytimes.com/2017/09/13/magazine/was-charlottesville-the-exception-or-the-rule.html. For more on Charlottesville and Trump's response, see Michael D. Shear and Maggie Haberman, "Trump Defends Initial Remarks on Charlottesville; Again Blames 'Both Sides,'" *New York Times*, August 15, 2017, https://www.nytimes.com/2017/08/15/us/politics/trump-press-conference-charlottesville.html.

22. Cara Buckley, "Powerful Hollywood Women Unveil Anti-Harassment Action Plan," *New York Times*, January 1, 2018, https://www.nytimes.com/2018/01/01/movies/times-up-hollywood-women-sexual-harassment.html?hp&action=click&pgtype=Homepage&clickSource=story-heading&module=first-column-region&region=top-news&WT.nav=top-news. On the rise of #MeToo, see Jodi Kantor and Megan Twohey, *She Said: Breaking the Sexual Harassment Story That Sparked a Movement*, 2nd ed. (New York: Penguin, 2020), 1–56; Tarana Burke, *Unbound: My Story of Liberation and the Birth of the Me Too Movement* (New York: Macmillan, 2021), 1–15, 89–140.

23. On Kavanaugh's reputation and nomination, see "Trump Picks Conservative Judge for Supreme Court Opening," *NPR*, July 10, 2018, https://www.npr.org/2018/07/10/627610086/trump-picks-conservative-judge-for-supreme-court-opening.

24. For examples of Aden's early cases at AUL, see *Planned Parenthood of Greater Ohio v. Hodges*, 917 F.3d 908 (6th Cir. 2019) (Aden contributing amicus brief in case involving statute barring funding for organizations that performed abortions); *California by and through Becerra v. Azar*, 950 F.3d 1067 (9th Cir. 2020) (Aden participating in amicus brief defending Title X rules barring the promotion of abortion).

25. For a sample of Aden's and Foster's early work at AUL, see Steven H. Aden, "Americans Increasingly Understand that Pro-Abortion Arguments Are Based in Ignorance," *Americans United for Life*, October 16, 2017, https://aul.org/2017/10/16/americans-increasingly-understand-that-pro-abortion-arguments-are-based-in-ignorance/; "AUL Says Planned Parenthood's Annual Report Shows That Abortion Is Business as Usual," *Americans United for Life*, May 30, 2017, https://aul.org/2017/05/30/aul-says-planned-parenthoods-annual-report-shows-that-abortion-is-business-as-usual/. For Foster's account: Catherine Glenn Foster, "I Was Pressured to Abort My Children. For My First Baby, I Gave In," *USA Today*, October 28, 2020, https://www.usatoday.com/story/opinion/voices/2020/10/28/abortion-amy-coney-barrett-genetic-testing-life-column/3745396001/.

26. On the support for Kavanaugh's nomination, see Opheli Garcia Lawler, "Men Celebrate Kavanaugh's Win with #BeersforBrett," *The Cut*, October 6, 2018, https://www.thecut.com/2018/10/men-celebrate-kavanuaughs-win-with-beersforbrett.html. On the confirmation vote, see Sheryl Gay Stolberg, "Kavanaugh Is Sworn in After Close Confirmation Vote in the Senate," *New York Times*, October 26, 2018, https://www.nytimes.com/2018/10/06/us/politics/brett-kavanaugh-supreme-court.html.

27. James Bopp and Corinne L. Youngs to Indiana Right to Life (October 19, 2018), JBP, NRLC 2018 Pro-Life Strategy; James Bopp Jr. and Corinne L. Youngs to Tennessee Right to Life (August 12, 2019), JBP, Digital Files, Tennessee Right to Life Folder.

28. Pro-Life Generation Action, "Launch Summary," December 15, 2018, SBL, Pro-Life Generation Action Folder. On the rise of single-party state legislatures, see Adam Nagourney and Sydney Ember, "Election Consolidates One-Party Control over State Legislatures," *New York Times*, November 7, 2018, https://www.nytimes.com/2018/11/07/us/politics/statehouse-elections.html. On the sources of state polarization, see Joshua Zingher and Jesse Richman, "Polarization and the Nationalization of State Legislative Elections," *American Politics Review* 47 (2018): 1036–1054; Boris

Shor, "Polarization in American State Legislatures," in *American Gridlock: The Sources, Character, and Impact of Political Polarization*, ed. James A. Thurber and Antoine Yoshinaka (New York: Cambridge University Press, 2015), 201–215.

29. Alabama Constitution, Amendment 903 (2019). On trigger bans, see Elizabeth Nash et al., "13 States Have Trigger Bans—Here's What Happens When *Roe* Is Overturned," *Guttmacher Institute*, June 2022, https://www.guttmacher.org/article/2022/06/13-states-have-abortion-trigger-bans-heres-what-happens-when-roe-overturned.

30. Mary Ziegler, *Roe: The History of a National Obsession* (New Haven: Yale University Press, 2023), 121–140; Janet Folger Porter, *A Heartbeat Away: How the Heartbeat Bill Will Pierce the Heart of* Roe v. Wade (Shippensburg, PA: Destiny, 2020), 101–134.

31. " 'Heartbeat Bill' Divides Ohio Anti-Abortion Leaders," *Columbus Dispatch*, September 27, 2011, https://www.dispatch.com/story/news/politics/2011/09/27/heartbeat-bill-divides-ohio/23618938007/ (OH). On divisions within the movement, see Erik Eckholm, "Anti-Abortion Groups Are Split on Legal Tactics," *New York Times*, December 4, 2011, https://www.nytimes.com/2011/12/05/health/policy/fetal-heartbeat-bill-splits-anti-abortion-forces.html. For Porter's statement: Porter, *A Heartbeat Away*, 130–135.

32. On Mitchell: Jonathan Mitchell, interview with Mary Ziegler, May 12, 2023; Jonathan Mitchell, email interview with Mary Ziegler, August, 25, 2024; Michael S. Schmidt, "Behind the Texas Law, A Persevering Conservative Lawyer," *New York Times*, September 12, 2021, https://www.nytimes.com/2021/09/12/us/politics/texas-abortion-lawyer-jonathan-mitchell.html; Jeannie Suk Gersen, "The Conservative Who Wants to Bring Down the Supreme Court," *New Yorker*, January 5, 2023, https://www.newyorker.com/news/annals-of-inquiry/the-conservative-who-wants-to-bring-down-the-supreme-court. On Dickson: Ziegler, *Roe*, 152–165; Mark Lee Dickson, interview with Mary Ziegler, September 9, 2021; Mark Lee Dickson, interview with Mary Ziegler, October 19, 2021.

33. On SB8 and the arguments for it, Sanctuary Cities for the Unborn, "The Effort to Outlaw Abortion in Cisco, Texas: Factsheet," SCFU; see also Ziegler, *Roe*, 163–165.

34. Jazmin Orozco Rodriguez, "Small, Rural Communities Are Becoming Abortion Access Battlegrounds," *NBC News*, May 21, 2023, https://www.nbcnews.com/health/womens-health/small-rural-communities-are-becoming-abortion-access-battlegrounds-rcna84921; see also Ziegler, *Roe*, 163–165. On the ordinances passed by 2022, see Sanctuary Cities for the Unborn, "Cities that Have Voted on Ordinances Prohibiting Abortion within Their City Limits" (November 2022), SCFU.

35. On Fisher, Free the States, and Abolish Human Abortion, see Irin Carmon, "Meet the Rebels of the Anti-Abortion Movement," *MSNBC*, March 7, 2014, https://www.msnbc.com/melissa-harris-perry/meet-the-rebels-the-anti-abortion-movement-msna281321; Free the States, "Abolitionist, Not Pro-Life" (n.d., ca. 2023), https://abolishhumanabortion.com/abolitionism/.

36. On End Abortion Now, see "Is Abortion Murder?" *End Abortion Now*, January 11, 2022, https://endabortionnow.com/abortion-is-murdering-humans/; Elisabeth Dias, "Inside the Extreme Effort to Punish Women for Abortion," *New York Times*, July 1, 2022, https://www.nytimes.com/2022/07/01/us/abortion-abolitionists.html. On Durbin's perspective on gender roles, see "Women behind the Pulpit: What Does the Bible Say?" *Apologia Studios*, February 26, 2018, https://apologiastudios.com/episode/women-behind-the-pulpit-what-does-the/ (Tempe, AZ).

37. Lyanne Gueracuco, "Meet the Abolitionists: The Most Extreme Anti-Abortion Group at the Texas Legislature," *Texas Observer*, March 22, 2017, https://www.texas-observer.org/meet-texas-abortion-abolitionists-group-pro-life/ (Austin); Bud Kennedy, "Activists Urge House Committee to Make Abortion a Felony Crime," *Fort Worth Star-Telegram*, March 10, 2017, A5 (TX).

38. For Serratore's argument: Serratore, "Coerced into Unwanted Abortion," *American Feminist*, December 2018. For AUL's model law: "Coercive Abuse against Mothers Prevention Act," in *Defending Life 2019* (Washington, DC: Americans United for Life, 2020), 416–424. After the reversal of *Roe,* some abortion opponents invested further in laws to punish what they called abortion coercion. See Monica Snyder et al., "Pivoting to Unwanted and Coerced Abortion: A Manifesto," *Public Discourse*, June 16, 2024, https://www.thepublicdiscourse.com/2024/06/95171/ (arguing that a focus on coerced abortion represented "an unprecedented opportunity to find common ground").

39. Students for Life, "Life After *Roe* Tour Training" (2019), SFL, Trainings Folder; see also "Life After *Roe* Tour Talking Points" (Fall 2019), SFL, 2019–2020 Talking Points Folder.

40. Brief of Alliance Defending Freedom and the Radiance Foundation, 14–15. For the statement about sex-selection abortions: Americans United for Life Fundraising Letter (1987), PAW, Carton 9, Folder 3.

41. *Box v. Planned Parenthood of Indiana and Kentucky*, 139 S. Ct. 1780, 1789–1790 (2019) (Thomas, J., concurring). For analysis of Thomas's concurrence, see Melissa Murray, "Race-ing *Roe*: Racial Justice, Reproductive Justice, and the Battle for *Roe v. Wade*," *Harvard Law Review* 134 (2021): 2025–2045; Melissa Murray, "Abortion, Sterilization, and the Universe of Reproductive Rights," *William & Mary Law Review* 63

(2022): 1607–1610; Khiara M. Bridges, "The Supreme Court, 2021 Term—Foreword: Race in the Roberts Court, *Harvard Law Review* 136 (2022): 24–66; Reva B. Siegel and Mary Ziegler, "Abortion-Eugenics Discourse in *Dobbs*: A Social Movement History," *Journal of American Constitutional History* 2 (2024): 71–98.

42. For examples of pre-*Box* arguments about eugenics, see Pamphlet, Erma Clardy Craven, "Abortion, Poverty, and Black Genocide: A Gift to the Poor?" (n.d., ca. 1987), LMP, Box 82, Folder 11; Archdiocese of New York, "The Racism of Abortion" (n.d., ca. 1988), LMP, Box 82, Folder 11; "Black & Unwanted," *TooManyAborted. Com* (2009), https://perma.cc/9GNV-AVAX; Brief Amici Curiae of the Ethics and Religious Liberty Commission of the Southern Baptist Convention et al., 9, *Box v. Planned Parenthood of Indiana and Kentucky*, 139 S. Ct. 1780 (2019) (No. 17-3163). For post-*Box* arguments of this kind, see Americans United for Life, *Defending Life 2021*, 10–11 (citing Thomas and arguing that "if government desires to eradicate discrimination predicated on race, sex, disability, and genetic makeup, it must ensure that this protection begins in the womb"); Carole Novielli, "Planned Parenthood Says That Idea That Abortion Is 'Black Genocide' Is Offensive, But There Is Good Reason to Believe It," *Live Action*, July 12, 2020, https://www.liveaction.org/news/planned-parenthood-falsely-dismisses-abortion-black-genocide-claim/ (linking Thomas to the Black genocide argument).

43. On COVID and its racially disparate impacts, see Samantha Artiga et al., "Racial Disparities in COVID-19: Key Findings from Available Data and Analysis," *Kaiser Family Foundation*, August 17, 2020, https://www.kff.org/racial-equity-and-health-policy/issue-brief/racial-disparities-covid-19-key-findings-available-data-analysis/.

44. On Floyd and his life, see Adrian Florido et al., "Many Know How George Floyd Died. A New Biography Reveals How He Lived," *NPR*, May 18, 2022, https://www.npr.org/2022/05/18/1099585400/george-floyd-biography-book.

45. On Floyd's murder and Trump's response, see Evan Hall et al., "How George Floyd Was Killed in Police Custody," *New York Times*, May 31, 2020, https://www.nytimes.com/2020/05/31/us/george-floyd-investigation.html. On Taylor and Arbery, see Richard Oppel Jr. et al., "What to Know About Breonna Taylor's Murder," *New York Times*, December 13, 2023, https://www.nytimes.com/2020/05/31/us/george-floyd-investigation.html; Richard Fausset, "What to Know About the Shooting Death of Ahmaud Arbery," *New York Times*, August 8, 2022, https://www.nytimes.com/article/ahmaud-arbery-shooting-georgia.html.

46. Kim Parker et al., "Amid Protests, Majorities across Racial and Ethnic Groups Express Support for Black Lives Matter Movement," *Pew Forum*, June 12, 2020, https://www.pewresearch.org/social-trends/2020/06/12/amid-protests-majorities-

across-racial-and-ethnic-groups-express-support-for-the-black-lives-matter-move
ment/. On corporate giving to racial justice causes, see "Corporate America's $50 Bil-
lion Promise," *Washington Post*, August 23, 2021, https://www.washingtonpost.com/
business/interactive/2021/george-floyd-corporate-america-racial-justice/. For examples of the spread of claims about systemic racism, see Courtland Milloy, "Biden
Speaking about Structural Racism Is a Win. But the Battle Is Ongoing," *Washington
Post*, November 13, 2020, https://www.washingtonpost.com/local/biden-systemic-
racism/2020/11/13/c99ec540–239a-11eb-952e-0c475972cfc0_story.html. On the history and expansion of Black Lives Matter, see Christopher J. Lebron, *The Making of
Black Lives Matter: The Brief History of an Idea,* 2nd ed. (New York: Oxford University Press, 2023), xiii, 2–15, 23–101; Veronica Chambers and Jennifer Harlan, *Call and
Response: The Story of Black Lives Matter* (New York: Harper Collins, 2021). On the
number of Americans participating in the rallies, see Larry Buchanan et al., "Black
Lives Matter May Be the Largest Movement in U.S. History," *New York Times*, July 3,
2020, https://www.nytimes.com/interactive/2020/07/03/us/george-floyd-protests-
crowd-size.html.

47. For the USCCB's teaching on systemic racism: USCCB, "What Is Systemic Racism?" (n.d., ca. 2019), https://www.usccb.org/systemic-racism; see also Press Release,
"Statement of U.S. Bishops' President on the Killing of George Floyd," May 31, 2020.

48. For James's statement: "Kay C. James and Penny Nance Talk about American
Greatness," *Heritage Foundation*, June 25, 2020, https://www.heritage.org/article
/kay-c-james-and-penny-nance-talk-life-race-and-americas-greatness. For Bomberger's
statement: "Abortion and Racism: A Conversation with Three Black Pro-Life Leaders," *Catholic World*, October 27, 2020, https://www.catholicworldreport.com/
2020/10/27/abortion-and-racism-conversations-with-three-black-pro-life-leaders/.
For the statement about Black Lives Matter, see Paul Stuber to Representative J. Bris-
coe, "Re: The Shocking Truth about the 'Marxists' Behind the Black Lives Matter
Organization," July 3, 2020, *Utah State Legislature,* https://le.utah.gov
/publicweb/BRISCJK/PublicWeb/43194/43194.html.

49. Students for Life, *Students for Life 2020–2021 Board Report*, 22, 28; see also Students for Life Action, Press Release, "Black Preborn Lives Matter Billboards Launched
across the Country," September 1, 2020, https://www.studentsforlifeaction.org
/black-preborn-lives-matter-billboards-launched-across-the-country-with-calls-for-
defunding-planned-parenthood/; Students for Life, Press Release, "Students for Life
Joins with Frederick Douglass Foundation, the Human Action Coalition, and Black
Community Leaders to Unveil the Next Step in the Black Preborn Lives Matter,"
August 31, 2020. For criticism of the abortion-is-eugenics argument, see Murray,

"Race-ing *Roe*," 2025–2045; Bridges, "The Supreme Court, 2021 Term," 24–66; Siegel and Ziegler, "Abortion-Eugenics Discourse," 71–98.

50. For Roberts's decision: *June Medical Services v. Russo*, 591 U.S. 299, 327–345 (2020) (Roberts, C. J., concurring).

51. For the Court's decision in *Bostock*, see *Bostock v. Clayton County, Georgia*, 590 U.S. 644, 660–681 (2020).

52. For Hammer's argument: Josh Hammer, "Common Good Originalism: Our Tradition and Our Path Forward," *Harvard Journal of Law and Public Policy* 44 (2021): 916–935. For Vermeule's March piece, see Adrian Vermeule, "Beyond Originalism," *Atlantic*, March 31, 2020, https://www.theatlantic.com/ideas/archive/2020/03/common-good-constitutionalism/609037/; see also Adrian Vermeule, *Common Good Constitutionalism* (New York: Polity, 2022). For more on reaction to these ideas, see Ian Ward, "Critics Call It Theocratic and Authoritarian. Young Conservatives Call It an Exciting New Legal Theory," *Politico*, December 9, 2022, https://www.politico.com/news/magazine/2022/12/09/revolutionary-conservative-legal-philosophy-courts-00069201.

53. Students for Life, Talking Points, "SCOTUS Pick and What's at Stake" (September 26, 2020), SFL, 2019–2020 Talking Points Folder. On Barrett's ties to ADF and the movement, see Ariane De Vogue, "Barrett Signed a 'Right to Life' Letter in Ad That Also Called to End *Roe v. Wade*," *CNN*, October 1, 2020, https://www.cnn.com/2020/10/01/politics/amy-coney-barrett-abortion-rights/index.html; Trudy Ring, "Amy Coney Has Ties to Group in Anti-LGBTQ Rights Group," *Advocate*, September 9, 2020, https://www.advocate.com/law/2022/9/09/amy-coney-barrett-has-ties-right-wing-group-lgbtq-rights-case.

54. Nicholas Fandos, "Senate Confirms Barrett, Delivering for Trump and Reshaping the Court," *New York Times*, October 26, 2020, https://www.nytimes.com/2020/10/26/us/politics/senate-confirms-barrett.html.

55. Josh Craddock, interview with Mary Ziegler, September 15, 2023.

56. For a sample of Craddock's work during his time at Personhood USA, see Josh Craddock, "Fetal Pain Hurts (The Pro-Life Cause)" *Life Site News*, June 23, 2013, https://www.liveaction.org/news/why-fetal-pain-hurts-the-pro-life-cause/; Josh Craddock, "Personhood Wins Supreme Court Battle in Mississippi," *Life Site News*, September 10, 2011, https://www.liveaction.org/news/personhood-wins-supreme-court-battle-in-mississippi/; Josh Craddock, "Personhood Challenges Legally Recognized Abortion in the United States," *Life Site News*, August 4, 2012, https://www.liveaction.org/news/personhood-challenges-nationally-legalized-abortion-at-the-u-s-supreme-court/.

57. Chapter 2 canvasses these earlier arguments.

58. For AUL's proposal: Catherine Glenn Foster, Chad Pecknold, and Josh Craddock, "The Lincoln Proposal: An Executive Order to Restore Constitutional Rights to All Human Beings," Americans United for Life, 2020, https://aul.org/law-and-policy/lincoln-proposal/. For Craddock's article: Josh Craddock, "Protecting Prenatal Persons: Does the Fourteenth Amendment Prohibit Abortion?" *Harvard Journal of Law and Public Policy* 40 (2017): 543–569.

59. On Trump's efforts to subvert the election, see Hannah Grabenstein et al., "Read the Full Indictment against Trump for His Alleged Efforts to Overturn the 2020 Elections," *PBS NewsHour*, August 1, 2023, https://www.pbs.org/newshour/politics/read-full-the-indictment-against-trump-for-his-efforts-to-overturn-the-2020-election; Alan Feuer and Katie Benner, "The Fake Electors Scheme, Explained," *New York Times*, July 27, 2023, https://www.nytimes.com/2022/07/27/us/politics/fake-electors-explained-trump-jan-6.html.

60. For the text of SB8, see Act of September 1, 2021, 87th Leg., Ch. 171, § 201, 2021 Tex. Gen. Laws 2882.

61. See *Whole Woman's Health v. Jackson*, 595 U.S. 30, 39–51 (2021).

62. *Whole Woman's Health v. Jackson*, 642 S.W.3d 569, 578–583 (Tex. 2022).

63. Food and Drug Administration, "Information about Mifepristone for Medical Termination of Pregnancy through Ten Weeks Gestation, 2023," (2023) https://www.fda.gov/drugs/postmarket-drug-safety-information-patients-and-providers/information-about-mifepristone-medical-termination-pregnancy-through-ten-weeks-gestation; see also Greer Donley, "Medication Abortion Exceptionalism," *Cornell Law Review* 107 (2022): 640–642.

64. On the rising number of mifepristone abortions, see Rachel K. Jones et al., "Medication Abortion Accounted for More Than 63 Percent of All Abortions in 2023—An Increase from 53 Percent in 2020," *Guttmacher Institute*, March 2024, https://www.guttmacher.org/2024/03/medication-abortion-accounted-63-all-us-abortions-2023-increase-53-2020. On the changing landscape of telehealth abortions, see David Cohen, Greer Donley, and Rachel Rebouché, "Abortion Pills," *Stanford Law Review* 76 (2024): 320–391.

65. For Rufo's original piece, see Christopher Rufo, "Cult Programming in Seattle," *City Journal*, July 8, 2020, https://www.city-journal.org/article/cult-programming-in-seattle. For more on Rufo and the spread of anti-CRT politics, see Benjamin Wallace-Wells, "How a Conservative Activist Invented the Conflict over Critical Race Theory," *New Yorker*, June 18, 2021, https://www.newyorker.com/news/annals-of-inquiry/how-a-conservative-activist-invented-the-conflict-over-critical-race-

theory. On declining support for Black Lives Matter, especially among conservatives, see Julia Menasce Horowitz et al., "Views on the Black Lives Matter Movement," *Pew Forum*, June 13, 2023, https://www.pewresearch.org/social-trends/2023/06/14/views-on-the-black-lives-matter-movement/.

66. For DeSantis's statement: Tanner Stewart, "Northwest Florida Citizens Weigh in on Critical Race Theory in Schools," *WEAR News*, June 9, 2021, https://weartv.com/news/local/northwest-florida-citizens-weigh-in-on-critical-race-theory-in-schools (Pensacola, FL); see also Valeria Olivares, "Governor Greg Abbott Signs Tougher Anti–Critical Race Theory Law," *Dallas Morning News*, September 17, 2021, https://www.dallasnews.com/news/education/2021/09/17/gov-greg-abbott-signs-tougher-anti-critical-race-theory-law/ (TX).

67. See Erika Bachiochi, *The Rights of Women: Reclaiming a Lost Vision* (Notre Dame: Notre Dame University Press, 2021). For the encyclical, see Pope Francis, *Fratelli Tutti* (October 2020), https://www.vatican.va/content/francesco/en/encyclicals/documents/papa-francesco_20201003_enciclica-fratelli-tutti.html. For Coakley's statement: "U.S. Bishops Lament Continued Poverty, Sex Discrimination in Labor Day Statement," *Catholic News Service*, September 3, 2021.

68. For Pope John Paul's statement: John Paul II, *Evangelium Vitae* (Washington, DC: United States Conference of Catholic Bishops, 1995), 59, 99. For Pope Francis's letter: Pope Francis, "Misericordia et Misera," November 20, 2016, https://www.vatican.va/content/francesco/en/apost_letters/documents/papa-francesco-lettera-ap_20161120_misericordia-et-misera.html.

69. Southern Baptist Convention, "On Abolishing Abortion," June 21, 2021, https://www.sbc.net/resource-library/resolutions/on-abolishing-abortion/. On the debate prompted by the resolution: Lisa Misner, "SBC Resolution on Abortion Creates Strategy Debate among Pro-Life Baptists," *Illinois Baptist News*, June 30, 2021, https://illinoisbaptist.org/sbc-resolution-on-abortion-creates-strategy-debate-among-pro-life-baptists/ (Springfield); Bob Smietana, "Evangelical Pro-Lifers Clash over Criminalizing Abortion," *Christianity Today*, May 19, 2022, https://www.christianitytoday.com/news/2022/may/abortion-abolition-criminalize-women-tom-ascol-roe-v-wade-n.html.

70. Students for Life, Talking Points, "Confronting the Falsehood That Women Will Be Prosecuted if *Roe* Falls" (May 18, 2021); SFL, 2021–2022 Talking Points Folder; see also Students for Life, Talking Points, "On Why We Don't Support Prosecuting Women" (November 2021), SFL, 2021–2022 Talking Points Folder.

71. Students for Life, IVF Talking Points (May 31, 2022), SFL, 2022–2023 Talking Points Folder. On conflict within the movement around IVF, see Oriana González

and Caitlin Owens, "Republicans' Thorny Path ahead on Fertility Policy," *Axios*, November 29, 2022, https://www.axios.com/2022/11/29/republicans-abortion-fertility-ivf-pence. On the prevalence of IVF, see Isabelle Goddard and Caroline Aragao, "A Growing Share of Americans Say They've Had a Fertility Treatment or Know Someone Who Has," *Pew Forum*, September 14, 2023, https://www.pewresearch.org/short-reads/2023/09/14/a-growing-share-of-americans-say-theyve-had-fertility-treatments-or-know-someone-who-has/.

72. Students for Life, Talking Points, "Contraception" (May 10, 2022), SFL, 2022–2023 Talking Points Folder.

73. For the story about the leak: Josh Gerstein and Alexander Ward, "Supreme Court Voted to Overturn Abortion Rights, Leaked Draft Shows," *Politico*, May 2, 2022, https://www.politico.com/news/2022/05/02/supreme-court-abortion-draft-opinion-00029473. For coverage of the passage of Mississippi's law, see Jenny Jarvie, "Mississippi Leads War on Abortion," *Los Angeles Times*, March 9, 2018, A6. For ADF's perspective, see Press Release, Alliance Defending Freedom, "U.S. Supreme Court to Weigh in on MS Law Protecting Mothers, Unborn Babies from Late-Term Abortions," Alliance Defending Freedom, May 17, 2021, https://adflegal.org/press-release/us-supreme-court-weigh-ms-law-protecting-mothers-unborn-babies-late-term-abortions.

74. *Dobbs v. Jackson Women's Health Organization*, 597 U.S. 215, 231 (2022).

75. Ibid., 230, 250. For the work of Dellapenna, see Joseph Dellapenna, *Dispelling the Myths of Abortion History* (Durham, NC: Carolina Academic Press, 2006). The Court also cited the work of Eugene Quay, the Christian bioethicist John Keown, Joseph Witherspoon, the Texas law professor who had served on the board of the National Right to Life Committee, and pioneering antiabortion scholar Eugene Quay. See John Keown, *Abortion, Doctors, and the Law: Some Aspects of the Legal Regulation of Abortion in England from 1803 to 1982* (New York: Cambridge University Press, 2009); Joseph Witherspoon, "Reexamining *Roe:* Nineteenth-Century Abortion Statutes and the Fourteenth Amendment," *St. Mary's Law Journal* 17 (1985): 34–36; Eugene Quay, "Justifiable Abortion—Medical and Legal Foundations," *Georgetown Law Journal* 49 (1961): 447–520. Chapter 1 discusses the scholarly consensus on pre-quickening abortion.

76. *Dobbs v. Jackson Women's Health Organization*, 597 U.S. 215, 286, 289 (2022).

77. For Kavanaugh's opinion: ibid., 336–347 (Kavanaugh, J., concurring). For Thomas's opinion: ibid., 331–336 (Thomas, J., concurring). For examples of personhood briefs submitted in the case, see Brief Amici Curiae Scholars of Jurisprudence John Finnis and Robert George, 5–23, *Dobbs v. Jackson Women's Health Organization*, 597 U.S. 215 (2022) (No. 19-1392); Brief Amicus Curiae of the National Catholic

Bioethics Center et al., 7–11, *Dobbs v. Jackson Women's Health Organization*, 597 U.S. 215 (2022) (No. 19-1392); Brief Amici Curiae of the Foundation to Abolish Abortion et al., 25–34, *Dobbs v. Jackson Women's Health Organization*, 597 U.S. 215 (2022) (No. 19-1392); Brief Amici Curiae of Illinois Right to Life and Dr. Steve Jacobs, 3–12, *Dobbs v. Jackson Women's Health Organization*, 597 U.S. 215 (2022) (No. 19-1392); Amicus Brief of Human Coalition Action and Students for Life of America in Support of Petitioners, 14–15, *Dobbs v. Jackson Women's Health Organization,* 597 U.S. 215 (2022) (No. 19-1392).

78. On the foundation laid in Dobbs for the potential recognition of personhood, see Katherine Shaw and Melissa Murray, "*Dobbs* and Democracy," *Harvard Law Review* 137 (2024): 730–806.

79. On the effects of post-*Dobbs* criminal laws on patients experiencing pregnancy complications, see Kate Zernike, "Medical Impact of *Roe* Reversal Goes Well beyond Abortion Clinics, Doctors Say," *New York Times*, September 10, 2022, https://www.nytimes.com/2022/09/10/us/abortion-bans-medical-care-women.html; Pam Belluck, "They Had Miscarriages, and New Abortion Laws Obstructed Treatment," *New York Times*, July 17, 2022, https://www.nytimes.com/2022/07/17/health/abortion-miscarriage-treatment.html. For a snapshot of early state litigation, see Rachel Roubein, "These State Courts Are Considering Abortion Bans," *Washington Post*, June 5, 2023, https://www.washingtonpost.com/politics/2023/06/05/these-state-supreme-courts-are-weighing-abortion-bans/. On new bans, see "Abortion Policy Tracker,*" Kaiser Family Foundation*, June 6, 2023, https://www.kff.org/other/state-indicator/abortion-policy-tracker/?currentTimeframe=0&sortModel=%7B%22colId%22:%22Location%22,%22sort%22:%22asc%22%7D. On polls documenting the unpopularity of *Dobbs*, see Lydia Saad, "Broader Support for Abortion Rights Continues After *Dobbs*," *Gallup*, June 14, 2023, https://news.gallup.com/poll/506759/broader-support-abortion-rights-continues-post-dobbs.aspx#:~:text=Since%20then%2C%20the%20preference%20for,13%25%20in%202022%20and%202023; "Majority Disapproves Supreme Court Decision to Overturn *Roe v. Wade*," *Pew Forum*, July 6, 2022, https://www.pewresearch.org/politics/2022/07/06/majority-of-public-disapproves-of-supreme-courts-decision-to-overturn-roe-v-wade/. On the number of abortions after *Dobbs*, see Claire Cain Miller and Margot Sanger-Katz, "Despite State Bans, Legal Abortions Didn't Fall in the Year After *Dobbs*," *New York Times*, October 24, 2023, https://www.nytimes.com/2023/10/24/upshot/abortion-numbers-dobbs.html; Suzanne O. Bell et al., "Texas' 2021 Ban on Abortion in Early Pregnancy and Changes in Live Births," *Journal of the American Medical Association* 330 (2023): 281–282; Isaac Maddow-Zimet and Candace Gibson, "Despite Bans, Number of

Abortions in the United States Increased in 2023," *Guttmacher Institute*, March 2024, https://www.guttmacher.org/2024/03/despite-bans-number-abortions-united-states-increased-2023. For criticism of the Court's historical account, see Serena Mayeri, "The Critical Role of History After *Dobbs*," *Journal of American Constitutional History* 131 (2024): 173–269; Reva B. Siegel, "Memory Games: *Dobbs's* Originalism as Anti-Democratic Living Constitutionalism—and Some Pathways for Resistance," *Texas Law Review* 101 (2023): 1127–1140; Reva B. Siegel, "The History of History and Tradition: The Roots of *Dobbs's* Method (and Originalism) in the Defense of Segregation," *Yale Law Journal Forum* (2023): 99–112.

80. "New North Star Letter," 1–2; Lila Rose et al., "The Pro-Life Movement Should Follow Its North Star: Equal Protection," *National Review*, June 15, 2023, https://www.nationalreview.com/2023/06/the-pro-life-movement-should-follow-its-north-star-equal-protection/. For Forsythe's argument: Clarke Forsythe, "The Fourteenth Amendment's Personhood Mistake," *National ReviewPlus*, February 2024, https://www.nationalreview.com/magazine/2024/02/the-14th-amendments-personhood-myth/. For Bachiochi's argument: Erika Bachiochi, "What Makes a Fetus a Person?" *New York Times*, July 1, 2022, https://www.nytimes.com/2022/07/01/opinion/fetal-personhood-constitution.html.

81. "New North Star Letter," 1–2; see also Rose et al., "The Pro-Life Movement."

82. "New North Star Letter," 1–2; see also Rose et al., "The Pro-Life Movement."

83. For the USCCB's statement: Katie Yoder, "U.S. Bishops Back Bill to Protect Pregnant Workers as Some Warn It's Paid Abortion Leave," *Catholic News Agency*, December 7, 2022, https://www.catholicnewsagency.com/news/253014/pregnant-workers-bill-tk#:~:text=The%20USCCB%20has%20repeatedly%20expressed,of%20the%20unborn%20in%20abortion. For the Pregnant Workers Fairness Act, see 42 U.S.C. § 2000gg (2022). On the spread of maternity homes, see Katia Riddle, "Maternity Homes Provide Support in a Post-*Roe* World, but Not without Conditions," *NPR*, May 9, 2023, https://www.npr.org/2023/05/09/1174323027/maternity-homes-provide-support-in-a-post-roe-world-but-not-without-conditions. On the proposal to make "birth free," see Catherine Glenn Foster and Kristen Day, "Make Birth Free: A Vision for Congress to Empower American Mothers, Families, and Communities," *Americans United for Life* (January 2023), 1–3. On state support for crisis pregnancy centers, see Kimberly Kindy, "Partisan Battle Grows over State Funding for Antiabortion Centers," *Washington Post*, September 14, 2023, https://www.washingtonpost.com/politics/2023/09/14/gop-lawmakers-crisis-pregnancy-centers-state-funding/.

84. On Tiller's killing, see Stephanie Simon, "Anti-Abortion Activist Charged in Killing of Doctor," *Wall Street Journal*, June 3, 2009, A6. On Operation Rescue's

targeting of Tiller, see Robin Abcarian and Nicholas Riccardi, "Abortion Doctor Fatally Shot," *Chicago Tribune*, June 1, 2009, 1. On the conflict between Terry and Newman, see Robin Abcarian, "The Abortion Battle Within," *Los Angeles Times*, August 26, 2009, https://www.latimes.com/archives/la-xpm-2009-aug-26-na-operation-rescue26-story.html; see also *Terry v. Newman*, No. 92047809 (T.T.A.B. April 22, 2013).

85. On Storms and the new Operation Save America, see Martha Kelner, "'Babies Are Murdered Here': The Anti-Abortion Activist Using His Family to Protest outside Abortion Clinics," *Sky News*, June 14, 2022, https://news.sky.com/story/us-abortion-debate-action-outside-planned-parenthood-clinic-in-wisconsin-is-on-frontline-in-a-divided-america-12633602; Sofia Resnick, "A Men's Movement Takes Reins in Quest to End Abortion," *Louisiana Illuminator*, September 13, 2023, https://lailluminator.com/2023/09/13/a-mens-movement-takes-reins-in-a-nationwide-quest-to-end-abortion/ (Baton Rouge).

86. For the brief, see Brief Amici Curiae Foundation to Abolish Abortion et al., 5–34, *Dobbs v. Jackson Women's Health Organization*, 597 U.S. 215 (2022) (No. 19-1392). On the Louisiana bill: Greg Hilborn, "Louisiana Legislature Guts Controversial Abortion Bill, Removes Murder Penalty for Moms," *Daily Advertiser*, May 13, 2022, https://www.theadvertiser.com/story/news/2022/05/12/louisiana-guts-contro versial-abortion-bill-removes-mom-murder-penalties/9743252002/ (Lafayette, LA). For an example of the language of the foundation's model bill, see House Bill 2181, 2023–2024 Kansas State Legislative Session (2023), https://www.kslegislature.org/li/b2023_24/measures/documents/hb2181_00_0000.pdf. For Pierce's statement: Maia Bond, "Missouri Republican Proposes Bill to Enable Murder Charges for Getting an Abortion," *Kansas City Star*, May 3, 2023, https://www.kansascity.com/news/politics-government/article275017471.html (MO).

87. James Bopp Jr. to National Right to Life Committee et al., July 4, 2022, https://www.bopplaw.com/wp-content/uploads/2022/06/NRLC-post-roe-model-abortion-law.pdf. On the Idaho law: David W. Chen, "Idaho Bans Out-of-State Abortions for Minors without Parental Consent," *New York Times*, April 5, 2023, https://www.nytimes.com/2023/04/05/us/idaho-out-of-state-abortions-minors-ban.html.

88. Amy Littlefield, "The Poison Pill in the Mifepristone Lawsuit That Could Trigger a National Abortion Ban," *Nation*, April 26, 2023, https://www.thenation.com/article/society/comstock-act-jonathan-mitchell; Mark Lee Dickson, "Lee County in New Mexico Becomes Sanctuary County for the Unborn After Final Vote," *Live Action*, December 9, 2022, https://www.liveaction.org/news/lea-county-new-mexico-sanctuary-county-unborn. On ADF's suit, see Complaint, *Alliance for*

Hippocratic Medicine v. U.S. Food and Drug Administration, 2:22-cv-00223-Z (N.D. Tex. November 18, 2022). Arguments that pregnancy was not a disease had a history in the movement. See Clipping, Judie Brown, "Repeat After Me: Pregnancy Is Not a Disease," *Washington Dispatch*, January 7, 2005, MFJ, Box 12, Folder 7.

89. Project 2025, *Mandate for Leadership: The Conservative Promise, Project 2025 Presidential Transition Project* (Washington, DC: Heritage Foundation, 2023), 459, 562. On Trump's ascendancy, see "Inside Donald Trump's Dominance of the Republican Primary," *New York Times*, December 7, 2023, https://www.nytimes.com/2023/12/07/podcasts/run-up-donald-trump-gop-primary.html.

90. "New North Star Letter," 2–3. On the *Dobbs* anniversary rally and call for personhood, see Amy Littlefield, "The Anti-Abortion Movement Gets a Dose of Post-*Roe* Reality," *Nation*, June 28, 2023, https://www.thenation.com/article/politics/anti-abortion-activists-dobbs/. On Hawkins's statement about Comstock: Caroline Kitchener et al., "Trump Wins Back Antiabortion Activists as Activists Plot 2025 Crackdowns," *Washington Post*, January 5, 2024, https://www.washingtonpost.com/politics/2024/01/05/trump-abortion/. On Hawkins's lifestyle: Kristan Hawkins, interview with Mary Ziegler, April 17, 2023; Kristan Hawkins, interview with Mary Ziegler, December 21, 2022.

91. Robert P. George and Josh Craddock, "On the Constitutional Authority of Congress to Protect Unborn Persons," *National Review*, July 3, 2022, https://www.nationalreview.com/bench-memos/on-the-constitutional-authority-of-congress-to-protect-unborn-persons/; Robert George and Josh Craddock, "A National Abortion Ban Is Constitutional," *Wall Street Journal*, September 15, 2022, https://www.wsj.com/articles/national-abortion-ban-graham-15-week-constitution-law-equal-protection-11663286642. For George and Ponnuru's piece, see Robert George and Ramesh Ponnuru, "Why We Shouldn't Punish Women for Abortions," *National Review*, May 2016, https://www.nationalreview.com/2016/05/abortion-punishment-donald-trump-doctors-mothers-prosecuted/.

92. For Craddock's perspective: Craddock, interview.

93. "New North Star Letter," 1–2.

94. On the Fifth Circuit's ruling, see *Alliance for Hippocratic Medicine v. Food and Drug Administration*, 78 F.4th 210 (5th Cir. 2023). For Kacsmaryk's conclusion, see *Alliance for Hippocratic Medicine v. Food and Drug Administration*, 2023 WL 2825871 at *16–32 (N.D. Tex. 2023).

95. On *Zurawski* and related cases, see Plaintiffs' Second Amended Petition for Declaratory Judgment and Application for Temporary and Permanent Injunction, Case No. D-1-GN-23-000968, (Tex. Dist. Ct., 353d Dist., November 14, 2023);

Memorandum Decision and Order on Motion to Dismiss, *Adkins v. Idaho*, No. CV01-23-14744 (Id. 4th Dist., December 29, 2023); Plaintiffs' Motion for Temporary Injunction, Case No. 23-1196-I (Davidson Cty., TN, Chancery Ct., January 8, 2024). Some groups opposed to abortion had long opposed *all* exceptions. See Judie Brown, American Life League to Mildred Jefferson, March 29, 1996, MFJ, Box 12, Folder 7 (organizing antiabortion doctors to lobby against life exceptions in abortion bans). The Texas Supreme Court rejected Zurawski's argument. See *State v. Zurawski,* 2024 WL 2787913, at *10–15 (Tex. 2024). Other state courts have recognized narrow rights to life or health. *Wrigley v. Romanick,* 988 N.W. 2d 231, 245 (N.D. 2023) (concluding that the state constitution protected a right to access abortion in cases of threats to life or health); *Oklahoma Call for Reproductive Justice v. Drummond,* 526 P.3d 1123, 1130 (Okla. 2023); *Members of the Medical Licensing Board of Indiana v. Planned Parenthood Great Northwest,* 211 N.E. 3d 957, 976 (Ind. 2023).

96. On the ballot initiatives supporting abortion rights, see Michelle Long, "2022 State Ballot Initiatives on Abortion," *Kaiser Family Foundation*, September 20, 2022, https://www.kff.org/policy-watch/2022-state-ballot-initiatives-abortion-rights/. For the ballot initiatives potentially up in 2024, see "Ballot Tracker: Status of Abortion-Related State Constitutional Amendment Measures for the 2024 Election," *Kaiser Family Foundation*, June 28, 2024, https://www.kff.org/womens-health-policy/dashboard/ballot-tracker-status-of-abortion-related-state-constitutional-amendment-measures/.

97. For the Court's immunity decision, see *Trump v. United States*, 144 S. Ct. 2312, 2328–2346 (2024). On Vance's previous views about abortion and the Comstock Act, see Carter Sherman, "JD Vance Called for 'Federal Response' to Block Women from Traveling for Abortion," *Guardian*, July 26, 2024, https://www.theguardian.com/us-news/article/2024/jul/26/jd-vance-abortion-ban-travel; Dan Diamond and Meryl Kornfield, "Vance Asked DOJ to Enforce Comstock Act, Crack Down on Abortion Pills," *Washington Post*, July 17, 2024, https://www.washingtonpost.com/health/2024/07/17/jd-vance-abortion-comstock-vice-presidential-nominee/.

98. For the 2024 GOP platform, see "2024 Republican Party Platform: Make America Great Again!" (July 8, 2024), https://www.presidency.ucsb.edu/documents/2024-republican-party-platform. For Martin's perspective: Julianne McShane, "RNC Official: Nothing in Our Platform Says We Won't Ban Abortion Nationwide," *Mother Jones*, July 15, 2024, https://www.motherjones.com/politics/2024/07/rnc-platform-ed-martin-abortion-ban-softening-gop/. For Hawkins's perspective: Press Release, "Students for Life Action Calls GOP Platform Support of 14th Amendment Protections for the Pre-Born a 'Significant' Contribution to

Restoring Legal Protections for ALL," *Students for Life*, July 8, 2024, https://www.studentsforlifeaction.org/students-for-life-action-calls-gop-platform-support-of-14th-amendment-protections-for-the-pre-born-a-significant-contribution-to-restoring-legal-protections-to-all/.

99. For the chief justice's statement: *LePage v. Center for Reproductive Medicine*, *13, 2024 WL 656591 (Al. 2024) (Parker, C. J., concurring). On Republicans' damage control after the ruling, see Jessica Piper and Megan Messerly, "Trump Says He Supports IVF After Alabama Supreme Court Decision," *Politico*, February 23, 2024, https://www.politico.com/news/2024/02/23/trump-says-he-supports-ivf-after-alabama-court-decision-00142994. On the new challenge to Alabama's shield law, see Emily Cochrane, "Alabama's Shield Law Faces New Constitutional Challenge," *New York Times*, June 14, 2024, https://www.nytimes.com/2024/06/14/us/politics/alabamas-ivf-shield-law.html.

100. Students for Life, "IVF Industry Talking Points Post-Alabama SCOTUS Ruling" (February 2024), SFL, 2023–2024 Talking Points Folder. For AUL's statement: Mary Ann Pazanowski, "In Vitro Embryos Are Children, Alabama Supreme Court Says," *Bloomberg Law*, February 20, 2024, https://news.bloomberglaw.com/health-law-and-business/in-vitro-embryos-are-children-alabama-supreme-court-says. For Aden's statement: "Blanket Immunity?" *World Magazine*, March 7, 2024, https://wng.org/articles/blanket-immunity-1709783134. For the SBC resolution: "On the Ethical Realities of Reproductive Technologies and the Dignity of the Human Embryo" (June 2024), https://sbcannualmeeting.net/wp-content/uploads/2024/06/Final-Resolutions-2024.pdf.

101. For the Court's decision in the EMTALA case, see *Moyle v. United States*, 144 S. Ct. 2015, 2015 (2024). For Alito's dissent, see *id.* at 2018-2037 (Alito, J., dissenting). For the Court's decision in the mifepristone case, see *Food and Drug Administration v. Alliance for Hippocratic Medicine*, 602 U.S. 367, 370–381 (2024).

102. For French's piece, see David French, "The Supreme Court Puts the Pro-Life Movement to the Test," *New York Times*, June 30, 2024, https://www.nytimes.com/2024/06/30/opinion/moyle-idaho-abortion-emtala.html.

103. Hawkins, April interview; Hawkins, December interview.

Conclusion

1. For an overview of these arguments, see Mary Ziegler, *After Roe: The Lost History of the Abortion Debate* (Cambridge, MA: Harvard University Press, 2015), 353, n. 23.

2. Chapter 6 discusses these developments.

3. For the South Korea decision, see *Case on the Crime of Abortion, Apr. 11, 2019/* Case No.: 2017Hun.-Ba127, KCCR (Constitutional Court of Korea). For the German decisions, see *Schwangerschaftsabbruch I* (1975) 39 BVerfGE 1 (Fed Const Ct) (Germany); *Schwangerschaftsabbruch II* (1993) 88 BVrfGE 203 (Fed Const Ct) (Germany). For discussion of the rules in Germany, see Vanessa MacDonnell and Julia Hughes, "The German Abortion Decisions and the Protective Function in German and Canadian Constitutional Law," *Osgoode Hall Law Journal* 50 (2013): 1006–1022. On polls suggesting that some Americans both believe in fetal protection of some kind and oppose the criminalization of abortion or pregnancy, see "America's Abortion Quandary," *Pew Research Center*, May 16, 2022, https://www.pewresearch.org/religion/2022/05/06/americas-abortion-quandary/; Americans United for Life and YouGov, "Abortion" (May 6–13, 2022), https://aul.org/wp-content/uploads/2022/06/2022-05-AUL-YouGov-National-Survey.pdf.

4. Steven Teles, *The Rise of the Conservative Legal Movement: The Battle for Control of the Law* (Princeton: Princeton University Press, 2010); Amanda Hollis-Brusky, *Ideas with Consequences: The Federalist Society and the Conservative Counterrevolution* (New York: Oxford University Press, 2015); Michael Avery and Danielle McLaughlin, *The Federalist Society: How Conservatives Took the Law Back from Liberals* (Nashville: Vanderbilt University Press, 2021); Kenneth Kersch, *Conservatives and the Constitution: Imagining Constitutional Restoration in the Heyday of American Liberalism* (New York: Cambridge University Press, 2019); Amanda Hollis-Brusky and Joshua Wilson, *Separate but Faithful: The Christian Right's Radical Struggle to Transform Law and Legal Culture* (New York: Oxford University Press, 2020); Andrew Lewis, *The Rights Turn in Conservative Christian Politics: How Abortion Transformed the Culture Wars* (New York: Cambridge University Press, 2017).

Index

equality: (*continued*)
40, 53, 60, 64, 70, 142, 196, 200, 223; Nixon's view of, 63; and personhood, 55; racial, xv, 3, 9, 22, 40, 41, 77; Reagan's view of, 73, 80; and the right to life, 26; socioeconomic xiii; for women, xiii, xvi, 12, 13, 60–61, 71, 176, 180, 221. *See also* inequality
Eshoo, Anna, 183
Ethics and Public Policy Center, 180
Eubanks, Robert Royce, 144–145
eugenics movement, 13, 14, 42, 166, 190, 192, 193
euthanasia, 113
Evangelium Vitae (John Paul II), 200
Ex parte Young, 197
extramarital sex, 102, 120–121, 145, 148, 150, 221

FACE (Freedom of Access to Clinic Entrances) Act, 116, 207
Fair Housing Act, 41
Falkenberg, Nanette, 75
Falwell, Jerry, 87, 139, 188
family leave, 200, 221
family planning, 16, 151. *See also* contraception
Family Research Council, 142, 145
FDA. *See* Food and Drug Administration (FDA)
Federal Constitutional Court (Germany), 220
Federal Election Commission, 161
Federal Election Commission v. Massachusetts Citizens for Life, 161–162
Federalist Society, xv, 83, 88–91, 93–94, 155, 156, 182, 183, 221
Feldt, Gloria, 134

feminist movement: and abortion rights, xvi, 35, 36, 72, 75, 105, 124, 176, 177; and the ERA, 60, 61; falsehoods of, 181; and fetal rights, viii, 180; and Operation Rescue, 106; opposition to, 61, 149, 162; and sexual difference, 177; and women's victimhood, 113–114.
feminists: Black, 42; as clinic escorts, 107–108; opposing abortion, 36, 61, 101, 189; pro-choice, 104, 107, 113, 138, 161, 176; protesting Trump election, 180
Feminists for Life, 61, 189
fetal equality, ix, xvi, xvii, xviii, 29–32, 34, 52, 73, 91, 102–103, 122. *See also* fetal personhood
fetal heartbeat bill, 186
fetal personhood: abolitionist ideas, 188; advocacy for, 56, 129, 142, 184, 187, 195; and the antiabortion movement, 71, 138, 189, 215–216; Byrn's writings on, 30–32; and common-good constitutionalism, 193–194; and the Constitution, 72, 87, 111; and contraception, 175; and critical race theory, 199; defined, vii–viii; disagreements regarding, 57–58; fight for, ix, 174, 175, 219; and the Fourteenth Amendment, ix, xii, xvi, 63–64, 210, 213; and the heartbeat ban, 185; and the Human Life Bill, 77–79; marketing of, 115; and newborns with disabilities, 83–84; and politics, 105; and race, 182; recognition of, 138–139, 159, 206, 214; and religious liberty, 134, 140, 146, 149–150, 170; and reproductive justice, 114, 151–152; and the